AF753833

Consumption Tax Trends 2020

VAT/GST AND EXCISE RATES, TRENDS AND POLICY ISSUES

OECD
BETTER POLICIES FOR BETTER LIVES

This work is published under the responsibility of the Secretary-General of the OECD. The opinions expressed and arguments employed herein do not necessarily reflect the official views of OECD member countries.

This document, as well as any data and map included herein, are without prejudice to the status of or sovereignty over any territory, to the delimitation of international frontiers and boundaries and to the name of any territory, city or area.

The statistical data for Israel are supplied by and under the responsibility of the relevant Israeli authorities. The use of such data by the OECD is without prejudice to the status of the Golan Heights, East Jerusalem and Israeli settlements in the West Bank under the terms of international law.

Note by Turkey
The information in this document with reference to “Cyprus” relates to the southern part of the Island. There is no single authority representing both Turkish and Greek Cypriot people on the Island. Turkey recognises the Turkish Republic of Northern Cyprus (TRNC). Until a lasting and equitable solution is found within the context of the United Nations, Turkey shall preserve its position concerning the “Cyprus issue”.

Note by all the European Union Member States of the OECD and the European Union
The Republic of Cyprus is recognised by all members of the United Nations with the exception of Turkey. The information in this document relates to the area under the effective control of the Government of the Republic of Cyprus.

Please cite this publication as:
OECD (2020), *Consumption Tax Trends 2020: VAT/GST and Excise Rates, Trends and Policy Issues*, OECD Publishing, Paris, *https://doi.org/10.1787/152def2d-en*.

ISBN 978-92-64-76386-9 (print)
ISBN 978-92-64-46591-6 (pdf)

Consumption Tax Trends
ISSN 1562-8752 (print)
ISSN 1999-0979 (online)

Corrigenda to publications may be found on line at: *www.oecd.org/about/publishing/corrigenda.htm*.
© OECD 2020

The use of this work, whether digital or print, is governed by the Terms and Conditions to be found at *http://www.oecd.org/termsandconditions*.

Foreword

This is the thirteenth edition of *Consumption Tax Trends*, a biennial OECD publication. It presents cross-country comparative data on consumption taxes in OECD member countries, as at 1 January 2020. Tables using data from the *National Accounts* and data on tax revenue from *Revenue Statistics 2020* are updated up to and including 2018. Price levels for fuel oils are updated as at 4th Quarter 2019 from *Energy Prices and Taxes - Quarterly Statistics* issued by the International Energy Agency. The country data for the report have, for the most part, been provided by delegates to the Committee on Fiscal Affairs' Working Party N°9 on Consumption Taxes. The exchange rates used to convert national currencies into US dollars (USD) are average market rates for 2019 taken from the OECD *Monetary and Financial Statistics*, except for Annex Tables 3.A.5 where market rates for 2018 are used as taxes and prices refer to the year 2018; and Annex Tables 2.A.5 and 2.A.9 where the Purchase Power Parity (PPP) rates for GDP are used as they provide for a better comparison of the value of VAT relief thresholds (PPP rates for GDP 2019 are extracted from the OECD Statistics Database). These exchange rates are available in Annex B to this publication.

This publication illustrates the evolution of consumption taxes as instruments for raising tax revenue and, sometimes, to influence customer behaviour. It identifies and documents the large number of differences that exist in respect of the consumption tax bases, rates and implementation rules while highlighting the features underlying their development. It looks, in particular, at revenue and policy trends and developments in the Value Added Tax/Goods and Services Tax (VAT/GST) area (referred to as "VAT" in this publication). It notably presents an updated estimate of the VAT Revenue Ratio (VRR) for OECD countries, providing an indicator of the loss of VAT revenue as a consequence of exemptions and reduced rates, fraud and non-compliance. It provides an update on the implementation of the OECD International VAT/GST Guidelines as the international standard for the application of VAT to cross-border trade in services and intangibles and, in particular, on the implementation of the recommended rules and mechanisms for the efficient and effective collection of VAT on digital sales. This edition of *Consumption Tax Trends* also includes a special section outlining the VAT measures taken by OECD countries as part of their tax policy responses to the COVID-19 outbreak. These measures have been particularly important in supporting business cash flow, reducing tax compliance burdens and supporting the healthcare sector.

Chapter 1 summarises trends in consumption taxes and their main features. It shows the evolution of consumption tax revenues between 1965 and 2018 and looks in some more detail at the challenges of applying VAT to international trade and at policy responses particularly in the context of the digitalisation of the economy. Chapter 2 describes the key features of VAT regimes in OECD countries, i.e. tax rates, exemptions, specific restrictions to input tax credit, registration and collection thresholds, and special tax collection methods. It provides updated estimates of OECD countries' VAT Revenue Ratio (VRR) as an indicator of the effect of exemptions, reduced rates and non-compliance on government revenues. It considers evolutions in countries' strategies to counter VAT fraud and developments in international administrative co-operation. This chapter finally provides an overview of the VAT measures included in OECD countries' tax responses to the COVID-19 crisis. Chapter 3 describes the main features of excise duties and their impact on revenue, customer behaviour and markets. It shows the detailed excise tax rates on beer, wine, alcoholic beverages, tobacco, and fuel oil for households in OECD countries. It also provides an estimate of the total tax burden in a pack of cigarettes in OECD countries. Chapter 4 describes the main features of vehicle taxes and their use for influencing customer behaviour. It provides detailed information on taxes on sale and registration and recurrent taxes on vehicles and on taxes of the main road fuels (i.e. unleaded gasoline and diesel). It finally provides information on the taxation of aviation fuels in OECD countries.

This publication was prepared under the auspices of the Working Party N°9 on Consumption Taxes of the Committee on Fiscal Affairs. It was written by Stéphane Buydens of the OECD Centre for Tax Policy and Administration (CTPA) under the supervision of Piet Battiau, Head of the Consumption Taxes Unit in the CTPA.

Acknowledgements

Acknowledgements are due to: David Bradbury (Head, Tax Policy and Statistics Division); Piet Battiau (Head, Consumption Taxes Unit), Kurt Van Dender (Head, Tax and Environment Unit); Michelle Harding (Head, Statistical Analysis Unit); Emmanuelle Modica (Statistician/Analyst), Nicolas Miranda (Statistician), Michael Sharratt (Website and Database Developer), Marie-Aurélie Elkurd (Assistant), Karena Garnier (Communications), and Alexandra Le Cam (Assistant), CTPA; Anne-Marie Perucic (World Health Organisation) and Professor Walter Hellerstein (Distinguished Research Professor & Francis Shackelford Distinguished Professor in Taxation Law, University of Georgia).

Table of contents

FIGURES

TABLES

Acronyms

B2B	Business-to-business
B2C	Business-to-consumer
BEPS	Base erosion and profit shifting
BIAC	Business and Industry Advisory Committee to the OECD
CFA	Committee on Fiscal Affairs
EU	European Union
GST	Goods and Services Tax
ICAO	International Civil Aviation Organization
OECD	Organisation for Economic Co-operation and Development
RST	Retail Sales Tax
RSP	Retail Selling Price (for cigarettes)
VAT	Value Added Tax. In this publication, VAT is used to refer to any national tax that embodies the basic features of a value added tax by whatever name or acronym it is known, e.g. Goods and Services Tax or GST
WHO	World Health Organisation

Executive Summary

Consumption tax revenues in OECD countries have remained stable at 10.3 % of GDP on average, equal to the record level reached in 2016 (and an increase of 0.1% compared to 2015). These taxes represent almost one-third (30.8%) of total tax revenues in the OECD. Although the overall share of taxes on consumption in total tax revenues has remained relatively stable since 1975, the composition of these taxes has changed fundamentally. OECD countries' reliance on taxes on general consumption (which includes VAT) has increased by more than 70%, from 4.1% in 1975 to 7.1% of GDP in 2018. This is primarily due to the introduction of VAT in most OECD countries. VAT is now the largest source of taxes on consumption, accounting for 6.8% of GDP and 20.4% of total tax revenue in OECD countries in 2018 on average.

Consumption taxes generally consist of general taxes on goods and services ("taxes on general consumption") and taxes on specific goods and services. Taxes on general consumption comprise value added tax (VAT) and its equivalent in several jurisdictions (goods and services tax, or GST), sales taxes, and other general taxes on goods and services. Taxes on specific goods and services consist primarily of excise taxes, customs and import duties, and taxes on specific services (such as insurance and financial services).

Main consumption tax trends in OECD countries

- Consumption tax revenues in OECD countries in 2018 ranged from 3.8% of GDP in the United States to 16.4% of GDP in Hungary. As a share of tax revenues in the OECD, these taxes represented between 15.4% of total taxes in the United States and 49.5% in Chile.
- VAT revenues have remained stable in 2018 as the largest source of taxes on consumption in the OECD on average. VAT accounts for one-fifth of total tax revenues (20.4%) on average, representing 20% or more of total taxes in 21 of the 36 OECD countries that operate a VAT. As a share of GDP, VAT revenues in 2018 ranged from 3.3% of GDP in Australia and Switzerland to 9.7% of GDP in Denmark and New Zealand. An increase in VAT-to-GDP levels was seen between 2015 and 2018 in 25 of the 36 OECD countries that operate a VAT, while these revenues fell as a share of GDP in 8 countries and 3 countries saw no change.
- Standard VAT rates across OECD countries stabilised in 2020 at the record level of 19.3% on average that was first reached in 2017. One OECD country increased its standard VAT rate in 2019 (Japan, from 8% to 10%). Two OECD countries (Germany and Ireland) introduced a temporary reduction of their standard VAT rate in 2020 (from 19% to 16 % and from 23% to 21% respectively) as part of their economic stimulus packages in response to the COVID-19 crisis.
- Most OECD countries' COVID-19 emergency responses included expansions of reduced VAT rates or further reductions of these rates to support the healthcare sector. Several countries introduced specific VAT rate reductions to support the sectors most affected by the crisis (primarily hospitality, tourism). Most OECD countries have included a range of broader VAT measures in

their short-term tax responses to the COVID-19 outbreak, which have been particularly important in supporting business cash flow and reducing tax compliance burdens.

- Almost all OECD countries with a VAT have now implemented the OECD standards for the collection of VAT on online sales of services and digital products from offshore e-commerce vendors. The surge in e-commerce following the COVID-19 outbreak has further emphasised the importance of reform to ensure the proper collection of VAT on these sales. Many OECD countries are now focusing on further expanding their e-commerce VAT regimes, in particular to include online sales of small parcels that are often imported from abroad by foreign electronic marketplaces and other digital vendors. Three OECD countries have already implemented such reform (Australia, New Zealand and Norway), supported by OECD guidance, while similar measures will enter into force in European Union countries and the United Kingdom in 2021.
- Revenues from taxes on specific goods and services, the bulk of which are excise taxes, have further declined both as a percentage of GDP (to 3.2% in 2018; a decline of 0.1 percentage point since 2015) and as a percentage of total tax revenue (to 9.6% in 2018; a decline of 0.5 percentage points since 2015).
- Excise duties are increasingly used to influence consumer behaviour, in particular to reduce pollution through taxes on motor fuels and improve health by heavier taxation of tobacco products. The total tax burden on cigarettes is above 60% of the consumer price in almost all the OECD countries and above 75% in 21 OECD countries. The total tax burden for premium unleaded gasoline exceeds 100% of pre-tax prices in all but nine OECD countries. Excise levels for diesel fuel remain lower than those for gasoline in all but five OECD countries. From an environmental point of view, this is peculiar, as diesel consumption in vehicles has a much greater environmental impact than unleaded gasoline, largely due to the significant differences in nitrogen oxides (NOx) and particulate emissions.
- Car taxation is increasingly used to influence customer behaviour and encourages the use of low polluting vehicles. In 2020, almost all OECD countries take environmental or fuel efficiency criteria into account when determining the level of taxation for the purchase or use of vehicles and 24 of these countries apply tax rebates or exemptions for electric or hybrid vehicles.

The VAT Revenue Ratio for OECD countries

Across the OECD, the unweighted average VAT Revenue Ratio (VRR) has remained stable at 0.56 in 2018, suggesting that 44% of the theoretical potential VAT revenue is not collected. The VRR provides a comparative measure of the difference between the VAT revenue collected and what would theoretically be raised if VAT was applied at the standard rate to the entire potential tax base in a "pure" VAT regime. It provides an indicator that combines the effect of loss of revenues as a consequence of exemptions and reduced rates, fraud and non-compliance. Although the VRR has to be interpreted with care and tax base erosion may be caused by a variety of factors, this VRR estimate suggests that there remains significant potential for raising additional revenues by improving VAT systems' performance.

1 Consumption tax figures: Main trends and figures

1.1. Introduction

Consumption taxes account for approximately one third of the total taxes collected in OECD countries. They have two common forms: taxes on general consumption (value added taxes and retail sales taxes) and taxes on specific goods and services (mainly excise duties).

1.1.1. VAT has become the main consumption tax for countries worldwide

Since the mid-1980s, VAT (also called Goods and Services Tax – GST) has become the main consumption tax both in terms of revenue and geographical coverage. VAT is designed to be a tax on final consumption that is broadly neutral towards the production process and international trade. It is widely seen as a relatively growth-friendly tax. Many developing countries have introduced a VAT during the last two decades to replace lost revenues from trade taxes following trade liberalisation. Some 170 countries operate a VAT today (see Annex A), including 36 of the 37 OECD member countries, the only exception being the United States although most states within the US employ some form of retail sales tax. This is more than twice as many as 25 years ago. VAT raises approximately a fifth of total tax revenues in the OECD and worldwide.

The evolution of VAT as an increasingly important source of tax revenues for countries around the world, and its application to an increasingly large share of the world's economic activity, have raised its importance in the global tax policy debate. The global spread of the VAT coincided with the rapid expansion of the international trade in goods and services in an increasingly globalised economy. Most international trade is now subject to VAT and the interaction of national VAT regimes can potentially have a major impact in either facilitating or distorting trade. Against this background, tax authorities worldwide noted that the absence of an internationally agreed framework for the application of VAT to cross-border trade created growing risks of under-taxation and loss of revenue for governments, and of trade distortion due to double taxation. The need for a consistent global response to the challenge of applying VAT to international trade became particularly urgent due to the strong growth of international trade in services, digital products and goods from online sales as a consequence of the expansion of the digital economy. In response to the strong international call for a global standard on VAT design and operation, the OECD's Committee on Fiscal Affairs (CFA) developed the International VAT/GST Guidelines, which were adopted as a Recommendation by the Council of the OECD in September 2016.

This Recommendation is the first OECD legal instrument in the area of VAT. It incorporates the International VAT/GST Guidelines, presenting a set of internationally agreed standards and recommended approaches for the consistent application of VAT to international trade, with a particular focus on trade in services and intangibles. Their main objective is to reduce the uncertainty and the risks of double taxation and unintended non-taxation that result from inconsistencies in the application of VAT in a cross-border context. The Guidelines were developed through an inclusive process, with the active involvement of international organisations and jurisdictions beyond the current OECD membership and with intense consultation of the business community. These Guidelines have been complemented with detailed implementation guidance focusing in particular on effective and consistent methods and strategies for the collection of VAT on online sales of goods, services and digital products (see Section 1.8 below).

These OECD standards for the effective collection of VAT on online sales of goods, services and digital products are influencing VAT reform in a growing number of countries worldwide, including outside the OECD membership. Over 60 countries have implemented these standards while several other countries are preparing to implement these standards or are considering doing so. The OECD's standards and expertise in VAT are also increasingly in demand from developing countries. In common with other areas of international tax standards, the OECD is progressively increasing the engagement of non-OECD member countries in the design of standards in the VAT area, while expanding the guidance and support available to developing countries seeking to implement the standards. The OECD is developing specific regional toolkits to support developing countries wishing to implement its standards and guidance on VAT. The continuously growing impact of these standards reflects their significant importance for countries' VAT revenues and for minimising competitive distortions between online traders and traditional businesses. This has become even more relevant in light of the outbreak of COVID-19 in 2020, as containment and mitigation measures taken in response to the pandemic have notably led to spikes in online shopping and increased demand for digital products and online services.

VAT policy design and administration has been an important component in most government's fiscal policy responses to mitigate the impact of the COVID-19 crisis in 2020. The outbreak of COVID-19 resulted in a health and economic crisis that was without precedent in recent history. Governments around the world introduced expansive containment and mitigation measures to slow down and reduce infection rates. Together with the overall health crisis, these necessary containment measures have had sudden and profound impacts. These measures reduced production and coupled with the overall health crisis they reduced business and household demand. With containment measures in place, governments' early policy reactions were aimed in particular at alleviating economic hardship and maintaining the productive capacity of the economy. Economic policy measures have focused primarily on providing liquidity support to businesses to help them stay afloat and providing income support to vulnerable households. As the duration of the pandemic lengthens and uncertainty about its development remains high, countries have been extending and expanding these emergency policy measures. VAT policy and administration measures have been a key component of these economic policy responses. These VAT measures are discussed in further detail in Chapter 2 of this publication.

1.1.2. Excise duties as an instrument to influence consumer behaviour

Whilst VAT was first introduced about 60 years ago, excise duties have existed since the dawn of civilisation. They are levied on a specific range of products and are assessed by reference to various characteristics such as weight, volume, strength or quantity of the product, combined in some cases with ad valorem taxes. Although they generally apply to alcoholic beverages, tobacco products and fuels in all OECD countries and beyond, their tax base, calculation method and rates vary widely between countries, reflecting local cultures and historical practice. Excise duties are increasingly being used to influence consumer behaviour to achieve health and, increasingly, environmental objectives.

1.1.3. Structure of this chapter

This chapter first provides an overview of the statistical classification of consumption taxes (Section 1.2). In then shows the evolution of consumption tax revenues between 1965 and 2018 (Section 1.3) and the geographical spread of VAT (Section 1.4). This is followed by an overview of the main features of VAT design (Section 1.5), of the main design features of retail sales taxes (Section 1.6) and of the main characteristics of consumption taxes on specific goods and services (Section 1.7). Section 1.8 of this chapter provides a further detailed discussion of the application of VAT to cross-border sales of goods, services and intangibles and the main recommendations included in the International VAT/GST Guidelines developed by the OECD as the internationally agreed standard for addressing the VAT challenges of international, particularly in the context of the continuously growing digital economy. It finally outlines the follow-up work carried out by the OECD to support the consistent and effective implementation of these standards.

1.2. Classification of consumption taxes

In the OECD classification, "taxes" are confined to compulsory, unrequited payments to general government. According to the OECD nomenclature, taxes are divided into five broad categories: taxes on income, profits and capital gains (1000); social security contributions (2000); taxes on payroll and workforce (3000); taxes on property (4000); and taxes on goods and services (5000) (OECD, 2020[1])

Consumption taxes (Category 5100 "Taxes on production, sale, transfer, leasing and delivery of goods and rendering of services") fall mainly into two sub-categories:

- *General taxes on goods and services* (5110 "taxes on general consumption"), which includes value added taxes (5111), sales taxes (5112) and other general taxes on goods and services (5113).
- *Taxes on specific goods and services* (5120) consisting primarily of excise taxes (5121), customs and import duties (5123) and taxes on specific services (5126, e.g. taxes on insurance premiums and financial services).

Consumption taxes such as VAT, sales taxes and excise duties are often categorised as *indirect taxes* as they are generally not levied directly on the person who is supposed to bear the burden of the tax. They are rather imposed on certain transactions, products or events (OECD Glossary of Tax Terms). They are not imposed on income or wealth but rather on the expenditure that the income and wealth finance. Governments generally collect the tax from producers and distributors at various points in the value chain, while the burden of the tax falls in principle on consumers assuming that it will be passed on to them in the prices charged by suppliers.

1.3. Evolution of consumption tax revenues

In 2018, consumption taxes accounted for 30.8% of the total tax revenue in OECD countries on average representing 10.3% of the GDP in these countries on average (unweighted average, (Annex Table 1.A.1). Approximately two thirds of revenue from consumption taxes is attributable to taxes on general consumption and one third to taxes on specific goods and services (see Annex Table 1.A.2 and Annex Table 1.A.3).

Figure 1.1. Average tax revenue as a percentage of aggregate taxation by category of tax, 2018

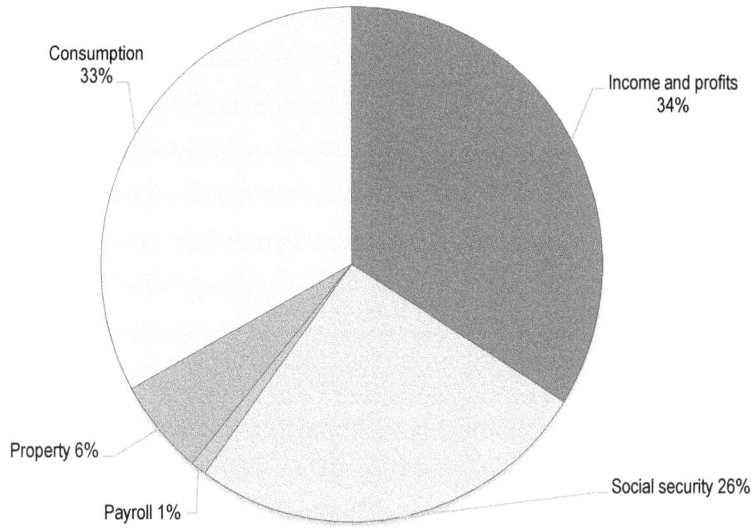

Source: OECD *Adapted from Revenue Statistics 2020, OECD publishing Paris.* (OECD, 2020[1])

StatLink https://doi.org/10.1787/888934219831

Three groups of countries can be distinguished depending on their level of consumption tax revenues as a share of GDP: low (consumption tax-to-GDP ratios below 9%), mid (between 9% and 13%) and high (above 13%). The high consumption tax-to-GDP group in 2018 was entirely composed of European Union (EU) countries, while all countries with low consumption tax-to-GDP ratios were non-EU countries, except for Ireland.

Between 2015 and 2018, the average consumption tax-to-GDP ratio increased slightly by 0.1 percentage point. Over this period, 19 countries reported an increase in their consumption tax-to-GDP ratios while 15 recorded a decrease and 3 saw no change. Greece and Poland recorded the largest increase (of 1.3 and 1.2 percentage points respectively) whereas Turkey recorded the largest decrease (of 1.2 percentage points).

The overall share of taxes on consumption in total tax revenue has remained relatively stable since 1995, except during the 2007-9 global economic crisis, where consumption tax revenues as a share of GDP declined by 0.33 percentage points on average. This decrease was largely driven by a fall in VAT revenues, with both consumption tax and VAT revenues only returning to their pre-crisis level in 2012. Recent OECD analysis shows that the overall level of consumption remained relatively stable during the 2007-9 global crisis. The fall in consumption tax and VAT revenues was primarily due to a shift in consumer spending towards necessity goods and services, often exempt or taxed at lower VAT rates, as well as an increase in the consumption of government and public sector services, which are exempt from VAT. Partly offsetting these impacts, the size of the consumption tax base actually increased as a share of GDP, largely due to strong decreases in investment. In general, however, revenues from taxes on consumption have generally been less affected by the global economic crisis and have been more stable over time than revenues from other bases such as corporate income (Simon and Harding, 2020[2]) (see special feature of Revenue Statistics 2020 (OECD, 2020[1])).

1.3.1. Taxes on general consumption now account for more than 21% of total taxation

Taxes on general consumption include VAT, sales taxes and other general taxes on goods and services. These taxes accounted for 21,2% of total tax revenues in OECD countries on average in 2018, up from

21,1% in 2015, representing 7.1% of GDP on average, up from 6.9 % in 2015. Their importance varies considerably between countries both as a share of GDP and of total taxation (see Annex Table 1.A.2). In Australia, Mexico, Switzerland, and the United States, taxes on general consumption account for less than 4% of GDP while they account for more than 9% in Denmark, Estonia, Finland, Hungary, Latvia, New Zealand and Sweden. Revenues from those taxes account for less than 15% of total taxation in Australia, Canada, Italy, Japan, Switzerland and the United States and for more than 29% in Chile, Colombia, Hungary, Israel, Latvia and New Zealand. Taxes on general consumption account for more than 20% of total taxation in 21 of the 37 OECD countries, with an OECD unweighted average of 21.2%.

Between 2015 and 2018, the vast majority OECD countries recorded an increase in revenues from taxes on general consumption, with 23 countries reporting an increase of revenues from these taxes as a share of GDP while 9 recorded a decrease and 5 saw no change.

Over the longer term, OECD member countries have relied increasingly on taxes on general consumption. Since 1975, the share of these taxes as a percentage of GDP in OECD countries has almost doubled, from 4.1% to 7.1% in 2018. They accounted for only 13.4% of total tax revenue in OECD countries in 1975 compared to 21.2% in 2018.

1.3.2. VAT remains the largest source of consumption tax revenues, by far

In 2018, VAT has remained stable as the largest source of revenue from taxes on general consumption in the OECD, on average, and as a key source of these countries' total tax revenues (see Annex Table 1.A.4). Revenues from VAT as a percentage of GDP slightly increased from 6.7% in 2015 to 6.8% in 2018 on average and as a share of total taxation from 20.3% to 20.4% over the same period.

25 of the 36 countries that operate a VAT reported an increase in their VAT revenues as a share of GDP between 2015 and 2018, while 8 countries reported a decrease and 3 countries reported no change. Poland and Greece recorded the largest increase (of 1.1 and 1.0 percentage points respectively) whereas decreases remained relatively small with Luxemburg reporting the largest decrease at 0.4 percentage points.

VAT is now operated in 36 of the 37 OECD countries, the United States being the only OECD country not to have adopted a VAT. In 1975, thirteen of the current OECD member countries had a VAT (see Annex Table 2.1 in Chapter 2). Colombia, Greece, Iceland, Japan, Mexico, New Zealand, Portugal, Spain and Turkey introduced VAT in the 1980s while Switzerland followed shortly afterwards. Central European economies introduced VAT in the late 1980s and early 1990s, often based on the European Union (EU) model in anticipation of their future EU membership. Australia implemented a VAT ("Goods and Services Tax – GST) in 2000.

The share of VAT in total tax revenues in the 36 OECD countries that operate a VAT shows a considerable spread, ranging from 12-13 % in Australia, Canada, Japan, Switzerland to 26-27% in Estonia, Latvia, Lithuania; and to 29.4% and 29.8 % in Colombia and New Zealand and 41.2 % in Chile (see Figure 1.2 and Annex Table 1.A.4). VAT produces 15% or more of total tax revenues in 31 of the 36 OECD countries that operate a VAT and it exceeds 20% of total taxation in 21 of these countries.

Figure 1.2. Value added taxes as a percentage of total tax revenues, 2018

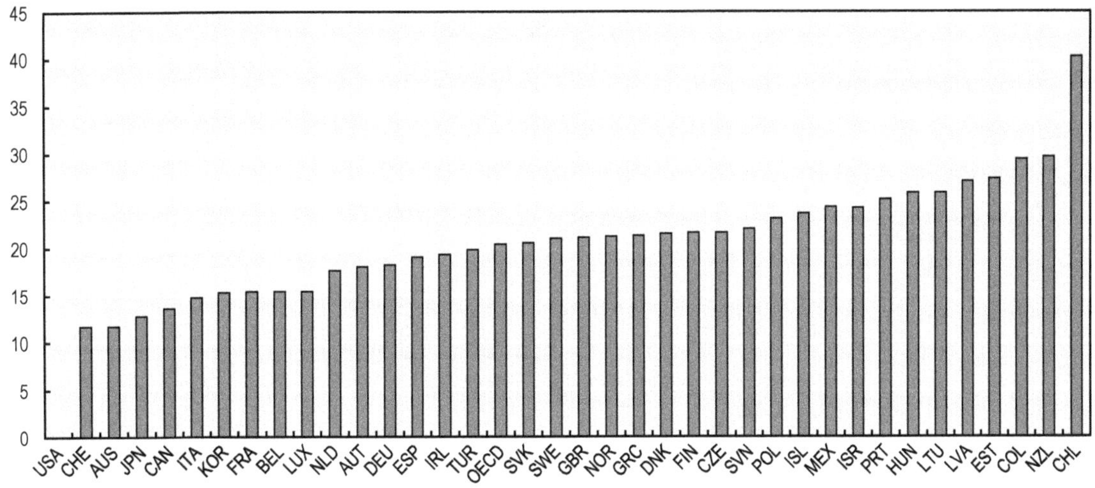

Source: *Adapted from Revenue Statistics 2020, OECD publishing Paris.* (OECD, 2020[1]).

StatLink https://doi.org/10.1787/888934219850

Many factors influence VAT revenue and their importance in the countries' tax mix. Tax policy decisions regarding the balance between the various sources of government revenue obviously play a key role but the efficiency of the tax system to collect VAT revenue effectively is also crucial. The most powerful of the drivers of (changes in) VAT revenues is countries' capacity to collect the tax on its natural base, i.e. final consumption, as influenced by the application of reduced rates and exemptions and the capacity to combat fraud, evasion and tax planning. The capacity of collecting the VAT on inbound supplies in the context of the digitalisation of the economy also plays a growing role. These efficiency factors, the impact of which is estimated in countries' VAT Revenue Ratio (see Chapter 2), often play a greater role in countries' VAT revenues than the level of the standard VAT rate (Michael Keen, 2013[3]).

1.3.3. Taxes on specific goods and services now account for less than 10% of total taxation

Annex Table 1.A.3 shows that revenues from taxes on specific goods and services have decreased steadily as a percentage of GDP between 1975 (4.6%) and 2010 (3.3%) and have remained stable on average since then at 3.2% in 2018. The evolution of the share of taxes on specific goods and services in total taxation has followed the same pattern and decreased from 17.7% in 1975 to 10.1% in 2015 and falling further to 9.6% on average in 2018. The share of taxes on specific goods and services in total tax revenues fell in almost all OECD countries since 1975.

Excise taxes form the bulk of taxes on specific goods and services, accounting for 2.4% of GDP on average in 2018 down from 2.5% in 2015. Between 2015 and 2018, 19 OECD countries recorded a drop in revenues from excise duties as a share of GDP, with only 7 countries reporting an increase and 11 countries reporting no change. The taxes are discussed in greater detail in Chapters 3 and 4.

As a result of this long-term trend, the composition of consumption taxes has fundamentally changed over time. The substantially increased importance of VAT has effectively balanced the diminishing share of taxes on specific goods and services (see Figure 1.3). Only Turkey still collects more than 15% of its revenues by way of taxes on specific goods and services, i.e. 19.2% of its total tax revenue against an OECD average of 9.6%.

Figure 1.3. Share of consumption taxes as a percentage of total tax revenues, 1968-2018

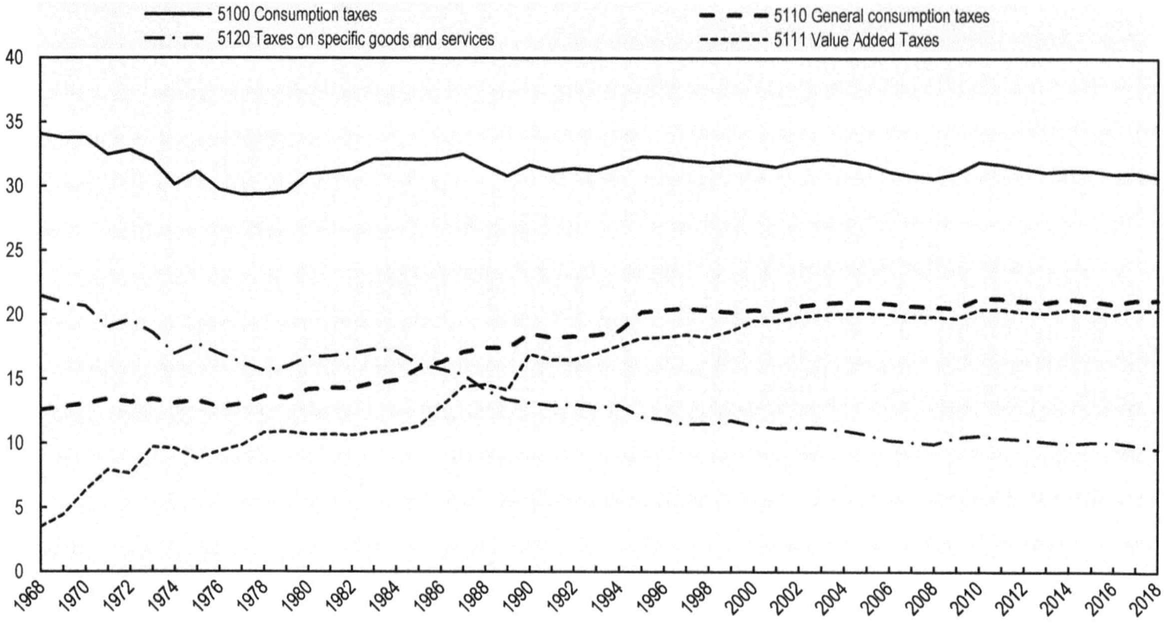

Source: Adapted from *Revenue Statistics 2020*, OECD Publishing, Paris. (OECD, 2020[1]).

StatLink https://doi.org/10.1787/888934219869

Figure 1.3 and Figure 1.4 show the evolution of the tax structure or tax mix in OECD countries between 1965 and 2018. Tax structures are measured by the share of major taxes in total tax revenue. On average, taxes on personal income (personal income tax and social security contributions) increased slightly over this period, representing together about 50% of total tax revenue in 2018. With a share of 20%, VAT is the third largest source of tax revenue for OECD countries on average, ahead of corporate income taxes, payroll and property taxes. The share of corporate income taxes remained relatively stable over the long time, reaching 10% of total tax revenue in 2018.

1.4. Spread of VAT

The spread of VAT has been among the most important developments in taxation over the last half century. Limited to less than 10 countries in the late 1960s, it is today an important source of revenue in 170 countries worldwide (see Figure 1.5 and Annex 1.A).

Figure 1.4. Evolution of the tax mix as a percentage of total tax revenues, 1965-2018

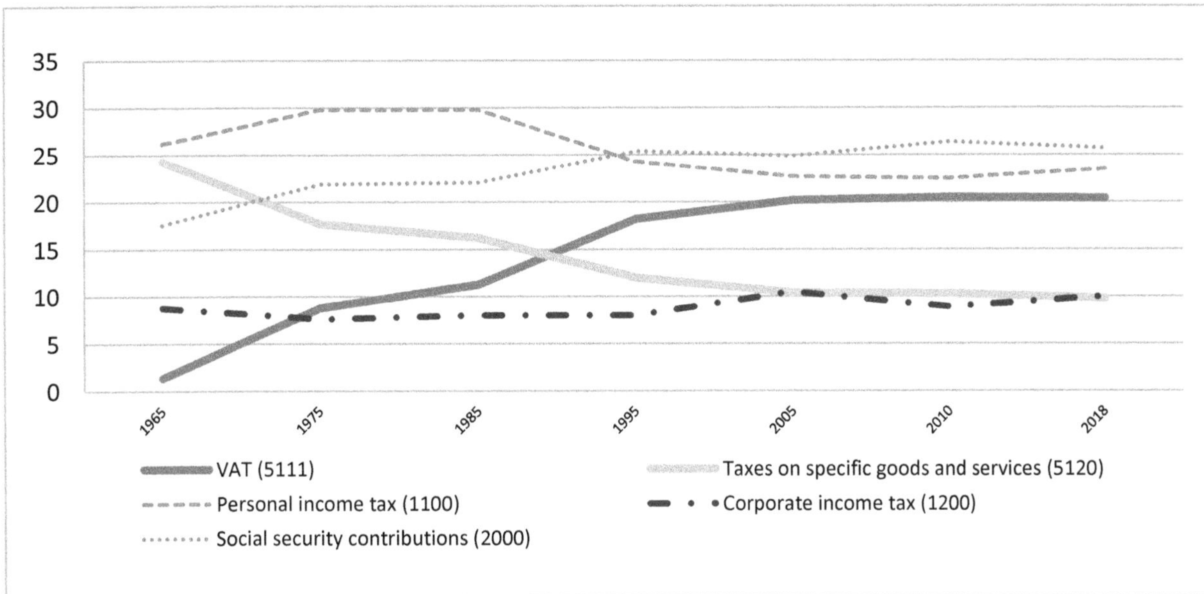

Source: Adapted from *Revenue Statistics 2020*, OECD Publishing, Paris (OECD, 2020[1]).

StatLink https://doi.org/10.1787/888934219888

The domestic and international neutrality properties of the VAT have encouraged its global spread. Many developing countries have introduced a VAT during the last decades to replace lost revenues from trade taxes following trade liberalisation. In the European Union, VAT is directly associated with the development of its internal market. The adoption of a common VAT framework in the European Union was intended to remove the trade distortions associated with cascading indirect taxes that it replaced and to facilitate the creation of a common market in which member states cannot use taxes on production and consumption to protect their domestic market or to gain a competitive advantage compared to other member states. A VAT is operated in 36 of the 37 OECD countries, the only exception being the United States.

Figure 1.5. Countries with VAT 1960-2020

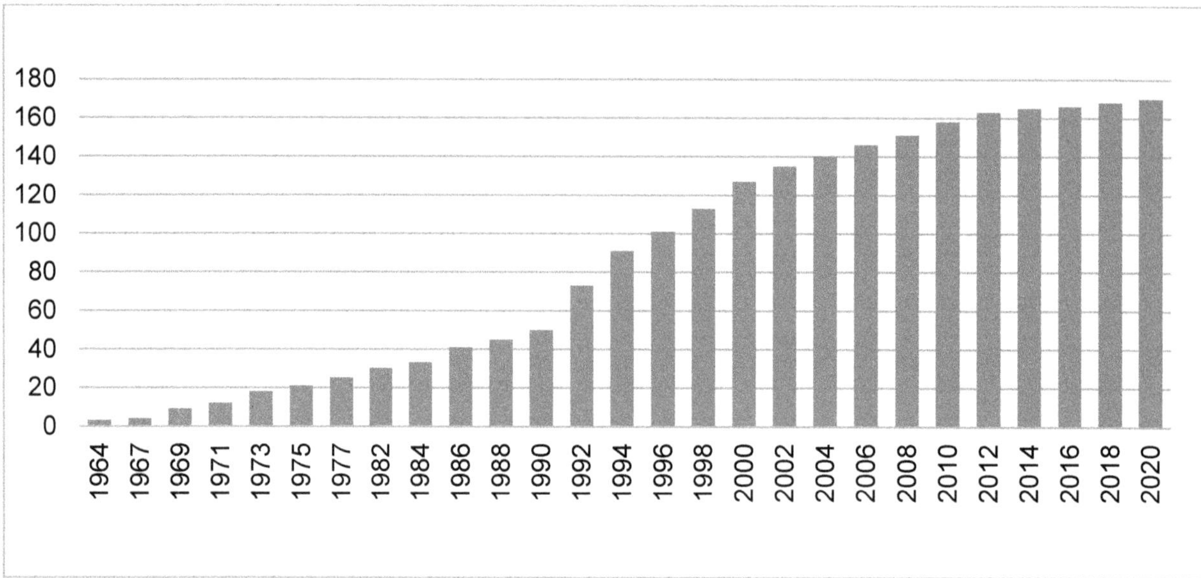

Source: Author's work based on Fabiola Annacondia 2019.

StatLink https://doi.org/10.1787/888934219907

1.5. The main features of VAT design

Although there is a wide diversity in the way VAT systems are implemented, this tax can be defined by its purpose and its specific tax collection mechanism. The *OECD International VAT/GST Guidelines* (OECD, 2017[4]) provide an overview of the core features of VAT, which are summarised below.

1.5.1. VAT is a tax on final consumption

The overarching purpose of a VAT is to impose a broad-based tax on final consumption, which is understood to mean final consumption by households. In principle, only private individuals, as distinguished from businesses, engage in the consumption at which a VAT is targeted. "Businesses buy and use capital goods, office supplies and the like - but they do not consume them in this sense" (Hellerstein, 2010[5]) In practice, however, many VAT systems impose VAT burden not only on consumption by private individuals, but also on various entities that are involved in non-business activities.

From a legal and practical standpoint, VAT is essentially a transaction tax. In "real life", things can be consumed in many ways. Some can be consumed fully and immediately (like a taxi ride), some can be bought and fully consumed later (like a sandwich), some can be consumed over a longer period of time (like a desk or a subscription to an on-line database). However, VAT does not actually tax such material consumption. Rather, it aims at taxing the sale to the final consumer through a staged collection process along the supply chain.

The staged collection process means that VAT is in principle collected on sales to businesses (B2B) as well as on sales to private consumers (B2C). However, since its purpose is to impose a tax on final consumption by households, the burden of the VAT should in principle not rest on businesses, except where explicitly provided for in legislation (e.g. where purchases are made for the private consumption of the business owners or their employees). This is achieved by giving businesses the right to deduct the

VAT they incur on their inputs from the VAT they collect on their outputs and to remit only the balance to the tax authorities.

It can be argued, however, that the economic burden of the VAT may effectively lie in a variable proportion on business and consumers. Indeed, the effective incidence of VAT, like that of any other tax, is determined not only by its formal nature but also by market circumstances, including the elasticity of demand and the nature of competition between suppliers (LEbrill@imf.org/MKeen@imf.org/VSummers@imf.org, 2001[6]).

1.5.2. The tax is collected under a staged collection process

The central design feature of a VAT, and the feature from which it derives its name, is that the tax is collected through a staged process on the value added at each stage of production and distribution. Each business in the supply chain takes part in the process of controlling and collecting the tax, remitting the proportion of tax corresponding to its margin, i.e. on the difference between the VAT imposed on its taxed inputs and the VAT imposed on its taxed outputs. Businesses collect VAT on the value of their outputs from their customers and are entitled to deduct the tax they have paid on purchases and must account and remit the difference (or receive a refund from) to the tax authorities. In this respect, the VAT differs from a retail sales tax ("RST"), which taxes consumption through a single-stage levy imposed in theory only at the point of final sale.

This mechanism reflects the central design feature of the VAT as a tax collected by businesses through a staged payment process coupled with the fundamental principle that the burden of the tax does not rest on businesses but on final consumers. This requires a mechanism for relieving businesses of the burden of the VAT they pay when they acquire goods, services or intangibles.

There are two main approaches for operating the staged collection process:

- Under the invoice credit method (which is a "transaction based method"), each trader charges VAT at the rate specified for each supply and passes to the purchaser an invoice showing the amount of tax charged. The purchaser is in turn able to credit that input tax against the output tax it charges on its sales, remitting the balance to the tax authorities and receiving refunds when there are excess credits. This method is based on invoices that could, in principle, be crosschecked to pick up any overstatement of credit entitlement. By linking the tax credit on the purchaser's inputs to the tax paid by the purchaser, the invoice credit method is designed to discourage fraud.
- Under the subtraction method (which is an "entity based method"), the tax is levied directly on an accounts-based measure of value added, which is determined for each business by subtracting the VAT calculated on allowable purchases from the VAT calculated on taxable supplies.

Almost all jurisdictions that operate a VAT use the invoice-credit method. In the OECD, only Japan uses "credit subtraction VAT", where the VAT on taxable sales (output tax) is calculated by multiplying the total taxable sales by the VAT rate while the amount of deductible input VAT is calculated by extracting the VAT from the total VAT inclusive amount of purchases as recorded in the business's purchase records. This includes the purchases from exempt suppliers such as unregistered small businesses so that there is no incentive to purchase from taxable businesses, but excludes exempt supplies such as financial services. The VAT-liability is calculated on an annual basis, except for certain businesses which can elect for quarterly accounting periods (e.g. exporters that are eligible for VAT refunds). There is no requirement to issue VAT invoices; businesses are required to document their VAT liability and this documentation can include invoices.

1.5.3. VAT is a neutral tax

The staged collection process, whereby tax is in principle collected from businesses only on the value added at each stage of production and distribution, gives to the VAT its essential character in domestic trade as an economically neutral tax. The full right to deduct input tax through the supply chain, except by the final consumer, ensures the neutrality of the tax, whatever the nature of the product, the structure of the distribution chain, and the means used for its delivery (e.g. retail stores, physical delivery, Internet downloads). As a result of the staged payment system, VAT "flows through the businesses" to tax supplies made to final consumers.

Where the deductible input VAT for any period exceeds the output VAT collected, there is an excess of VAT credit, which should in principle be refunded. This is generally the case in particular for exporters, since their output is in principle free of VAT (i.e. exempt with right to deduct the related input tax) under the destination principle, and for businesses whose purchases are larger than their sales in the same period (such as new or developing businesses or seasonal businesses). These are especially important groups in terms of wider economic development, so it is important that VAT systems provide for an effective treatment of excess credits to avoid the risk that VAT introduces significant and costly distortions for these groups of business. At the same time, however, the payment of refunds evidently can create significant opportunities for fraud and corruption. It is important therefore that an effective refund system is administered properly, supported by a well-designed and operated risk based compliance strategy and by a comprehensive audit strategy (LEbrill@imf.org/MKeen@imf.org/VSummers@imf.org, 2001[7]).

When the right to deduct input VAT covers all business inputs, the final burden of the tax does not lie on businesses but on consumers. This is not always the case in practice, as the right to deduct input tax may be restricted in a number of ways. Some are deliberate and some result from imperfect administration (see Chapter 2).

Restrictions to the deduction of input VAT result in particular from the application of VAT exemptions. When a supply is VAT-exempt, the supplier does not charge any VAT on the supply while it is not entitled to deduct the VAT it has incurred on the related inputs. Many VAT systems apply exemptions for social (health, education and charities), practical (financial services, insurance) or historical (immovable property, land) reasons.

Another set of restrictions to the right of deduction of input VAT relates to purchases used, or deemed to be used, for the private consumption of the owners of a business, or of its employees or clients (e.g. cars and entertainment).

Chapter 2 of the OECD's *International VAT/GST Guidelines* presents the key principles of VAT-neutrality and a set of internationally agreed standards to support neutrality of VAT in international trade.

1.6. Man design features of Retail Sales Taxes

A retail sales tax is a tax on general consumption charged only once on products at the last point of sale to the end user. In principle, only consumers are charged the tax; resellers are exempt if they are not final end users of the products. To implement this principle, business purchasers are normally required to provide the seller with a "resale certificate," which states that they are purchasing an item to resell it, or with equivalent evidence that the business will fulfil whatever tax obligations it may have (e.g. a so-called "direct pay" permit, which is analogous to the "reverse charge" concept). The tax is charged on each item sold to purchasers who do not provide such a certificate or equivalent evidence. The retail sales tax covers not only retailers, but all businesses dealing with purchasers who do not provide a resale or other evidence signifying that no tax is due (e.g. a public body or a charity, unless specific exemption applies).

The basis for taxation is the sales price. Like the VAT and unlike multi-stage cumulative taxes, this system allows the tax burden to be calculated precisely and it does not in principle discriminate between different forms of production or distribution channels. In practice, however, at least in the United States, the failure of the retail sales tax to reach many services and the limitation of the resale exemption to products that are resold in the same form that they are purchased, or are physically incorporated into products that are resold, leads to substantial taxation of business inputs.

In theory, the final outcomes of VAT and retail sales tax should be identical: they both ultimately aim to tax final consumption of a wide range of products where such consumption takes place. They also both tax the consumption expenditure i.e. the transaction between the seller and the buyer rather than the actual consumption. In practice, however, the end result may be somewhat different given the fundamental difference in the way the tax is collected. Unlike VAT where the tax is collected at each stage of the value chain under a staged payment system (see Section 1.5 above), sales taxes are collected only at the very last stage i.e. on the sale by the retailer to the final consumer. The latter method has significant disadvantages: the higher the rate the more pressure is placed on the weakest link in the chain i.e. on the retailer and in particular on numerous small retailers. All the revenue is at risk if the retailer fails to remit the tax to the authorities and the audit and invoice trail is poorer than under a VAT, especially for services. In addition, revenue is not secured at the time of importation and this can be crucial for many developing countries. As a result, a single point resale sales tax is efficient at relatively low rates, but is increasingly difficult to administer as rates rise (Smith and Tait, 1990[8]).

The United States is the only OECD country that employs a retail sales tax as the principal consumption tax. However, the retail sales tax in the United States is not a national tax. Rather, it is a subnational tax imposed at the state and local government levels. Currently, 45 of the 50 States as well as thousands of local tax jurisdictions impose broad-based retail sales taxes. In general, the local taxes are identical in coverage to the state-level tax, are administered at the state level and amount in substance simply to an increase in the state rate, with the additional revenues distributed to the localities. Retail sales taxes are complemented in every state by functionally identical "use" taxes imposed on goods purchased from out-of-state vendors, because the state has no power to tax out-of-state "sales" and therefore imposes a complementary tax on the in-state "use" (Jerome R. Hellerstein, 2020[9])

Combined state and local sales tax rates vary widely in the United States, from 1.76% (Alaska), 4.44% (Hawaii) and 5.46% (Wisconsin) to 9.53% (Tennessee), 9.52% (Louisiana), and 9.47% (Arkansas). Five states do not have a state-wide sales tax (Alaska, Delaware, Montana, New Hampshire, and Oregon and, of these, only Alaska generally allows localities to charge local sales taxes and Montana permits special taxes in local resort areas (Janelle Cammenga, 2020[10]). These rates are much lower than the applicable VAT rates in OECD countries (except Canada, Japan and Switzerland). This is due to two main factors: the compliance risks associated with the sales tax collection method (see above) and the competition between jurisdictions (see below).

Retail sales and use taxes in force in the United States are subject to significant competitive pressure, especially in the context of interstate and international trade. Prior to the US Supreme Court's decision in *South Dakota v. Wayfair, Inc.* (June 2018), Supreme Court rulings interpreting constitutional restraints on state taxation prohibited states from requiring vendors to collect tax with respect to cross-border sales when they were not physically present in the purchaser's state. States were therefore unable effectively to collect use taxes with respect to cross-border sales from remote sellers, a problem that became increasingly significant with the advent of the Internet and online sales. In *Wayfair*, the Court overruled the physical-presence requirement for enforcing tax collection obligations on remote vendors as "unsound and incorrect," and it sustained a South Dakota statute imposing such obligations on remote vendors whose annual sales into the state exceeded USD 100,000 or who annual engaged in 200 or more separate transactions in the state. In place of the physical-presence nexus rule for requiring remote vendors to collect tax on sales to in-state customers, the Court adopted a nexus rule that looks to whether the taxpayer tax collector "avails itself of the substantial privilege of carrying on business" in the state based on its "economic and virtual contacts" with the state.

Although the general standards the Court articulated in *Wayfair* provide little concrete guidance to state tax administrators and state tax advisors as to the nature and level of "economic and virtual" contacts that will satisfy constitutional nexus norms for remote sellers, the Court did identify several features of the South Dakota statute that, in its view, were designed to prevent undue burdens upon interstate commerce and thus implicitly provided guidance to the states in designing their tax enforcement regimes. First, the nexus statute provided a safe harbour for those who transact only limited business in the state. Second, the statute did not apply retroactively. Third, South Dakota was one of more than 20 states that have adopted the Streamlined Sales and Use Tax Agreement (SSUTA - available at www.streamlinedsalestax.org), which "standardizes taxes to reduce administrative and compliance costs." As the Court elaborated: "It requires a single, state level tax administration, uniform definitions of products and services, simplified tax rate structures, and other uniform rules. It also provides sellers access to sales tax administration software paid for by the State. Sellers who choose to use such software are immune from audit liability." Indeed, as of November 2020, 42 of the 45 states with sales taxes have adopted legislation or administrative guidance imposing tax collection obligations on remote vendors, as well as on digital platforms, based on thresholds analogous to those sustained by the Court in *Wayfair*, and more than half of these states are members of SSUTA, a number that is likely to increase in the future. It is also worth noting that the US Congress possesses the ultimate power (regardless of pre-existing judicially created nexus rules) to prescribe the terms under which remote vendors must collect tax on cross-border sales and could approve proposed legislation authorising states to require such collection if they have adopted SSUTA or similar measures to ease compliance burdens for vendors.

1.7. Main characteristics of consumption taxes on specific goods and services

In the OECD nomenclature, taxes on specific goods and services (5120) include a range of taxes such as excises, customs and import duties, taxes on exports and taxes on specific services. Consumption Tax Trends focuses on excise duties only.

A number of general characteristics differentiate excise duties from value added taxes:

- They are levied on a limited range of products.
- They are not normally due until the goods enter free circulation, which may be at a late stage in the supply chain.
- Excise charges are generally assessed by reference to the weight, volume, strength or quantity of the product, combined in some cases, with *ad valorem* taxes.
- Consequently, and unlike VAT, the excise system is characterised by a small number of taxpayers at the manufacturing or wholesale stage (although, in some cases they can also be levied at the resale stage).

As with VAT, excise taxes aim to be neutral internationally. As the tax is normally collected when the goods are released into free circulation, neutrality is often ensured by exempting the targeted goods from excise duties under controlled regimes (such as bonded warehouses) and certification of final export (again under controlled conditions) by customs authorities. Similarly, imported excise goods are levied at importation although frequently the goods enter into controlled tax-free regimes until released into free circulation.

Excise taxes may cover a very wide range of products like salt, sugar, matches, fruit juice or chocolates. However, the range of products subject to excise has declined with the expansion of taxes on general consumption. On the other hand, excise taxes on alcohol, tobacco and hydrocarbon oils are increasingly used by governments to influence consumers' behaviour and continue to raise significant revenues for governments (see Chapter 3 and 4).

There has indeed been a discernible trend in recent decades to ascribe to these taxes characteristics other than simply revenue raising. A number of excise duties have been adjusted with a view to discouraging certain behaviours considered harmful, especially for health and environmental reasons. This is particularly the case for excise duties on tobacco and alcohol whose rates have increased over time with the aim of reducing consumption of these products. The structure of certain excise duties, for example on road fuels and vehicles, has also gradually changed to encourage more responsible behaviour towards the collective welfare, especially the environment (see Chapter 3).

1.8. VAT and international trade - The destination principle

1.8.1. The choice for the destination principle

The overarching purpose of the VAT as a levy on final consumption coupled with its central design feature of a staged collection process lays the foundation for the core VAT principles bearing on international trade. The fundamental issue of economic policy in relation to the international application of the VAT is whether the levy should be imposed by the jurisdiction of origin or destination. Under the destination principle, the tax is fully levied on the final consumption that occurs within the taxing jurisdiction. Under the origin principle, the tax is levied in the various jurisdictions where the value is added. The key economic difference between the two principles is that the destination principle places all firms competing in a given jurisdiction on an even footing whereas the origin principle places consumers in different jurisdictions on an even footing.

There is a strong economic and policy case for countries adopting the destination principle. First, a destination principle VAT guarantees the independence of countries in determining the rates at which they wish to tax domestic consumption. Second, in the absence of global uniform VAT rate and exemptions, the adoption of the origin principle would result in price differences within the country for the same goods since they may include different value-added tax burdens, which may also be different from those on domestic production. The origin principle therefore introduces production inefficiencies and implies some degree of positive or negative protection of domestic production for each country, depending upon its tax rate relative to its trading partners. (Victoria J Perry ; Katherine Baer ; Emil M Sunley, 1996[11])

In contrast, the application of the destination principle in VAT achieves neutrality in international trade. Under the destination principle, exports are exempt with refund of input taxes (that is, free of VAT) and imports are taxed on the same basis and at the same rates as domestic supplies. Accordingly, the total tax paid in relation to a supply is determined by the rules applicable in the jurisdiction of its consumption and therefore all revenue accrues to the jurisdiction where the supply to the final consumer occurs.

For these reasons, there is widespread consensus on the destination principle, which is actually the international norm. It is sanctioned by the World Trade Organisation rules and it is one of the key principles on which the OECD's *International VAT/GST Guidelines* are grounded.

Sales tax systems, although they work differently in practice, also set out to tax consumption of goods, and to some extent services, within the jurisdiction of consumption. Exported goods are usually relieved from sales tax to provide a degree of neutrality for cross-border trade. However, in most sales tax systems, businesses do incur some irrecoverable sales tax on their inputs and, if they subsequently export goods, there will be an element of sales tax embedded in the price.

The application of the destination principle is not without its own difficulties. First, as already noted, the usual way of implementing this principle for VAT involves exemption of exports, which means that goods and services circulate free of tax in cross-border trade. The possibilities of fraud are evident. Second, although most of the rules currently in force are generally intended to tax supplies of goods and services within the jurisdiction where consumption takes place in application of the destination principle, practical means of implementing this intention are diverse across countries. This can, in some instances, lead to double taxation or unintended non-taxation and create uncertainties for both business and tax administrations. The adoption of the OECD International VAT/GST Guidelines responds to these challenges (see below).

1.8.2. Implementing the destination principle

While the destination principle has been widely accepted as the basis for applying VAT to international trade, its implementation is nevertheless diverse across jurisdictions. This can lead to double taxation or unintended non-taxation and to complexity and uncertainty for businesses and tax administrations.

In order to apply the destination principle, VAT systems must have a mechanism for identifying the destination of supplies. Because VAT is generally applied on a transaction-by-transaction basis, VAT systems contain "place of taxation" rules that address all transactions, building on "proxies" that indicate where the good or service supplied is expected to be used by a business in the production and distribution process (if the supply is made to a business) or consumed (if the supply is made to a final consumer).

The following paragraphs provide a concise overview of the mechanisms for identifying the destination of a supply, focusing on supplies of goods first and then on supplies of services.

1.8.3. Application to the cross-border trade in goods

The term "goods" generally means "tangible property" for VAT purposes. The VAT treatment of supplies of goods normally depends on the location of the goods at the time of the transaction and/or their location as a result of the transaction. The supply of a good is in principle subject to VAT in the jurisdiction where the good is located at the time of the transaction. When a transaction involves goods being moved from one jurisdiction to another, the exported goods are generally "free of VAT" in the origin's jurisdiction (and are freed of any input VAT via successive businesses' deductions of input tax), whilst imports are subject to the same VAT as equivalent domestic goods in the importing jurisdiction. The VAT on imports is generally collected at the same time as customs duties, although in some countries collection is postponed until declared on the importer's next VAT return. Deduction of the VAT incurred at importation, in the same way as input tax deduction on a domestic supply, ensures neutrality and limits distortions in relation to international trade.

Within the European Union, which abolished internal customs barriers and tax frontiers in 1993, the system of intra-Community delivery (free of VAT in the Member State of origin) and intra-Community acquisition (taxed in the Member State of destination) for business-to-business supplies allows the application of the destination principle even in the absence of customs procedures.

Many VAT systems apply a "*de minimis*" exemption for the importation of relatively low value goods. These exemptions are generally motivated by the consideration that the administrative costs of bringing these low value items into the customs and tax system were likely to outweigh the revenue gained. Most OECD countries currently apply such a VAT relief arrangement, with thresholds varying widely across countries, from USD 11 in Denmark to USD 200 in Colombia. For European Union countries, legislation in place until 1 July 2021 provides that Member States must exempt from VAT the import of goods whose value does not exceed EUR 10, and are permitted to grant an exemption for imported goods with a value of more than EUR 10 but not exceeding EUR 22. All EU Member States that are members of the OECD had opted for the higher threshold of EUR 22, except Denmark that applied the lower threshold of EUR 10 and France and Poland where there was no threshold for goods imported on mail order. This exemption in the EU did not apply to tobacco or tobacco products and alcoholic products. Turkey does not apply any threshold and tax at the border all imports of goods regardless of their value.

These VAT exemptions for low value imports have become increasingly controversial in the context of the growing digital economy. This was one of key the findings of Action 1 of the OECD/G20 Base Erosion and Profit Shifting (BEPS) project, on *Addressing the Tax Challenges of the Digital Economy* (OECD, 2015[12]). At the time when most low value import relief provisions were introduced, internet shopping did not exist and the level of imports benefitting from the relief was relatively low. In recent years, however, many countries have seen a significant and rapid growth in the volume of low value imports of physical goods from online sales on which VAT is not collected. This results in potentially unfair competitive pressures on domestic retailers who are required to charge VAT on their sales to domestic consumers and in decreased VAT revenues for governments. It also creates an incentive for domestic suppliers to relocate to an offshore jurisdiction in order to sell their low value goods free of VAT. The 2015 BEPS Action 1 report recognised that the difficulty lies in finding the balance between the need for appropriate revenue protection and avoidance of distortions of competition and the need to keep the cost of collection proportionate to the amounts of VAT to be collected. The report observed that tax authorities could be in a position to remove or lower their VAT exemption threshold for imports of low value goods, if they were able to improve the efficiency of processing such low value imports and of collecting the VAT on such imports. The report outlines and assesses the main available approaches to address this challenge, noting that a vendor collection model offered the most promising solution. Under this model, the (online) vendor of the low value goods or the digital platform through which these goods are sold is required to register in the jurisdiction of importation and to remit the VAT on these sales in that jurisdiction via the same simplified registration and collection mechanism that is recommended for the taxation of remote supplies of services and intangibles to final consumers (see below). Such a model limits or removes the need for customs authorities to intervene in the collection of VAT collection on the importation of these low value goods, since this VAT is collected directly from the vendor or digital platform at the time of sale. This collection method can apply to goods that are only subject to VAT on importation, which are in practice goods that have a value below the customs "de minimis" threshold (generally significantly higher than the VAT de minimis thresholds). Goods subject to specific duties such as excise would in principle be excluded from the vendor collection approach.

The OECD subsequently complemented the conclusions and recommendation for addressing the VAT challenges of the digital economy included in the 2015 BEPS Action 1 report with further detailed guidance to support their consistent and effective implementation. A first report on "Mechanisms for the effective collection of VAT/GST" (OECD, 2017[13]) includes detailed guidance on the design and implementation of the vendor collection model and on the simplified registration and compliance mechanism. A second report on "The role of digital platforms in the collection of VAT/GST on online sales" (OECD, 2019[14]) provides guidance on the available models for enlisting online marketplaces and other digital platforms in the collection of VAT on e-commerce, focusing in particular on the implementation of the vendor collection mechanism for the effective collection of VAT on imports of low value goods.

Australia was the first country to implement a vendor collection model for the collection of GST on imports of low value goods as of 1 July 2018, in accordance with the OECD guidance. The GST relief for imports of goods with value of AUD 1 000 or less remains in place and no GST on these imports is collected through border processes. A requirement was implemented for foreign vendors and digital platforms that supply more than AUD 75 000 of taxable goods to consumers in Australia per year, to register for GST in Australia and charge the tax on their sales to final consumers in Australia. The GST on the importation of these goods is collected from these foreign vendors through a simplified "pay only" registration regime, in line with OECD guidance. The threshold of AUD 75 000 is the same as the local registration threshold, below which Australian businesses are relieved from the collection of the GST. It aims to relieve small foreign vendors for whom the compliance cost of registering and remitting the GST on their goods sales to Australian consumers, from the requirement to do so.

New Zealand implemented a similar regime from 1 December 2019 where imports of low-value goods from foreign supplies to final consumers in New Zealand are taxed if the foreign supplier sells goods for more than NZD 60 000 per annum in the country, the same registration threshold as for domestic businesses. The GST relief for imports of goods with value of NZD 1000 or less supplied by foreign vendors to New Zealand final consumers was also repealed from that date. As for remote services, a simplified "pay only" registration is available to foreign suppliers, with the option to do a full registration to claim input credits for business-related purchases sourced from New Zealand. This system is very similar to the Australian system. One important difference is that New Zealand implemented a simplification measure allowing suppliers whose shipments to consumers in New Zealand comprise at least 75 percent of goods below the

NZD 1000 threshold, are allowed to make an election to apply the simplified "pay only" regime to the entire shipment, including the goods with a value above NZD 1000.

Under both Australian and New Zealand regimes, goods purchased from abroad via an online marketplace are considered to have been supplied by this online marketplace, which are required to collect and remit the GST on supplies made through them. This requirement also includes so-called "re-deliverers". This applies when a foreign vendor or a digital platform is requested to deliver the goods outside Australia or New Zealand without knowing that the goods are destined for one of these countries, and the consumer contracts to have those goods re-delivered to Australia or New Zealand. Then the re-deliverer is responsible for the collection of GST on the sale of these goods to the final consumers.

Norway was the next country to implement a vendor collection regime for the collection of VAT on the importation of low value goods in accordance with OECD guidance, as of 1 April 2020. Under that regime, foreign vendors and digital marketplaces that sell goods with value below NOK 3 000 to final consumers in Norway must register and account for VAT under a simplified "pay only" registration regime (VOEC) if they sell goods for more than NOK 50 000 per annum in the country, the same registration threshold as for domestic businesses. The VOEC is not available for goods with value at or above NOK 3 000, foodstuffs, restricted goods, and goods subject to excise duties, which are subject to border collection of VAT, excise duties and customs duties.

The EU is following the same trend. EU Member States adopted the so-called VAT e-commerce package in December 2017, with a view to enhancing and simplifying VAT compliance for online businesses. One of the key measures included in this package is the removal of the VAT exemption for imports of low-value goods (i.e. goods worth not more than EUR 22) from outside the EU as of 1 July 2021 (European Commission, 2017[15]). From that date, EU and non-EU vendors will have the option to charge and collect the VAT on distance sales of imported low value goods to EU consumers at the time of sale and to declare and pay this VAT through the EU's online digital portal (One Stop Shop; OSS). These goods will then be exempt from VAT at importation, allowing a fast release at customs. If EU and non-EU vendors do not opt for this simplified registration and collection regime, import VAT will be collected from customers by the customs declarant (e.g. postal operator, courier firm, customs agents) which will remit it to the customs authorities via a monthly payment rather than on a transactional basis. These new rules will apply to distance sales of goods by EU and non-EU vendors with a value of EUR 150 or below. Imports of goods above the EUR 150 (customs) threshold will still require a full customs declaration. Where such distance sales are facilitated by electronic marketplaces, these will be considered as the suppliers of the goods for VAT purposes and be liable for collecting and declaring the VAT on these sales. This requirement will include sales of goods that are already being stored by non-EU vendors in warehouses (so-called "fulfilment centres") within the EU, which have been increasingly used to sell goods fraudulently without VAT to consumers in the EU.

Switzerland implemented a regime since 1 January 2019 requiring foreign vendors and digital platforms to register for VAT in the country and to remit the tax on imports of low value goods to final consumers. Unlike the Australian and New Zealand rules, there is no simplified "pay only" registration available and the vendor or digital platform must register under the standard registration procedure. In Switzerland, low value goods are defined by the VAT amount due, i.e. when this amount exceeds CHF 5, which means that the value of the goods subject to that regime is of CHF 200 for those subject to the reduced rate of 2.5% and CHF 65 for those subject to the standard rate of 7.7%. Foreign vendors selling goods to consumers in Switzerland for a total amount of at least CHF 100 000 per annum (i.e. the same as the domestic registration threshold) are required to register and remit the VAT on these sales in Switzerland.

The common features of all these regimes is that the imports of low value goods destined to final consumers are not relieved from VAT any more, placing foreign and domestic vendors of such goods on an equal footing. The VAT is not collected upon importation by customs authorities but by the tax administration at the point of sale, i.e. when the good is sold by the foreign vendor or digital platform to the final consumer. Imports of goods that are not considered as "low value" goods i.e. whose value is above the value set by legislation or possibly subject to other taxes such as excise duties are taxed upon importation according to the standard customs procedures.

1.8.4. The destination principle also applies to the cross-border trade in services and intangibles

The VAT legislation in many countries tends to define a "service" negatively as "anything that is not otherwise defined", or to define a "supply of services" as anything other than a "supply of goods". While this generally also includes a reference to intangibles, some jurisdictions regard intangibles as a separate category. For the purposes of this section, references to "services" include "intangibles" unless otherwise stated.

While the application of the destination principle is relatively straightforward for the cross-border trade in goods, since their supply is in principle subject to VAT in the jurisdiction where they are physically located at the time of the supply or where they are imported, it is much less so for services. Given its intangible nature, it is more challenging for VAT systems to determine the destination of a service and thus to determine the jurisdiction that has the right to apply the VAT to the supply of this service. A variety of models for determining the place of taxation of internationally traded services can be observed in VAT systems around the world. Many systems for determining the place of taxation of services operate on the basis of a categorisation approach, in which supplies are divided into categories of services with a place of taxation specified for each category. Other models favour an iterative approach, in which the principle underlying the place of taxation rule is described in more general terms and where a series of rules are applied consecutively to determine the appropriate place of taxation. A combination of both approaches may also be applied. The key common feature among these various VAT models for determining the place of taxation of internationally traded services is that they generally aim to implement the destination principle, under which the place of taxation rules are intended to impose tax at the place of consumption. The OECD's International VAT/GST Guidelines have been designed to enhance consistency in the design and application of country's place of taxation rules by presenting an internationally accepted understanding of what is the place of taxation of internationally traded services and intangibles and by setting out consistent and effective approaches for determining this place of taxation with a view to minimising uncertainty, revenue risks, compliance costs and administrative burdens for tax authorities and businesses. These Guidelines are discussed in further detail in the closing section of this Chapter. The following paragraphs of this section provide an overview of some of the models for determining the place of taxation of internationally traded services that are operated around the world.

In the European Union, the determination of the "place of supply" (i.e. the place of taxation) depends on the status of the customer receiving the service and the nature of the service supplied. B2B supplies are in principle taxed at the customer's place of establishment (or at the fixed establishment of the customer to which it is provided), implementing the destination principle for both supplies within the EU and with customers in third countries. On the other hand, supplies of services to final consumers (B2C supplies) are still, in principle, taxed at the supplier's place of establishment. This latter rule does not reflect a will to apply the "origin principle" to B2C supplies but rather the historical reality that most services were consumed where they were provided and it was technically difficult to provide services at a distance to final consumers. There are, however, many exceptions aiming at aligning the place of taxation with the place where consumption is likely to take place. These exceptions include notably the services connected with immovable property (taxed where the property is located); services relating to cultural, artistic, sporting, scientific, educational, entertainment etc. (taxed at the place where they are physically carried out) and the B2C electronically supplied services, that are taxed where the customer resides (since 2003 for services provided by non-EU suppliers and since 2015 also for EU suppliers).

To facilitate compliance by non-EU suppliers, the EU member states created an online digital portal ("Mini One Stop Shop" - MOSS), allowing these suppliers to register at a distance in only one Member State and account in this Member State for the VAT due in all the Member States of the EU where their customers are located.

Although this model for determining the place of supply applies in the Member States of the Union and in a number of other countries such as Norway, Switzerland, and Russia, it is not the international norm. A number of countries (e.g. Australia, Canada, New Zealand, Singapore, South Africa) have adopted different models. While the EU model is based on an approach by category of supplies, where a "place of supply" (which is also the place of taxation) is determined for each category according to its nature and the status (business or consumer) of the customer, other models systematically apply a series of proxies for place of consumption or use to all kinds of services. Such systems work in steps: first a connection with the country is established (e.g. the supplier or the customer are established there; the service is performed or can be acquired there). Then, a number of proxies are applied to determine the actual place of taxation, e.g. a connection with a tangible property; the customer location and/or residence; the location of the person to whom the services are delivered or who uses the service.

For example, in New Zealand (which adopted the GST in 1986) the place of taxation for supplies made by non-residents is generally presumed to be outside New Zealand, except when the service is performed in New Zealand or supplied to a customer who is resident in New Zealand and the recipient is either a final consumer or a registered business who has agreed to have the transaction treated as being made in New Zealand. In contrast, the place of taxation for supplies by residents is presumed to be New Zealand, unless the supply is a zero-rated export of services. These services include international transport and related services; services physically performed outside New Zealand; services supplied to a non-resident who is outside New Zealand at the time the services are performed; services directly in connection with land or goods located outside New Zealand and supplies in relation to intellectual property rights for use outside New Zealand. From 1 October 2016, New Zealand applies GST to supplies of services and intangibles made by non-resident suppliers to final consumers who are usually resident in New Zealand (see section below).

In Australia (which adopted GST in 2000), supplies are taxable (unless GST-free) in Australia and the GST collected through the supplier when the supplies are "connected with Australia". Supplies made through an Australian based business or performed in Australia for a final consumer are connected with Australia. To prevent GST applying to services not consumed or used in Australia, the Australian GST law includes broad, proxy-based zero-ratings ("GST-free") similar to those used in New Zealand. The Australian GST rules were amended as from 1 July 2017, to make supplies of services and intangibles made by non-residents to final consumers who are residents of Australia generally taxable unless the GST-free provisions apply.

The different ways in which the VAT systems have attempted to bring consumption within the scope of the tax during the second half of the 20th century and the new interactions between national VAT systems have become increasingly problematic as volumes of cross-border trade in services and intangibles were growing. VAT systems have experienced considerable difficulties in determining where services are deemed to be consumed, to monitor these transactions and to ensure collection of the tax, particularly where businesses sell services in jurisdictions where they do not have a physical presence. In the absence of adjustment, from a government's viewpoint there is a risk of under-taxation and loss of revenue, or distorting trade through double taxation; from a business viewpoint, there are large revenue risks and high compliance costs.

The OECD developed the *International VAT/GST Guidelines* as the international standard for applying VAT to cross-border trade in services and intangibles, to minimise the risks of double taxation and unintended double non-taxation resulting from mismatches between national VAT systems.

1.8.5. The OECD International VAT/GST Guidelines are setting global standards for determining the place of taxation for internationally-traded services and intangibles

The OECD released the International VAT/GST Guidelines in November 2015 at the third meeting of its Global Forum on VAT, where they were endorsed as the international standard for the application of VAT to the international trade in services and intangibles by over 100 countries, jurisdictions and international organisations. These Guidelines were subsequently adopted as a Recommendation by the Council of the OECD in September 2016 (OECD, 2017[4]). This is the first OECD legal instrument in the area of VAT.

The Guidelines present a set of global standards and recommended approaches for the consistent VAT treatment of international transactions, focusing in particular on trade in services and intangibles. They include chapters on the principle of VAT neutrality and its implementation in practice, and on the implementation of the destination principle for allocating the taxing rights on cross-border supplies of services and intangibles. For business-to-business supplies, the Guidelines establish that, the taxing rights on cross border supplies of services and intangibles are to be allocated to the jurisdiction where the business customer has located its permanent business presence. For business-to-consumer supplies, the Guidelines recommend that the taxing rights over "on-the-spot supplies" be allocated to the jurisdiction in which the supply is physically performed; and that the taxing rights over all other supplies and services be allocated to the jurisdiction in which the customer has its usual residence. These include remote supplies of services and digital products over the Internet (e.g. apps, streaming of music and movies, online gaming) by foreign suppliers. The Guidelines recommend that these foreign suppliers be required to register and remit VAT in the jurisdiction of taxation and that countries implement a simplified registration and compliance regime to facilitate compliance for non-resident suppliers. They finally recommend that the taxing rights be allocated to the jurisdiction where immovable property is located when they are closely connected with such property.

The Guidelines do not aim at providing detailed prescriptions for national legislation. Jurisdictions are sovereign with respect to the design and application of their laws. Rather, the Guidelines seek to provide guidance to jurisdictions in developing national legislation with a view to facilitating a coherent application of national VAT systems to international trade, taking into account their specific economic, legal, institutional, cultural and social circumstances and practices.

These Guidelines are further complemented with guidance and technical standards to support their coherent implementation and application (implementation packages). A first report on "Mechanisms for the effective collection of VAT/GST" was delivered in 2017. (OECD, 2017[13]). This report provides further detailed practical guidance to support the implementation of the rules and mechanisms for the efficient and the effective collection of VAT on inbound digital services from offshore suppliers, as recommended in the International VAT/GST Guidelines and in the 2015 Final Report on Action 1 "Addressing the Tax Challenges of the Digital Economy" of the BEPS project. A second report "The role of digital platforms in the collection of VAT/GST on online sales" (OECD, 2019[14]) focuses on possible approaches for enlisting online marketplaces and other digital platforms in the collection of VAT on e-commerce and to support and coordinate country reform in this context.

Annex Table 2.A.8 presents a broad overview of the approaches adopted by OECD countries for collecting VAT on cross-border supplies of services and intangibles from foreign suppliers (i.e. on remote "inbound supplies"). This overview shows that the EU rules determine the place of taxation for cross-border supplies of services and intangibles (i.e. transactions with non-EU Member States) in principle by reference to the customer's location (for business-to-business supplies - B2B) and to the customer's usual residence (for business-to-consumer supplies - B2C), in line with the OECD Guidelines. The VAT on inbound supplies is collected through a reverse charge (self-assessment) mechanism, for B2B supplies, and through a simplified vendor registration and compliance regime ("Mini One Stop Shop") for B2C supplies of telecommunication, broadcasting and electronic services. This regime is operated by the 23 OECD member countries that belong to the EU (Austria, Belgium, Czech Republic, Denmark, Estonia, Finland,

France, Germany, Greece, Hungary, Ireland, Italy, Latvia, Lithuania, Luxembourg, Netherlands, Poland, Portugal, Slovak Republic, Slovenia, Spain, Sweden and the United Kingdom until 31 January 2020).

Ten other OECD countries use (some variation of) the customer's location (usual residence, head office, etc.) as the main proxy for determining the place of taxation for cross-border supplies of services and intangibles (Australia, Canada, Iceland, Israel, Japan, Korea, New Zealand, Norway, Switzerland and Turkey). Most OECD countries make a distinction between B2B and B2C supplies for determining the place of taxation as well as for determining the mechanism to collect the VAT on inbound supplies. The tax status of customers in this context is generally determined on the basis of the presence of a VAT registration number or on the basis of the customer's business tax identification number. Two countries (Japan and Korea) distinguish between B2B and B2C supplies on the basis of the nature of the services provided. In these countries, services that are considered to be generally used by final consumers such as provision of e-books, digital newspapers, music, videos, games, etc. are deemed to be B2C services while others are considered B2B supplies. Some countries do not systematically distinguish between B2B and B2C supplies (Canada, Chile, and Mexico).

Most OECD countries apply a reverse charge mechanism to collect VAT on inbound B2B supplies of services and intangibles. In Australia, Canada and New Zealand this mechanism only applies when the customer has a limited right to deduct the input tax, and no tax is due when the customer has a full right to deduction. In Switzerland, the application of the reverse charge mechanism is limited to situations where the place of taxation is determined according to the customer's residence proxy. When the supply is taxed in Switzerland according to other proxies (e.g. the location of the immovable property to which the supply is connected), the reverse charge mechanism does not apply and the supplier must register in Switzerland according to the standard procedure and account for VAT. In addition, foreign suppliers that are registered in the Switzerland to account for VAT on their B2C supplies, must also account for their B2B supplies under that local registration and the reverse charge does not apply. In Korea, inbound B2B supplies are considered out of scope and no VAT is due on such supplies. In Iceland, inbound supplies of services are VAT exempt if the business customer has a full right to deduction. If not, the supplier must register for VAT in Iceland.

For B2C supplies, all OECD countries that operate a VAT now require the foreign supplier to register and account for VAT, except Canada and Israel where the customer is liable to account for the tax on inbound supplies of services and intangibles. A simplified registration and collection regime (without right to deduct input taxes in the taxing jurisdiction - "pay-only registration") applies in these countries (generally with an option for standard registration), except in Japan and Switzerland where only the standard registration is available (with the right to deduct the input tax incurred in the country) and where the foreign supplier must appoint a local tax agent.

Six of the countries requiring foreign suppliers to register to account for VAT on their B2C supplies into the country do not impose such a requirement when the annual turnover of these suppliers in the country remains below a threshold that is set at the same level as the registration threshold for domestic taxpayers. These countries are Australia, Iceland, Japan, New Zealand, Norway and Switzerland.

The OECD standards and guidance for the application of VAT to international trade are influencing VAT reform in a growing number of countries worldwide, including in countries outside the OECD membership. The standards for the effective collection of VAT on online sales of goods, services and digital products have been particularly influential. Over 60 countries have implemented these standards while several other countries are preparing to implement these standards or are considering doing so. Very positive results have been reported in terms of compliance and revenue collected from these measures.

The continuously growing impact of these standards reflects their significant importance for countries' VAT revenues and for minimising competitive distortions between online traders and traditional businesses. This has become even more relevant in light of the outbreak of COVID-19, as containment and mitigation measures taken in response to the pandemic have notably led to spikes in online shopping and increased demand for digital products and online services.

The OECD's standards and expertise in VAT are also increasingly in demand from developing countries. In common with other areas of international tax standards, the OECD is progressively increasing the engagement of non-OECD member countries in the design of standards in the VAT area, while expanding the guidance and support available to developing countries seeking to implement the standards.

To support developing countries wishing to implement the OECD standards and guidance in the area of VAT, the OECD has committed to developing specific regional toolkits. These toolkits will provide further detailed, practical guidance for the implementation of the internationally agreed VAT standards and best-practice solutions, targeted at developing countries.

For the tables in annex, references to the 'European Union and its Member States' includes the UK as a Member State for January 2020 and as an addition to the Member States ('Member States and the UK') for the period 1 February 2020 until the end of December 2020.

Annex 1.A. Consumption Tax Revenue

Annex Table 1.A.1. Consumption taxes (5100) as a percentage of GDP and total taxation

	Tax revenue as % of GDP					Tax revenue as % of total taxation				
	1975	2005	2010	2015	2018	1975	2005	2010	2015	2018
Australia	6.5	7.6	6.5	6.6	6.3	25.8	25.4	25.7	23.8	21.9
Austria	12.3	11.1	10.9	10.9	10.7	33.9	27.1	26.5	25.3	25.3
Belgium	10.1	10.5	10.5	10.3	10.5	26.0	24.2	24.6	23.2	23.9
Canada	8.1	7.7	7.0	7.1	7.3	26.0	23.7	22.5	21.5	21.9
Chile	..	10.1	9.4	10.4	10.4	..	48.7	48.2	50.8	49.5
Colombia	..	8.1	8.1	8.0	8.1	..	44.4	44.7	40.4	42.0
Czech Republic	..	10.1	10.2	10.7	10.8	..	29.5	31.8	32.3	30.8
Denmark	12.0	15.2	14.0	13.4	13.5	32.7	31.8	31.2	29.2	30.3
Estonia	..	12.1	13.0	13.6	13.3	..	40.7	39.6	41.2	40.3
Finland	11.4	13.0	12.6	13.6	13.7	31.6	30.8	31.0	31.3	32.4
France	11.3	10.7	10.8	11.4	11.9	32.4	25.0	25.5	25.1	25.8
Germany	8.7	9.7	10.2	9.9	9.8	25.4	28.1	28.7	26.7	25.3
Greece	7.9	10.1	11.3	12.1	13.4	42.2	31.7	35.2	33.2	34.3
Hungary	..	14.3	15.7	16.7	16.4	..	39.1	42.1	42.8	43.7
Iceland	18.3	14.9	10.7	10.9	11.7	62.2	37.8	33.1	30.8	31.3
Ireland	12.4	10.8	9.1	6.9	6.4	44.4	35.8	33.0	29.4	28.1
Israel	..	11.0	11.2	11.0	10.4	..	32.8	36.5	35.2	33.8
Italy	6.9	9.4	10.0	10.5	10.5	28.3	24.1	23.9	24.5	25.0
Japan	3.0	4.5	4.4	6.0	5.8	15.1	17.2	16.7	19.5	18.1
Korea	8.7	7.2	7.3	6.2	6.6	60.0	33.3	32.6	26.2	24.7
Latvia	..	11.4	11.3	12.5	13.3	..	40.6	39.3	41.6	42.7
Lithuania	..	10.9	11.5	11.2	11.4	..	37.2	40.4	39.0	37.7
Luxembourg	6.5	10.8	10.1	9.4	9.3	20.6	28.5	26.9	25.3	23.3
Mexico	..	4.2	4.7	6.0	5.8	..	37.1	36.7	37.9	35.9
Netherlands	8.5	10.2	10.1	10.0	10.5	22.5	29.3	28.2	27.1	27.1
New Zealand	6.8	10.8	11.2	11.5	11.6	22.8	30.0	37.1	36.3	35.3
Norway	14.2	11.1	11.0	11.0	11.1	36.6	26.1	26.3	28.6	28.1
Poland	..	12.2	12.2	11.5	12.7	..	37.2	38.8	35.3	36.0
Portugal	7.6	13.3	11.9	12.9	13.3	40.1	43.0	39.2	37.4	38.1
Slovak Republic	..	11.6	9.7	10.7	11.2	..	37.1	34.3	32.9	32.6
Slovenia	..	12.7	13.3	13.7	13.0	..	32.5	35.2	36.8	34.9
Spain	4.3	9.3	7.9	9.6	9.5	24.0	26.3	25.3	28.2	27.3
Sweden	8.7	11.9	12.3	11.7	12.0	22.7	25.5	28.6	27.3	27.2
Switzerland	4.6	5.4	5.3	5.1	5.0	20.6	20.3	19.9	18.7	17.8
Turkey	4.7	11.0	11.3	10.6	9.4	40.9	47.4	45.8	42.7	39.0
United Kingdom	8.1	9.6	9.7	10.5	10.4	23.7	29.4	30.2	32.2	31.5
United States	4.2	3.8	3.6	3.8	3.8	17.1	14.7	15.5	14.6	15.4
OECD unweighted average	8.6	10.2	10.0	10.2	10.3	31.1	31.7	31.9	31.2	30.8

Source: OECD Revenue Statistics 2020 (OECD, 2020[1]).

StatLink https://doi.org/10.1787/888934219926

Annex Table 1.A.2. General taxes on goods and services (5110) as a percentage of GDP and total taxation

	Tax revenue as % of GDP					Tax revenue as % of total taxation				
Year	1975	2005	2010	2015	2018	1975	2005	2010	2015	2018
Australia	1.7	4.0	3.5	3.7	3.4	6.7	13.4	13.8	13.3	12.0
Austria	7.2	7.6	7.7	7.6	7.6	19.8	18.6	18.7	17.7	18.0
Belgium	6.3	7.0	7.0	6.7	6.8	16.2	16.2	16.4	15.1	15.5
Canada	3.9	4.8	4.3	4.6	4.7	12.5	14.8	14.0	13.9	14.2
Chile	..	7.8	7.5	8.3	8.5	..	37.8	38.5	40.8	40.2
Colombia	..	5.9	6.1	6.1	6.5	..	32.3	33.9	30.4	33.8
Czech Republic	..	6.5	6.6	7.2	7.6	..	19.1	20.5	21.7	21.6
Denmark	6.4	9.7	9.4	9.1	9.5	17.5	20.2	21.0	19.9	21.5
Estonia	..	8.0	8.5	9.0	9.0	..	26.9	25.8	27.2	27.3
Finland	5.7	8.3	8.3	9.0	9.1	15.6	19.9	20.4	20.6	21.6
France	8.2	7.4	7.5	7.7	7.9	23.4	17.3	17.9	16.9	17.1
Germany	5.0	6.1	7.0	7.0	7.0	14.6	17.8	19.8	18.8	18.2
Greece	3.4	6.9	7.3	7.4	8.3	18.3	21.6	22.8	20.3	21.4
Hungary	..	10.2	11.0	11.8	11.8	..	28.0	29.7	30.3	31.6
Iceland	8.4	10.8	7.3	8.0	8.8	28.6	27.3	22.7	22.6	23.6
Ireland	4.1	7.3	6.0	4.5	4.4	14.7	24.2	21.7	19.3	19.3
Israel	..	9.3	9.1	9.2	8.8	..	27.5	29.8	29.6	28.5
Italy	3.5	5.7	6.1	6.1	6.2	14.3	14.6	14.5	14.2	14.8
Japan	0.0	2.5	2.5	4.2	4.1	0.0	9.5	9.6	13.7	12.8
Korea	1.8	3.8	3.9	3.6	4.1	12.7	17.4	17.5	15.3	15.3
Latvia	..	7.4	7.2	8.7	9.3	..	26.4	25.2	29.0	29.7
Lithuania	..	7.5	7.8	7.8	7.8	..	25.8	27.5	27.2	26.0
Luxembourg	3.8	6.0	6.4	6.5	6.1	12.1	16.0	17.0	17.5	15.4
Mexico	..	3.3	3.8	3.8	3.9	..	29.3	29.4	23.9	24.3
Netherlands	5.4	6.7	6.7	6.5	6.8	14.4	19.2	18.7	17.6	17.6
New Zealand	2.7	8.6	9.3	9.5	9.7	9.0	23.8	30.7	30.2	29.6
Norway	8.0	7.7	7.8	8.2	8.4	20.5	18.2	18.6	21.4	21.3
Poland	..	7.7	7.6	7.0	8.1	..	23.2	24.2	21.5	23.1
Portugal	2.1	8.2	7.5	8.6	8.7	11.2	26.6	24.7	24.9	25.1
Slovak Republic	..	7.7	6.1	6.8	7.1	..	24.6	21.8	20.8	20.5
Slovenia	..	8.5	8.1	8.3	8.2	..	21.6	21.3	22.2	22.0
Spain	2.7	6.2	5.2	6.4	6.6	15.3	17.7	16.6	19.1	19.1
Sweden	4.6	8.5	9.1	9.0	9.2	12.0	18.3	21.2	21.0	21.0
Switzerland	2.0	3.6	3.4	3.5	3.3	8.7	13.6	13.0	12.6	11.9
Turkey	0.0	5.1	5.4	5.1	4.8	0.0	21.8	21.7	20.6	19.8
United Kingdom	3.0	6.1	6.1	6.9	7.0	8.9	18.6	19.0	21.4	21.1
United States	1.7	2.1	2.0	2.1	2.0	7.0	8.0	8.4	7.9	8.2
OECD unweighted average	4.1	6.8	6.7	6.9	7.1	13.4	21.0	21.3	21.1	21.2

Source: OECD Revenue Statistics 2020 (OECD, 2020[1]).

StatLink https://doi.org/10.1787/888934219945

Annex Table 1.A.3. Taxes on specific goods and services (5120) as a percentage of GDP and total taxation

	Tax revenue as % of GDP					Tax revenue as % of total taxation				
Year	1975	2005	2010	2015	2018	1975	2005	2010	2015	2018
Australia	4.9	3.6	3.0	2.9	2.8	19.1	12.0	11.9	10.4	9.9
Austria	5.1	3.5	3.2	3.3	3.1	14.0	8.4	7.8	7.6	7.3
Belgium	3.8	3.5	3.5	3.6	3.7	9.8	8.1	8.2	8.1	8.4
Canada	4.2	2.9	2.6	2.5	2.5	13.6	8.9	8.5	7.7	7.7
Chile	..	2.3	1.9	2.0	2.0	..	10.9	9.8	10.0	9.3
Colombia	..	2.2	2.0	2.0	1.6	..	12.1	10.9	10.0	8.2
Czech Republic	..	3.5	3.6	3.5	3.2	..	10.3	11.3	10.6	9.2
Denmark	5.6	5.5	4.5	4.3	3.9	15.2	11.6	10.1	9.3	8.8
Estonia	..	4.1	4.5	4.6	4.3	..	13.8	13.8	13.9	13.0
Finland	5.8	4.6	4.3	4.7	4.6	16.0	11.0	10.6	10.7	10.8
France	3.2	3.3	3.2	3.7	4.0	9.0	7.7	7.6	8.2	8.7
Germany	3.7	3.5	3.1	2.9	2.7	10.8	10.2	8.8	7.9	7.1
Greece	4.5	3.2	3.9	4.6	4.9	23.9	9.9	12.3	12.7	12.7
Hungary	..	4.1	4.6	4.9	4.6	..	11.1	12.4	12.6	12.2
Iceland	9.9	4.2	3.4	2.9	2.9	33.6	10.6	10.5	8.2	7.7
Ireland	8.3	3.5	3.1	2.4	2.0	29.7	11.6	11.3	10.1	8.8
Israel	..	1.8	2.1	1.8	1.6	..	5.3	6.8	5.6	5.3
Italy	3.4	3.7	3.9	4.5	4.3	14.0	9.5	9.4	10.4	10.2
Japan	3.0	2.0	1.9	1.8	1.7	15.1	7.7	7.2	5.8	5.3
Korea	6.9	3.4	3.4	2.6	2.5	47.3	15.9	15.1	10.9	9.4
Latvia	..	4.0	4.1	3.8	4.1	..	14.2	14.1	12.6	13.0
Lithuania	..	3.3	3.6	3.4	3.5	..	11.4	12.8	11.8	11.7
Luxembourg	2.6	4.7	3.7	2.9	3.1	8.4	12.5	9.9	7.8	7.9
Mexico	..	0.9	0.9	2.2	1.9	..	7.8	7.3	14.0	11.6
Netherlands	3.1	3.5	3.4	3.5	3.7	8.1	10.1	9.5	9.6	9.6
New Zealand	4.1	2.2	1.9	1.9	1.9	13.8	6.2	6.4	6.1	5.8
Norway	6.3	3.4	3.2	2.8	2.7	16.1	7.9	7.6	7.2	6.8
Poland	..	4.6	4.6	4.5	4.5	..	13.9	14.6	13.8	12.9
Portugal	5.5	5.1	4.4	4.3	4.5	28.9	16.4	14.4	12.5	13.0
Slovak Republic	..	3.9	3.5	4.0	4.1	..	12.5	12.5	12.1	12.0
Slovenia	..	4.2	5.3	5.4	4.8	..	10.8	13.9	14.5	12.9
Spain	1.6	3.0	2.7	3.1	2.9	8.7	8.6	8.7	9.2	8.2
Sweden	4.1	3.4	3.2	2.7	2.7	10.7	7.2	7.4	6.4	6.2
Switzerland	2.7	1.8	1.8	1.7	1.6	11.9	6.7	6.9	6.0	5.9
Turkey	4.7	5.9	5.9	5.5	4.6	40.9	25.5	24.1	22.0	19.2
United Kingdom	5.1	3.5	3.6	3.5	3.4	14.8	10.8	11.2	10.8	10.3
United States	2.5	1.7	1.7	1.8	1.8	10.0	6.7	7.2	6.7	7.3
OECD unweighted average	4.6	3.4	3.3	3.3	3.2	17.7	10.7	10.6	10.1	9.6

Source: OECD Revenue Statistics 2020 (OECD, 2020[1]).

StatLink https://doi.org/10.1787/888934219964

Annex Table 1.A.4. Value added taxes (5111) as a percentage of GDP and total taxation

	Tax revenue as % of GDP					Tax revenue as % of total taxation				
Year	1975	2005	2010	2015	2018	1975	2005	2010	2015	2018
Australia	0.0	3.9	3.4	3.6	3.3	0.0	13.1	13.4	13.0	11.7
Austria	7.2	7.6	7.7	7.6	7.6	19.8	18.6	18.7	17.7	18.0
Belgium	6.3	6.9	7.0	6.6	6.8	16.2	15.9	16.2	15.0	15.4
Canada	0.0	3.2	4.2	4.4	4.5	0.0	9.9	13.7	13.3	13.6
Chile	..	7.8	7.5	8.3	8.5	..	37.8	38.5	40.8	40.2
Colombia	..	5.2	5.3	5.2	5.7	..	28.2	29.3	26.0	29.4
Czech Republic	..	6.5	6.6	7.2	7.6	..	19.1	20.5	21.7	21.6
Denmark	6.4	9.7	9.4	9.1	9.5	17.5	20.2	21.0	19.9	21.5
Estonia	..	8.0	8.5	9.0	9.0	..	26.9	25.7	27.2	27.3
Finland	5.7	8.3	8.3	9.0	9.1	15.6	19.9	20.4	20.6	21.6
France	8.1	7.2	6.8	6.9	7.1	23.1	16.7	16.1	15.2	15.4
Germany	5.0	6.1	7.0	7.0	7.0	14.6	17.8	19.8	18.8	18.2
Greece	0.0	6.7	7.1	7.3	8.3	0.0	21.1	22.0	20.0	21.3
Hungary	..	8.2	8.5	9.5	9.7	..	22.5	22.9	24.5	25.8
Iceland	0.0	10.8	7.3	8.0	8.8	0.0	27.3	22.7	22.6	23.6
Ireland	4.1	7.3	6.0	4.5	4.4	14.7	24.2	21.7	19.3	19.3
Israel	..	7.5	7.5	7.8	7.5	..	22.3	24.4	24.9	24.2
Italy	3.3	5.7	6.1	6.1	6.2	13.7	14.6	14.5	14.2	14.8
Japan	..	2.5	2.5	4.2	4.1	..	9.5	9.6	13.7	12.8
Korea	0.0	3.8	3.9	3.6	4.1	0.0	17.4	17.5	15.3	15.3
Latvia	..	7.4	6.7	7.7	8.4	..	26.4	23.3	25.6	27.0
Lithuania	..	7.1	7.8	7.7	7.8	..	24.3	27.5	27.0	25.8
Luxembourg	3.8	6.0	6.4	6.5	6.1	12.1	16.0	17.0	17.5	15.4
Mexico	..	3.3	3.8	3.8	3.9	..	29.3	29.4	23.9	24.3
Netherlands	5.4	6.7	6.7	6.5	6.8	14.4	19.2	18.7	17.6	17.6
New Zealand	0.0	8.6	9.3	9.5	9.7	0.0	23.8	30.7	30.2	29.6
Norway	8.0	7.7	7.8	8.2	8.4	20.5	18.1	18.6	21.3	21.2
Poland	..	7.7	7.6	7.0	8.1	..	23.2	24.2	21.5	23.1
Portugal	0.0	8.2	7.5	8.6	8.7	0.0	26.6	24.7	24.9	25.1
Slovak Republic	..	7.7	6.1	6.8	7.1	..	24.6	21.8	20.8	20.5
Slovenia	..	8.5	8.1	8.3	8.2	..	21.6	21.3	22.2	22.0
Spain	0.0	6.2	5.2	6.4	6.6	0.0	17.7	16.5	19.0	19.0
Sweden	4.6	8.5	9.0	8.9	9.2	12.0	18.1	21.0	20.8	21.0
Switzerland	0.0	3.6	3.4	3.4	3.3	0.0	13.4	12.7	12.4	11.7
Turkey	..	5.1	5.4	5.1	4.8	..	21.8	21.7	20.6	19.8
United Kingdom	3.0	6.1	6.1	6.9	7.0	8.9	18.6	19.0	21.4	21.1
United States	0.0	0.0	0.0	0.0	0.0	0.0	0.0	0.0	0.0	0.0
OECD unweighted average	3.1	6.5	6.4	6.7	6.8	8.8	20.2	20.5	20.3	20.4

Source: OECD Revenue Statistics 2020 (OECD, 2020[1]).

StatLink https://doi.org/10.1787/888934219983

Annex Table 1.A.5. Excise (5121) as a percentage of GDP and total taxation

	Tax revenue as % of GDP					Tax revenue as % of total taxation				
Year	1975	2005	2010	2015	2018	1975	2005	2010	2015	2018
Australia	3.0	2.3	1.9	1.4	1.3	11.8	7.6	7.5	4.9	4.4
Austria	2.9	2.6	2.3	2.3	2.1	7.9	6.3	5.7	5.2	5.0
Belgium	2.6	2.3	2.1	2.1	2.2	6.6	5.3	5.0	4.7	5.0
Canada	2.0	1.6	1.4	1.3	1.3	6.3	4.9	4.5	3.9	3.8
Chile	..	1.6	1.4	1.5	1.5	0.0	7.8	7.1	7.4	6.9
Colombia	..	1.4	1.1	1.4	1.2	..	7.5	6.1	7.1	6.3
Czech Republic	..	3.4	3.5	3.3	3.1	0.0	9.8	10.8	10.0	8.7
Denmark	5.1	4.9	4.1	3.9	3.6	13.8	10.3	9.1	8.5	8.0
Estonia	..	3.6	4.2	4.2	3.9	0.0	12.2	12.6	12.6	11.9
Finland	4.2	3.6	3.3	3.6	3.6	11.5	8.6	8.2	8.3	8.5
France	2.3	2.4	2.3	2.6	2.7	6.5	5.7	5.4	5.7	6.0
Germany	3.0	2.8	2.5	2.2	2.0	8.8	8.3	7.0	5.8	5.1
Greece	2.5	2.6	3.3	3.9	3.9	13.6	8.1	10.4	10.7	9.9
Hungary	..	3.5	3.4	3.2	3.0	..	9.7	9.2	8.3	7.9
Iceland	0.9	3.6	2.8	2.5	2.5	3.0	9.2	8.6	7.0	6.7
Ireland	7.2	3.2	2.9	2.1	1.7	26.0	10.5	10.5	8.9	7.5
Israel	0.0	1.5	1.8	1.5	1.4	0.0	4.5	5.8	4.8	4.6
Italy	2.5	2.2	2.3	2.8	2.7	10.2	5.6	5.4	6.5	6.4
Japan	2.3	1.8	1.7	1.6	1.5	11.3	6.9	6.5	5.1	4.6
Korea	3.2	2.6	2.4	1.9	1.9	22.0	12.0	10.6	8.1	7.1
Latvia	..	3.5	3.6	3.3	3.6	0.0	12.6	12.5	11.0	11.5
Lithuania	..	2.9	3.2	3.1	3.2	0.0	10.0	11.4	10.9	10.6
Luxembourg	2.3	4.5	3.5	2.6	2.6	7.3	11.8	9.3	7.1	6.5
Mexico	0.0	0.6	0.6	1.9	1.5	0.0	5.1	5.0	12.2	9.4
Netherlands	2.4	3.1	2.9	2.6	2.7	6.3	8.7	8.1	7.1	7.0
New Zealand	2.8	1.4	0.9	0.9	0.9	9.4	3.9	2.9	2.8	2.6
Norway	4.0	3.2	2.9	2.5	2.4	10.3	7.4	7.0	6.6	6.0
Poland	..	4.3	4.3	3.9	3.9	0.0	13.0	13.7	12.1	11.0
Portugal	2.5	3.7	3.2	2.9	3.0	13.0	11.9	10.4	8.4	8.8
Slovak Republic	..	3.6	3.1	3.2	3.3	0.0	11.4	10.9	9.9	9.5
Slovenia	..	3.4	4.3	4.2	3.7	0.0	8.8	11.3	11.2	9.8
Spain	0.4	2.5	2.3	2.4	2.2	2.2	7.1	7.3	7.1	6.4
Sweden	3.4	2.8	2.6	2.1	2.1	8.8	6.0	5.9	5.0	4.8
Switzerland	1.7	1.4	1.4	1.2	1.2	7.7	5.4	5.1	4.5	4.4
Turkey	2.0	4.9	4.9	4.5	3.6	17.6	21.2	19.9	18.1	14.9
United Kingdom	4.3	2.8	2.8	2.5	2.3	12.7	8.6	8.8	7.6	7.0
United States	1.9	1.0	1.0	0.9	0.8	7.6	3.9	4.2	3.3	3.3
OECD unweighted average	2.9	2.8	2.6	2.5	2.4	10.5	8.6	8.4	7.8	7.2

Source: OECD Revenue Statistics 2020 (OECD, 2020[1]).

StatLink https://doi.org/10.1787/888934220002

Annex Table 1.A.6. Tax structures in the OECD area as a percentage of total taxation

Revenue from main categories of taxes as a percentage of total taxation							
	1965	1975	1985	1995	2005	2010	2018
Taxes on income, profits and capital gains (1000)	34.7	37.1	36.9	33.5	34.3	32.6	34.3
Personal income tax (1100)	26.2	29.8	29.8	24.3	22.7	22.5	23.5
Corporate income tax (1200)	8.8	7.6	8.0	8.1	10.5	8.9	10.0
Social security contributions (2000)	17.6	21.9	22.1	25.4	24.9	26.4	25.7
Payroll taxes (3000)	1.0	1.3	1.1	0.9	1.0	1.0	1.2
Property taxes (4000)	7.9	6.4	5.4	5.2	5.6	5.5	5.6
Taxes on goods and services (5000)	38.4	32.8	33.7	34.1	33.6	33.8	32.7
General consumption taxes (5110)	11.5	13.4	15.8	20.2	21.0	21.3	21.2
Value added taxes (VAT) (5111)	1.4	8.8	11.3	18.2	20.2	20.5	20.4
Specific consumption taxes (5120)	24.3	17.7	16.2	12.1	10.4	10.7	9.6

Source: OECD Revenue Statistics 2020 (OECD, 2020[1]).

StatLink https://doi.org/10.1787/888934220021

2 Value-added taxes - Main features and implementation issues

2.1. Introduction

Although most VAT systems are built on the same core VAT principles (see Chapter 1), there is considerable diversity in the design of VAT systems in OECD countries. This is notably illustrated by the variety of reduced rates, exemptions and other preferential treatments and special regimes that are widely used in OECD countries, for practical or historical reasons, to support certain economic sector or to achieve equity or social objectives.

This chapter presents an overview of the VAT rate structures in OECD countries and their evolution between 1975 and 2020 (Section 2.2) and looks in some detail at the VAT exemptions that exist in these countries (Section 2.3). This is followed by an overview and analysis of the wide variety of special regimes used in OECD countries on the following aspects: specific restrictions to the right to deduct VAT on specific inputs (Section 2.4), registration and collection thresholds (Section 2.5), and the application of margin schemes (Section 2.6). It also presents the VAT Revenue Ratio as an indicator of the revenue effect of VAT exemptions, reduced rates and non-compliance (Section 2.7) and the measures taken by governments to combat VAT fraud and avoidance (Section 2.8).

This Chapter concludes with a special section on the VAT policy and administration measures introduced by OECD countries as part their fiscal and tax policy responses to the COVID-19 outbreak. These VAT measures have been particularly important in supporting business cash flow and in alleviating tax compliance burdens for businesses given the restrictions in place in many countries. Most OECD countries have also taken VAT measures to facilitate emergency medical responses and to support the healthcare sector. These measures are discussed in further detail in the special section on COVID-19 VAT measures below. In addition, a comprehensive overview of temporary change to VAT rates implemented by countries in this context is included in Section 2.2 and country notes to Annex Table 2.A.2 below.

2.2. The evolution of standard and reduced VAT rates

2.2.1. Standard VAT rates have remained stable in recent years

The evolution of VAT rates in the OECD can be divided into five periods. The first period between 1975 and 2000 has seen a progressive increase in the average standard VAT rates from 15.6% in 1975 to 18.1% in 2000.

During a second period, between 2000 and 2009, the standard rate of VAT remained stable in most countries, with 26 out of 36 countries maintaining a rate between 15% and 22%. As of 1 January 2009, only four countries had a standard rate above 22% (Denmark, Iceland, Norway and Sweden –see Annex Table 2.A.1).

The third period, between 2009 and 2014, was marked by a considerable increase in the standard VAT rate in many countries, often in response to financial consolidation pressures caused by the economic and financial crisis. VAT standard rate increases have played a key role in many countries' consolidation strategies, since raising additional revenue from VAT rather than from other taxes (such as income taxes) is often considered more effective (it generates immediate additional revenue) and less detrimental to economic growth and competitiveness than income taxes (Jens Matthias Arnold, 2011[1]). Between January 2009 and December 2014, 23 OECD countries raised their standard VAT rate at least once. These changes occurred principally in European Union (EU) countries (Czech Republic, Estonia, Finland, France, Greece, Hungary, Ireland, Italy, Latvia, Lithuania, the Netherlands, Poland, Portugal, Slovak Republic, Slovenia, Spain and United Kingdom) but also in a number of non-EU countries (Iceland, Israel, Japan, Mexico, New Zealand, and Switzerland). Two OECD countries lowered their standard VAT rate temporarily and then raised it again during this period (Ireland and the United Kingdom). This evolution resulted in a hike of the unweighted OECD average standard VAT rate from 17.7% in January 2009 to an all-time record level of 19.2% on 1 January 2015. Ten OECD countries operated a standard VAT rate above 22% on 1 January 2015 against only four in 2009. All these countries belong to the European Union, except Iceland and Norway.

The increases in standard VAT rates observed until the end of 2014 have not continued and OECD countries have entered a new period of relatively stable standard VAT rates. Only four OECD countries have increased their standard VAT rate between January 2015 and January 2020, i.e. Colombia (from 16% to 19%), Greece (from 23% to 24%), Japan (from 8% to 10%) and Luxemburg (from 15% to 17%). During the same period, two OECD countries have reduced their standard VAT rate, i.e. Iceland (from 25.5% to 24%) and Israel (from 18% to 17%). As a result of these changes in various directions, the increase in the unweighted OECD average standard VAT has remained limited, from 19.2% in 2015 to 19.3% in 2020 (see Figure 2.1).

Figure 2.1. Evolution of standard VAT rates - OECD average 1976-2020

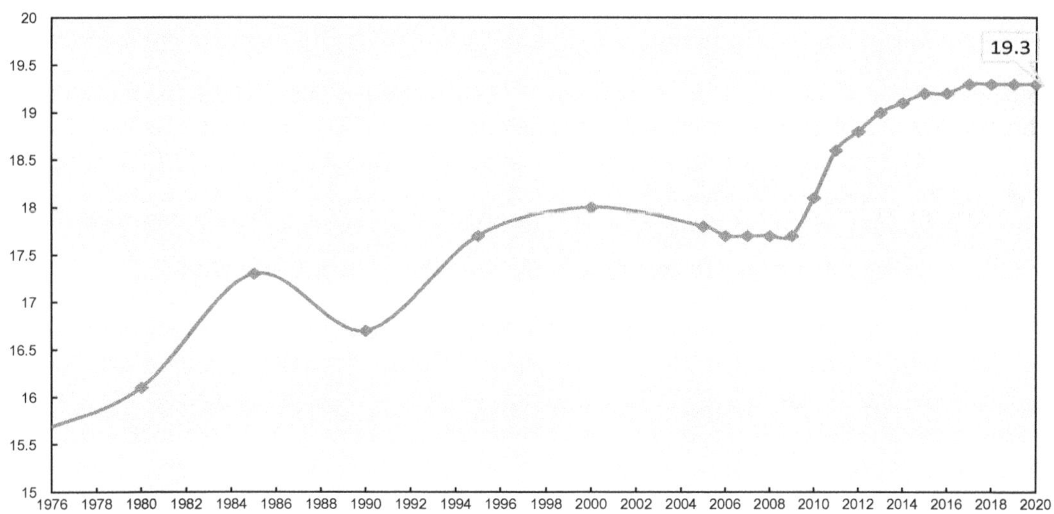

Note: Unweighted average
Source: Author's calculations

StatLink https://doi.org/10.1787/888934220040

Major differences in standard VAT rates can be observed among OECD countries, with rates ranging from 5% in Canada (note, however, that most Canadian provinces levy specific sales taxes or Harmonised Sales Taxes alongside the Federal 5% GST), 7.7% in Switzerland and 10% in Australia, Japan and Korea to 25% in Denmark, Norway and Sweden and 27% in Hungary (see Figure 2.2). On 1 January 2020, 23 OECD countries operated a standard VAT rate of 20% or more, with 9 of these countries having a standard VAT rate of 23% or more. All these countries are EU Member States, except for Norway (with a 25% VAT standard rate).

Figure 2.2. Standard rates of VAT in OECD countries 2020

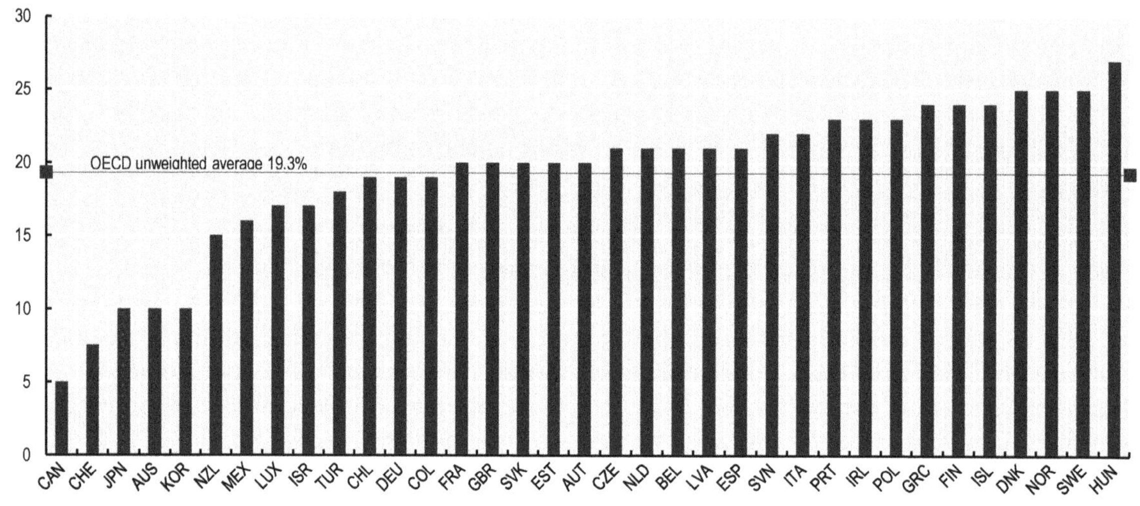

Source: Author's work

StatLink https://doi.org/10.1787/888934220059

The average standard VAT rate of the 23 OECD countries that are members of the EU (including the UK until 1 February 2020) is at 21.8%, which is significantly above the OECD average (19.3%). EU Member States are bound by common rules regarding VAT rates (VAT Directive 2006/112/EC), which set the minimum level of the standard VAT rate at 15%.

2.2.2. OECD countries continue to apply a wide variety of reduced rates

Most OECD countries continue to apply a wide variety of reduced VAT rates and exemptions (see Annex Table 2.A.2 and Annex Table 2.A.3). With the exception of Chile, all OECD countries that have a VAT apply one or more reduced rates to support various policy objectives. A major reason for the application of reduced rates is the promotion of equity. Countries generally consider it desirable to alleviate the VAT burden on necessity goods and services (e.g. food, water), which typically form a larger share of expenditure of lower income households by taxing them at a preferential VAT rate. Most countries also apply reduced VAT rates or exemptions to medicine, health, education and housing. Reduced VAT rates have also been used to stimulate the consumption of "merit goods" (such as cultural products) or promoting locally supplied labour-intensive activities (e.g. tourism) and addressing environmental externalities.

Evidence suggests that exemptions and reduced VAT rates are not an effective way of achieving such objectives (OECD/KIPF, 2014[2]) and can be even regressive in some instances. Other measures, such as providing targeted through the income tax and/or the social transfer and benefit system, tend to be more effective in addressing equity concerns and to pursue policy objectives other than raising tax revenues

(Thomas, 2020[3]). Reduced VAT rates that are targeted at supporting lower-income households (i.e. to address distributional goals) typically do have the desired progressive effect. Notably reduced rates for basic food generally provide greater support to the poor than to the rich as a proportion of household income and as a proportion of expenditure. However, despite their progressive effect, research led notably by the OECD has shown that these reduced VAT rates remain a very poor distributive tool. This is because better-off households tend to benefit more in absolute terms from VAT reduced rates than low-income households. As richer households tend to consume more, and more expensive products than poorer households, their consumption of the tax-favoured goods and services is generally greater than that of poorer households. Research has also demonstrated that preferential VAT rates to stimulate employment (e.g. in the tourism or hospitality sectors), or to support cultural activities (e.g. theatre) or pursue other non-distributional goals, clearly benefit richer households more than lower-income categories of the population, and often considerably so.

Preferential VAT regimes such as reduced rates and exemptions (see Section 2.3) also tend to considerably add to the complexity of the VAT system, increase the compliance burden for businesses and negatively impact on compliance levels (C. Evans; R. Highfield; B. Tran-Nam; M. Walpole, 2020[4]). A more effective policy to achieve distributional objectives is generally to reduce the scope for reduced VAT rates where possible and use measures that are directly targeted at increasing the real incomes of poorer households and public services for these households. It is recognised, however, that although this analysis is widely shared, it is often difficult if not impossible to implement it in practice. The political economy obstacles to broadening the VAT base (in particular their perceived distributional impact) can indeed be formidable, and often insurmountable, particularly where the social transfer and benefit system may not be sufficiently effective to ensure that poorer households are properly compensated for the impact of a VAT increase on the cost of their consumption basket.

EU Member States are bound by common rules regarding the operation of reduced VAT rates (VAT Directive 2006/112/EC). This common framework allows Member States to apply one or two reduced rates of not less than 5% to a restricted list of goods and services set out the VAT Directive. Some EU countries are allowed to apply special VAT rates below the standard rate of not less than 12% for goods not in the list of possible reduced rates (a “parking rate”) and super-reduced rates below 5% on certain supplies. For the time being, over 40 different standard and reduced VAT rates are being applied in the EU, often based on specific derogations granted to individual Member States.

Between 2018 and 2020, a number of countries have expanded the application of their reduced VAT rates. Greece reclassified a number of basic foodstuffs to include them in the scope of its 13% reduced VAT rate. The scope of this 13% VAT rate was also extended to restaurants and hotels, to infant food and other baby products, such as diapers and car seats, and to bicycle helmets. Greece also reduced its VAT rate for the supply of electricity and domestic gas from 13% to 6%. Spain expanded the application of its super reduced VAT rate of 4% to a wider range of bread products. The Slovak Republic extended the list of food items, including fruit and vegetables, which are subject to the 10% reduced VAT rate. Poland introduced an updated and simplified VAT rate structure along with the possibility for businesses to acquire certainty on the applicable VAT rate through a binding decision (WIS). Italy, Belgium, Germany and Iceland reduced their VAT rates for feminine hygiene products from 22% to 5%, from 21% to 6%, from 19% to 7% and from 24% to 11% respectively. The UK announced that it will apply a zero-rate to feminine hygiene products as of 1 January 2021. Germany extended the application of its 7% reduced rate to long-distance rail travel as part of environmental policy measures. Sweden made its 6% reduced rate applicable to the exploitation of natural areas outside urban areas, national parks, nature reserves and national city parks. Some countries have expanded the scope of their reduced VAT rates to support specific economic sectors. Hungary and the Slovak Republic reduced their VAT rate on accommodation services from 18% to 5% and from 20% to 10% respectively. The Czech Republic lowered its VAT rate on hairdressing and clothing repair services to 10%. Portugal extended the application of its reduced VAT rate of 6% to domestic assistance services by telephone to the elderly and chronic patients, as well as to admissions to cultural exhibitions, zoos, parks, aquariums, botanic gardens, museums and buildings of national interest. Slovenia introduced a new reduced VAT rate of 5% for printed and electronic publications (incl. e-books). A number of EU countries have reduced their VAT rates on electronic publications following an EU Council agreement in 2018 that EU Member States are allowed to apply reduced rates on these publications (e.g. e-books and e-newspapers) thereby aligning EU VAT rules for electronic and physical publications. Reduced rates now apply to e-books and e-publications in 16 of the 36 OECD countries that have a VAT – these are all EU Member States, except Norway.

Japan has moved from a single VAT rate to a dual rate system, by introducing a new reduced rate of 8% on a number of food and beverage items, when it increased its standard rate from 8% to 10%. Chile is now the only OECD country with one single VAT rate.

Given the political difficulty to significantly reduce the scope of reduced rates (and exemptions) and the limited scope for increasing standard VAT rates, which are already at a relatively high level in many cases, countries are increasingly looking at other measures to raise additional VAT revenue and improve the efficiency of their VAT systems (OECD, 2018[5]). These measures mainly include the collection of VAT on the supplies of goods and services from online sales (see Chapter 1) and measures designed to improve compliance and combat fraud (see Section 2.8).

2.2.3. Temporary VAT rate reductions have been introduced in response to the COVID-19 crisis

Several OECD countries have included temporary VAT rate reductions, including zero rates, in their tax responses to the COVID-outbreak. Most of these measures have been aimed at supporting the healthcare sector. Some countries have introduced temporary rate reductions to stimulate consumption and/or to support specific economic sectors that have been hardest hit by the COVID-19 crisis (e.g. tourism, hospitality). A comprehensive overview and description of these VAT rate reductions in OECD countries is included in the Country notes to Annex Table 2.A.2 (*in italics*).

Most OECD countries have introduced zero rates or reduced rates for supplies and imports of medical equipment and sanitary products (gloves, masks, hand sanitiser…) and for healthcare services where these were not yet VAT exempt or subject to reduced rates under normal rules. The European Union introduced a six-month suspension of VAT and customs duties on protective equipment, testing kits and medical equipment such as ventilators. The European Commission published an indicative list of goods potentially covered by this relief but leaves it to the discretion of Member States to decide according to their particular national needs. This relief applies to goods imported by or on behalf of state organisations or charitable or philanthropic organisations approved by the competent authorities of the Member States. The initial measure applied for a period of six months and was further extended until the end of April 2021.

A number of OECD countries apply temporary reduced VAT rates (including zero-rates) to supplies of a range of medical products and equipment needed to combat the COVID-19 outbreak, including Austria, Belgium, France, Germany, Greece, the Netherlands, Portugal and Spain. Germany, the Netherlands, Poland and Portugal apply a 0% VAT rate to donations of certain medical material and equipment to hospitals. In the Netherlands, a rate of (effectively) 0% is applied to the hiring of healthcare workers by healthcare facilities or institutions qualifying for the VAT exemption of medical services.

Some countries have introduced VAT rate reductions to support specific economic sectors, such as restaurants (Austria, Belgium, Germany, Greece); accommodation (Austria, Czech Republic, cinema, culture or sports (Austria, Greece, the Netherlands, United Kingdom); or passenger transport (Greece and Turkey). The United Kingdom introduced a temporary reduced rate of 5% for certain supplies relating to hospitality, holiday accommodation and admissions to certain attractions from 15 July 2020 to 31 March 2021.Poland introduced a temporary 0% VAT rate for the supplies of laptops and tablets to educational institutions.

A few OECD countries have introduced more general temporary rate reductions. Germany reduced its standard VAT rate from 19% to 16% and its reduced VAT rate from 7% to 5% from 1 July to 31 December 2020. Ireland reduced its standard VAT rate from 23% to 21%, with effect from 1 September 2020 until 28 February 2021. Norway decreased its 12% reduced VAT rate to 6% from 1 April until 31 December 2020.

The VAT component of OECD countries' tax responses to the COVID-19 crisis is discussed further in the Special section at the end of this Chapter.

2.3. Exemptions

VAT regimes in the OECD make extensive use of exemptions, in addition to reduced rates (see Annex Table 2.A.3). In this context, exemption means that the supplier does not charge the VAT on its outputs and, as a consequence, has no right to recover the VAT on its related inputs. In some jurisdictions, exemption is referred to as "input taxation" to indicate that the supply is not free of VAT but that there is a "hidden VAT" in the price of the exempt supply - i.e. the VAT burden incurred on the inputs is embedded in the price of the exempt outputs. Exemption is thus not the same thing as absence of taxation.

Although it is a significant departure from the basic concept of VAT, all OECD countries apply a number of exemptions. A wide variety of motivations exist for the application of VAT exemptions. These include the difficulty to determine the tax base (e.g. financial and insurance services) or the desire to exclude activities from the VAT base that are considered as public service or as serving a purpose of general and/or social interest (education, health, postal services, charities). A number of other exemptions have their roots in tradition, such as letting of immovable property and the supply of land and buildings. Certain sectors that are exempt from VAT may also be subject to other specific taxes (e.g. property, insurance, financial services).

Exemptions beyond these core items are also numerous and cover a wide diversity of sectors such as culture, legal aid, passenger transport, public cemeteries, waste and recyclable material, water supply, precious metals and agriculture (see Annex Table 2.A.3). To this regard, EU Member States are subject to common rules providing for the exemption of supplies considered as in the public interest such as postal services, healthcare, social services, education, public broadcasting and charities but also for a number of specific supplies such as financial and insurance services, transactions involving immovable property and gambling. However, EU Member States may choose to allow business to opt to tax certain transactions and set specific conditions for some exemptions.

A number of services that are generally exempt in OECD countries are taxed in certain countries. For example, postal services is taxed in Australia, Canada, Japan, New Zealand and Norway; betting or gambling is taxed in Australia, Canada, Korea, New Zealand, Turkey and the United Kingdom; and insurance services are taxed in Mexico, New Zealand and Turkey and zero-rated in Australia. On the other hand, the transportation of passengers, which is taxed in most countries, is exempt (to some extent) in Chile, Denmark, Ireland and Korea. Chile treats, services that are not specifically listed in the law as "out of scope" of its VAT i.e. they are actually treated in a similar way as exemptions. These include legal, accounting, engineering, architecture and other professional services.

The standard advice in VAT design is to have a short list of exemptions, limited to basic health, education and perhaps financial services. By not allowing the deduction of input tax, VAT exemptions create an important exception to the neutrality of VAT (see Chapter 1). The following paragraphs provide an overview of the main, often adverse consequences of exemptions.

VAT exemptions introduce a cascading effect when applied in a B2B context. The business making an exempt supply can be expected to pass on the uncreditable input tax by including it in the price of this supply. This "hidden tax" will subsequently not be deductible/recoverable by the recipient business. If the outputs of this recipient business are not also exempt, this hidden VAT will presumably be part of the price for the supplies on which it will charge output VAT. The result is a hidden tax at a variable rate depending on the number of production stages that are subject to the tax. This distorts businesses' production decisions and choices of organisational form. The size of this cascading effect depends on where the exemption is applied in the supply chain. If the exemption is applied at the stage of the final consumption, there is no cascading effect and the consequence is simply a loss of tax revenue since the value added at the final stage escapes tax. If the exemption occurs at some intermediate stage, the consequence of the cascading effect may be an increase of net revenues in a non-transparent manner.

Exemptions create incentives for reducing tax liability by vertical integration ("self-supply") and disincentives for outsourcing as firms have an incentive to produce their inputs internally rather than to purchase externally and incur irrecoverable VAT. This may lead to economic inefficiencies from the distortion of the structure of the supply chain. It can also initiate a dynamic whereby exemptions feed on each other resulting in "exemption creep": once a sector receives an exemption, it has an incentive to lobby for exemptions for those from whom it buys its inputs in order to avoid paying hidden VAT on its inputs.

Exemptions generally lead to the under-taxation of supplies to consumers, who face a tax burden equal to the tax on inputs used by the businesses without its value-added, and an over-taxation of businesses who are unable to deduct the "hidden" tax embedded in their inputs. It also leads to the taxation of investments rather than consumption, which is in contradiction with the main purpose of the tax.

The VAT exemption of financial services is often mentioned as one that is increasingly problematic. In a recent paper (GFV N°087 of March 2019), the European Commission recalled that the European Union's VAT exemption rules for financial and insurance services have not kept pace with developments in these sectors, which makes these rules increasingly complex and difficult to apply in practice. This has led to rising litigation rates, legal uncertainty, and high administrative and regulatory costs. These rules are also interpreted and applied inconsistently across Member States, leading to competitive distortion within the EU. The European Commission has therefore launched a public consultation on this topic in October 2020.

In the international context, exemptions compromise the destination principle for taxation of internationally traded goods and services (see Chapter 1). When an exporter uses exempt inputs, it is not possible to remove the irrecoverable VAT resulting from the exemption applied at an earlier stage in the production chain. The export thus becomes effectively "input taxed". On the other hand, businesses that use exempt inputs have an incentive to import from countries where these inputs are zero rated for export instead of purchasing them from exempt domestic providers. It has been suggested that managing exemptions also imposes increased administrative and compliance costs. As is the case for differentiated rate structures, it may often be difficult for businesses and tax administrations to distinguish between exempt and taxable supplies, in particular in complex areas such as financial services. Businesses that make both taxable and exempt supplies are often faced with complex allocation rules to determine the share which is attributable to taxed outputs and for which it is thus entitled to an input tax credit. However, there is little evidence on the quantitative extent to which exemptions increase administration and compliance costs (Bird and Gendron, 2007[6]).

For further reading on the theoretical and practical justification of exemptions, see (de la Feria, n.d.[7]); and on the potential of broadening the tax base by reducing the scope of exemptions as an alternative to increasing VAT rates, see (European Commission, 2011[8]).

2.4. Restrictions to the right to deduct VAT on specific inputs

Although the burden of the tax should not fall on businesses, the right to deduct the VAT on inputs is limited to the extent that those inputs are used for producing taxable outputs. The right to input VAT deduction is legitimately denied in cases where inputs are used to make onward supplies that are not taxable, i.e. exempt without credit (e.g. health care, financial services – see Section 2.3 above) or outside the scope of

VAT (e.g. supplies for no consideration). Input-VAT deduction is also denied when purchases are not (wholly) used for the furtherance of taxable business activity, for example, when they are used for the private needs of the business owner or its employees (i.e. final consumption). All these limitations to the right to deduct input VAT result from the application of the basic principles of VAT design.

In addition to the rules described above, most OECD countries have legislation in place that provides for restrictions to input VAT deduction on a number of goods and services because of their nature rather than because of their use by businesses. This is often with a view to ensuring the (input)taxation of their deemed final consumption (see Annex Table 2.A.4).

Restrictions to the deduction of input VAT on entertainment costs are the most widespread, although the items included in that category may vary widely. These restrictions may include VAT incurred on restaurant meals; on (alcoholic) beverages; reception costs; hotel accommodation; attendance at sporting or cultural events; and on gifts and transport services. Seven OECD countries (Chile, Colombia, France, Israel, Japan, Switzerland and Turkey) have not implemented such specific limitation to the right of deduction. The deduction of input VAT on the purchase and/or the use of cars is also subject to limitations in 23 out of the 36 OECD countries operating a VAT. On the other hand, Israel, Japan and Switzerland do not report any of these specific restrictions. In Mexico, there are no specific restrictions but the law provides that input VAT deduction is allowed only on inputs that are "strictly indispensable" for the principal activity. The expenses deductible for VAT purposes must also be deductible under the Income Tax Law, which provides a list of "Authorised deductions" for each type of regime.

The restriction to input-VAT deduction may often be limited to a portion of the VAT incurred. This can for instance be the case for the VAT incurred on the use of cars by the employees of a business, which can be limited to a fixed percentage. Some countries restrict the deduction of input VAT on cars to 50%, even if the car is fully used for business purposes.

The rationale behind those limitations is generally threefold. First, it aims at avoiding the administrative burden associated with the need to control the actual use of goods and services that may easily be used for dual business/private purposes due to their very nature. Second, it is a way of reducing the risks of fraud. Third, such commodities often contain an element of "consumption" - for example restaurant meals. This third justification may be considered inconsistent with the main features of the VAT system. Indeed, businesses (or their employees) never actually "consume" goods and services within the meaning of the VAT when they are used in the furtherance of a taxable activity.

2.5. Registration and collection thresholds

All taxes impose compliance costs on businesses and administrative costs on tax authorities, but VAT is often considered as particularly burdensome for small and medium size businesses (SMEs) to comply with (European Commission, 2013[9]) (Evans et al., 2018[10]). Many countries have therefore introduced simplified regimes for SMEs to ease their compliance burden. These regimes can be grouped into three main categories: those that provide for an exemption from the VAT regime (exemption thresholds); those that facilitate the calculation of the VAT liability; and those that simplify accounting, filing and/or payment obligations (OECD, 2015[11]).

Most OECD countries (except Chile, Mexico and Spain) apply exemption thresholds below which small businesses are not required to charge and collect the tax on their outputs and their input VAT is not deductible. In Colombia and Turkey, the exemption threshold only applies to individuals and not to companies or incorporated businesses. The consequences of such exemptions are equivalent to treating small businesses as non-taxable businesses. There are two kinds of exemption thresholds: registration thresholds that relieve suppliers from both the requirement to register for VAT and to collect the tax; and collection thresholds for which taxpayers, even those below the threshold, are required to register for VAT, but are relieved from collecting the tax until they exceed the threshold. Different types of activities (e.g. supply of services vs supply of goods) or sectors (e.g. the non-profit sector) may be subject to different thresholds or even be excluded from their application (e.g. the construction sector). In most cases registration thresholds do not apply to foreign businesses and in some cases collection thresholds apply only to individuals or to businesses for which commercial accounting is not compulsory.

Annex Table 2.A.5 provides an overview of applicable collection and registration thresholds in OECD countries. In principle, the calculation of thresholds is generally based on annual turnover. In Japan, businesses (companies and individuals) are not required to register and account for VAT during the first two years of establishment if they remain below a capital-based threshold; a threshold based on an annual taxable turnover applies after the first two years (with some exceptions, based on levels of turnover). Although thresholds are generally based on annual turnover, their application may be subject to additional rules and conditions.

The levels of these thresholds vary significantly across OECD countries. Three broad groups can be distinguished.

Twenty countries have a relatively high general threshold above USD 30 000 of turnover per year: Australia, Austria, Belgium, Czech Republic, Estonia, France, Hungary, Ireland, Italy, Japan, Korea, Latvia, Lithuania, Luxembourg, New Zealand, Poland, Slovak Republic, Slovenia, Switzerland and the United Kingdom. Of these France, Italy, Japan, Poland, Slovak Republic and the United Kingdom have a particularly higher threshold of more than USD 90 000.

Nine countries have a relatively low threshold between USD 5 000 and 30 000: Canada, Denmark, Finland, Germany, Greece, Iceland, Israel, Netherlands and Portugal. Two countries have a low threshold below USD 5000: Norway and Sweden.

Since 2018, six OECD countries have raised their threshold: Austria, France, Germany, Hungary, Israel, Korea, Netherlands and Portugal while none has reduced it.

There are no definitive arguments on the need for, or the level of, thresholds. The main reasons for excluding small businesses (a notion that may vary considerably across countries) are that the costs of tax administration are disproportionate to the VAT revenues raised and, similarly, the VAT compliance costs can be disproportionate for many small businesses compared to their turnover. It is also assumed that smaller businesses may be less compliant. A relatively high threshold may give an advantage to small businesses, distorting competition with larger companies. A relatively low threshold may act as a disincentive for businesses to grow or as an incentive to avoid VAT by splitting activities artificially. It can also frustrate policy efforts to formalise the economy. However, the latter may be at least partly addressed by applying a simpler alternative tax to businesses below the VAT threshold and thus bring them into the "formal" economy. The level of the threshold is often the result of a trade-off between minimising compliance and administration costs, and the need to protect revenue and avoid competitive distortion.

All OECD countries that have a registration or collection threshold give the option to businesses below the threshold to register and account voluntarily for VAT, except Israel and Korea. Voluntary registration is often intended to provide an option for small businesses to avoid the disadvantages of non-registration - but they increase tax administration costs and impose compliance costs on entities that elect to be in the system. This also increases the risk of VAT fraud by "fly-by-night" traders, who register and claim VAT refunds before disappearing again. Countries therefore often impose a minimum period of time during which taxpayers that have registered voluntarily must remain registered. This period varies from one year (Australia, Canada, Czech Republic, Greece, Hungary, Japan, Slovak Republic and Switzerland) to two years (Denmark, France, and Norway) or in some cases, three years (Netherlands and Sweden) or five years (Austria, Germany, Portugal and Slovenia).

Recent research (Li Liu, 2019[12]) shows that firms tend to bunch below the registration threshold by restricting their reported turnover to avoid having to register for the VAT when they have a high share of sales to private consumers (B2C) but tend to register voluntarily, even when their turnover is below the threshold, in cases where they have a low share of such B2C sales, a high input-cost ratio, and more competition in the industry.

One challenge of VAT thresholds is to minimise incentives for small businesses to underreport turnover so as to remain below the exemption threshold, and/or to incentivise small businesses to grow their business. The adoption of a flexible threshold is one option. Under such a regime, small businesses that exceed the regular VAT threshold are not obliged to register immediately but are allowed to continue to benefit from the exemption as long as they do not exceed the threshold by a significant percentage. For example in France, businesses that exceed the regular thresholds of EUR 85 800 (for goods) and EUR 34 400 (for most services) may continue to benefit from the exemption if their turnover does not exceed EUR 94 300 and EUR 36 500 respectively for more than a year.

Other ways exist to reduce compliance costs for SMEs while avoiding the disadvantages of the exemption. One way used in many countries is to apply simplified presumptive schemes to facilitate the calculation of the VAT liability. For example, certain small businesses may be allowed to apply a single flat rate to turnover for determining the amount of VAT to be remitted to tax authorities instead of requiring a detailed VAT calculation of input and output VATs. An alternative simplification scheme for calculating VAT liability relies on simplified input tax credit calculations. A more detailed description of such regime is given in an OECD study on SME taxation (OECD, 2015[11]).

In most cases, registration thresholds do not apply to foreign businesses. However, the OECD VAT/GST Guidelines recommend that jurisdictions implementing a vendor registration regime for collecting the VAT on B2C supplies of services and intangibles by foreign suppliers do so without creating compliance and administrative burdens that are disproportionate to the revenues involved or to the objective of achieving neutrality between domestic and foreign suppliers. They specifically acknowledge that thresholds have been implemented by some jurisdictions to achieve this objective, adding that a balance should be sought between the desire to minimise administrative costs and compliance burdens for tax administrations and foreign suppliers and the need to maintain an even playing field between domestic and foreign businesses. The report on Mechanisms for the Effective Collection of VAT/GST where the Supplier is not Located in the Jurisdiction of Taxation (OECD, 2017[13]) provides further guidance on key policy aspects to consider for the possible implementation of such a threshold. These include neutrality aspects on the competitive position of domestic and foreign suppliers; simplification aspects on the potential reduction of compliance costs for foreign businesses and tax administrations; and the determination of the level of the threshold, including the calculation method (based on the supplier's turnover in the taxing jurisdiction or its worldwide turnover).

Among the 12 OECD jurisdictions requiring foreign suppliers of inbound services and intangibles to final consumers to register and account for the VAT in their jurisdiction, six apply a registration turnover threshold below which foreign suppliers are relieved from that obligation, i.e. Australia, Iceland, Japan, New Zealand, Norway and Switzerland. In these countries, the registration threshold is the same for domestic and foreign vendors. The EU is considered as one single jurisdiction in this context, as the absence of a registration threshold for non-EU suppliers of remote telecommunication, broadcasting and electronically supplied services under its Mini One Stop Shop (MOSS) regime (non-Union scheme) is set at EU level. A voluntary threshold of 10 000 EUR was implemented as of 1 January 2019 for remote intra-EU supplies of these services to final consumers by EU vendors (Union scheme).

2.6. Usage of margin schemes

Most countries allow or utilise specific methods for determining the VAT liability in special circumstances. The purpose of these methods is usually to simplify VAT administration and compliance and/or to address specific circumstances. Typical examples are the margin schemes, which are often used when the deduction of input tax according to the normal rules is considered too difficult or impossible – see for instance the resale of second-hand goods bought from private individuals, and the activities of travel agencies. Under a margin scheme, the tax base is calculated on the difference between the price paid by the taxpayer and the price of resale rather than on the full selling price. The reseller is not allowed to deduct the input VAT embedded in the buying price of the items that are resold under the margin scheme.

The

Annex Table 2.A.6 shows that all the EU countries employ a margin scheme for travel agencies, second-hand goods, works of art, collector's items and antiques since they share the same legislative root. Beyond the EU, eight other OECD countries employ margin schemes, i.e. Australia (on new residential property, gambling and second hand goods); Chile (second-hand real property); Colombia (sale of used cars, sale of fixed assets made by an intermediary, sale of gasoline); Israel (on coins and postal stamps, furniture, dwellings, used vehicles and foreign currency exchange); Mexico (second hand cars); Norway (on second hand goods, works of art, collectors' items and antiques); Switzerland (Collector's items such as works of art and antiques); and Turkey (on travel agencies).

2.7. Measuring performance of VAT: the VAT Revenue Ratio

VAT performance can be measured through different methods, depending on the dimension of the performance to be measured. It has traditionally been estimated by the "efficiency ratio", defined as the ratio of VAT revenues to GDP divided by the standard rate (expressed as a percentage). Although the efficiency ratio has been widely used as a diagnostic tool in evaluating VATs, it does not distinguish a product-type VAT from a consumption-type VAT. This difficulty is addressed by taking final consumption as a reference for the potential tax base rather than production (Ebrill et al., 2001[14]). If measured by the ratio of revenue from the tax to the product of the standard VAT rate and aggregate consumption, a benchmark VAT levied at a uniform rate on all consumption would have "C-Efficiency" of 100% provided that all the tax due is collected by the tax administration.

The estimates of the VAT Revenue Ratio (VRR) for OECD countries presented in this section builds on the "C-Efficiency ratio" principles. It provides an indicator that combines the effect of loss of revenues as a consequence of exemptions and reduced rates, fraud, evasion and tax planning. Although the VRR has to be interpreted with care and erosion of the tax base may be caused by a variety of factors, it may support policymakers in assessing the revenue raising performance of their VAT system and in identifying opportunities to raise additional revenues by improving VAT performance.

2.7.1. What does the VRR measure?

The aim of the VRR is to provide a measure of the extent to which a country collects its VAT on the natural base of the tax: final consumption expenditure. The VRR thus measures the difference between the VAT revenue actually collected and what would theoretically be raised if VAT was uniformly applied at the standard rate to the entire potential tax base and all revenue was collected:

$$\mathrm{VRR} = \frac{\mathrm{VR}}{\mathrm{B}\,.\,\mathrm{r}}$$

Where: VR = actual VAT revenues; B = potential tax base and r = standard VAT rate

The 'standard' rate refers to the default rate applicable to the tax base, unless otherwise advised by legislation. Legislation can (and many countries do) provide that lower (or higher) rates are applicable to a defined list of products. Reduced VAT rates are still widely used in OECD countries, mainly for equity or social objectives (basic essentials, health, education, etc.). No OECD countries apply higher VAT rates (see Annex Table 2.A.1).

In the VRR calculation formula as presented above, the potential tax base (B) is based on the Final Consumption Expenditure under Item P3 in the national accounts. However, the SNA measures consumption expenditures at market prices, i.e. including VAT. This VAT element must be deducted from the amount under P3 for the VRR calculation, because the theoretical basis for taxation should not include the tax itself.As a result, the VRR estimates presented in Annex Table 2.A.1 have been calculated as follows:

$$\text{VRR} = \frac{\text{VR}}{(\text{FCE} - \text{VR}).\text{r}}$$

Where: VR = actual VAT revenues; FCE = Final Consumption Expenditure (Item P3 in National Accounts); and r = standard VAT rate.

2.7.2. The challenge of assessing the tax base

The main methodological difficulty in the calculation of the VRR lies in the assessment of the potential tax base, since no standard assessment of the potential VAT base for all OECD countries is available. The potential VAT base includes all supplies of goods, services and intangibles made for consideration (or deemed to be made for consideration) by businesses or any other entity acting as a business (e.g. individuals, government entities providing supplies for direct consideration, etc.) to final consumers. In principle, the tax base ultimately corresponds to the expenditure made by final consumers to obtain goods, services and intangibles. In practice, however, many VAT systems impose VAT burden not only on final household consumption, but also on various entities that are involved in non-business activities or in VAT exempt activities (Chapter 1 and this chapter). In such situations, VAT can be viewed as treating such entities as if they were end consumers, or as "input taxing" the supplies made by such entities on the presumption that the burden of the VAT imposed will be passed on in the prices of the outputs of those non-business activities. The tax ultimately collected by the government in these situations is the tax on these inputs.

In the absence of a standard assessment of the potential VAT base for all OECD countries, the closest statistic for that base is final consumption expenditure as measured in the national accounts, VAT is indeed, ultimately a tax on final consumption. Final consumption expenditure in national accounts is calculated according to a standard international norm, the System of National Accounts (SNA 2008 - except for Turkey, Chile and Japan that still use SNA 1993) under Item P3 Final consumption expenditure.

2.7.3. The average VRR for OECD countries has remained stable

Across the OECD, the unweighted average VRR has remained relatively stable at 0.56 in 2017 and 2018, up 0.1% compared to 2016, as is shown in Annex Table 2.A.7. This OECD average has remained around this level since 2010 (0.55), after it had declined during the financial and economic crisis in 2008-9 (from 0.59 in 2007 to 0.53 in 2009). This estimate suggests that, on average, 44% of the theoretical potential VAT revenue is not collected.

The VRR estimates vary considerably among OECD countries. In 2018 the estimates ranged from 0.34 in Mexico and 0.38 in Colombia and Italy, to 0.89 in Luxembourg and 0.99 in New Zealand. An additional four OECD countries have an estimated VRR above 0.65, i.e. Estonia (0.74), Japan (0.72), Switzerland (0.69) and Korea (0.68). All the other OECD countries that operate a VAT (30 out of 36) have a VRR below 0.65; eleven of these countries have a ratio below 0.50. This suggests that a considerable part of the theoretical potential VAT revenue remains uncollected in many OECD countries. The VRR rose in 26 countries compared to 2016, with Poland's estimated VRR showing the biggest increase from 0.45 to 0.52 and Latvia's and Hungary's estimated VRR rising from 0.55 to 0.59 and from 0.54 to 0.58 respectively. The impact of the increase of the estimated VRR of these 26 countries on the OECD average was partly offset by the introduction of Colombia with a VRR considerably below the OECD average of 0.38, and the drop in the estimated VRRs for Australia (from 0.50 to 0.47) and Luxemburg (from 0.92 to 0.89). The VRR estimates remained unchanged for eight OECD countries.

The VRR levels notably reflect the fact that preferential treatments, such as reduced rates and exemptions, are still widely used in OECD countries (see Annex Table 2.A.2 and Annex Table 2.A.3). This is confirmed by tax expenditures data, which reflect the cost of tax concessions (OECD, 2010[15]).

It appears that there is no direct correlation between the level of the standard VAT rate and the VRR. Countries with very different VAT rates may have comparable VRRs. Australia and Ireland, for example, have a very similar VRR estimate 0.47 and 0.49 respectively while their standard VAT rates are at very different levels, i.e. 10% and 23% respectively. Although two thirds of countries (25 out of 36) have a VRR between 0.45 and 0.65, they have standard VAT rates that vary widely from 5% (Canada) to 25% (Denmark, Norway, and Sweden) and 27% (Hungary). These last four countries combine high standard VAT rates (25% and 27%) with a VRR above the OECD average, at respectively 0.62, 0.58, 0.59 and 0.59; while Mexico and Turkey combine lower standard VAT rates (respectively 16% and 18%) with a VRR estimate considerably below the OECD average (respectively 0.34 and 0.40). Japan combines a low VAT rate (8% in 2017-18) and the absence of reduced rates with a relatively high VRR (0.72).

Figure 2.3. VAT Revenue Ratio (VRR) 2018

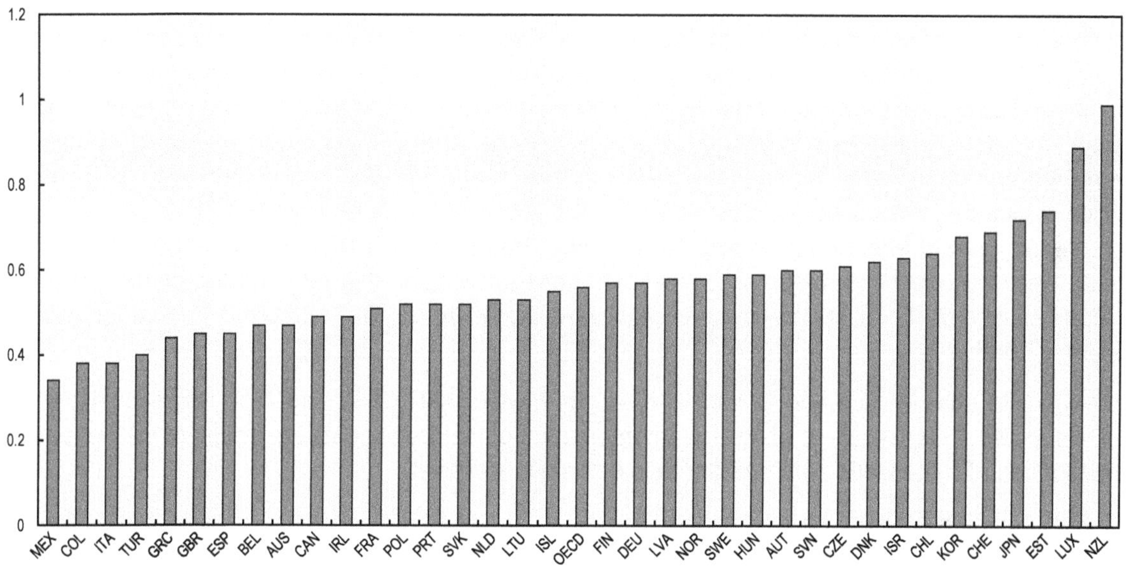

Note: OECD = OECD unweighted average
Source: Author's calculations

StatLink https://doi.org/10.1787/888934220078

The respective weight of the different factors that affect the VRR may vary widely across countries depending on the circumstances. The two countries with the highest VRR, New Zealand and Luxembourg, are both far above the OECD average (with respectively 0.99 and 0.89 compared to an average of 0.56) and even significantly above the country that immediately follows (Estonia with a VRR of 0.74). However, the reasons behind these high ratios are very different.

The VRR for Luxembourg has increased constantly between 1996 (0.54) and 2014 (1.23). This increase was correlated with deep changes in the EU marketplace, in particular the liberalisation of financial services and the boom of e-commerce. It is reasonable to assume that these market factors and the specific VAT treatment of these markets have had a strong upward effect on Luxembourg's VRR. It may be assumed that Luxembourg's position as an international financial centre has resulted in additional VAT revenue for the country. The supply of financial services is generally exempt from VAT in Luxembourg without the right to deduct the input tax, in accordance with EU VAT rules, including when supplied to customers in other EU Member States. This means that the non-deductible VAT incurred by financial service providers in Luxembourg increases Luxembourg's VAT revenues while a large share of the corresponding final consumption occurs in other EU Member States, as a result of the increased cross-border trade in financial services. Luxembourg had also become an international centre for e-commerce, notably as a consequence of the VAT treatment of this activity under EU VAT legislation until 1st January 2015. According to this legislation, e-commerce supplies to final consumers in other EU Member States were taxed in the Member State where the supplier was established. The low standard VAT rate in Luxembourg, the lowest in the EU (15 % until 2014), acted as an incentive to e-commerce suppliers to establish in Luxembourg; and this generated additional and continuously increasing revenue for the country as internet trade continued to grow. This changed as of 1 January 2015. Since that date, intra-EU e-commerce sales to final consumers are no longer subject to VAT in the Member State where the supplier is established (which was often Luxemburg). These sales are now subject to VAT in the Member State of these consumers' residence and at the rate applicable in that Member State. The loss of VAT revenues for Luxemburg from this change of the intra-EU place of taxation rules for e-commerce is reflected in the VAT revenue and VRR estimates for Luxembourg (which have declined from 1.25 in 2014 to 0.89 in 2018).

The factors underlying the constant very high VRR since the implementation of the VAT (GST) in New Zealand are very different from the Luxembourg ones. First, unlike Luxembourg, New Zealand operates a very broad GST tax base with limited exemptions (see Annex Table 2.A.3) and a limited use of zero rates (see Annex Table 2.A.2). Second, New Zealand treats public services as GST taxable (see Chapter 1). Although this does not generate actual additional revenue (the GST charged by public bodies to the government is compensated through budgetary transfers and the GST collected on local government activities is included in local taxes), this increases the share of revenues from GST in total tax revenues, which has an upward effect on the VRR. On the other hand, the potential GST base determined on the basis of the national accounts (see section above) does not include the value added by the government. The combination of these factors may explain why the VRR for New Zealand is so high and even sometimes above 1.

At the opposite end, Mexico and Colombia have the lowest VRR (0.33 and 0.38 respectively) amongst OECD countries. This is likely to be due to a combination of factors such as the scope of VAT exemptions, the application of a domestic zero rate and a low compliance level.

2.7.4. A number of factors influence the VRR

In theory, the closer the VAT system of a country is to a "pure" VAT as a broad-based tax on all final household consumption, the closer its VRR is to 1. A VRR close to 1 can be taken as an indicator of a VAT bearing uniformly on a broad base with effective tax collection. A lower value reflects such factors as the effects of reduced rates, exemptions or a failure to collect all tax due. A VRR above 1 is possible in theory, notably where almost all the tax base is covered by a VAT at a single standard rate and a number of exemptions without right to deduction apply so that the cascading effect of the exemption provides additional revenue for the government that exceeds the cost of the exemption. In practice, the VRR rarely equals 1 and a number of complex factors, alone or in combination, may influence the results positively or negatively. These include:

- The application of lower VAT rates to a number of goods and services and the level of such lower rates that reduce the tax revenue and have a negative impact on the VRR.
- The level of the registration and/or collection threshold under which small businesses do not account for VAT. These thresholds reduce the amount of VAT collected, although it could be argued that the adverse revenue consequences of such thresholds are likely to be limited since the businesses under the thresholds will generally not be able to deduct any input VAT and their value added can be expected to be modest.
- The scope of the exemptions. Depending on the features of the exemptions and market structures, exemptions may influence the VRR upwards or downwards. Exemptions may reduce the tax revenue when the exemption applies to goods or services directly supplied to final consumers

without requiring much investment or expenditure other than the supplier's own labour. They may increase revenue when the exemption occurs early in a supply chain and the revenue arising from the non-recoverable input VAT and its cascading through the value chain exceeds the potential tax arising from taxation at standard rates with the deduction of input tax (e.g. financial service supplied to businesses). The application of a VAT exemption for financial services in particular may have a considerable impact on the VRR, given the economic importance of this sector in many countries.

- The VAT treatment of public sector activities. Final consumption by government is the second largest final use in national accounts after household consumption. From a VAT perspective, governments' activities are exempt or outside the scope of VAT in most countries, New Zealand being the notable exception treating all governments activities as taxable. As a consequence, public bodies cannot deduct the input VAT paid on their taxable expenditure, again with the exception of New Zealand that provides a full right to deduct input tax for government activities. A number of countries have created mechanisms for balancing the adverse effects of the exemption of public sector activities, such as targeted VAT refunds, full or partial right to deduct input VAT, budgetary compensations or extended taxation of government activities. The different options chosen by governments may have varied impacts on the VRR. Compensations outside of the VAT system (e.g. a simple budgetary compensation) have no direct effect on the VRR. The government activities remain input taxed, generating the corresponding VAT revenue, before and after the compensation measures. A measure that provides the right to input-VAT deduction to government bodies will normally reduce VAT revenue if the outputs remain exempt, and hence influence the VRR downwards. Applying VAT to government activities like New Zealand does, on the other hand, will increase the amount of VAT collected and influence the VRR upwards, as it results in the taxation of the total output rather than just the inputs.
- The implementation of an effective regime for the collection of VAT on supplies of goods, services and digital products from online sales by foreign vendors and electronic marketplaces. Many VAT regimes have struggled to ensure the proper collection of VAT on online trade, in particular when faced with the challenge of collecting these taxes from non-resident vendors, which has caused increasingly important revenue losses as the value and volume of digital trade has continued to increase (see Chapter 1).
- The capacity of the tax administration to manage the VAT system efficiently and the degree of compliance by taxpayers influences the VRR as low compliance has a negative impact on VAT revenues. The level of taxpayer insolvencies and bankruptcies can also influence the VRR.
- The failure of a tax administration to operate an appropriate VAT refund process (with timely refunds of excess input-VAT credits to domestic businesses and/or refunds to non-resident businesses), which is contrary to the fundamental principle of VAT-neutrality, may influence the VRR upwards (for the "wrong" reasons).
- Similarly, the failure of a VAT regime to ensure the proper implementation of the destination principle to the exportation of goods and/or services, notably by taxing exports in the origin jurisdiction or by exempting exports without a right for the exporter to recover the associated input-VAT, my influence the VRR upwards "for the wrong reasons".
- The evolution of consumption patterns may also affect the tax revenue. The VRR can for instance decline, all other things equal, when the share of consumption of necessities that are taxed at the lower VAT rate increases, e.g. as a result of an economic crisis (OECD, 2020[16]).
- Finally, also the possible impact of the differences between the measurement of final consumption expenditure in the national accounts and countries' potential VAT base should be taken into account when interpreting the VRR.

For further technical discussion on the factors influencing the calculation of the VRR see (OECD, 2016[17]).

2.7.5. Policy and compliance factors influencing the VRR

The level of the VRR rarely depends on one factor in isolation but rather on the interaction between them. For example, a high standard rate may create an incentive for evasion while multiple lower rates may lead to revenue loss due to misclassifications. Exemption of certain sectors of activity may create distortions and incentives for avoidance, which require additional administrative capacities that cannot be used for the efficient collection of VAT. Inefficient tax administration, burdensome administrative requirements and complex VAT mechanisms may reduce taxpayer compliance levels.

These potentially influencing factors can be divided in two main categories:

- Those resulting from policy decisions, mainly affecting the tax base or the coverage of the standard rate (i.e. reduced VAT rates and exemptions – "policy gap"), and
- Those related to the efficiency of the tax collection and compliance levels ("compliance gap").

The VRR is a combination of the result of policy decisions and the "compliance gap". Analysis to further break down the composition of the VRR can be carried out. One method to decompose the VRR into its policy and compliance components consists in using tax expenditure data from VAT preferential regimes (i.e. the revenue cost of a system's departure from the application of the standard VAT rate to the entire theoretical tax base) to estimate the "policy gap". The remaining difference between 1 and a given country's VRR then provide an estimate of the "compliance gap by" deduction. However, given the number of other factors that may influence the VRR, such figures should be used with caution.

Another method is to calculate the "compliance gap" (or "VAT gap"), i.e. the difference between tax collected and the tax that should be collected if all consumers and businesses fully complied with a given jurisdiction's VAT rules. This method is employed for the annual VAT Gap estimates in the European Union where the VAT Gap is defined as the difference between the amount of VAT actually collected and the theoretical tax liability according to tax law (VAT Total Tax Liability VTTL). (Institute for Advanced Studies, 2015[18]). (CASE – Center for Social and Economic Research, 2020[19]). The VAT Gap is estimated using a "top-down" approach that applies a jurisdiction's respective VAT rates to the relevant components of consumption (including final consumption of households; final consumption of government and non-profit institutions, intermediate consumption for partially exempt businesses; expenditure on housing, country-specific, adjustments, etc.). Australia uses a similar method (Australian Taxation Office, 2020[20]). The International Monetary Fund RA-GAP framework (Eric Hutton, 2017[21]) uses national accounts data to calculate the potential VAT base per economic sector. It calculates the potential VAT revenues for a given VAT system by applying its current tax schedule (exemptions, zero-rates, reduced rates) to that VAT base. Potential VAT revenues under the reference policy are calculated by applying the current standard VAT rate to the base. The VAT gap is calculated by comparing actual VAT revenue with potential revenues under the current policy and the reference policy.

2.8. Combatting VAT fraud and non-compliance

2.8.1. VAT revenue losses from fraud and non-compliance remain significant

Reducing the revenue losses from VAT non-compliance remains a key challenge and a priority for countries around the world. Many tax administrations carry out research to estimate their country's VAT compliance gap, i.e. the revenue loss from VAT fraud, non-compliance and bankruptcies. The VAT Gap in the European Union (EU) was estimated at EUR 140 billion for the 28 EU Member States for 2018 in the latest VAT Gap report (CASE – Center for Social and Economic Research, 2020[19]). Although it remains very high, the EU Commission observed that this VAT Gap has improved marginally in recent years in both relative and nominal terms. In relative terms, the EU-wide VAT Gap fell to 11% of the VAT total tax liability (VTTL) in 2018, from 12.3% in 2016 and 14.3% in 2014. In nominal terms, the overall EU VAT Gap slightly decreased by almost EUR 1 billion to EUR 140.04 billion in 2018, slowing down from a decrease of EUR 2.9 billion in 2017. However, figures for 2020 forecast a reversal of this trend, with a potential loss of EUR 164 billion in 2020 due to the effects of the coronavirus pandemic on the economy.

The smallest VAT Gaps in the EU were observed in Sweden (0.7 percent), Croatia (3.5 percent), and Finland (3.6 percent); the largest in Romania (33.8 percent), Greece (30.1 percent), and Lithuania (25.9 percent). The United Kingdom estimated its VAT Gap at GBP 10.0 billion in 2018-19, i.e. 7.0% of the estimated net VTTL (HMRC, 2020[22]), declining from 13.3 billion and 9.6% of the VTTL in 2017-18. A number of other OECD countries provide public estimates of their VAT gap. In Australia the GST gap is estimated at AUD 5.8 billion or 8.1% of VTTL (Australian Taxation Office, 2020[20])); in Canada, the multi-year average GST/HST gap for 2000-2014 is estimated at 5.6% VTTL (CRA, 2016[23]). In Latin America, the VAT gaps showed a wide diversity in 2017 (CEPAL, 2020[24]) but OECD countries in this region had a relatively low VAT gap compared to others, i.e. 21.4% in Chile, 23.6% in Colombia and 16.4% in Mexico (compared to e.g. 45.3% in Panama and 43.8 in the Dominican Republic).

Losses of VAT revenue from non-compliance can result from a number of factors. In addition to "traditional" VAT avoidance (i.e. arrangements intended to reduce the tax liability that could be strictly legal but in contradiction with the intent of the law) and evasion (illegal arrangements where liability to tax is ignored or hidden) VAT systems have often been the target of organised criminal attacks. This organised and criminal VAT fraud has been shown to have connections with other criminal activities such as terrorism and money laundering in a number of cases (EUROPOL, 2020[25]).

The most common type of organised VAT fraud is the "missing trader" or "carousel" fraud. It arises when a business makes a purchase without paying VAT (typically a transaction for which tax self-assessment applies), then collects VAT on an onward supply and disappears without remitting the VAT collected. Originally, the fraud involved primarily high-value goods that can easily be moved across borders, such as computer chips and cell phones - but it expanded to services that can be bought and sold like goods. Organised VAT fraud in CO_2 emission trading, for instance, caused billions of Euros of VAT revenue losses in a range of countries. Energy markets are also vulnerable to organised VAT fraud. European energy regulators, energy trading firms and gas and electricity operators notably warned EU authorities about the serious impact of VAT carrousel fraud on the functioning of European gas and electricity markets (Europex – Association of European Energy Exchanges, 2018[26]). They reported signs of "a major penetration of the gas and electricity markets by VAT fraudsters". Research in the past also showed that certain accounting software products contained hidden tools (zappers) for the manipulation of VAT receipts (OECD, 2013[27]). The digitalisation of the economy creates new challenges for VAT regimes in addressing fraud and non-compliance, notably in light of the exponential growth of cross-border e-commerce (OECD, 2015[28]).

Tax authorities are developing, and implementing, a growing variety of responses to the increasingly complex challenge of protecting important VAT revenues against VAT fraud and non-compliance. The following sections look in slightly more detail at three categories of responses that can be observed among OECD countries: changes in VAT collection mechanisms; reinforcement in taxpayer's reporting obligations and data analysis; and international administrative cooperation and exchange of information.

2.8.2. Changes in the VAT collection methods: domestic reverse charge and split payment

Domestic reverse charge (see

Annex Table 2.A.12)

In a standard VAT regime, the VAT is collected from suppliers through a staged process whereby the supplier collects the VAT from its customer and remits it to the authorities after having deducted any recoverable input VAT (see Chapter 1). Under a reverse charge mechanism, the liability for remitting the VAT to the tax authorities is shifted from the supplier to its business customer (i.e. in B2B transactions). Shifting the VAT liability from the supplier to the customer removes the possibility for dishonest suppliers to disappear with VAT that they collected from their customers without remitting it to the tax authorities, which is for example typical for so-called "missing trader" fraud. Nor can businesses claim the deduction or refunds of VAT that they have not paid (e.g. VAT on false invoices) or that has not been remitted to the tax authorities, which it typical for "carrousel fraud" schemes.

OECD countries that are using the domestic reverse charge mechanism have typically limited its application to economic sectors that are particularly vulnerable to such organised fraud schemes. It is particularly used to counteract missing trader and carousel fraud in sectors such as trade in mobile phones; integrated circuit devices; game consoles; tablet PCs and laptops; cereals and industrial crops; raw and semi-finished metals; gas and electricity; and telecom services.

No OECD country operates a more generalised reverse charge regime for the collection of all VAT on domestic transactions between businesses. Although this would reduce the risks of specific fraud types, as described above, it would also have several drawbacks including new burdens for businesses and tax administrations and growing risks of other types of fraud at the retail level (e.g. sales suppression, misuse of VAT identification numbers). One concern is that it would effectively transform the VAT into a retail sales tax, with the concentration of all revenue risks at the stage of the final sale or at a limited number of points, with the inherent weaknesses of such a system.

In the EU, Member States can apply a domestic reverse charge mechanism to a determined list of supplies, on an optional and temporary basis. EU Member States have also been allowed since 2013 to apply a domestic reverse charge to any kind of supply in case of sudden and massive VAT fraud.

Annex Table 2.A.12 shows that the use of domestic reverse charge as a means of combatting VAT fraud is widely used in the 23 OECD countries that are EU Member States, in particular for the supply of CO_2 emission certificates (all except Estonia, Poland, Latvia and Lithuania); scrap materials and waste (all except Belgium, Luxembourg Poland, and the United Kingdom); and construction work (all except Estonia, Luxembourg, Poland and the United Kingdom). The domestic reverse charge is also applied by many EU countries to the supply of gold (14 countries); electronic devices such as laptops, chips, mobile phones etc. (11 countries) and the supply of gas and electricity to taxable dealers (10 countries). Also other OECD countries use a domestic reverse mechanism albeit to a much lesser extent i.e. Canada (supplies of real property by non-residents and some supplies between provinces); Chile (supplies of rice, construction works, waste and certain plants and animals); Israel (metal debris); Mexico (waste, some supplies made by individuals); New Zealand (supplies of land incorrectly zero rated); Norway (supply of CO_2 emission allowances and investment gold) and Turkey (some supplies made by non-taxable persons). More than half of the OECD countries (19 out of 36) apply the reverse-charge to supplies in the construction sector.

Domestic reverse-charge has not been implemented in Colombia, Iceland, Japan, Korea, and Switzerland. Poland replaced its domestic reverse charge arrangements with a mandatory split payment mechanism in November 2019 (applicable only to the supplies that were previously subject to the domestic reverse charge; see also the section below).

The split payment mechanism (see

Annex Table 2.A.12)

Another means of reducing the vulnerability of VAT regimes to fraud and non-compliance is through the implementation of a so-called split payment (or withholding) mechanism. Under such a mechanism, the supplier charges the VAT on its domestic supplies to the customer according to normal rules, but the VAT paid by the customer (or part of it) is either directly remitted to the tax authorities ("withholding scheme") or deposited on the supplier's special VAT account ("split payment") rather than to the supplier. The supplier can generally use the amounts deposited in its special VAT account under a split payment regime only to pay VAT either to the tax administration or to another supplier (and to this supplier's VAT account only). Poland, which operates such a split payment regime (see previous section), has extended the possible use of amounts on special VAT accounts to pay certain other public levies.

A split-payment or withholding regime has a similar fraud-prevention effect as a domestic reverse-charge mechanism in that it removes the possibility for a supplier to collect the VAT without remitting it to the tax authorities. Among the drawbacks of these regimes are the added complexity (incl. the requirement for suppliers to determine for each transaction whether or not it is in the scope of the regime) and the cash-flow impact for businesses, which can be significant particularly under a withholding regime as businesses receive no/less output VAT against which they can offset deductible input-VAT (and this could result in a perennial excess-input VAT position). Some have observed that split-payment mechanisms may not prevent more complex missing trader frauds (Bartosz Gryziak, 2020[29]).

Annex Table 2.A.12 shows that such a regime has been implemented in only five OECD countries and these are all targeted at specific sectors or types of supplies.

In Poland, a mandatory split payment mechanism applies to business-to-business (B2B) supplies of a defined list of goods and services that are considered to be sensitive to fraud (such as scrap metal, of CO_2 emission allowances, mobile phones, tablets, construction services etc. which were previously subject to a domestic reverse charge), if the invoiced gross amount exceeds PLN 15 000. Upon decision of the customer, an optional split payment mechanism can be applied to B2B supplies that are not covered by the mandatory split payment.

Italy requires public authorities or government bodies, public owned companies and companies listed on the Italian Stock Market to remit the VAT on their purchases of goods and services directly to the tax authorities instead of to their suppliers. Under this withholding regime, suppliers are entitled to faster refunds of excess input VAT credits. Korea applies a withholding regime for the supplies of gold, copper and scrap gold and iron. In the Czech Republic, such a system is only optional for customers that wish to avoid possible joint and several liability for the supplier's unpaid taxes. Turkey operates a partial withholding regime whereby customers are required to withhold a percentage of the VAT charged to them by suppliers and remit it directly to the tax authorities for supplies in certain sectors, such as construction, scrap metal, glass, plastic and paper, advisory and audit services, some repair services etc. Australia requires recipients of new residential property suppliers to effectively withhold GST from payment to the supplier and they are instead obliged to remit the full amount of the GST to the tax authority which is reconciled against taxable amounts of GST required to be reported for these supplies by the supplier.

Colombia, Chile and Mexico operate a withholding requirement as a fallback for the collection of VAT on inbound business-to-consumer (B2C) supplies of services and intangibles by foreign vendors. Where the foreign supplier of such B2C services and intangibles does not register to account for the VAT in the country, payment providers that facilitate the payment for these supplies (credit and debit cards; payment wallets; and banks) are required to withhold VAT on the payment for these supplies and remit it to the tax authorities.

2.8.3. Collecting transaction data from the taxpayers

Many OECD countries have used technology to enhance the reporting of tax relevant data to tax authorities. After a generalisation of mandatory e-filing of VAT returns (OECD, 2015[30]), many OECD countries have introduced or consider introducing a requirement for taxpayers to provide transaction data to tax authorities, sometimes in real time. These measures typically require detailed information to be provided in an electronic format at individual taxable transaction level. This information can include invoicing information and accounting data or any other information that allows tax authorities to monitor supplies made and/or received by individual taxpayers.

Annex Table 2.A.11 shows that most OECD countries have implemented transaction information reporting obligations since 2000, except Belgium, Canada, Finland, Iceland and Japan. Amongst the countries that have implemented transaction information reporting obligations, nineteen impose a specific format for such reporting (Chile, Colombia, Czech Republic, France, Greece, Israel, Italy, Korea, Lithuania, Luxembourg, Mexico, Netherlands, Norway, Poland Portugal, Slovak Republic, Slovenia, Spain and Turkey). Eight of them use (a variation of) the Standard Audit File for Tax (SAF-T) format developed by the OECD Forum on Tax Administration (OECD, 2005[31]). This involves the use of accounting software to create an electronic file (the SAF-T) containing tax-relevant accounting data. The SAF-T format enables the transfer of these data from the taxpayer to the tax authorities in a standardised electronic format.

Half of the countries requiring electronic transaction reporting (16 out of 31) require the systematic transmission of such information to the tax administration (Chile, Colombia, Czech Republic, Estonia, Greece, Hungary, Israel, Italy, Korea, Lithuania, Mexico, Poland, Portugal, Slovak Republic, Spain and Turkey) and eight of these require this transmission to happen in (near) real time (Chile, Colombia, Hungary, Italy, Korea, Mexico, Spain and Turkey).

Countries are also increasingly concerned with the monitoring of transactions in cash in the business-to-consumer (B2C) environment and more than one third of OECD countries (16 out of 36) have implemented requirements for suppliers to use electronic cash registers (Austria, Belgium, Czech Republic, France, Greece, Hungary, Israel, Italy, Korea, Latvia, Lithuania, Norway, Poland, Slovak Republic, Slovenia, and Sweden). Six of these countries require the systematic transmission of data to the tax administration (Austria, Greece, Israel, Korea, Slovak Republic and Slovenia, in (near) real time for Korea, Slovak Republic and Slovenia.

The volume of information collected by tax administrations has increased dramatically in recent years. In order for countries to take advantage of the opportunities that such data collection provides, countries and their taxpayers need to have confidence in the security and confidentiality of the information gathered by tax administrations. Facing the risks of inappropriate disclosure of information whether intentionally or by accident (e.g. hacking of tax administration databases), countries must ensure that both the legal framework and appropriate data protection systems are in place (OECD, 2012[32]).

2.8.4. International administrative cooperation

There is also a growing recognition that effective strategies to tackle VAT fraud and evasion would benefit from the enhanced international administrative co-operation. Governments increasingly recognise that information exchange and administrative co-operation play a significant role in combatting international VAT fraud and ensuring effective tax collection, not least in the context of the digitalisation of the economy (OECD, 2015[28]); (Court Auditors, 2015[33]). This need was also recognised in the 2015 OECD Report on Tax Challenges Arising from Digitalisation (OECD, 2015[34]) and the OECD is developing work in this context.

A number of instruments already exist that provide the legal foundation for the international administrative co-operation in the area of VAT. These include the Multilateral Convention on Mutual Administrative Assistance in Tax Matters (OECD/Council of Europe, 2011[35]), the bilateral treaties implementing the current Articles 26 and 27 of the OECD and UN Model Tax Conventions, and Tax Information Exchange Agreements (TIEAs) based on the OECD Model. Regional agreements also provide legal base for such co-operation. These include EU Regulation No 904/2010, the Nordic Mutual Assistance Convention on Mutual Administrative Assistance in Tax Matters, the CIAT Model Agreement on the Exchange of Tax Information, and the African Tax Administration Forum Agreement on Mutual Assistance in Tax Matters.

Amongst these instruments, the Multilateral Convention on Mutual Administrative Assistance in Tax Matters (the Convention) is considered the most promising. The Convention was developed jointly by the Council of Europe and the OECD. It was opened for signature by the member states of both organisations in 1988. It was then aligned with the internationally agreed standard on transparency and exchange of information and opened to all countries in 2011. It provides for all possible forms of administrative co-operation between the Parties in the assessment and collection of taxes, in particular with a view to combating tax avoidance and evasion. The Convention has a very wide scope and covers all forms of compulsory payments to general governments (i.e. the central government and its political subdivisions) including VAT (although the obligations set forth in the Convention are subject to any reservations by the Parties). As of November 2020, 141 jurisdictions participate in the Convention.

Within the EU, the VAT Directive (2006/112/EC) and implementing regulation (904/2010) provide legal background for administrative co-operation and exchange of information among members. It is supported by an operational network of tax officials, Eurofisc. In December 2018, the European Commission adopted a proposal to reinforce administrative cooperation within the EU to improve the exchange and analysis of information between the Member States' tax administrations and with law enforcement bodies. The VAT e-commerce package applicable as from July 2021 will remove the VAT exemption on imports of low value goods this obliging suppliers to pay the VAT on all goods imported into the EU. These measures will reduce the possibility for certain fraud involving these goods and they are accompanied by reinforced co-operation between tax and customs authorities. Eurofisc has also strengthened its co-operation and exchange of information with the European Anti-Fraud Office (OLAF) and Europol. In addition, the Council has adopted in February 2020 a legislative package requesting payment service providers to transmit information on cross-border payments originating from Member States and on the beneficiary of these payments. A new central electronic system of payment information ("CESOP") will be set up for storage of the payment information and for further processing of this information by national anti-fraud officials. The EU also signed a bilateral agreement on the VAT exchange of information with Norway in February 2018.

2.9. Special section: VAT measures in response to the COVID-19 crisis

Governments have taken rapid and unprecedented action to address the health crisis and the drop in economic activity caused by the outbreak of COVID-19. Containing and mitigating the spread of the virus has been the first priority of public authorities. With containment measures in place, countries' immediate policy reactions focused on alleviating hardships and maintaining the productive capacity of the economy. As the duration of the pandemic lengthens and uncertainty about its development remains high, governments have begun extending and expanding emergency policy measures. Some countries have started relaxing their containment rules and are announcing economic recovery and stimulus packages.

This section takes stock of the tax measures that have been introduced to mitigate the impact of the COVID-19 crisis, with a particular focus on the VAT measures that were included in most countries' fiscal and tax policy responses. After recalling the broader policy background to countries' responses to the COVID-19 outbreak, this section outlines the measures in the area of VAT policy and administration introduced in OECD countries focusing on countries' immediate, short-term responses to the outbreak of the pandemic. It looks consecutively at the VAT measures aimed at supporting businesses cash flow, at reducing business compliance burden and at supporting the healthcare sector, before concluding and looking ahead at possible post-pandemic policies.

This section is based on a database (https://oecd.org/tax/covid-19-tax-policy-and-other-measures.xlsm) compiled by the OECD on tax policy responses to the COVID-19 crisis. Other important sources are the OECD reports on Tax Policy Reforms 2020 – OECD and Selected Partner Economies (OECD, 2020[36])and on Tax and Fiscal Policy in Response to the Coronavirus Crisis: Strengthening Confidence and Resilience (OECD, 2020[37]).

2.9.1. Policy background

Uncertainty about the development of the COVID-19 health and economic crisis remains high. To discuss the policy responses to this crisis, it is useful to break down the crisis into different phases that may each require their own policy approaches. Recognizing that they may overlap and vary across countries, and that countries have moved at different paces through the crisis as the epicentre of the pandemic has shifted between regions, Figure 2.4 presents a schematic view of these different phases and how policy responses may be expected to evolve.

In the initial phase (Phase 1), countries confronted with a virus outbreak have implemented containment and mitigation measures, aimed primarily at halting the outbreak. In this phase, tax and broader fiscal policies have tended to focus on liquidity and income support. As the health crisis continues and containment measures remain in place, tax and fiscal measures have evolved gradually into a more sustained effort to reduce the adverse impacts of containment (Phase 2). As countries have begun to relax containment and mitigation measures, the focus on keeping businesses and households afloat and on limiting hardship has begun to shift towards an emphasis on economic recovery, including through fiscal stimulus policies (Phase 3). The progression towards recovery may not be linear: there may be some overlap with Phase 2, where containment and mitigation measures are only being removed gradually or partially. Containment measures are likely to be reinstated in countries that are confronted to a second wave of the pandemic. Once economies have recovered, a shift towards restoring public finances can be anticipated, during which there may be renewed attention on strengthening resilience to health risks but also to other known risks, including climate change (Phase 4).

Figure 2.4. Schematic policy phases during and after the pandemic

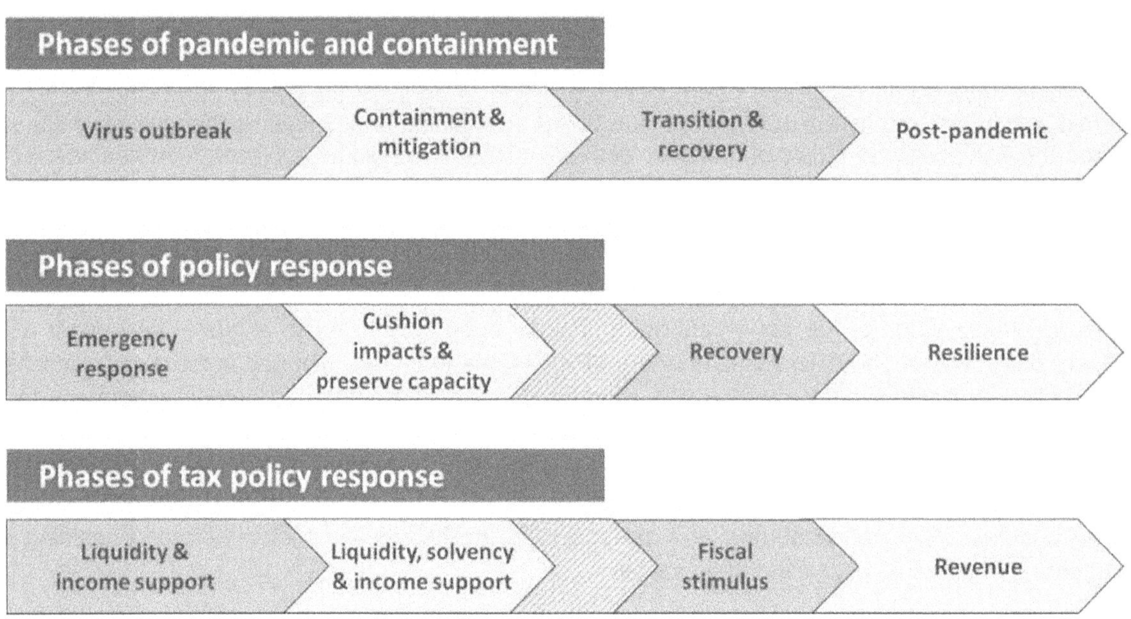

Source: Based on (OECD, 2020[38]).

Fiscal policy responses by OECD countries have focused on cushioning the immediate impact of the crisis, with very similar objectives across countries: preventing hardship and reducing burdens for households and businesses caused by the COVID-19 outbreak and by the restrictions introduced to contain the virus; and ensuring that households and businesses are able to resume economic activity when the worst of the health crisis has passed. For businesses, this has generally meant providing liquidity support to help them stay afloat. For individuals, the priority has been to provide income support to the most directly affected households. Most OECD countries have also introduced measures to reduce compliance burdens for businesses and to secure the continuity of public administration, as well as to enhance the funding and functioning of the healthcare sector. Most of the measures introduced in the emergency phase have taken effect immediately and have been time-bound. These rapid responses may often have been introduced based on the assumption that containment phases would be shorter than what has proved to be the case. As the crisis has continued, countries have retained their focus on keeping businesses and households afloat and have often expanded their initial packages of measures. Some countries have prolonged existing crisis measures and expanded support to groups that were not covered by the initial measures.

2.9.2. VAT measures as part of countries' tax policy response to the COVID-19 crisis

This overview focuses on the measures taken by OECD countries in the area of VAT as part of their fiscal and tax policy responses to support households and businesses during the emergency and the mitigation and containment phases of the COVID-19 crisis (Phases 1 and 2 as described above). Measures for individual taxpayers have generally focused on preventing hardship and reducing burdens in light of the restrictions from mitigation and containment strategies. Most countries have introduced measures to provide income support to households, generally through enhanced cash benefits targeted at the most vulnerable households. This support to households has largely been provided through direct transfers rather than through the tax system.

VAT measures have primarily been part of countries' COVID-19 tax responses aimed at supporting businesses. Tax measures for businesses, both legal entities and the self-employed, have generally focused on alleviating cash-flow problems to help avoid escalating problems such as the laying off workers, inability to pay suppliers and closure or bankruptcy. Liquidity support has been provided through a mix of tax and non-tax measures. The most common non-tax instrument used by OECD and partner economies throughout the crisis has been loan guarantee schemes, where the government guarantees all or part of the value of loans granted to eligible businesses. Other measures have included small interest-free loans and cash grants, typically targeted toward small businesses or businesses in the most affected sectors. The most common type of tax measure to enhance business cash flow has been the deferral of tax payments. Many countries have complemented these business cash flow support measures with measures to alleviate tax reporting and other compliance burdens during the mitigation and containment phase of COVID-19 crisis. Most countries have also taken tax measures to support the healthcare sector and facilitate medical urgency responses to the crisis.

VAT policy and administration measures have been an important component of countries' COVID-19 tax responses to support businesses and the healthcare sector during the mitigation and containment phases. This section hereafter first provides an overview of the VAT measures aimed at supporting business cash flow. This is followed by an outline of VAT measures taken to alleviate tax compliance burdens for businesses and, finally, by an overview of VAT measures aimed at supporting the healthcare sector.

2.9.3. Measures to support business cash flow

The majority of measures in OECD countries have sought to ensure that businesses have sufficient cash flow through a mix of tax and non-tax measures. The most common type of tax measure to enhance business cash flow has been the deferral of tax payments. These measures have generally applied to taxes that require frequent (monthly or quarterly) payments, including advance payments of corporate income tax (CIT) or personal income tax (PIT) and social security contributions (SSCs).

Measures to defer the payment of VAT have played a critical role in countries' tax policy and administration responses to support business cash flow. VAT can often be due before businesses have effectively received payment from their customers (e.g. at the time of invoicing). When the volume of payment delays or defaults escalates during the mitigation and containment phases of the COVID-19 crisis, businesses face growing pressure to pre-finance VAT on their sales that they have not, and may never receive, from their customers. Given the typically short VAT filing and payment obligations (monthly or quarterly), the pressure on businesses to pre-finance potentially considerable amounts of VAT that they have not received from their customers can add very quickly and significantly to businesses cash flow burdens. VAT deferrals have therefore been a key component of the tax measures introduced by most OECD countries to reduce business cash flow pressures. These measures have not only granted a temporary relief from the burden of having to pre-finance VAT on unpaid invoices, but have also proven to be and efficient and easy-to-implement manner of providing financial support to businesses by allowing them to deploy any received VAT amounts temporarily as working capital.

Most countries have complemented VAT payment deferrals with a suspension, or reduction, of penalties and/or interest charges that are normally applied for late tax payments. Such penalties or interest payments can both add to businesses' cash flow problems as well as cause significant stress for taxpayers during periods of mitigation and containment, particularly if there are difficulties in communicating with the administration on these issues or in exercising appeal rights. Similar payment deferrals and suspensions of penalties and/or late payment interest have been introduced for Retail State Taxes in most US States.

The process and conditions for obtaining deferral of VAT payments and the suspension of penalties and/or interest for late tax payments have varied across countries, along with the duration and other modalities of these measures. Most countries have required businesses to apply for the relief and/or to prove a link with the COVID-19 crisis. Some countries have applied these measures automatically. Several countries made these measures available to all businesses, while others have limited them to certain sectors (e.g. tourism, retail, entertainment and hospitality) or have targeted small and medium size enterprises (SMEs) or self-employed businesses. Some countries offered businesses flexibility to opt for partial deferral or to negotiate a flexible payment plan with their tax administration.

Several countries (approximately one third of OECD countries) have taken measures to accelerate and/or to enhance the processing of excess input VAT refund claims. These measures have primarily been introduced through adjustments to administrative practice rather than through legislative or regulatory change. Enhancing the refunding of excess VAT credits is arguably as important for improving business cash flow as VAT payment deferrals. While output VAT is falling for many businesses as a result of declining sales, the input VAT on fixed costs and other business purchases keeps accruing. These may be significant as many businesses may face payment obligations under longer-term contracts, e.g. for key functions that they may have outsourced to third-party contractors. This may lead to growing amounts of excess input VAT credits, i.e. VAT incurred on costs and investment that cannot be credited against VAT collected on sales. This may generate spillover effects, with businesses potentially defaulting on their invoices to avoid the growing cost of non-refundable VAT, and defaults rippling through supply chains.

The measures taken by tax administrations to enhance VAT refunds include the internal reprioritisation of activities to fast track the treatment of refund claims, notably by redirecting administrative capacity to expedite the process; the simplification of procedures notably through the increased use on electronic/online processes instead of paper-based ones; relaxing the risk checks that are normally done before making refunds; facilitating the offsetting of VAT refunds against other tax or similar liabilities (e.g. social security contributions). Tax administrations have typically restricted simplified or expedited VAT refunds to claims below a certain threshold (typically EUR 10.000 - 30.000) or to businesses with a good compliance history to limit fraud risks.

A temporary relaxation of the conditions for claiming relief from VAT on bad debts is another possible measure for tax authorities to support business cash flow as well as broadening the access to cash-accounting schemes. Bad debt relief regimes allow businesses to claim relief from the VAT on the supplies for which they have not been paid. Most VAT systems provide for such relief under relatively strict conditions. A temporary relaxation of these conditions (e.g. shortening the period for which the debt must have remained unpaid) may be an efficient measure to further alleviate cash flow pressure for businesses that are likely to see payment delays and defaults escalating as the COVID-19 crisis continues. Cash accounting schemes, on the other hand, allow businesses to account for the VAT on their sales on the basis of the payments they receive, rather than on the tax invoices they issue. They can only reclaim the VAT on their inputs once they pay their suppliers. Such a scheme supports cash flow, as VAT does not have to be remitted to the tax authorities until payment has been received from the customer. These schemes are typically available to small and medium enterprises subject to several conditions. Although a temporary relaxation of these regimes could further support cash flow for businesses during the COVID-19 crisis, such measures have generally not been considered necessary by tax authorities in OECD countries. Most OECD countries have relied primarily on the deferral of VAT payments, and on the extension of such measures where necessary, to support business cash flow as the COVID-19 crisis continues.

While the deferral of VAT payments is generally considered as an effective and relatively straightforward approach to supporting cash flow, tax authorities have highlighted that this measure requires careful management notably to minimise risks of fraud (e.g. deferred payments siphoned off in fraudulent schemes) and to avoid VAT debts building up to unsustainable levels or deferred payments leading to severe cash-flow problems at a later date making it more difficult for taxpayers to return to normal conditions.

2.9.4. Measures to alleviate business compliance burden

Tax authorities in many OECD countries have introduced measures to reduce compliance burdens on businesses in light of the restrictions in place during the mitigation and containment phases of the COVID-19 crisis. Measures to facilitate VAT compliance are particularly important in this context, given the volume and frequency of filing and reporting requirements associated with the operation of these taxes (incl. returns, invoices, sales listings etc.).

Over one third of OECD countries has extended deadlines for the filing of VAT returns and related forms, typically on request, along with the waiver of penalties for late filing. Some tax authorities have introduced further reporting simplifications, such as allowing VAT liabilities to be computed on a "best estimate" basis. Several tax administrations reported the increased use of digital communication channels to simplify compliance processes (incl. VAT registration), to facilitate the interaction with taxpayers and to help reduce physical contacts. This includes the enhanced use of direct digital messaging, of web chat, social media, mobile applications, hotlines (possibly with call-back facilities), changes to mobile applications, virtual assistants, etc. This is particularly important where taxpayers require the assistance of intermediaries or specialised staff and systems to file returns, process invoices, manage VAT registrations, claim VAT refunds, produce listings, etc. Remote working may often make these tasks more difficult or even impossible for taxpayers, for example for systems security and access reasons, and key staff may not always be available due to illness or caring responsibilities.

Tax authorities have typically made the extension of filing and reporting deadlines available only on request and/or in limited cases, in light of the various possible consequences of these measures for both taxpayers and tax administrations. VAT returns are notably an important source of information to monitor and understand the economic impact of COVID-19, to identify which businesses and/or sectors require additional assistance, to support a proper management of compliance risks and tax debts, and to see when the economy is starting to recover. VAT returns may also be used to provide cash support or other government benefits. For businesses, the filing of VAT returns is generally required to claim refunds of excess VAT credits so that extending the filing deadlines would add to these businesses' cash flow pressure rather than to reduce business burdens.

Several countries have temporarily suspended audits and other enforcement and/or recovery actions to limit the additional stress and diversion of resources and time that these actions may cause during the

COVID-19 crisis. Cases involving fraud or tax businesses with a high-risk profile have typically been excluded from these measures.

Some countries have delayed reforms that were due to be implemented. The European Union postponed the implementation of its new e-commerce VAT rules from 1 January 2021 to 1 July 2021. This reform comprises a comprehensive package of VAT measures relating to e-commerce, incl. abolishment of the VAT exemption for the importation of low-value goods and its replacement by a special import scheme that requires the seller or the online marketplace to account for the VAT at the point of payment by the customer. Delays of reforms in other countries include the postponement of real-time reporting requirements and delays in the introduction of new e-invoicing rules, e-filing requirements and formats and of electronic cash registers, and the postponement of VAT rate changes.

2.9.5. Measures to support the healthcare sector

Most OECD and partner economies have adopted measures to strengthen patient care and reduce the pressure on healthcare systems. VAT measures have been a core component of these healthcare and medical support packages. Most OECD countries have introduced zero (or reduced) rates for supplies and imports of medical equipment and sanitary products (gloves, masks, hand sanitiser…) and for healthcare services where these were not yet VAT exempt or subject to reduced rates under normal rules. The European Union introduced a six-month suspension of VAT and customs duties on the importation of protective equipment, testing kits and medical equipment such as ventilators. This measure has since then been extended for another six months. Several countries implemented temporary VAT zero-rating of staff secondments to healthcare institutions and measures to safeguard the deduction of input VAT on items donated by businesses to healthcare institutions or to avoid a donation triggering any VAT liability (see Country notes to Annex Table 2.A.2 and Section 2.2. above).

2.9.6. Conclusions and looking ahead

This section has provided an overview of the main VAT policy and administration components of OECD countries' short-term fiscal and tax policy responses during the mitigation and containment phases of the COVID-19 crisis. As the crisis has continued, countries have retained their focus on keeping businesses and households afloat and have often expanded their initial packages of measures. Some countries have prolonged existing crisis measures and expanded support to groups that were not covered by the initial measures. Countries' experience and feedback from the business community through Business@OECD suggest that the VAT measures to support cash flow and to reduce VAT compliance burden have been particularly important in helping to mitigate the impact of the crisis for businesses. VAT payment deferrals, fast and flexible refunds of excess VAT and enhanced relief of VAT on bad debts have been flagged up as particularly important measures to support business cash flow. Measures to temporarily simplify VAT procedures and formalities notably by moving away from paper-based to electronic and online processes have been highlighted as critical in alleviating compliance burdens and in allowing business to continue given the mitigation and containment restrictions in place in many countries.

The transition from containment and mitigation to recovery is likely to be gradual and to differ across countries. While economic activity will gradually be allowed to resume, severe restrictions could continue to apply for specific sectors or restrictions could be tightened again as renewed outbreaks arise. As economies recover, countries are likely to continue re-evaluating their short-term measures, removing some while extending or expanding others and implementing stimulus where such policies would be most effective to boost economic recovery. The extension of support for businesses, such as tax payment deferrals, will require careful consideration notably to mitigate risks of fraud and of negative impact on compliance culture, and to limit damage to countries' medium-term tax revenue raising capacity. This may require the further targeting of support, notably to businesses with a low risk profile and/or with a positive compliance history, and to economically healthy or viable businesses to avoid maintaining 'zombie' firms that would not have survived in the absence of containment and mitigation measures. The removal of short-term measures will need to avoid spikes in tax liabilities. The removal of measures such as tax deferrals will need to ensure that where tax payments were deferred, large tax liabilities do not generate cliff-edges that could result in solvency problems for recovering businesses and jeopardise recovery.

Recent announcements and discussions suggest that the recovery phase will be supported by expansionary fiscal policy. Discussions have begun both in countries that are removing containment measures and in countries that are still in mitigation and containment phases. Most countries have signalled that government stimulus will be a key pillar of a recovery effort that aims to be inclusive and sustainable. This may include measures to support consumption through temporary cuts in VAT rates that apply to all consumption (e.g. Germany and Ireland) or to specific categories supplies or sectors such as tourism and hospitality (e.g. Belgium, Norway, United Kingdom). Questions have been raised about the effectiveness of such temporary VAT rate reductions, notably as evidence suggests that the impact of lower VAT rates on consumption and consumer prices may be short-lived and difficult to roll back once they have been introduced, even on a temporary basis, or lead to net price increases when they are rolled back. VAT rate cuts are also likely to give the greatest benefit to those who spend most, i.e. those with medium and high incomes. Feedback from the business community suggests that the additional compliance burden from implementing VAT rate changes may often be considerable. On the other hand, temporary VAT cut could boost investment and consumer confidence and induce people to make certain purchases earlier than they had planned, particularly of durable goods.

Tax policy is likely to remain an important part of countries' strategies to support recovery and to restore public finances in a fair and sustainable way after the crisis. Countries are expected to explore a wide range of options. These may include efforts to address the international tax challenges posed by the digitalisation of the economy (Pillar 1) and to introduce a minimum corporate tax (Pillar 2), to enhance the progressivity of tax systems, and to strengthen the role of carbon taxation. Governments may also consider new and under-used tax bases. Where governments need to expand tax revenues, efforts can focus on raising revenues from tax bases that will be the least detrimental to growth, including recurrent taxes on immovable property and general consumption taxes.

The OECD will keep monitoring countries' responses to the COVID-19 crisis. Monitoring tax policy measures is crucial to informing tax policy discussions and assisting governments in their response to the crisis.

For the tables in annex, references to the 'European Union and its Member States' includes the UK as a Member State for January 2020 and as an addition to the Member States ('Member States and the UK') for the period 1 February 2020 until the end of December 2020.

Annex 2.A. Data on VAT rates and structures

Annex Table 2.A.1. VAT rates

Countries	Implemented	2005	2007	2008	2009	2010	2011	2012	2013	2014	2015	2016	2017	2018	2019	2020[2]	Reduced rates[1]	Regional rates
Australia	2000	10	10	10	10	10	10	10	10	10	10	10	10	10	10	10	0	-
Austria*	1973	20	20	20	20	20	20	20	20	20	20	20	20	20	20	20	10.0/13.0	19
Belgium*	1971	21	21	21	21	21	21	21	21	21	21	21	21	21	21	21	0.0/6.0/12.0	-
Canada*	1991	7	6	5	5	5	5	5	5	5	5	5	5	5	5	5	0	13.0/15.0
Chile	1975	19	19	19	19	19	19	19	19	19	19	19	19	19	19	19	-	-
Colombia	1983	16	16	16	16	16	16	16	16	16	16	16	19	19	19	19	0.0/5.0	-
Czech Republic*	1993	19	19	19	19	20	20	20	21	21	21	21	21	21	21	21	10.0/15.0	-
Denmark*	1967	25	25	25	25	25	25	25	25	25	25	25	25	25	25	25	0	-
Estonia*	1992	18	18	18	18	20	20	20	20	20	20	20	20	20	20	20	0.0/9.0	-
Finland*	1994	22	22	22	22	22	23	23	24	24	24	24	24	24	24	24	0.0/10.0/14.0	-
France*	1968	19.6	19.6	19.6	19.6	19.6	19.6	19.6	19.6	20	20	20	20	20	20	20	2.1/5.5/10.0	0.9/2.1/10.0/13.0 & 1.05/1.75/2.1/8.5
Germany*	1968	16	19	19	19	19	19	19	19	19	19	19	19	19	19	19	0.0/7.0	-
Greece*	1987	18	19	19	19	19	23	23	23	23	23	23	24	24	24	24	6.0/13.0	4.0/ 9.0/17.0
Hungary*	1988	25	20	20	20	25	25	27	27	27	27	27	27	27	27	27	5.0/18.0	-
Iceland	1990	24.5	24.5	24.5	24.5	25.5	25.5	25.5	25.5	25.5	24	24	24	24	24	24	0.0/11.0	-
Ireland*	1972	21	21	21	21.5	21	21	23	23	23	23	23	23	23	23	23	0.0/4.8/9.0/13.5	-
Israel*	1976	17	15.5	15.5	15.5	16	16	16	17	18	18	17	17	17	17	17	0	0
Italy*	1973	20	20	20	20	20	20	21	21	22	22	22	22	22	22	22	4.0/5.0/10.0	-
Japan*	1989	5	5	5	5	5	5	5	5	5	8	8	8	8	8	10	8	-
Korea	1977	10	10	10	10	10	10	10	10	10	10	10	10	10	10	10	0	-
Latvia*	1995	18	18	18	21	21	22	22	21	21	21	21	21	21	21	21	5.0/12.0	-
Lithuania*	1994	18	18	18	19	21	21	21	21	21	21	21	21	21	21	21	5.0/9.0	-

Luxembourg*	1970	15	15	15	15	15	15	15	15	15	17	17	17	17	17	17	3.0/8.0/14.0	-
Mexico*	1980	15	15	15	15	16	16	16	16	16	16	16	16	16	16	16	0	8
Netherlands*	1969	19	19	19	19	19	19	19	21	21	21	21	21	21	21	21	9	-
New Zealand	1986	12.5	12.5	12.5	12.5	12.5	15	15	15	15	15	15	15	15	15	15	0	-
Norway*	1970	25	25	25	25	25	25	25	25	25	25	25	25	25	25	25	0.0/12.0/15.0	-
Poland*	1993	22	22	22	22	22	23	23	23	23	23	23	23	23	23	23	5.0/8.0	-
Portugal*	1986	19	21	21	20	20	23	23	23	23	23	23	23	23	23	23	6.0/13.0	4.0/9.0/18.0 & 5.0/12.0/22.0
Slovak Republic*	1993	19	19	19	19	19	20	20	20	20	20	20	20	20	20	20	10	-
Slovenia*	1999	20	20	20	20	20	20	20	20	22	22	22	22	22	22	22	5.0/9.5	-
Spain*	1986	16	16	16	16	16	18	18	21	21	21	21	21	21	21	21	4.0/10.0	0.0/2.75/3.0/7.0/9.5/13.5/20.0 & 0.5 to10.0
Sweden*	1969	25	25	25	25	25	25	25	25	25	25	25	25	25	25	25	0.0/6.0/12.0	-
Switzerland	1995	7.6	7.6	7.6	7.6	7.6	8	8	8	8	8	8	8	7.7	7.7	7.7	0.0/2.5/3.7	-
Turkey*	1985	18	18	18	18	18	18	18	18	18	18	18	18	18	18	18	1.0/8.0	-
United Kingdom*	1973	17.5	17.5	17.5	15	17.5	20	20	20	20	20	20	20	20	20	20	0.0/5.0	-
Unweighted average		17.8	17.7	17.7	17.7	18.1	13.6	18.8	19.0	19.1	19.2	19.2	19.3	19.3	19.3	19.3		

Notes:

* See country notes.

Yearly data: the rates shown in the table are rates applicable on 1 January of each year. Reduced rates and specific regional rates are those applicable as at 1 January 2020.

1. Reduced rates include zero-rates applicable to domestic supplies (i.e. an exemption with right to deduct input tax). They do not include zero-rated exports or other supplies subject to similar treatment such as international transport or supplies to embassies, international organisations and diplomatic missions. Detailed history of the VAT rates is available on the OECD Tax Database.

2. VAT rates changes or adoption of new VAT rates introduced after 1 January 2020 are mentioned in the Country notes to this table. Specific or temporary VAT rates applicable in the context of the Covid-19 crisis are shown in italics in the country notes.

Source: National delegates - position as at 1 January 2020.

StatLink https://doi.org/10.1787/888934220097

Annex Box 2.A.1. Country notes to Table 2.A.1

Austria*. A standard rate of 19% applies in Jungholz and Mittelberg. *Specific reduced VAT rates apply in the context of the Covid-19 pandemic – See country note to Table 2.2.*

Belgium*. *Specific reduced VAT rates apply in the context of the Covid-19 – See country note to Table 2.2.*

Canada. The following provinces have harmonised their provincial sales taxes with the federal Goods and Services Tax and therefore levy a GST/HST at the following rates: New Brunswick, Newfoundland and Labrador, Nova Scotia, Prince Edward Island: 15%; and Ontario: 13%. Québec applies GST at a rate of 5% and Québec Sales Tax at a rate of 9.975% (applied on the same tax base as the GST). With the exception of Canada's territories (Yukon, Northwest Territories and Nunavut) and the province of Alberta, other Canadian provinces apply a provincial sales tax to certain goods and services in addition to the federal GST.

Czech Republic*. *Specific reduced VAT rates apply in the context of the Covid-19 pandemic – See country note to Table 2.2.*

Denmark*. *Specific reduced VAT rates apply in the context of the Covid-19 pandemic – See country note to Table 2.2.*

Estonia*. *Specific reduced VAT rates apply in the context of the Covid-19 pandemic – See country note to Table 2.2.*

Finland*. *Specific reduced VAT rates apply in the context of the Covid-19 pandemic – See country note to Table 2.2.*

France*. Rates of 0.9%; 2.1%; 10.0%; 13.0% and 20.0% apply in Corsica; rates of 1.05%; 1.75%; 2.1% and 8.5% apply to overseas departments (DOM) excluding French Guyana and Mayotte. *Specific reduced VAT rates apply in the context of the Covid-19 pandemic – See country note to Table 2.2.*

Germany*. *The standard VAT rate is reduced from 19% to 16% and the reduced VAT rate from 7% to 5% from 1 July to 31 December 2020. Specific reduced VAT rates apply in the context of the Covid-19 pandemic – See country note to Table 2.2.*

Greece*. Specific regional rates of 4.0%; 9.0% and 17.0% apply in the islands of Leros, Lesbos, Kos, Samos and Chios until 31 December 2020. *Specific reduced VAT rates apply in the context of the Covid-19 pandemic – See country note to Table 2.2.*

Hungary*. *Specific reduced VAT rates apply in the context of the Covid-19 pandemic – See country note to Table 2.2.*

Ireland*. *The standard VAT rate is reduced from 23% to 21%, with effect from 1 September 2020 until 28 February 2021. Specific reduced VAT rates apply in the context of the Covid-19 pandemic – See country note to Table 2.2.*

Israel. The rate of 0% applies when an Eilat resident dealer buys goods from Eilat non-residents. Supplies made by an Eilat resident supplier (to be consumed in Eilat) are exempt from VAT.

Italy*. *Specific reduced VAT rates apply in the context of the Covid-19 pandemic – See country note to Table 2.2.*

Japan. The standard VAT rate was increased from 8% to 10% on 1 October 2019. A reduced VAT rate of 8% was introduced as of the same date for the supply of food, beverages (excluding alcoholic beverages and eating-out services) and certain subscription newspapers (see Table 2.2).

Latvia*. *Specific reduced VAT rates apply in the context of the Covid-19 pandemic – See country note to Table 2.2.*

Lithuania*. *Specific reduced VAT rates apply in the context of the Covid-19 pandemic – See country note to Table 2.2.*

Luxembourg*. *Specific reduced VAT rates apply in the context of the Covid-19 pandemic – See country note to Table 2.2.*

Mexico. A reduced VAT rate of 8% applies in the northern border region (Ensenada, Playas de Rosarito, Tijuana, Tecate and Mexicali in the state of Baja California; San Luis Río Colorado, Puerto Peñasco, General Plutarco Elías Calles, Caborca, Altar, Sáric, Nogales, Santa Cruz, Cananea, Naco and Agua Prieta in the state of Sonora; Janos, Ascensión, Juárez, Praxedis G. Guerrero, Guadalupe, Coyame del Sotol, Ojinaga and Manuel Benavides in the state of Chihuahua; Ocampo, Acuña, Zaragoza, Jiménez, Piedras Negras, Nava, Guerrero and Hidalgo in the state of Coahuila de Zaragoza; Anáhuac in the state of Nuevo León; and Nuevo Laredo, Guerrero, Mier, Miguel Alemán, Camargo, Gustavo Díaz Ordaz, Reynosa, Río Bravo, Valle Hermoso and Matamoros in the state of Tamaulipas) from 1 January 2019 until 31 December 2020.

Netherlands*. *Specific reduced VAT rates apply in the context of the Covid-19 pandemic – See country note to Table 2.2.*

Norway. *Specific reduced VAT rates apply in the context of the Covid-19 pandemic – See country note to Table 2.2.*

Poland*. *Specific reduced VAT rates apply in the context of the Covid-19 pandemic – See country note to Table 2.2.*

Portugal*. In the Islands of Azores, the standard VAT rate is 18% and the reduced rates are 4% and 9%. In the Islands of Madeira the standard rate is 22% and reduced rates are 5% and 12%. *Specific reduced VAT rates apply in the context of the Covid-19 pandemic – See country note to Table 2.2.*

Slovak Republic*. *Specific reduced VAT rates apply in the context of the Covid-19 pandemic – See country note to Table 2.2.*

Slovenia*. *Specific reduced VAT rates apply in the context of the Covid-19 pandemic – See country note to Table 2.2.*

Spain*. Rates of 0.0%, 2.75%; 3.0%; 7.0%, 9.50%; 13.50% and 20% apply in the Canary Islands. Rates of 0.5%; 1.0%, 2.0%; 4.0%; 6.0%; 8.0%; 9.0% and 10% apply in either Ceuta and Melilla. *Specific reduced VAT rates apply in the context of the Covid-19 pandemic – See country note to Table 2.2.*

Sweden. *Specific reduced VAT rates apply in the context of the Covid-19 pandemic – See country note to Table 2.2.*

Turkey. *Specific reduced VAT rates apply in the context of the Covid-19 pandemic – See country note to Table 2.2.*

United Kingdom. *Specific reduced VAT rates apply in the context of the Covid-19 pandemic – See country note to Table 2.2.*

***Member States of the European Union** apply a customs duties and VAT exemption for the importation of certain goods needed to combat the effects of the COVID-19 outbreak in 2020 See Table 2.2.

Note: Specific or temporary VAT rates applicable in the context of the Covid-19 crisis are shown in italics. Specific reduced VAT rates applicable in the context of the Covid-19 pandemic – are shown in country notes to Table 2.2.

Annex Table 2.A.2. Application of reduced VAT rates

Country	Reduced VAT rates, including domestic zero rate[1]
Australia	0%: most food and beverages for human consumption (excl. prepared food); most health and medical supplies; some education courses and students accommodation; some child care services; some religious services; some activities of charitable institutions; water (except supplied in, or transferred to, a container less than 100L); sewerage and drainage; sales of businesses as going concerns; precious metals (first supply after refinement); grants of freehold and similar interests by governments; farm land; cars for use by disabled people subject to a (general) threshold of AUD 57 466; supplies of accommodation and meals to residents of retirement villages by certain operators; certain government services; some telecommunication supplies made under arrangements for global roaming in Australia; international mail; certain menstrual products.
Austria*	10%: food; water supply; pharmaceuticals; passenger transport (except domestic flights); books; newspapers and periodicals; e-books and e-publications; pay television; some supplies of artists, writers and composers; forestry; restaurants (except beverages); collection of domestic waste and street cleaning; sewage. 13%: hotel accommodation, supply of wine by producing farmers; agricultural supplies; some supplies of artists, writers and composers; admission to cultural, sporting events and cinemas; domestic flights.
Belgium*	0%: cars for disabled persons; certain newspapers and periodicals, certain recovered materials and by products. 6%: food; some beverages; water supply; pharmaceuticals; feminine hygiene products and external defibrillators; equipment for the disabled; passenger transport; books; newspapers and periodicals; certain electronic publications and e-books; culture; sport; works of art, collectors' items and antiques; works of art delivered by their authors/creators; agriculture; hotel accommodation and camping sites; renovation of dwellings over 10 years old; private homes and establishments for disabled; subsidised social housing; some labour intensive services (small repair services); reconstruction subsequent to demolition works leading to the construction of new private housing (under strict conditions and specific limitations as to the amount); funeral services; cut flowers and plants. 12%: restaurants (except beverages); certain energy products (coal, coke; lignite); certain social housing.
Canada	0%: prescription medicine, basic groceries; certain financial services provided by financial institutions (usually to non-residents); certain agricultural and fishing products; certain medical devices; international bridge or tunnel authorities (on certain purchases only); precious metals; sales of 25 cents or less made through mechanical coin-operated devices.
Chile	–
Colombia	0%: food for human consumption; some health products such as medicines, antibiotics and blood, medical consultations, diagnostic images, books and newspapers; personal hygiene products. 5%: certain agricultural products; agricultural equipment; some electric or hybrid vehicles; agricultural and health insurances; safety and cleaning services; wine and liquors; some food products; aviation fuels.
Czech Republic*	10%: essential child nutrition; gluten-free products; certain pharmaceutical products; certain printed books; hairdressing and clothing repair. 15%: food; pharmaceutical products and printed books (when not subject to the lower rate of 10%) some beverages; water supply; medical services (if not exempt); equipment and repair for the disabled; passenger transport; art; cultural services; newspapers and periodicals; construction of private dwellings and social housing; renovation and repair of private dwellings; collection and treatment of waste and waste water; hotel accommodation; health care and domestic care services; cleaning in households; funeral services; sport activities; agricultural products; cut flowers and plants; heating.
Denmark*	0%: newspapers and periodicals. 5%: first time sale of products of artistic work valued over DKK 300 000 (the standard rate of 25% applies to 20% of the tax base resulting in an effective rate of 5%).
Estonia*	0%: certain commercial aircraft and sea-going vessels and certain supplies of goods and services related to them; international transport of passengers. 9%: pharmaceuticals; medical equipment or devices for disabled; books; newspapers and periodicals; hotel accommodation.
Finland*	0%: printing services for certain membership publications; certain vessels. 10%: pharmaceuticals; passenger transport; books, subscribed newspapers and periodicals; certain electronic publications and e-books; hotel accommodation; admission to cultural, entertainment and sporting events and cinema performances; use of sports facilities; works of art supplied by their creators or imported; copyrights to literary and artistic works; TV licence fees; *supply of services by athletes and performing artists, provided that they have opted for VAT liability.* 14%: food; non-alcoholic drinks; animal food; restaurants (except alcoholic beverages).

France*	2.1%: newspapers and periodicals; pharmaceuticals. 5.5%: most food products and beverages (except alcoholic beverages); water supply; equipment for the disabled; books and e-books; admission to cultural services; work on dwellings over 2 years old under certain conditions; domestic care services; subscription fees to natural gas and electricity networks; district heating; supplies of works of art by their creators; women's sanitary products; some social housing 10%: passenger transport; social housing; admission to exhibitions, sites and facilities of a cultural, recreational, educational or professional nature; pay TV; domestic care services; restaurant services and catering (except alcoholic beverages); hotel accommodation; farm products; gardens, plants and flowers; treatment of waste; sewage; passenger transport; author's rights.
Germany*	7% food; water supply; equipment for the disabled; medical services (if not exempt); books and newspapers; certain electronic publications and e-books;plants; flowers; certain cultural events; museums; zoos; circuses; charitable work (if not exempt); author's rights; local public passenger transport within a municipality or if the distance covered is not more than 50 km; long-distance rail travel; hotel accommodation; cut flowers and plants; works of art supplied by their creator or successors in title and importation of collector's items; feminine hygiene products; long-distance travel by rail.
Greece*	6% pharmaceutical drugs and vaccines for human medicine; books; children's picture books; newspapers, journals and periodicals; admission to theatres (theatrical plays) and concerts, supply of natural gas and electricity and district heating. 13%: basic food goods (meat and abattoir by-products; meat preparations; fish, squid, octopus and cuttlefish excluding livers, eggs and semen; milk and dairy products; birds' eggs; natural honey; vegetables, plants, some types of roots and tubers; animal food falling within CN code 230990, oil cake, seeds for sowing; fruit and nuts; cereal; flour and flour products; olive oil; pasta not baked or stuffed or otherwise processed; bread; fruit and vegetable juices excluding the undermentioned subject to the standard rate: most types of processed food, farm supplies that are usually intended to be used as intermediate inputs by farmers and farm industries (excluding capital goods such as machinery or buildings); live plants and their roots, cuttings and slips; pharmaceutical products (besides those subject to 6%); medical equipment and other appliances for the disabled persons; intrauterine contraceptives; catheters; feeding syringes; «talking» sphygmomanometers; needles for insulin pens and dialysis needles; water supply; accommodation provided in hotels and similar establishments, including the provision of holiday accommodation and the letting of places on camping or caravan sites; services provided by restaurants and similar businesses, excluding nightclubs, and with the exception of the disposal of alcoholic and non-alcoholic beverages, juices and beverages; domestic care services such as home help and care of young, elderly, sick or disabled; services by retirement homes and establishments for disabled and mentally retarded persons or persons suffering from mental disorders or substance abuse insofar as those transactions are subject to VAT and not exempt as welfare or social security work; the provision of services for farming production(excluding capital goods such as machinery or buildings); infant food and other baby products, such as diapers and car seats; bicycle helmets.
Hungary*	5% pharmaceuticals for humans; certain equipment for the blind; books, newspapers and sheet music; live pigs and carcasses of pig; certain live cattle, sheep, lamb, goat, and their meat in bulk; meat of domestic pig; meat and edible offal of poultry; fresh eggs; fresh milk; edible offal and inner parts of domestic swine; live fish (excluding ornamental fish) and the body/parts/fillet of fish for human consumption; district heating; services supplied by performing artists; internet access services; restaurant meals and supply of non-alcoholic beverages prepared on site; provision of accommodation. 18%: milk and dairy products; products containing cereals, flour, starch or milk; certain open-air concerts.
Iceland	0% shipbuilding and maintenance of ships and aircraft; services to foreign fishing vessels related to landing and sale of fish in Iceland; direct payments to farmers. 11%: food and beverages; passenger transport (if not exempted); services of travel agencies, travel organisers and touring associations; travel guidance; books including music books and e-books; audio recordings of books. CD's and similar media with text as well as electronic version of such books; magazines, newspapers and countryside- and district newspapers with text as well as electronic version of such papers and magazines; periodicals with text as well as electronic version of such periodicals; subscriptions to radio and TV; rental of hotels, guestrooms and other guest services; hot water, electricity and fuel oil used for the heating of houses and swimming pools; admission tolls to land transportation projects; CD disks, records, magnetic tapes and other similar means of music recordings, other than visual records. Electronic version of music other than visual; condoms; diapers for children; admission fees to bathhouses, bathings, saunas and spas (if not exempted); contraceptive products and feminine hygiene products.
Ireland*	0% books; children's clothing and footwear; oral medicine; certain medical equipment; certain food products; seeds for food production; fertilisers; certain aircraft and sea-going vessels 4.8%: livestock and horses for food or agricultural production. 9% newspapers and certain periodicals, e-books; certain electronic publications; provision of sporting facilities; 13.5%: waste disposal; energy for heating and light; fuel for certain purposes; gas; electricity; building services; immovable goods; repair services; tour guide services; photographic prints; works of art; short-term car and boat hire; driving instruction; veterinary services; certain plants and flowers; seeds for plants and flowers; medical services (if not exempt); admission to cinemas/certain

	musical performances; holiday accommodation; restaurant/hotel meals; certain agricultural services; hairdressing. .
Israel	0%: hotel accommodation for foreign tourists and another hotel services (serving food and beverage, laundry, pool, gym, etc.); sale of, to a foreign tourist, tickets for an international conference in which more than 50 foreign tourists are in attendance; rental of a private motor vehicle to a tourist to drive himself; transportation of tourists in a private motor vehicle, a bus or an airplane; hospitalization of a foreign tourist; sale of fruits and vegetables; sale of dealer's/dealers' assets to a company in exchange for the company's stock only, provided that the dealer/dealers owns 90%, or more, of the voting power immediately after the assets transfer; sale of all of the company's assets to its shareholders in a liquidation process, in which, the assets are divided amongst the said shareholders in proportion to the shares respectively held by them; supplies of goods to who would be exempted from sales tax due to entry to Israel (supplies of certain goods to new immigrants and to students returning from study abroad); sale of a real estate by a non-profit organization or by a financial institution to a non-profit organization or to a financial institution as part of restructuring; renting exhibition space by non-resident; services given by an Israeli production company to a non-resident for film production in Israel; services given to a non-resident in respect of human clinical trials; an Eilat resident dealer buys goods from an Eilat non-resident.
Italy*	4%: certain food; medications and health products/services and equipment for the disabled; supply of services for certain residential housing constructions; books; newspapers; weekly magazines; supply of food by schools, canteens and "soup kitchens". 5%: aromatic herbs, fresh or chilled truffles, social and health service for the elderly, drug addicts, migrants, prisoners, handicapped, AIDS patients, transport services on urban waterways (see, river, lake or lagoon); compostable feminine hygiene products. 10%: certain food and beverage, water supply; pharmaceutical products (for humans and animals); medical services (if not exempt); passenger transport; combustible gas for cooking; mineral oil; electricity; gas; urban waste; purification stations; livestock meat and fish; renewable-source energy; works of art; admission to shows and cultural events; letting of immovable property by building enterprises; renovation and maintenance work for residential housing; restaurants; construction of urban development; hotel and similar accommodation services.
Japan	8% food, beverages (excluding alcoholic beverages and eating-out services) and certain newspapers under subscription.
Korea	0%: supply of certain machinery and materials for agriculture; fishery; livestock and forestry; supply of mineral oil used for certain purposes in agriculture, fishery and forestry; certain equipment for the disabled.
Latvia*	12%: medicinal products; medical devices; food for infants; pharmaceutical products; inland passenger transport services; books, newspapers and periodicals; hotel accommodation; district heating, firewood for household needs. 5%: Certain supplies of fresh fruits, berries and vegetables.
Lithuania*	9%: heating power used for heating residential premises, hot water (including cold water used for preparing hot water and to heating power used for preparation of hot water) supplied to residential premises; books, non-periodical information; inland regular passenger transport; accommodation services; firewood and wood products for heating supplied for domestic energy consumers. 5%: certain medicines and medical aid equipment (including prescription drugs); technical aids for disabled persons and repairs of such aids; newspapers, magazines and periodical publications.
Luxembourg*	3%: food for human and animal consumption; water supply; pharmaceutical products including products used for contraception and sanitary protection; certain medical equipment; certain aids and other appliances normally intended to alleviate or treat disability; passenger transport; accommodation; books, newspapers and periodicals supplied on physical means of support or electronically, but excluding material with predominantly adult content; admission to cultural and sporting events; use of sporting facilities; restaurant services but excluding alcoholic beverages; services by writers, composers and performing artists, or of the royalties due to them; goods and services of a kind normally intended for use in agricultural production; services supplied in connection with waste collection and treatment; children's clothing and footwear; housing used by the owner, for his own use, as principal dwelling; substantial works on housing used as principal dwelling and (i) constructed more than 20 years prior to the start of the works (ii) newly acquired, the works to be completed in the five years following the acquisition; funeral services; reception of radio and television broadcasting services but excluding exclusively adult content services. 8%: certain labour intensive services; works of art delivered by their authors/creators or by their heirs or imported; gas; electricity; firewood; district heating; flowers and ornamental plants; certain plant protection products allowed for organic production. 14%: certain wines; certain fuels; washing and cleaning products; printed advertising; heat and air conditioning; certain financial services.

Mexico	0%: sale of non-industrialised animals (except dogs, cats and small species used as home pets) and vegetables (except rubber); patent medicines; milk; bottled water; juices, nectar and concentrated fruits and vegetables; ice; food (except sale of processed food in restaurants and food establishments, chewing gum, caviar, smoked salmon, eels, pet food and soft drinks); agricultural equipment; machinery and fishing boats; wholesale of gold; gold bullion (with a content of at least 80% of gold) and jewellery; some agricultural and fishing services; magazines, books and newspapers printed by the taxpayer himself; domestic water supply; hotel services provided to foreign tourists participating in congresses, conventions and trade shows; use of convention centres by event organisers who are residents abroad; call centre services for telephone calls originated abroad, as long as the services are contracted and paid a foreign resident without a permanent establishment in Mexico. 8%: sale of goods, provision of independent services, and granting of the temporary use or enjoyment of goods in the premises or establishments located in the northern border region. This reduced rate does not apply with respect to certain digital commerce transactions, sale of real estate and intangible assets, and imports.
Netherlands*	9%: food; catering; goods and services for the disabled; medicine; accommodation; books; certain electronic publications and e-books; lending of books; newspapers; magazines; passenger transport (except passenger transport by air); water supply; entrance fees for sports events; amusement; parks; museums; cinemas; zoos and circuses; cut flowers and plants; restaurant and hotel meals; aids for the visually disabled; use of sports accommodation; art and antiques; hotel and holiday accommodation; certain labour intensive services like some specific services for the maintenance and isolation of dwellings; cleaning of dwellings and hairdressing.
New Zealand	0%: supply of taxable activity (business) as a going concern; supply of fine metal (gold, silver or platinum) from a refiner in fine metal to a dealer in fine metal; supply by local authorities of the local authorities petroleum tax; supply of financial services to GST registered businesses. Supply of land by and to a GST registered person when the recipient intends to use it to make taxable supplies and it is not intended to be used as a principal place of residence (this zero-rating between GST-registered persons is equivalent to the domestic reverse charge). Long-term stay in a commercial dwelling; certain services provided as part of the right to occupancy (taxed at the standard rate on 60% of the value of the supply).
Norway	0%: books; newspapers; certain periodicals and publications; certain electronic publications and e-books; electronic news services; electricity and energy supplied from alternative energy sources for household use in the counties of Finnmark, Troms and Nordland; the purchase and leasing/hiring of electric motor vehicles and batteries; second-hand vehicles covered by re-registration tax; supply of certain ships, aircrafts and drilling platforms and hiring out such vessels; services that are directly related to the construction of embassy buildings (to final consumer); goods and services to specific international military forces and command units; supply of taxable activity (business) as a going concern; supply of human organs, blood; supply by funeral directors of services relating to the transportation of deceased persons. 12%: accommodation, passenger transport and transport of vehicles by ferries or other vessels in connection with the domestic road network; public broadcasting; admission to sporting events, museums, cinemas and amusement parks. 15%: food and non-alcoholic beverages.
Poland*	5% - certain foodstuffs (e.g. bread, meat, fish, fruits and vegetables, eggs, dairy products, bakery products, juices); products for children and hygiene products; books and regional or local magazines; e-books (other than publications consisting of video content or audible music). 8% - certain foodstuffs; newspapers and periodicals; goods and services of a kind normally intended for use in agricultural production; pharmaceutical products; medical devices; certain disinfectants applied in health protection; transport of passengers and their accompanying luggage; supply of water; admission to shows, theatres, circuses, amusement parks, concerts, museums, zoos, cinemas etc.; reception of radio and television broadcasting services (excluding VOD); provision, construction, renovation and alteration of housing, as part of a social policy; maintenance of private dwellings; accommodation provided in hotels and similar establishments; restaurant and catering services; admission to sporting events and use of sporting facilities; funeral services; supply of services provided in connection with street cleaning, refuse collection and waste treatment, other than the supply of such services by public bodies; lending in libraries of books and newspapers; some labour intensive services; animal feeding stuffs; veterinary services; certain equipment for blind persons and certain animal semen (as of 31 August 2020).
Portugal*	6%: essential food; water supply; pharmaceutical products; devices for the disabled; medical services (if not exempt); books, newspapers and periodicals; certain electronic publications and e-books; passenger transport; hotels and similar services; social housing; some goods used in agriculture; certain agriculture products and certain agriculture services; home care services for elderly people, children and drug addicts, as well as phone assistance services to elderly people or chronically ill patients; admission to cultural events as well as to admissions to exhibitions, zoos, parks, aquariums, museums and buildings of national interest. 13%: some other food; still wine; diesel fuel for agriculture; machinery mainly used in agricultural production; restaurant services. .
Slovak Republic*	10%: certain food; radioactive elements and isotopes and compounds for health service; pharmaceutical products; diagnostic or laboratory reagents; certain medical and sanitarian means; printed books and newspapers, brochures, leaflets and similar printed matter; music; orthopedic appliances; contact and spectacle lenses; certain means for blind and partly blind persons, hard-of-hearing persons and hard health-disabled persons; accommodation services.

Slovenia*	9.5%: foodstuff (for human and animal consumption); preparation of food; water supply; medicine, devices for the disabled; passenger transport; admission to cultural and sporting events; author's rights; import and supply of certain works of art, collectors' items or antiques; social housing; renovation and maintenance work of residential housing not provided as part of a social policy; livestock and certain supplies in connection with agricultural production; hotel accommodation; restaurant (except beverages); use of sporting facilities; supplies by undertakers and cremation services; public hygiene services; window-cleaning and cleaning in private households; minor repairing of bicycles, shoes and leather goods; domestic care services; hairdressing; cut flowers and plants. 5.0%: books, including books form libraries, newspapers and periodicals.
Spain*	4%: basic foodstuff (bread, flour, milk, cheese, eggs, vegetables and fruit); certain supplies to the disabled (e.g. wheelchairs); ; medicines and other medical devices for human use (e.g. lenses); books, newspapers and periodicals; supply of new buildings for social housing and social accommodation; supply of dwelling to certain house lease entities. 10%: foodstuff (for human or animal consumption); water supply; medicines for animal use; certain medical equipment and certain pharmaceutical products; passengers transport; sale (also restoration or construction works under conditions) of building or parts of buildings susceptible of use as private housing; minor works on private housing; restaurants and catering; certain cultural and entertainment services; hotel accommodation and alike; amateur sport events; commercial fairs; animals as well as agriculture and forestry products for obtaining foodstuffs; goods and services used in agricultural, livestock and forestry undertakings, including flowers and plants; waste treatment; cleaning of public sewage; burial services; cleaning and maintenance services of public areas.
Sweden*	0%: commercial aircraft and ships and certain services related to these; aircraft fuel; prescribed medicine; printing of certain membership publications. 6%: passenger transport; books, newspapers and magazines, including in electronic format; certain electronic publications and e-books; culture (theatre, cinema, etc.); author's rights; zoos; commercial sports events; commercial museums, exploitation of natural areas, parks and nature reserves. 12%: food and restaurants services; accommodation; works of art owned by the originator; import of antiques, collector's items and works of art; repair of bikes, shoes and other leather goods and household linen.
Switzerland	0%: Supply of services by travel agents and organisers of events, if they make use of supplies of goods and services by third parties that are provided abroad; certain supplies of goods and services to international airlines; state minted gold coins, fine gold for investment purposes and gold destined for refining or recovery. 2.5%: tap water; food; cattle; poultry; fish; grains; seeds; planting roots and bulbs; living plants; cuttings; scions and cut flowers and branches; animal feed; silage acids; scatterings for animals; fertilisers; pesticides; mulch; medication; books, newspapers and magazines, including in electronic format; non-commercial services of radio and television companies, certain supplies in connection with agricultural production. The 2.5% rate also applies to certain cultural services supplied directly to the public, considerations demanded for sporting events, cultural services and the supply of works by their creators when the suppliers have opted for taxation (otherwise those supplies are exempt without right of deduction). 3.7%; accommodation services.
Turkey	0%: supply of ships, aircraft, and rail transportation vehicles; supply of services related to the manufacture, repair, maintenance of such vehicles; supply of services to ships and aircraft at harbours or airports; supply of goods and services for the exploration, management and refining of gold, silver, platinum, and oil; supply of machinery and equipment to persons who have an investment incentive document; goods and construction works for the construction, restoration and enlargement of seaports and airports; some goods and services related to national security; international roaming services supplied in Turkey according to the reciprocity principle; supply of goods that are listed in the second list of excise duty tax law to the Presidency central organisation; the first supply of product certificate that are drawn up according to agricultural product license warehousing law via commodity exchange market; exemption for delivery of equipment produced for the disabled; deliveries and services made to Turkey Red Crescent Society; fertilizer and feed deliveries; resident or workplace deliveries to non-residents in Turkey; deliveries of goods and services made in the scope of construction of organized industrial zones and small industrial sites; deliveries and services made to donators in the scope of facilities that are donated to general and special budget public administrations, special provincial administrations, municipalities and villages by these donators; health services provided to foreigners; new machinery and equipment deliveries to those that perform R & D, innovation and design activities; printed books and periodicals. 1%: some agricultural products; second-hand cars; funeral services; supply of residential housing under 150 m2 in cities other than metropolitan ones and in metropolitan cities if land value per m^2 lower than TRY 500 for building permit delivered between 1/1/2013 and 31/12/2016 and lower than TRY 1000 for building permits delivered since 1/1/2017; lease of specified machinery and equipment; seeds. 8%: basic food; books; blood and blood component; cinema; theatre; opera and ballet tickets; private educational service; vaccines; some medical products and services; ambulance services; medicine; medical equipment; textile and confection products and custom manufacturing of them; accommodation services; meal services at non-luxury restaurants (excluding alcoholic beverages); services provided by orphanage and nursing homes; some constructional and agricultural machines; some furniture; clothing; stationery goods; waste water services; supply of residential housing under 150 m^2 in metropolitan cities and with land value per m^2 is between TRY 500 and TRY 999 for building permits delivered between 1/1/2013 and 31/12/2016 and with

	land value per m² between TRY 1000 and TRY 2000 for building permits delivered since 1/1/2017 .
United Kingdom*	0% food; certain services and goods supplied to charities; children's clothing; passenger transport; books; newspapers; domestic sewage and water; prescribed drugs; medicine; certain aids and services for disabled people; new housing, including the construction of new houses; residential and some charitable buildings. 5% fuel and power for domestic and charity use; certain energy saving materials supplied together with fitting services to recipient of benefits; certain grant-funded installations of heating equipment; children car seats; certain pharmaceutical products.

Notes:

VAT rates changes introduced after 1 January 2020 are mentioned in the country notes to this table.

1. For the purpose of this table, reduced rates also include "domestic zero rates" (0%), i.e. instances where VAT is not charged by the supplier on domestic supplies while related input VAT is deductible. In some countries, these supplies are called "exempt with right of deduction" and in others "GST free". They do not include zero-rate applied to exports, supplies of goods or services used or consumed abroad or other supplies subject to similar treatment such as international transport or supplies to embassies, international organisations and diplomatic missions.

Source: National delegates. Data as of 1 January 2020.

Annex Box 2.A.2. Country notes to Table 2.A.2.

Austria*. *A rate of 0% applies to imports of goods needed to combat the Covid-19 pandemic from 30 January until 31 October 2020. The same applies to supplies and Intra-Community acquisition of some of these goods from 14 April until 31 July 2020. From 30 June 2020 to 31 December 2020 a rate of 5% applies to restaurants, certain supplies by artists, writers and composers; admission to cultural events and cinemas, hotel accommodation, books, newspapers and periodicals (both physical and electronic).*

Belgium*. *A rate of 0% applies from 13 March until 31 October 2020 to imports of certain goods needed to combat the Covid-19 pandemic; a rate of 6% applies to the supply, intra-Community acquisition and importation of masks and hydro alcoholic gels from 4 May until 31 December 2020; a rate of 6% applies to restaurant and catering services, excluding alcoholic beverages from 8 June 2020 until 31 December 2020.*

Colombia. The Colombian VAT legislation distinguishes three categories of supplies: (i) "taxable supplies" (subject to VAT); (ii) "exempt supplies" (zero-rated with the right in some cases to credit VAT paid on inputs); and (iii) "excluded supplies" (not subject to VAT nor with the right to credit VAT paid on inputs).

Czech Republic*. From 1 May 2020 the reduced rate of 10 % applies to supplies of certain e-publications and e-books, passenger transport, water, collection and treatment of waste and waste water, restaurant and catering services, domestic care services, cleaning in private households, domestic care services, hairdressing, and repairs of clothing, shoes and leather goods. From 1 July 2020, the reduced rate of 10 % applies to supplies of passenger transport, accommodation, admission to cultural events and facilities, admission to sporting events and use of sporting facilities. *A rate of 0% applies to imports of certain goods needed to combat the Covid-19 from 1 January until 31 October 2020.*

Denmark*. *A rate of 0% applies to imports of certain goods needed to combat the Covid-19 pandemic from 1 January until 31 July 2020.*

Estonia*. Certain electronic publications and e-books became subject to the reduced rate of 9% as from 1 May 2020 *A rate of 0% applies to imports of certain goods needed to combat the Covid-19 pandemic from 1 January until 31 July 2020.*

Finland*. *A rate of 0% applies to imports of certain goods needed to combat the Covid-19 from 1 January until 31 July 2020.*

France*. Rates of 0.9%; 2.1%; 10.0%; 13.0% and 20.0% apply in Corsica; rates of 1.05%; 1.75%; 2.1% and 8.5% apply to overseas departments (DOM) excluding French Guyana and Mayotte. *Reduced rates of 0% or 5.5% apply to imports of certain goods needed to combat the Covid-19 from 1 January until 31 July 2020. A rate of 5.5 % also applies to supplies of certain goods needed to combat the Covid-19 from 1 march 2020 until 31 December 2021.*

Germany*. *A rate of 0% applies to donations of certain medical material and equipment to hospitals from 1 March 2020 to 31 July 2020. A rate of 0% applies to imports of goods needed to combat the Covid-19 pandemic from 1 January until 31 July 2020. Restaurant and catering services are subject to the reduced rate of 5% from 1 July 2020 until 31 December 2020 and 7% from 1 January 2021 until 30 June 2021.*

Greece*. Specific regional rates of 4.0%, 9.0% and 17.0% apply in the islands of Leros, Lesbos, Kos, Samos and Chios until 31 December 2020. *A rate of 0% applies to imports of certain goods needed to combat the Covid-19 pandemic from 1 January 2020 until 30 April 2021. Sanitary products essential for the protection of public health during the COVID-19 pandemic (masks, gloves, etc.) are subject the reduced rate of 6% from 20 March until 31 December 2020. Between 1 June 2020 and 30 April 2021, the reduced rate of 13% applies to admission to cinemas; transport of passengers and their accompanying luggage. In the same period, the reduced rate applies to the supply of non-alcoholic beverages in restaurants and similar businesses, excluding nightclubs. Also, between 1 September 2020 and 30 June 2021 the reduced rate of 13% applies to sports tickets.*

Hungary*. *A rate of 0% applies to imports of certain goods needed to combat the Covid-19 pandemic from 1 January until 31 July 2020.*

Ireland*. *A rate of 0% applies to imports of certain goods needed to combat the Covid-19 pandemic from 1 January until 31 July 2020.*

Israel. The rate of 0% applies when an Eilat resident dealer buys goods from Eilat non-residents. Supplies made by an Eilat resident supplier (to be consumed in Eilat) are exempt from VAT.

Italy*. *A rate of 0% applies to imports of certain goods needed to combat the Covid-19 pandemic from 30 January until 31 December 2020. A rate of 0% applies to the supplies of same goods from 19 May until 31 December 2020. From 1 January 2021 a VAT rate of 5% will apply to the supplies of goods deemed necessary to fight the spread of COVID-19.*

Japan. The standard VAT rate was increased from 8% to 10% on 1 October 2019.

Latvia*. *A rate of 0% applies to imports of certain goods needed to combat the Covid-19 pandemic from 1 January until 31 October 2020.*

Lithuania*. *A rate of 0% applies to imports of certain goods needed to combat the Covid-19 pandemic from 1 January until 31 July 2020.*

Luxembourg*. *A rate of 0% applies to imports of certain goods needed to combat the Covid-19 pandemic from 1 January until 31 October 2020.*

Mexico. A reduced VAT rate of 8% applies to sale of goods, provision of independent services, and granting of the temporary use or enjoyment of goods in the premises or establishments located in the northern border region from 1 January 2019 until 31 December 2020.

Netherlands*. *A rate of (effectively) 0% applies to the hiring of healthcare workers by healthcare facilities or institutions qualifying for the VAT exemption of medical services. The measure applies from 16 March 2020 to 1 January 2021. The rate of (effectively) 0% also applies to donations of Covid-19 related medical material and equipment to healthcare facilities or institutions and to general practitioners from 16 March 2020 to 1 January 2021. A rate of 0% applies to imports of certain goods needed to combat the Covid-19 pandemic from 30 January to 1 November 2020. A rate of 0% applies to the purchase in the Netherlands of mouth masks (medical and non-medical) from 25 May 2020 to 1 January 2021. The reduced rate of 9% applies to online fitness classes from 16 March to 1 July 2020.*

Norway. *The reduced rate of 12% is temporarily reduced to 6% from 1 April until 31 December 2020.*

Poland*. As of November 2019, taxpayers have the right to obtain, upon request, an administrative decision (Binding Rate Information - WIS) to ensure the correct application of VAT rates. This administrative decision provides the taxpayers with legal protection in this respect. *A rate of 0% applies to donations of certain medical material and equipment to hospitals; supply of imported pharmaceutical products imports of certain goods needed to combat the Covid-19 pandemic from 1 January until the epidemic state in Poland is terminated; supplies of laptops and tablets made until 30 June 2020 by VAT payers to educational institutions.*

Portugal*. In the Islands of Azores, the standard VAT rate is 18% and the reduced rates are 4% and 9%. In the Islands of Madeira the standard rate is 22% and reduced rates are 5% and 12%. *A rate of 0% applies to donations of certain medical material and equipment to hospitals from 1 March 2020. A rate of 0% applies to supplies, intra-community acquisition and imports of certain goods needed to combat the Covid-19 pandemic acquired by the State and other public entities, the national health service, private hospitals contracted by the State to fight COVID-19 and NGOs, from 30 January until 31 October 2020. A rate of 6% applies to imports, supplies and intra-community acquisitions of protective masks and disinfectant gel, from 8 May until 31 December 2020.*

Slovak Republic*. *A rate of 0% applies to imports of certain goods needed to combat the Covid-19 pandemic from 30 January until 31 October 2020.*

Slovenia*. *A rate of 0% applies to imports of certain goods needed to combat the Covid -19 from 30 January 2020 until 30 April 2021. The same applies to supplies and Intra-Community acquisition of these goods from 13 March until 31 July 2020.*

Spain*. Rates of 0.0%, 2.75%, 3.0%, 7.0%, 9.50%; 13.50%, 20% apply in the Canary Islands. Rates of 0.5%, 1.0%, 2.0%, 4.0%, 6.0%, 8.0%, 9.0% and 10% apply in either Ceuta and Melilla. Certain electronic publications and e-books are subject to the reduced rate of 4% from 23 April 2020. *A rate of 0% applies to the supply of medical equipment from national producers to public entities, NGOs and hospitals until 31 October 2020. A rate of 0% applies to imports of certain goods needed to combat the Covid-19 pandemic from 1 January until 31 July 2020.*

Sweden*. *A rate of 0% applies to imports of certain goods needed to combat the Covid-19 pandemic from 1 January 2020 until 30 April 2021.*

Turkey. *A rate of 1% applies to the supply of domestic air transport from 1 April to 30 June 2020.*

United Kingdom. Certain electronic publications are subject to a rate of 0% from 1 May 2020. *A rate of 0% applies to imports of certain goods needed to combat the Covid-19 pandemic from 30 January until 31 December 2020. A temporary reduced rate of 5% was also introduced for certain supplies relating to hospitality, holiday accommodation and admissions to certain attractions from 15 July 2020 to 31 March 2021 as an urgent response to the Covid-19 crisis.*

*According to the European Commission Decision C(2020)491 (as amended), a rate of 0% for VAT and import duties applies to the importation in the European Union of goods needed to combat the effects of the COVID-19 outbreak during 2020.

Specific or temporary VAT rates applicable in the context of the Covid-19 crisis are shown in italics

Annex Table 2.A.3. VAT Exemptions

Country	Exemptions	Taxation of "common exemptions" in the country
Australia	Financial services; residential rent and residential premises (other than new residential premises); certain supplies of precious metals; school canteens operated by non-profit bodies (optional); certain fund raising events conducted by charitable institutions.	Domestic postal services; sporting services; cultural services excluding religious services (zero rate); insurance and reinsurance excluding health insurance (zero rate); gambling (including lottery tickets and betting); supplies of land and buildings (except certain supplies of farm land and supplies of going concerns– zero rate and existing residential premises – exempt).
Austria	Common exemptions[2]	Letting (private housing)
Belgium	Common exemptions[2]	-
Canada	Common exemptions[2]; legal aid; public transit; ferry, road and bridge tolls; child and personal care services; certain regulatory/administrative supplies by a government or a municipality.	Most betting, lotteries and gambling; supply and leasing of commercial land and buildings; sales of newly constructed or substantially renovated housing; domestic postal services; most cultural and sporting services e.g. adult programmes; services provided by other than public sector bodies; most admissions to a place of amusement (e.g. museums, films, professional performances and sporting events, etc.); human blood and certain biologicals (zero rate).
Chile	Services not specifically listed in the law are out of scope of VAT (e.g. legal, accounting, engineering, architecture and other professional services). VAT Exemptions apply to:used motor vehicles; goods provided by the employer to dependent employees; domestic raw materials used in the production, processing or manufacture of goods for export; some imports by the Ministry of Defense, the Army and other related organisms; some imports by the firefighting organisations (Cuerpos de Bomberos) and the Junta Nacional de Cuerpos de Bomberos; some imports by the Chilean Mint (Casa de Moneda de Chile S.A.) and other persons provided that the import is made in the context of operations with the Central Bank of Chile; capital goods imported and assigned to projects involving investments of USD 5 000 000 or more; income received from tickets to shows and meetings; international freight, passenger transport including the transport of passenger within the national territory; premiums and disbursements of reinsurance contracts; commissions earned by the Regional and Metropolitan Housing and Urbanisation Services and Social Security Institutions on mortgages; non-taxable income; income subject to additional income tax; income such as wages, salaries, pensions, income obtained by independent workers and directors fees if taxed with income tax; insertions and notices to be published and disseminated under the right of reply; certain insurance premiums; financial interests; commissions coming from guarantees issued by financial institutions; letting and lease with a purchase option of immovable property; remunerations linked to exports; income obtained from services rendered to persons domiciled or resident abroad and qualified as exportable services by Customs; income of hotels relating to services rendered to foreign tourists and income from letting of furnished immovable properties rented to foreign tourists; fees paid for managing retirement savings earned by specific authorized institutions; income obtained by independent professionals, where the physical effort is more relevant than the capital or materials used; construction contracts and finance lease of a house financed with a housing subsidy granted by the Ministry of Housing and Urban Development; broadcasting and television	Income from artistic shows or plays not sponsored by the Ministry of Culture, Arts and Heritage; income from certain circus and sports events if certain requirements are not met. Postal services are subject to VAT if they are not provided by "Correos de Chile" (Chilean postal service company). The transport of cargo within national territory is subject to VAT. Payments to be done when using a private health insurance if these payments exceed amount normally covered by the public health insurance. Educational services are exempted as long as they cover teaching activities only. Letting of immovable properties is exempted to the extent that the immovable property is not furnished and there is no commercial or industrial equipment to carry out any commercial or industrial activity.

	enterprises excluding income from advertisement; news agencies; educational services; health services; health contributions paid to Private Health Insurance Companies; manufacturing of currency by Casa de Moneda de Chile; postal services rendered by Servicio de Correos y Telégrafos de Chile; interests, premiums, commissions or other forms of remunerations paid by authorized lotteries (Polla Chilena de Beneficencia and Lotería de Concepción to individual) or legal entities for business services; other minor exemptions.	
Colombia	Financial services; reinsurance services and life insurance; education services provided by recognised establishments; public transport; contraceptives; certain agricultural products and inputs; live animals; salt; natural or artificial mineral water; medical services; public utility services (electricity, water and gas); leasing of real estate for housing; tickets for movies, sports and cultural events; funeral services.	Insurance services related to social security; life insurance; education insurances and reinsurance agreements; postal services.
Czech Republic	Common exemptions[2]; public television and radio.	Certain cultural services (e.g. admission to theatres, cinemas, concerts, etc. subject to reduced rates); sporting services provided by others than by non-profit making organisations; supply of construction land; supply of new building and building land (subject for the option to taxation).
Denmark	Hospital and medical care; dental care; social service; education; non-commercial activities of some non-profit making organisations; non-profit sport activities etc.; cultural services (some exceptions); literary and composing activities; creative artist; letting of immovable property; supply of immovable property; insurance and reinsurance; financial services; lotteries and gambling; postal service; stamps; transport of persons; funeral service; certain fund-raising events; charitable work	Cultural services as radio, television broadcasting, cinema, theatre, concerts etc.; short term letting of immovable property; option to tax commercial letting; supply of new building and building land; some commercial postal service
Estonia	Common exemptions[2]	Immovable property, except dwellings (optional); financial services (optional); cultural services
Finland	Common exemptions[2]; services of performers; copyright to literary and artistic works (excluding payments to or from an organisation representing the copyright holders); certain transactions by blind people; public cemetery services; self-picked natural berries.	Cultural services; letting of commercial buildings in certain cases (optional)
France	Common exemptions[2]; construction, improvement, repair and maintenance work on monuments, cemeteries and graves commemorating war victims undertaken for public authorities and non-profit bodies; commodity futures transactions carried out on a regulated market; services rendered by resource consortia to their members composed of natural or legal persons that are VAT exempt or not subject to VAT.	Letting of immovable property (full taxation for letting of developed immovable property and land for professional use; option to tax for letting of undeveloped immovable property for professional use in certain circumstances and letting of land and buildings for agricultural use); transport services for sick/injured persons in vehicles not specially equipped for this purpose and/or carried out by persons who do not have administrative certification; recreational and sporting services; cinemas, concerts and theatres.
Germany	Common exemptions[2]	
Greece	Common exemptions[2]; national radio and TV broadcasting activities other than those of commercial nature; remunerative contributions imposed by Organizations of Territorial Improvements to their members for the supply of irrigating water and relative supplies directly connected thereto; services provided by dental technicians and the supply of dental prosthetics by dentists and dental technicians; supply of breast milk; supply of goods of an enterprise, in whole or in part, to an existing legal person or one being set up against a consideration, or as a gift or as contribution, provided that the goods were used until then exclusively in an exempt from (or out of scope of) VAT activity (or supply of goods to special scheme farmers) and the supplier was not granted or exercised input tax	Postal services not rendered by the Greek Post Office (ELTA.); charitable work when provided by organisations without state recognition; hospital and medical care supplied by profit organisations or by non-profit private organisations under distortion of competition; sporting, cultural, religion related or philosophy related etc. services supplied by profit organisations or subject to distortion of competition; supply of new buildings; letting of immovable property for professional use (optional taxation).

	deduction.	
Hungary	Common exemptions[2]; public radio and TV broadcasting (except for commercial activities).	Supply of building land, supply of new buildings (taxation of further supplies and letting of immovable property is optional); certain cultural services (e.g. admission to theatres, cinemas, concerts), certain sporting services (e.g. swimming pool services, entrance tickets to sporting events).
Iceland	Common exemptions[2]; sports, admission fees to athletic events and health facilities; public transportation, organised transportation of disabled, elderlies and school children, taxi services; authors, composers, burials and church-related services; medical and social services; cultural services; operation of schools and educational institutions; rental of real properties and parking spaces; lotteries and betting pools, charities.	
Ireland	Common exemptions[2] ; passenger transport; national broadcasting; supply of water by public authorities; admissions to sporting events; funeral undertaking.	Letting of commercial immovable property (subject to the option for taxation by the landlord); supply of undeveloped land and buildings that are not new (subject to a joint option for taxation); recreational and sporting services.
Israel	Rentals for residential purposes for a period of not more than 25 years; the sale of a part of a building which was approved as a rental building; transactions of an exempt dealer, other than transactions that are sales of real estate; the sale of an asset, on which input tax in respect of its acquisition or importation could not be deducted lawfully at the time of its acquisition or importation; deposits in a financial institution or giving a loan to a financial institution; goods whose import is tax exempt in certain cases; supplies made by an Eilat resident supplier(to be consumed in Eilat); the sale of residential dwelling to Real Estate Investment Trust (REIT) by a person who is not a dealer and the sale of that dwelling by the REIT.	Non-commercial activities of non-profit making organisations; financial services (specific regime).
Italy	Common exemptions[2]; taxi; funeral services.	Supply and letting of land; supplies of buildings are taxed in the first five years when sold by building enterprises within five years from their construction or after five years if the latter has opted for non-exemption. This scheme applies in the case of commercial buildings, while for residential housing taxation only applies when let by building enterprises which have opted for non-exemption. Rates are 4% for non-luxury owner-occupied dwelling, 10% for other non-luxury houses and 22% for luxury housing. Certain social assistance services provided by public bodies and non-profit organisations; welfare services to employees.
Japan	Common exemptions[2]; social welfare services; sale of certain kinds of equipment for the disabled people; administrative services; alienation of securities, textbooks, tuition fees.	Postal services; supply of buildings; cultural and sporting services provided by others than non-profit organisations; letting of immovable property by business.
Korea	Common exemptions[2]; certain public transport; supply of water and certain coal; mineral oil used for certain purposes in agriculture and fishery; funeral undertaking; certain personal services similar to labour; books, newspapers and magazines; broadcasting services; supply of farm, marine and forest products.	Rental and supply of commercial buildings; commercial cultural services; gambling in licensed clubs.
Latvia	Common exemptions[2]; royalty received by the author.	Supply of used immovable property (only a registered taxable person has the right to apply tax on the supply thereof), letting of commercial buildings.
Lithuania	Common exemptions[2]; public television and radio, sale of postal and fiscal stamps, social welfare services and goods related to it, services supplied to members.	Supply of building land and new (24 months) buildings, short-term (up to 2 months) letting of residential premises, letting of parking spaces and similar, supply of land and used buildings when option to tax is exercised.

Luxembourg	Common exemptions[2].	-
Mexico	Common exemptions[2]; gold and silver coins; shares; foreign currency; retailing of gold bullion with a content of at least 99 % gold; authors' rights; urban, suburban and metropolitan public transport of passengers by land including by train (with the exception of public transport that is contracted through digital intermediation service platforms and the vehicles with which the service is provided for private use); sale of used movable property (with exception of those sold by companies); professional medical services.	Postal services; insurance services (except life and agricultural insurance); transport of sick/injured persons; public hospital and medical care, sports services; financial services for consumer and personal credits; certain kinds of public spectacles like movie tickets; supplies of land and buildings (except housing); certain fund raising events and sale of goods, provision of services and granting of the temporary use or enjoyment of goods carried out by non-profit institutions authorized for receive deductible donations for effects the CIT.
Netherlands	Common exemptions[2]; burials; cremations; public broadcasting; sports clubs; the services of composers, writers and journalists.	Cultural services (mostly lower rate); letting of immovable property other than houses (only at combined request by letter and hirer); supply of immovable property (only at the combined request of supplier and purchaser); the use of sports accommodation; recreational and sporting services; admission to cinemas, concerts and theatres; sporting events; museums and zoological gardens.
New Zealand	Financial services; supply of residential accommodation in a dwelling; fine metal; supply by a non-profit body of donated goods and services.	Postal services; human blood, tissues and organs; hospital and medical care; transport of sick/injured persons; dental care; charitable work; certain fund raising events; education; non-commercial activities of non-profit making organisations (other than unconditional gifts); cultural services; sporting services; insurance and reinsurance (other than life insurance and reinsurance); letting of immovable property (other than residential accommodation); betting, lotteries and gambling; supply of land and buildings (other than land and buildings which have been used for the provision of residential accommodation for five years or more).
Norway	Common exemptions[2]; certain alternative treatments/fringe medicine; burials; stamps and coins for collection purposes; management services by a housing association to an affiliated housing cooperative; services in the form of membership of a board, supervisory board, committee, council or similar if the consideration is included in the employer's National Insurance contributions; services in the form of offsetting emission allowances	Postal services; infrastructural services within the passenger transport sector; admission to sporting events, museums, cinemas and amusement parks; letting of commercial buildings (optional).
Poland	Common exemptions[2]; public radio and television.	Rental or tenancy of the dwelling buildings used for commercial purposes; supply of building land or land for development and buildings.
Portugal	Common exemptions[2], burials and cremations, copyright to the literature and works of art.	Option to tax the supply and letting of immovable property; option to tax training services
Slovak Republic	Common exemptions[2]; public television and radio; services supplied to members; sale of postal and fiscal stamps.	Supply of a construction, including the supply of building land, on which the structure is constructed, provided that the supply is made within five years after the first approval of the building or a part thereof based on which the building or a part thereof was approved for use or within five years from the day when the building or a part thereof was put in use for the first time; option to tax supply and letting of immovable property; training, educational, sporting and cultural services provided by others than by non-profit making organisations.
Slovenia	Common exemptions[2]; public television and radio.	Supply of new buildings; admission to cultural and sporting events; educational, sporting and cultural services provided by profit making organisations; option to tax letting of immovable property.
Spain	Common exemptions[2]; copyright to literature and works of art; services provided by associations, entities, groups (including "economic interest groupings) and other legal persons to their members when they are exclusively integrated by taxable persons carrying out economic activities exempted	Cultural and sporting services provided for taxable persons different from public bodies and non-profit making organisations; letting of commercial buildings; building land; supply of new buildings.

	or not subject to VAT; certain social assistance services provided by public bodies or not-for-profit organisations.	
Sweden	Common exemptions[2]; public television and radio; public cemetery services; social services; creative artists.	Most cultural services; letting of commercial buildings in certain cases (optional).
Switzerland	Common exemptions[2]; cultural services and the supply of cultural works by their creators, such as authors, composers, film makers, painters, sculptors and services supplied by publishers and collecting societies in order to circulate these works; the supply of used movable goods, which were used exclusively for the provision of supplies exempt from the tax without credit; the sale of agricultural, forestry and market garden products cultivated in their own business by farmers, foresters or gardeners, the sale of cattle by cattle dealers, and the sale of milk by milk collection points to milk processing plants; publicity services, which charitable organisations provide for the benefit of third parties or third parties for the benefit of charitable organisations; the exercise of arbitration functions. supplies between organisational units within the same public authority, between private or public law companies owned wholly by public authorities and the public authorities that own them or their organisational units, between institutions or foundations that were founded exclusively by public authorities and the public authorities that founded them or their organisational units; the provision of staff by public authorities to other public authorities; supplies between education and research institutions that are involved in education and research cooperation, provided those supplies are made as part of the cooperation, irrespective of whether the education and research cooperation is liable to value added tax.	The dispensing of artificial limbs and orthopedic equipment; renting of exhibition stands and individual rooms in exhibition and congress buildings.
Turkey	Importation of goods for cultural and educational purposes or for social purposes; restoration project related to cultural object; delivery of goods and provision of services to military factories, shipyards and factory plants; exempted taxpayers according to Income Tax Law; mergers and transfer according to Corporate Tax Law; transactions on leasing of real properties not included in economic enterprises; banking and insurance transaction; transactions of the Mint House and the Stamp Printing House; supply of precious mine and waste; supply of water used in agriculture; services supplied in free trade area; transportation of foreign oil and gas by pipelines; supply of land and workplace for organised industrial zone; supply of goods within the scope of financial restructuring; the transactions of Savings Deposit Insurance Fund; news service provided to General Directorate of Press and Information; renting work place in customs area; delivery and leasing of immovable property by the Treasury ; transfers and deliveries resulting from the sales of shares and real properties that have been included for at least two years in the assets of institutions; transfer of movable and immovable assets and intangible assets to the asset leasing company and the leasing of assets by asset leasing company; services provided by "Insurance Arbitration Commission" about settling disputes; roaming services received from abroad in the scope of international roaming agreements and reflection of these services to customers in Turkey.	Private education; private cultural services and sporting services; private hospital and medical care and dental care; human blood; transport of sick/injured persons(lower rate); postal services; sale of commercial buildings; letting; radio and television broadcasting; betting, lotteries and gambling; financial services that made by financial corporation; supply of land and buildings included in economic enterprises (standard rate); public hospital and medical care and dental care; public education; public cultural services and sporting services; tissues and organs; certain charitable work that is made by public organization or certificated institution; insurance and reinsurance; letting of immovable property not included in economic enterprises (exemption); non-commercial activities of non-profit making organisations; certain fund-raising events(non-taxable).
United Kingdom	Common exemptions[2]; burials and cremations; sports competitions; works of art.	Standard rated: freehold sales of new commercial buildings (standard rated for three years from completion date) and "option to tax" for other ordinarily exempted supplies of commercial buildings; gaming machines and certain gambling in licensed clubs Zero-rated: New housing, including construction of new houses; residential and some charity buildings.

Notes:

1. Exemptions: for the purposes of this table, "exemption" refers to supplies for which VAT is not levied on the amount charged by the supplier while the latter is not allowed to deduct related input tax. In some countries, such supplies are called "input-taxed supplies".

2. Common exemptions: in this table, "common exemptions" refers to exemptions generally applied in most OECD countries, i.e. postal services; transport of sick/injured persons; hospital and medical care; human blood, tissues and organs; dental care; charitable work; education; non-commercial activities of non-profit making organisations; sporting services; cultural services (except radio and television broadcasting); insurance and reinsurance; letting of immovable property; financial services; betting, lotteries and gambling; supply of land and buildings; certain fund-raising events

Source: National delegates; position as at 1 January 2020.

Annex Table 2.A.4. Restrictions to the right to deduct VAT on specific inputs

Country	Inputs on which the right to deduct VAT is denied or limited
Australia	**Entertainment:** recreational club leisure facility, entertainment, meal entertainment, family maintenance, relative's travel. **Vehicles:** the amount of GST recoverable on the acquisition of a car is limited to that applicable to the car depreciation limit for the income year, currently AUD 57 466. **Others:** penalties, non-compulsory uniforms. GST is not recoverable on the expenses above to the extent they are not eligible for a deduction under the income tax law.
Austria	**Entertainment:** all entertainment expenses. **Vehicles:** vehicles, except used for commercial passenger transport, for leasing purposes or used at least 80% for driving schools.
Belgium	**Entertainment:** full input tax block for restaurant and hotel (with a number of strict exceptions), certain alcoholic beverages (with a number of strict exceptions) and reception and hospitality costs. **Vehicles:** Expenses relating to vehicles for transport of persons and/or goods by road. The right to deduct input tax may in principle not exceed 50% (with a number of strict exceptions). **Others:** supplies relating to special VAT scheme (e.g. margin scheme, special VAT scheme for tobacco).
Canada	**Entertainment**: deduction restrictions apply to memberships in dining, recreational or sporting facilities clubs; deduction for food, beverages, and entertainment expenses generally limited to 50% of the GST/HST payable. Food and beverage expenses for long-haul truck drivers are limited to 80%. **Vehicles:** deduction is limited on passenger vehicles acquired as capital property to the GST/HST payable on the capital cost value (CAD 30 000); a higher deduction limit is available for zero emission passenger vehicles (CAD 55 000); deduction is limited on passenger vehicles leases to the GST/HST payable on CAD 800 monthly lease payments. **Others:** home office expenses restriction to the extent that the consumption or use of a property or service of such quality, nature, or cost is unreasonable given the person's commercial activity.
Chile	**Vehicles:** automobiles, station wagons and similar vehicles as well their lubricants, spare parts, repairs or maintenance unless the regular business activity of the taxpayer is the sale, rental or lease of automobiles or unless the Commissioner of the Internal Revenue Service consider the relevant expenses as deductible for income tax purposes. **Fuels**: products or components that have any form of subsidy for end consumers.
Colombia	VAT levied on the acquisition of fixed assets that are not deemed as productive fixed assets is denied. Such VAT will be deemed as a higher value of the asset and will be taken into account for depreciation or amortization
Czech Republic	**Entertainment:** representation expenditures as defined in the income tax law for which there is no tax allowance according to the income tax law (except small gifts).
Denmark	**Entertainment:** expenses of entertainment, restaurant and presents. **Vehicles:** supply of vans with a weight of 3000kg or less used for both taxable and non-taxable purpose; cars with room for less than 10 persons; leased cars. **Others:** employee telephones paid by employer; board of employees and owner of the company; other objects in favour of the employees.
Estonia	**Entertainment**: goods or services relating to the reception of guests or the provision of meals or accommodation for employees. This restriction does not apply to accommodation services received during a business trip. **Vehicles**: the right of deduction is limited to 50% on purchase, import, lease or hire of passenger cars not wholly used for business purposes and on the related expenditures, except for cars purchased for resale, hire or lease, for cars used for the transportation of passengers (e.g. taxis) and for cars used for driving lessons.
Finland	**Entertainment:** representation and entertainment expenses. **Vehicles,** boats and aircraft: used for sporting and leisure purposes, cars, motorcycles and caravans. However, any means of transport which are to be resold, rented out or used in professional passenger transport or in driving lessons as well as passenger cars used only for taxable transactions are deductible. **Others:** travelling costs of personnel between home and workplace; goods and services related to dwellings or buildings provided for the recreation of personnel.
France	**Vehicles**: vehicles or equipment, whatever their nature, designed to carry persons or mixed-use, except those for resale as new; leased, having in addition to the driver's seat more than eight seats used by companies to bring their staff on the workplace, assigned exclusively to the driving instruction, all type of road vehicles exclusively for the operation of ski lifts and ski areas, vehicles acquired by companies of public passenger transport and assigned exclusively to the realisation of such transport. Components, parts and accessories of vehicles and machines previously referred. **Others:** goods and services used by taxable persons for more than 90% for a non-business purpose; gifts

	above a certain value; goods or services linked to the free supply of housing to officers or employees of a company, except when it's for the security staff on construction sites or in company premises; goods or services used for advertising alcoholic beverages; supply of passenger transport and services ancillary to such transport, except those produced either on behalf of an enterprise of public passenger transport, or under a permanent contract of transport by companies to bring their staff on the workplace; most fuels not subsequently delivered or sold as is or as other petroleum products. **Partial restrictions**: The right of deduction is limited to 50% for gas oil and other hydrocarbons in gaseous state and kerosene used as fuel, when such products are used for vehicles and equipment mentioned above. The right of deduction is limited to 80% for gas oils and bio ethanol E85 used as fuel for vehicles and equipment mentioned above, except those used for testing for the purposes of making engines of motorised equipment and insofar as they are not subsequently delivered or sold as is or as other petroleum products. The right of deduction is limited to 60% for petrol used as fuel for vehicles.
Germany	**Entertainment:** representation expenditures as defined in the income tax law for which there is no tax allowance according to the income tax law (e.g. gifts except small gifts, restaurant, catering, entertainment expenditure except appropriate ones, expenditures on hunting and fishing, sailing yacht or motor yachts and expenditures of similar nature).
Greece	**Entertainment:** receptions, recreation and hospitality in general; accommodation, food, drinks, transport and recreation for the personnel or representatives of the business. **Means of transport:** motor passenger vehicles of "private use" of up to 9 seats; motorcycles and mopeds, vessels and aircrafts of "private use" intended for recreation or sports, and the related supplies of fuel, repair, maintenance, rental/leasing and circulation in general. The restriction does not apply to the aforementioned means of transport when they are intended for sale, rental/leasing or transport of persons for a fare. **Others:** spirituous or alcoholic beverages intended to be used in non-taxable activities; manufactured tobacco products.
Hungary	**Entertainment**: services of restaurants and other public catering services; entertainment services; food and beverages. **Vehicles:** passenger cars (except hearses), motorcycles above 125 cubic centimetres; yachts and vessels. **Others**: supplies of motor fuels, other fuels, other goods used in connection with the operation or maintenance of passenger cars; residential properties, goods and services used for the construction or remodeling of residential properties; taxi services, parking services, highway toll services; 30% of input tax regarding fixed phone, mobile phone and VOIP service; 50% of input tax regarding the services used for the operation or maintenance of passenger cars.
Iceland	**Entertainment**: all expenses related to catering and food for the taxable person. Vehicles: supply, running and rental of passenger cars; delivery trucks, trucks and off-road vehicles with a weight of 5.000 kg or less, unless used for specially regulated taxable purpose. **Others**: all expenses related to residential property for the owner and the employees of the taxable person. All expenses which come instead of salaries to the owner and the employees of the taxable person. All expenses related to summer houses and similar entertainment for the owner and the employees of the taxable person; presents.
Ireland	**Entertainment:** food, drink, accommodation (except for qualifying conferences), personal services, entertainment. **Vehicles:** purchase or hire of passenger vehicles (up to 20% of the VAT cost is allowed where the car meets certain conditions regarding business use and emission levels). **Others**: petrol (unless part of stock in trade).
Israel	None
Italy	**Entertainment**: entertainment expenses, food and beverages. **Vehicles**: means of transport and services of transport (motor vehicles, aircraft and yachts) – for means of transport 60% of the input VAT is not deductible; passenger transport. **Others**: luxury goods and connected services, buildings.
Japan	None
Korea	**Entertainment**: entertainment expenses and similar expenditures. **Vehicles**: purchase and maintenance of non-business small automobiles.
Latvia	**Entertainment**: 60 % shall not be deductible from the tax as input tax from the tax amount to be paid into the State budget for the goods acquired and services received for the representation needs. **Vehicles:** 50 % shall not be deductible from the tax as input tax from the tax amount to be paid into the State budget for an acquired, leased or imported passenger car the number of seats of which, not including the driver's seat, does not exceed eight seats, as well as the costs related to the maintenance of such car, including expenses for repair of the car and purchase of fuel. Fully non-deductible is the tax amount to be paid into the State budget for buying, renting and importing passenger car the number of seats of which, not including the driver's seat, does not exceed eight seats and value higher than EUR 50 000 (exclusive of VAT), as well as the costs related to the maintenance of such car, including expenses for repair of the car and purchase of fuel.

Lithuania	**Entertainment**: representation and entertainment expenditures as defined in the income tax law for which there is no tax allowance according to the income tax law and 50 % expenditures of representation and entertainment as defined in the income tax law for which there is tax allowance according to the income tax law. **Vehicles**: passenger cars (up to 8 passengers excluding driver), except in cases where the cars are supplied, leased, used for taxi services or where the cars are classified as special purpose vehicles.
Luxembourg	**Entertainment**: not strictly business expenditures such as luxuries, entertainment or amusements.
Mexico	No restrictions list. The law establishes that deductions must come from goods and services that are "strictly indispensable" for the principal activity. The expenses deductible for VAT purposes must be deductible in terms of the Income Tax Law. The Income Tax Law has list of "Authorised deductions" for each type of regime.
Netherlands	**Entertainment**: restaurant services. Also certain representation and gift expenditures.
New Zealand	**Entertainment**: entertainment expenses are in effect only 50% deductible. Businesses may claim a full deduction when the goods and services are acquired and must annually calculate and repay the deemed 50% private portion.
Norway	**Entertainment**: catering and hiring of locations related to catering; entertainment expenses; the construction, maintenance, renting or operation of real property for accommodation or welfare needs. **Vehicles**: procurement, operation or maintenance of passenger vehicles. **Others**: works of art or antiques; accommodation of- and remuneration in kind to the owner, management, employees or pensioners of an enterprise; business gifts, goods and services for distribution for advertising purposes; cash payments above NOK 10 000 (USD 1040).
Poland	**Entertainment**: restaurant services and accommodation. **Vehicles**: limitation to 50% of the right to deduct VAT on the purchase, intra- Community acquisition, import, hire or lease of motor vehicles as well as VAT charged on expenditure related to those vehicles, where the vehicle is not entirely used for business purposes. **Others**: limitation to 50% of the right to deduct VAT on the purchase of motor fuels, fuel oil &and natural gas used by aforementioned vehicles.
Portugal	**Entertainment**: transport, accommodation or meals (except connected with conferences, seminars, fairs or exhibitions, which, under certain conditions, are deductible in 25% or 50%). Luxury and entertainment expenses. **Vehicles**: acquisition or hiring of light vehicles deemed to be used for non-business purposes, as well as pleasure boats, helicopters, aircrafts and motorcycles (except if intended for sale or constitute the core of the business activity). **Others**: fuel used in motor vehicles are deductible at 50%. Full deduction is possible if used in public transport vehicles, certain heavy vehicles, machines or tractors.
Slovak Republic	**Entertainment**: goods and services for the purposes of treat and entertainment. **Others**: suspense items (Suspense items means expenses paid on behalf and for the account of the purchaser or the customer, which the supplier charges to the purchaser or the customer.
Slovenia	**Entertainment**: entertainment expenses (where entertainment expenses shall include only the costs of entertainment and amusement during business or social contacts); meals (including drinks) and accommodation expenses, except expenses incurred by taxable person in connection with these supplies in the ordinary course of his business. **Vehicles**: yachts and boats intended for sport and recreation; aircrafts other than those used for transport of passengers and goods, leasing, renting and resale. Passenger cars and motorcycles other than: vehicles used for transport of passengers and goods, leasing, renting and resale, vehicles used in driving schools for the provision of the driver's training program in accordance with the regulations in force and combined vehicles for carrying out an activity of a public line and special line transport, and special vehicles adapted exclusively for the transport of deceased people. **Others**: fuels, lubricants, spare parts and services which are closely linked to vehicles above.
Spain	**Entertainment:** access to shows and services of a recreational character; travel, accommodation and catering services, unless they are deductible as a cost in income taxes. **Others**: jewelry, gold and platinum objects, pearls, precious stones; food, drinks and tobacco; goods or services used as gifts to clients, employees or third parties.
Sweden	**Entertainment:** representation expenditures as defined in the income tax law for which there is no tax allowance according to the income tax law (costs of a maximum of a taxable amount of SEK 300 per person and occasion regarding restaurant services). **Vehicles:** cars with a weight of 3500 kg or less used for both taxable and non taxable purposes unless the purpose is for taxi, car renting, car sales or driving school. Limitation to 50 % of the right to deduct VAT on the purchase of fuel used by those vehicles. **Others**: Expenses connected to a permanent residence.
Switzerland	None

Turkey	**Cars**: purchases of cars except when used by car renting companies. **Others**: Missing and stolen stocks (excluding those lost due to earthquake, flood and fire in places of compelling reason declared by Ministry of Treasury and Finance).
United Kingdom	**Entertainment**: business entertainment; in general terms the free provision of any hospitality to business contacts is not recoverable. The exception is where the entertainment is provided to non-UK customers. However, it is likely that if recovery is granted it would be off-set by a private use charge that would effectively cancel out any credit obtained. **Vehicles**: motor cars in general, except motor cars that are stock in trade (car dealers etc.); tools of the trade (driving schools etc.) or exclusively used for business purposes with no availability for private use (leasing companies etc.); lease of a motor car (right to deduction is limited to 50%).

Notes

1. Restrictions to the right to deduct VAT on specific inputs: this table includes limitations of the right to deduct input VAT on specific goods, services and intangibles because of their nature, generally with a view to achieving the (input) taxation of their deemed final consumption. The table does not include input tax blockings related to the exemption of outputs (e.g. limited right of deduction for inputs used to provide financial and insurance services, medical care, education, etc. listed in Table 2.3 on VAT exemptions) or to VAT inputs that are not connected with the business taxable activity.

Source: National delegates; position as at 1 January 2020.

Annex Table 2.A.5. Annual turnover concessions for VAT registration and collection

Country>	National currency	Registration thresholds					Voluntary registration or collection[2]	Minimum registration period[3]	Limitations or specific rules for application of the thresholds[5]
		Registration or collection threshold	General threshold		Other thresholds				
			Nat. curr.	USD[4]	Nat. curr.	USD[4]			
Australia*	AUD	R	75 000	52 090	150 000	104 180	Yes	1 year	See note
Austria[6]	EUR	R	35 000	46 065			Yes	5 years	
Belgium[6]*	EUR	C	25 000	33 102			Yes	None	See note
Canada*	CAD	R	30 000	25 130	50 000	41 884	Yes	1 year	See note
Chile*	CLP	None	None						See note
Colombia*	COP	R	None		122 844 150	91 062	Yes		See note
Czech Republic[6]*	CZK	R	1 000 000	80 365			Yes	1 year	
Denmark[6]*	DKK	R	50 000	7 498	170 000	25 493	Yes	2 years	See note
					300 000	44 987			
Estonia[6]	EUR	R	40 000	73 454			Yes	None	
Finland[6]*	EUR	R	10 000	11 801	30 000	35 404	Yes	None	See note
France[6]*	EUR	R	85 800	117 259	34400	47 013	Yes	2 years	See note
					44500	60 816			
Germany[6]*	EUR	C	22 000	29 843	50 000	67 824	Yes	5 years	See note
Greece[6]*	EUR	C	10 000	17 950			Yes	1 year	See note
Hungary[6]	HUF	C	12 000 000	85 145			Yes	1 year	
Iceland	ISK	R	2 000 000	14 635			Yes	None	
Ireland[6]*	EUR	R	75 000	94 186	37 500	47 093	Yes	None	
Israel*	ILS	C	100 491	27 257			No	None	See note
Italy*	EUR	C	65 000	96 898			Yes	None	See note
Japan*	JPY	R	10 000 000	98 547			Yes	1 year	See note
Korea	KRW	C	30 000 000	34 875			No	None	
Latvia[6]	EUR	R	40 000	80 851			Yes	None	
Lithuania[6]*	EUR	R	45 000	98 949			Yes	None	See note
Luxembourg[6]*	EUR	C	30 000	35 513			Yes	None	See note
Mexico	MXN	None	None						
Netherlands[6]*	EUR	C	20 000	25 480			Yes	3 years	
New Zealand	NZD	R	60 000	41 284			Yes	None	
Norway*	NOK	R	50 000	5 035	3 000 000	302 091	Yes	2 years	See note
					140 000	14 098			
Poland[6]	PLN	R	200 000	114 295			Yes	None	See note
Portugal[6]*	EUR	C	10 000	17 640			Yes	5 years	See note
Slovak Republic[6]	EUR	R	49 790	98 558			Yes	1 year	
Slovenia[6]	EUR	R	50 000	88 414			Yes	5 years	
Spain[6]	EUR	None	None						
Sweden[6]	SEK	R	30 000	3 430			Yes	3 years	See note
Switzerland*	CHF	R	100 000	87 121	150 000	130 682	Yes	1 year	See note
Turkey*	TRY	R	None		See note				See note
United Kingdom[6]	GBP	R	85 000	124 935			Yes	None	

Notes

* See country notes

1. Registration/collection thresholds identified in this table are general concessions that relieve domestic suppliers from the requirement to register for and/or to collect VAT until such time as they exceed a specific annual turnover threshold. Except where specifically identified, registration thresholds also relieve suppliers from the requirement to charge and collect VAT on supplies made within a particular jurisdiction. Relief from collection and/or registration may be available to specific industries or types of traders (for example non-resident suppliers) under more detailed rules, or a specific industry or type of trader may be subject to more stringent registration and collection requirements. The "R" indicates countries where a registration threshold applies, i.e. where suppliers having a turnover below the threshold are not required to register for VAT and are relieved from any VAT obligation. The "C" indicates countries where a collection threshold applies, i.e. where all suppliers are required to register for VAT but are not required to charge and collect VAT until they exceed the collection threshold. Thresholds shown in this table apply to businesses established in the relevant country. In most countries, the registration threshold does not apply to foreign businesses, i.e. businesses having no seat, place of business, fixed establishment, domicile or habitual residence within the country.
2. "Yes" means a supplier is allowed to voluntarily register and collect VAT where its total annual turnover is less than the registration threshold.
3. Minimum registration/collection periods apply to general concessions. This period is the minimum term during which the concession is applied to taxpayers that have opted for it.
4. Exchange rates for conversion into USD are Purchase Parity Rates (PPPs) for GDP 2019.
5. Restrictions or conditions to the application of the tax relief for businesses below the threshold
6. Limitations for member states of the European Union. Directive 2006/112/EC excludes from the application of the threshold the supply of new buildings or building land, certain supplies of new means of transport and disposals of the assets of the enterprise. The threshold does not apply to non-resident businesses. Specific thresholds also apply for certain intra-EU supplies.
Source: National delegates; position as at 1 January 2020.

StatLink https://doi.org/10.1787/888934220116

Annex Box 2.A.3. Country notes to Table 2.A.5.

Australia. For taxi drivers, including chauffeur driven limousines, hire cars and sharing economy ride-share services, there is no registration threshold. The applicable registration threshold to not-for-profit organisations is AUD 150 000.

Belgium. The registration threshold for Belgium does not apply to several sectors: real estate; hotels and restaurants; sale of used and waste materials. A number of specific supplies are also excluded from the application of the threshold: several supplies of new real estate, supplies of certain products subject to excise duties and undeclared and illicit activities.

Canada. The registration threshold does not apply to certain selected listed financial institutions; non-residents who enter Canada to make taxable supplies of admissions to a place of amusement, a seminar, an activity or an event; and persons who carry on a taxi or limousine business (which include a commercial ride-sharing business). These persons are required to register for and collect GST/HST. An alternative threshold applies to charities and public institutions. A charity or public institution is not required to register if either its revenue from worldwide taxable supplies is CAD 50 000 or less in a calendar quarter and over the last four consecutive calendar quarters, or its gross revenue in either of its two preceding fiscal years is CAD 250 000 or less.

Chile. All taxpayers are required to register and obtain a taxpayer's identification number (this TIN is not required for VAT purposes only, but also for any other tax purpose). However, small businesses, craftsmen and small service providers may be eligible for a special simplified regime according to which they account, for output VAT purposes, a monthly fixed amount based on an average level of earnings. This special regime has to be calculated by taking into account the earnings from the last 12 months and there is a threshold of 20 Monthly Tax Units (CLP 940 380 - USD 1 530). This simplified tax regime does not apply to legal entities but to individuals only. This system must be adopted for at least for 12 months after which the taxpayer can return back to the ordinary regime.

Colombia. The VAT exemption threshold is mentioned in Tax Units (Unidad de Valor Tributario - TVU) in the tax code. The VAT exemption threshold is 3 450 TVU. The value of the TVU in Colombian Pesos (COP) is set every year by decree. The value for 1 TVU is COP 35 607 for fiscal year 2020. The VAT registration threshold for individuals is therefore 3 450 x 35 607 = 122 844 150 COP. There is no VAT registration thresholds for incorporated businesses.

Czech Republic. A taxable person that is not established in the Czech Republic should register immediately once he starts to provide any taxable supply within the territory of the country, except for supplies being subject to the reverse charge mechanism or to the mini one-stop shop (MOSS).

Denmark. A higher threshold of DKK 170 000 (EUR 22 840) applies to the blind, and a threshold of DKK 300 000 (EUR 40 300) applies to the first sale of works of art by their creator or his successors in title. For the purposes of the latter exemption, the threshold of DKK 300 000 must not have been exceeded in the current or preceding year.

Finland. Where a business has exceeded the registration threshold of EUR 10 000, it must register and is subject to VAT, but a graduated relief is available until they reach a second threshold of EUR 30 000. On 1 January 2021, the registration threshold will be increased to EUR 15 000.

France. The VAT relief applies to businesses whose annual turnover does not exceed EUR 85 800 or when their turnover does has not exceeded EUR 94 300 the preceding calendar year (when the turnover has not exceeded EUR 85 800 the penultimate year). For supplies of services (except hotel accommodation and food and drink in restaurants), the annual turnover must not exceed EUR 34 400 or EUR 36 500 the preceding calendar year (when the turnover has not exceeded EUR 34 400 the penultimate year). For lawyers (in the furtherance of their regulated business), writers and artists, the turnover must not exceed EUR 44 500 (the threshold is EUR 18 300 for their supplies outside the normal framework of their affairs). Experimentally, for a period of five years, a specific threshold of EUR 100000 has been implemented in Guadeloupe, Martinique and La Réunion.

Germany. Taxpayers are relieved from VAT obligations if their annual turnover does not exceed EUR 22 000 and their expected turnover for the current calendar year will not exceed EUR 50 000.

Greece. If the annual turnover from taxable supplies is less than EUR 10 000, the business can voluntarily enter the Special Scheme for small businesses under which no VAT is collected. New businesses may also enter the Special Scheme upon registration. Farmers under the flat-rate scheme are not eligible to enter the Special Scheme for small businesses. Small businesses that have entered the Special Scheme will be obliged to enter the "normal" scheme and collect VAT from the moment they perform a taxable supply on account of which they exceed the threshold (and for the full value of that supply). In case the administrative period is less than a year, then the value of the taxable supplies for the purpose of determining whether the business may enter the Special Scheme during the next year is calculated on a proportional basis.

Ireland. The general turnover threshold for the supply of goods is EUR 75 000. Persons supplying goods liable at the reduced or standard rates which they have manufactured or produced from zero-rated materials must however register if their turnover is EUR 37 500 or more. The general turnover threshold for the supply of services is EUR 37 500. For persons supplying both goods and services where 90% or more of the turnover is derived from supplies of goods (other than of the kind referred to in the previous sentence) are subject to the threshold for the supply of goods applies.

Israel. Self-employed persons with annual revenue below NIS 100 491 are considered "Exempt Dealers". Some professions are not allowed to be Exempt Dealers: agronomist, architect, technician, private investigator, rabbinical attorney, dental technician, organizational consultant, management consultant, scientific consultant, economist, engineer, surveyor, bookkeeper, translator, insurance agent, lawyer, accountant or appraiser, chemical or medical laboratory owner, artistes, various others in show business, doctor, psychologist, physiotherapist, veterinary surgeon, dentist, driving school owner, school owner, real estate agent or dealer.

Italy. The micro-sized taxpayers' scheme ("Regime forfetario") applies to individual businesses if, in the previous year, they earned revenues or received remuneration, calculated per year, not exceeding EUR 65 000. (in addition, the gross expenses for employees must not exceed EUR 20 000). The regime does not apply to persons who are members of partnerships, professional associations or SRLs (limited liability companies) and are subject to the "regime di trasparenza" for income tax; persons who carry out sale of buildings or land or intra-EU supplies of new cars and trucks. Are also excluded, foreign businesses not established in Italy, except for those that are established in one of the EU Member States, or in a State party of the European Economic Area, and produce in Italy at least 75 percent of their total revenue.

Japan. Domestic and foreign businesses (both companies and individuals) whose taxable sales in Japan are less than 10 million yen, as well as new businesses of up to 2 years (except for the subsidiary of a certain large corporation) are exempt from JCT return. Exempted businesses can opt to be liable for Consumption Tax, in which case they shall remain liable for at least two years.

Luxembourg. Taxpayers established in Luxembourg are entitled to opt for the special scheme; the exemption only applies to goods and services supplied in Luxembourg. Taxpayers can opt out of the special scheme but have then to apply the normal VAT rules for at least five years.

Netherlands. The special scheme for small businesses applies to all businesses, irrespective of their legal form and including corporate businesses (e.g. foundations, private and limited companies).

Norway. The higher threshold of NOK 3 000 000 applies for admission to sporting events. The higher threshold of NOK 140 000 applies to charitable institutions and organisations.

Poland. The registration threshold does not apply to taxpayers supplying (a) certain types of silver, gold, platinum, knives, cutlery, jewellery, non-hazardous metal waste, museum collections and coins; (b) goods subject to excise duty with a number of exceptions; (c) certain buildings, structures and their parts; (d) building land; (e) new means of transport. The threshold does also not apply to taxpayers supplying (a) legal services; (b) consulting and expert services with certain exceptions; (c) jeweller services and taxpayers not established in Poland. As of September 2019 also supplies of certain goods bought online such as computers, electrical and non-electrical household appliances, cosmetics and toilet preparations are excluded from the exemption.

Portugal. The collection threshold does not apply to commercial legal entities. The threshold has been raised to EUR 11 000 from the 1st April 2020 and will be raised to EUR 12 500 from the 1st January 2021.

Sweden. The threshold does not apply to taxable persons not established in Sweden, taxable persons voluntarily registered for VAT for rental of immovable property, trade with investment gold and artists.

Switzerland. The thresholds refer to the worldwide turnover. The higher threshold of CHF 150 000 applies to non-for-profit sport and cultural associations and to public interest institutions.

Turkey. Certain small individual taxpayers who are exempt from Individual Income Tax are also exempt from VAT.

Annex Table 2.A.6. Usage of margin schemes

Country	Usage of margin schemes[1]
Australia	A margin scheme can be used on certain sales of new residential or commercial property. It is generally based on the difference between the tax inclusive sale price and the original purchase price. Special rules apply in certain cases, such as sales between associates or members of the same GST group. Gambling: GST applies to the gambling margin calculated based on the total amount wagered less total monetary prizes awarded. Second hand goods: when second-hand dealers adopt a special 'global' accounting method. It applies when (1) second-hand goods are acquired from an unregistered supplier and are divided up for re-supply and (2) the dealer exercises the option to apply the global method over a specified category of second-hand good.
Austria	Travel agencies; second-hand goods, works of art, collector's items and antiques (EU Directive)
Belgium	Travel agencies; second-hand goods, works of art, collector's items and antiques (EU Directive)
Canada	-
Chile	Used real estate property in which no value added tax has been paid, made by a professional seller. The tax base is the difference between the sale and purchase prices. For these purposes, the acquisition value of the property must be readjusted in accordance with the variation percentage experienced by the consumer price index in the period between the month prior to the acquisition and the month prior to the sale date. However, in the determination of the referred tax base, the value of the land included in both operations must be deducted from the purchase price and the sale price. For these purposes, the seller must deduct from the sale price the commercial value of the land at the date of the operation. Once this deduction has been made, the seller must deduct from the purchase price of the property an amount equivalent to the percentage that represents the commercial value assigned to the land in the sale price.
Colombia	Sale of used cars, sale of fixed assets made by an intermediary, sale of gasoline.
Czech Republic	Travel agencies; second- hand goods; works of art; collector's items and antiques (EU Directive)
Denmark	Travel agencies; second-hand goods, works of art, collector's items and antiques (EU Directive)
Estonia	Travel agencies; second-hand goods, works of art, collector's items and antiques (EU Directive)
Finland	Travel agencies; second-hand goods, works of art, collector's items and antiques (EU Directive)
France	Travel agencies; second-hand goods, works of art, collector's items and antiques (EU Directive); supply of building land; supply of a building completed more than five years ago, when taxed (option).
Germany	Travel agencies; second-hand goods, works of art, collector's items and antiques (EU Directive)
Greece	Travel agencies; second-hand goods, works of art, collector's items and antiques (EU Directive); sales by public auction
Hungary	Travel agencies; second-hand goods; works of art, antiques, collectors' items (EU Directive)
Iceland	-
Ireland	Travel agencies; second-hand goods, works of art, collector's items and antiques (EU Directive). Mandatory margin scheme for auctioneers and travel agents.
Israel	Sale of used furniture by a dealer whose business is the sale of such furniture. Sale of used vehicle, motorcycle or cross-country vehicle by a dealer whose business is a purchase and sale of used vehicles. Sale of dwellings by a real estate dealer who acquired it from a person who is not a non-profit organisation, a financial institution nor a dealer. Sale of coins and medals, which the seller has purchased such coins and medals from a non-licensed dealer (i.e. not VAT registered business). Sale of postage stamps and revenue stamps by a person whose business is the sale of such stamps (deemed to be a service). Sale of foreign currency, securities or other negotiable instruments, including the acquisition of aforesaid securities and instruments in order to collect their redemption or retirement price, by a dealer whose business is the sale of such assets or the sale of foreign currency, shall be deemed to be a brokerage service rendered by the dealer, between the dealer's supplier and the dealer's customer.
Italy	Travel agencies; second-hand goods, works of art, collector's items and antiques (EU Directive)
Japan	-
Korea	-
Latvia	Travel agencies; second-hand goods, works of art, collector's items and antiques (EU Directive)
Lithuania	Travel agencies; second-hand goods, works of art, collector's items and antiques (EU Directive)
Luxembourg	Travel agencies; second-hand goods, works of art, collector's items and antiques (EU Directive)
Mexico	Sale of used cars, previously acquired by a company from an individual.
Netherlands	Travel agencies; second-hand goods, works of art, collector's items and antiques (EU Directive).

New Zealand	-
Norway	Voluntary margin scheme for second hand goods, works of art, collectors' items and antiques.
Poland	Travel agencies; second-hand goods; works of art; collector's items and antiques (EU Directive).
Portugal	Travel agencies; second-hand goods, works of art, collector's items and antiques (EU Directive) and fuel retailers.
Slovak Republic	Travel agencies; second-hand goods, works of art, collector's items and antiques (EU Directive).
Slovenia	Travel agencies; second-hand goods, works of art, collector's items and antiques (EU Directive).
Spain	Travel agencies; second-hand goods, works of art, collector's items and antiques (EU Directive).
Sweden	Travel agencies; second-hand goods, works of art, collector's items and antiques (EU Directive).
Switzerland	Collector's items such as works of art, antiques and suchlike.
Turkey	Travel agencies (commission taken from tour sold abroad is exempt; commission taken from tour sold in Turkey is subject to tax). Deliveries of second hand motor vehicles or immovable properties (without making any fundamental changes in their nature) by taxpayers that are in second hand motor vehicles or immovable property business after purchasing them from non-VAT-Taxpayers (including purchases from taxpayers in the scope of exemption); The tax base in the delivery and import of gold jewelry and coins is the amount remaining after the gold ingot is deducted.
United Kingdom	Travel agencies; second-hand goods, works of art, collector's items and antiques (EU Directive)

Note:
1. Margin scheme: In this context, a margin scheme means a scheme where the tax base is calculated on the difference between the price paid by the taxpayer for an item and the resale price rather than on the full selling price. The reseller is not allowed to deduct the input VAT embedded in the buying price of the items resold under the margin scheme.
Source: National delegates; position as at 1 January 2020.

Annex Table 2.A.7. VAT Revenue Ratio (VRR) 2018

Country	Standard VAT rate 2018	1992	1996	2000	2005	2006	2007	2008	2009	2010	2011	2012	2013	2014	2015	2016	2017	2018	Diff. 2016 2018
Australia	10.0				0.56	0.54	0.54	0.49	0.51	0.49	0.47	0.47	0.49	0.48	0.50	0.50	0.48	0.47	-0.03
Austria	20.0	0.61	0.60	0.61	0.58	0.57	0.58	0.59	0.58	0.58	0.58	0.59	0.58	0.58	0.59	0.59	0.60	0.60	0.01
Belgium	21.0	0.50	0.46	0.51	0.50	0.51	0.51	0.49	0.47	0.49	0.48	0.48	0.47	0.47	0.46	0.47	0.47	0.47	0.00
Canada	5.0	0.43	0.47	0.49	0.50	0.47	0.51	0.49	0.49	0.49	0.48	0.47	0.47	0.47	0.48	0.48	0.49	0.49	0.01
Chile	19.0	0.63	0.67	0.64	0.67	0.64	0.68	0.71	0.60	0.63	0.64	0.65	0.64	0.64	0.64	0.63	0.64	0.64	0.01
Colombia	19.0			0.35	0.42	0.47	0.45	0.48	0.43	0.44	0.49	0.46	0.41	0.42	0.41	0.38	0.37	0.38	0.00
Czech Republic	21.0		0.43	0.42	0.56	0.52	0.54	0.56	0.55	0.52	0.55	0.57	0.56	0.58	0.58	0.60	0.62	0.61	0.01
Denmark	25.0	0.56	0.57	0.59	0.62	0.64	0.65	0.61	0.58	0.57	0.58	0.59	0.57	0.57	0.58	0.60	0.61	0.62	0.02
Estonia	20.0		0.72	0.71	0.70	0.82	0.81	0.67	0.73	0.66	0.67	0.69	0.66	0.69	0.72	0.72	0.74	0.74	0.02
Finland	24.0		0.54	0.61	0.61	0.61	0.60	0.58	0.56	0.55	0.56	0.56	0.55	0.55	0.54	0.55	0.56	0.57	0.02
France	20.0	0.54	0.53	0.51	0.52	0.52	0.51	0.50	0.47	0.48	0.48	0.48	0.48	0.48	0.49	0.49	0.50	0.51	0.02
Germany	19.0	0.61	0.60	0.61	0.55	0.57	0.55	0.56	0.55	0.55	0.56	0.56	0.55	0.55	0.56	0.56	0.56	0.57	0.01
Greece	24.0	0.47	0.41	0.45	0.47	0.46	0.48	0.46	0.39	0.44	0.37	0.37	0.36	0.37	0.38	0.44	0.43	0.44	0.00
Hungary	27.0	0.30	0.43	0.52	0.48	0.54	0.58	0.56	0.61	0.52	0.51	0.52	0.52	0.56	0.59	0.55	0.56	0.59	0.04
Iceland	24.0	0.63	0.54	0.58	0.61	0.64	0.59	0.52	0.44	0.42	0.42	0.43	0.43	0.44	0.51	0.53	0.57	0.55	0.02
Ireland	23.0	0.45	0.52	0.61	0.66	0.67	0.63	0.55	0.46	0.47	0.46	0.44	0.45	0.48	0.48	0.49	0.48	0.49	0.00
Israel	17.0		0.66	0.62	0.61	0.62	0.66	0.65	0.65	0.65	0.66	0.64	0.65	0.63	0.63	0.63	0.63	0.63	0.00
Italy	22.0	0.37	0.39	0.43	0.39	0.41	0.41	0.39	0.36	0.40	0.40	0.37	0.37	0.37	0.37	0.37	0.39	0.38	0.01
Japan	8.0	0.68	0.71	0.68	0.70	0.70	0.68	0.66	0.66	0.68	0.68	0.68	0.69	0.69	0.73	0.72	0.72	0.72	0.00
Korea	10.0	0.62	0.57	0.58	0.61	0.60	0.60	0.60	0.62	0.64	0.64	0.66	0.64	0.66	0.60	0.66	0.69	0.68	0.02
Latvia	21.0		0.53	0.51	0.57	0.61	0.61	0.49	0.38	0.42	0.42	0.46	0.49	0.51	0.52	0.54	0.54	0.58	0.04
Lithuania	21.0		0.46	0.52	0.52	0.56	0.61	0.58	0.47	0.49	0.51	0.50	0.50	0.51	0.51	0.51	0.53	0.53	0.02
Luxembourg	17.0	0.45	0.54	0.68	0.85	0.82	0.96	0.96	0.97	0.99	1.06	1.11	1.16	1.23	0.95	0.92	0.86	0.89	-0.03
Mexico	16.0	0.30	0.21	0.25	0.29	0.32	0.32	0.33	0.30	0.32	0.31	0.31	0.28	0.32	0.32	0.33	0.32	0.34	0.01
Netherlands	21.0	0.55	0.54	0.57	0.55	0.57	0.58	0.56	0.52	0.54	0.52	0.52	0.47	0.47	0.49	0.51	0.52	0.53	0.02
New Zealand	15.0	0.96	0.99	0.99	1.03	1.03	0.96	0.96	0.97	1.10	0.93	0.94	0.94	0.96	0.97	0.96	0.99	0.99	0.03
Norway	25.0	0.58	0.61	0.67	0.57	0.61	0.63	0.57	0.55	0.56	0.56	0.57	0.57	0.56	0.56	0.57	0.57	0.58	0.01
Poland	23.0	0.00	0.42	0.42	0.47	0.51	0.53	0.50	0.45	0.47	0.47	0.43	0.42	0.44	0.44	0.45	0.50	0.52	0.07

Portugal	23.0	0.46	0.55	0.60	0.56	0.51	0.51	0.49	0.43	0.48	0.45	0.47	0.46	0.49	0.50	0.49	0.51	0.52	0.03
Slovak Republic	20.0	0.00	0.45	0.43	0.61	0.58	0.53	0.53	0.47	0.46	0.49	0.43	0.47	0.49	0.52	0.50	0.52	0.52	0.02
Slovenia	22.0	0.00	0.00	0.68	0.67	0.68	0.69	0.68	0.59	0.59	0.59	0.57	0.59	0.58	0.58	0.58	0.59	0.60	0.02
Spain	21.0	0.59	0.44	0.52	0.56	0.56	0.52	0.41	0.29	0.44	0.38	0.40	0.39	0.41	0.43	0.43	0.44	0.45	0.02
Sweden	25.0	0.40	0.49	0.51	0.54	0.55	0.56	0.57	0.55	0.57	0.57	0.55	0.55	0.55	0.57	0.58	0.59	0.59	0.01
Switzerland	7.7		0.67	0.73	0.72	0.74	0.73	0.74	0.70	0.72	0.71	0.71	0.71	0.70	0.69	0.68	0.69	0.69	0.01
Turkey	18.0	0.37	0.43	0.46	0.40	0.42	0.38	0.37	0.36	0.41	0.44	0.40	0.44	0.40	0.42	0.40	0.41	0.40	0.00
United Kingdom	20.0	0.42	0.43	0.44	0.44	0.44	0.44	0.43	0.43	0.44	0.44	0.43	0.44	0.44	0.45	0.45	0.45	0.45	0.00
Unweighted average		0.51	0.53	0.56	0.57	0.58	0.59	0.56	0.53	0.55	0.54	0.54	0.54	0.55	0.55	0.55	0.56	0.56	0.01

Notes

Calculation formula: VRR = VAT Revenue/[(Consumption - VAT revenue) x standard VAT rate]. Consumption = Final Consumption Expenditure (Heading P3) in national accounts. VAT rates used are standard rates applicable as at 1 January of each year.

Time series: Since data beyond 2018 is not available for all countries at the time of publication, VRR is not calculated after this date.

Canada: VRR Calculation includes federal VAT only.

Canada, Japan and New Zealand. Annual final consumption expenditure in national accounts was adjusted to ensure matching between the fiscal year for the VAT revenue and the civil year for final consumption figures.

Israel. Although VAT was implemented in Israel in 1976, the VRR is only calculated from 1996 onwards since tax revenue figures are not available before that year.

Japan: given the substantial VAT rate hike on 1 April 2014, an average VAT rate was used to calculate the VRR for 2014 i.e. (5X3+8X9)/12=7.25%.

Source: OECD.

StatLink https://doi.org/10.1787/888934220135

Annex Table 2.A.8. Mechanisms for collecting VAT on cross-border supplies of services and intangibles[1] from non-resident suppliers ("inbound supplies")

Country[5]	Regime for the collection of VAT on inbound supplies of services and intangibles by foreign suppliers[2]	Proxies for determining place of taxation[3]	Threshold[4]
Australia	**VAT collection mechanism**: ***B2C supplies***: the foreign supplier is required to register and collect the GST. Simplified "pay-only" registration and reporting is available; full standard GST registration is allowed Fully digital registration is available for the simplified "pay-only" registration The appointment of a tax representative is not required but is allowed Digital platforms (Electronic Distribution Platforms) are liable to collect GST on inbound supplies made through them. ***B2B supplies***: the customer is liable to account for GST under the reverse-charge mechanism only if the business customer cannot claim a full GST credit. **Criteria for distinguishing B2C from B2B supplies:** Australian Business Number (ABN) of the customer; and a statement that the business is registered for GST **Supplies covered by the B2C rule**[3]: inbound supplies of services and intangibles (anything other than goods or real property), including services such as architectural or legal services. **Implementation:** as of 1 July 2017	B2C: Customer's location B2B: Customer's tax residence status	AUD 75 000 (USD 52 000) Same as for domestic suppliers
Austria	European Union scheme (see below)		
Belgium	European Union scheme (see below)		
Canada	**VAT collection mechanism:** ***B2C and B2B supplies***: the customer is liable to account for GST under a reverse charge mechanism. For B2B supplies, the reverse-charge mechanism applies only if the customer cannot claim a full GST credit. **Criteria for distinguishing B2C from B2B supplies:** no distinction is made. **Supplies covered**[4]: supplies of services and intangible property. **Implementation:** as of 1 January 1991	B2C and B2B: recipient's usual residence or location	Not applicable
Chile*	**VAT collection mechanism:** ***B2C and B2B supplies***: the customer is liable to account for VAT under the reverse-charge mechanism **Criteria for distinguishing B2C from B2B supplies**: no distinction made **Supplies covered**[3]: selected services of a non-professional, consultancy and technical nature. **Implementation**: as of 1975		No threshold
Colombia	**VAT collection mechanism**: ***B2C supplies***: the foreign supplier is required to register and collect the VAT. Simplified "pay-only" registration and reporting is available; full standard VAT registration is allowed Fully digital registration is available for the simplified "pay-only" registration The appointment of a tax representative is not required.	B2C: Customer's location B2B: Customer's tax residence status	No registration threshold

	Digital platforms are liable to collect the VAT on inbound supplies made through them. ***B2B supplies***: the customer is liable to account for VAT under the reverse-charge mechanism. **Criteria for distinguishing B2C from B2B supplies:** the Colombian VAT registration number of the customer **Supplies covered by the B2C rule**[3]: inbound supplies of services and intangibles (anything other than goods or real property). **Implementation:** as of 1 July 2018		
Czech Republic	European Union scheme (see below)		
Denmark	European Union scheme (see below)		
Estonia	European Union scheme (see below)		
Finland	European Union scheme (see below)		
France	European Union scheme (see below)		
Germany	European Union scheme (see below)		
Greece	European Union scheme (see below)		
Hungary	European Union scheme (see below)		
Iceland	**VAT collection mechanism**: ***B2C supplies***: the foreign supplier is required to register and collect the VAT. Simplified "pay-only" registration and reporting is available; full standard registration is allowed. Fully digital registration is available for the simplified "pay-only" registration The appointment of a tax representative is not required Digital platforms are liable to collect the VAT on inbound supplies made through them ***B2B supplies***: exempt if the customer has a full right of deduction. If not, the same procedure as for B2C supplies applies. **Criteria for distinguishing B2C from B2B supplies**: VAT registration number of the customer **Supplies covered**[3]: electronically supplied services and non-digital services such as services of consultants, lawyers, accountants and other similar specialised services. **Implementation**: 1 November 2011	B2C: customer's usual residence B2B: customer's location (permanent place of business)	ISK 2 million (USD 14 600) Same as for domestic suppliers
Ireland	European Union scheme (see below)		
Israel	**VAT collection mechanism:** ***B2C supplies***: self-assessment by customer. ***B2B supplies***: reverse-charge mechanism applies. **Supplies covered**[3]**:** services, including digital services. **Criteria for distinguishing B2C from B2B supplies:** VAT registration number of the customer. **Implementation:** 1 November 2011	**B2C and B2B**: the residence of the customer is in Israel or the supply is connected to an asset in Israel.	N.A.
Italy	European Union scheme (see below).		
Japan	**VAT collection mechanism:**	**B2C and B2B:** the place where the customer is	JPY 10 million

	B2C supplies: the non-resident service provider, which does not maintain a branch or an office in Japan, must appoint a tax agent to register under the standard registration procedure. ***B2B supplies:*** reverse-charge mechanism applies. Foreign businesses are required to notify their Japanese customers that they (customers) are required to account for VAT under the reverse-charge mechanism. **Criteria for distinguishing B2C from B2B supplies:** the nature of the services provided. **Supplies covered by B2C rule[3]:** "Electronic services" as defined by law (e.g. online e-books, online game, music movies, cloud services, Internet shopping or auction site). **Implementation:** 1 October 2015	located (i.e., address or domicile for private customers and head office or principal office for businesses).	(USD 98.500) Same as for domestic suppliers
Korea	**VAT collection mechanism:** ***B2C supplies:*** the foreign supplier is required to register and collect the VAT. Simplified "pay-only" registration and reporting is available; full standard registration is allowed. Fully digital registration is available for the simplified "pay-only" registration The appointment of a tax representative is not required Digital platforms are liable to collect the VAT on inbound supplies made through them ***B2B supplies:*** out of the scope. **Criteria for distinguishing B2C from B2B supplies:** the nature of the services provided. **Supplies covered by the B2C rule[3]:** "Electronic services" as defined by law (e.g. applications, games, music, films, electronic documents, software, etc.). **Implementation:** 1 July 2015	**B2C**: customer location **B2B:** not applicable	No threshold
Latvia	European Union scheme (see below)		
Lithuania	European Union scheme (see below)		
Luxembourg	European Union scheme (see below)		
Mexico*	**VAT collection mechanism:** ***B2C supplies:*** final consumers are required to report transactions for statistical purposes. ***B2B supplies:*** the customer should self-assess the VAT (reverse-charge mechanism). **Criteria for distinguishing B2C from B2B supplies:** No distinction is made **Supplies covered[4]:** All services **Implementation:** 1980	**B2C and B2B:** Services: consumption or physical presence of the customer; Intangibles: residence of the acquirer or place of use	No threshold
Netherlands	European Union scheme (see below)		
New Zealand	**VAT collection mechanism:** ***B2C supplies:*** the foreign supplier is required to register and collect the GST. Simplified "pay-only" registration and reporting is available; full standard GST registration is allowed. Fully digital registration is available for the simplified "pay-only" registration The appointment of a tax representative is not required. Digital platforms (Electronic Distribution Platforms) are liable to collect GST on inbound supplies made through them. ***B2B supplies:*** out of scope; a reverse-charge mechanism applies if the purchaser's taxable supplies are	**B2C:** customer's tax residence **B2B:** Customer's tax residence	NZD 60 000 (USD 41 200) Same as for domestic suppliers

	mostly exempt from GST (e.g. financial services) or the services are partly used for personal consumption. **Criteria for distinguishing B2C from B2B supplies:** New Zealand GST registration number or business number. The Commissioner of Inland Revenue can prescribe or agree to an alternative method taking into account the nature of the supply, the value of the supply and the terms and conditions of the provision of services. **Supplies covered by the B2C rule[3]:** remote services, including digital services such as e-books, music, videos and software downloads and non-digital services such as general insurance, consulting, accounting and legal services. **Implementation:** 1 October 2016		
Norway	**VAT collection mechanism:** ***B2C supplies***: the foreign supplier is required to register and collect the VAT. Simplified "pay-only" registration and reporting is available; full standard VAT registration is allowed. Fully digital registration is available for the simplified "pay-only" registration The appointment of a tax representative is not required. Digital platforms (Electronic Distribution Platforms) are liable to collect VAT on inbound supplies made through them. ***B2B supplies***: the reverse-charge mechanism applies. **Supplies covered by the B2C rule[3]:** telecommunication, radio and television broadcasting and electronically supplied services (TBE services). **Criteria for distinguishing B2C from B2B supplies:** VAT registration number of the customer **Implementation**: 1 July 2011	B2C: Customer's usual residence B2B: Customer's location	NOK 50 000 (USD 5 000) Same as for domestic suppliers
Poland	European Union scheme (see below)		
Portugal	European Union scheme (see below)		
Slovak Republic	European Union scheme (see below)		
Slovenia	European Union scheme (see below)		
Spain	European Union scheme (see below)		
Sweden	European Union scheme (see below)		
Switzerland*	**VAT collection mechanism:** ***B2C supplies***: the foreign supplier must register for VAT under the standard registration procedure No simplified registration procedure is available The appointment of a tax representative is required. ***B2B supplies***: most of the inbound supplies of services and intangibles are taxed under the reverse-charge mechanism, unless the foreign supplier is registered for VAT (e.g. to account for B2C supplies). **Supplies covered by the B2C rule[3]:** Information and communication technology (ICT) services. **Criteria for distinguishing B2C from B2B supplies:** VAT registration number of the customer. **Implementation**: 1 January 2010	B2C: Customer's usual residence B2B: Customer's location	CHF 100 000 (USD 87 100) The threshold refers to the global turnover of the supplier

Turkey	**VAT collection mechanism:** ***B2C supplies***: the foreign supplier is required to register and collect the VAT. Simplified registration and reporting is available, with right to input VAT deduction Fully digital registration is available for the simplified registration The appointment of a tax representative is not required. Digital platforms (electronic marketplaces) are liable to collect GST on inbound supplies made through them. ***B2B supplies***: reverse-charge mechanism applies. **Supplies covered by the B2C rule[3]:** electronic services **Criteria for distinguishing B2C from B2B supplies**: VAT registration number of the customer **Implementation**: 1 January 2018	B2C: Customer's usual residence B2B: Customer's location	No threshold
United Kingdom	European Union scheme (see below)		
European Union*	**VAT collection mechanism:** **B2C supplies**: the foreign supplier is required to register and collect the VAT. Simplified "pay-only" registration and reporting is available; full standard GST registration is allowed Non-EU suppliers can opt to register for VAT under the "One Stop Shop" mechanism to collect and remit VAT due on their B2C supplies in all EU Member States. Fully digital registration is available for the simplified "pay-only" registration The appointment of a tax representative is not required **B2B supplies:** the reverse charge mechanism applies. **Criteria for distinguishing B2C from B2B supplies:** VAT registration number of the customer. **Supplies covered by the B2C rule[3]:** telecommunication, electronic and broadcasting services. **Implementation**: 2003 for non-EU suppliers; 2015 for intra-EU suppliers.	B2C: Customer's usual residence B2B: Customer's location	No threshold (EUR 10 000 for intra-EU supplies)

Notes

1. In the context of this table:

"Services and intangibles" refer to any supply of service or intangible by a non-resident supplier (with no establishment whatsoever in the customer's country);

"Pay only registration" refers to a VAT registration regime for non-resident suppliers that seeks only the collection of VAT on inbound supplies of services and intangibles from these suppliers, without granting the right for these suppliers to deduct any VAT incurred in the taxing jurisdiction (although a refund or other relief procedure may be available).

2. The supplies covered in this table are those covered by the International VAT/GST Guidelines 3.1 to 3.4 and Guideline 3.6. Are therefore not covered in this table, the on-the spot supplies (Guideline 3.5), and supplies of services and intangibles subject to specific place of taxation rules including supplies directly connected to a specific immovable property, which are covered by Guidelines 3.7 and 3.8. For the purpose of this table, the term "digital platform" refers to platforms that enable, by electronic means, direct interactions between buyers and sellers.

3. Some jurisdictions may limit the application of the International VAT/GST Guidelines 3.1 to 3.4 and/or Guideline 3.6 to certain categories of service supplies. Other place of taxation or VAT collection methods may therefore apply to supplies that are not covered by this definition.

4. The threshold applies for the registration of foreign suppliers in the jurisdiction of taxation. The amount in local currency is converted into USD according to the OECD Purchasing Power Parity price for GDP (PPPs) for 2019 (see Annex B).

5. Only national taxes are included in this table. Sub-national VATs are not included.

Source: National delegates; position as at 1 January 2020.

Annex Box 2.A.4. Country notes to Table 2.A.8.

Chile. From 1 June 2020, foreign (non-established) suppliers providing digital services to final consumers (B2C) in Chile (i.e. customers that are not registered for VAT purposes in Chile) are required to register under a simplified "pay only" registration and collection regime. Registration under the standard registration procedure is also available. Digital platforms are liable to collect the VAT on inbound supplies made through them and remit the tax in Chile. The services covered include notably the supply of digital entertainment content, software and data storage. Such supplies are taxable in Chile provided they are "consumed within the country". Foreign suppliers are able to use proxies as evidence to identify the place of consumption. These proxies include: the location of the IP address of the device used by the customer (or another geolocation mechanism) at the time of contracting or paying the services; the country of issuance or registration of the card, bank account or other method of payment used; the invoicing address; and/or the country code of the mobile phone´s SIM card being used. Two items of non-contradictory evidence are required. There is no registration threshold and foreign suppliers are in principle requested to register from the first sale to Chilean consumers. B2B supplies continue to be subject to a reverse charge mechanism if the customer is registered for VAT in Chile.

Mexico. From 1 June 2020, foreign (non-established) suppliers providing digital services to consumers (B2C and B2B) in Mexico are required to register under a simplified "pay only" registration and collection regime. This registration does not grant the right to the registered businesses to deduct VAT incurred in Mexico. The registration does not generate a permanent establishment for income tax purposes in Mexico. Digital platforms are liable to collect the VAT on inbound supplies made through them and to remit it to the Mexican tax authorities. The digital services covered include notably downloads or access to images, movies, text, information, videos, audio, music, games, as well as other multimedia content, but not e-books or electronic versions of newspapers and magazines. The defined digital services also include distance learning, tests, and exercises and online clubs. Such supplies are taxable in Mexico provided they "take place" in the country. Foreign suppliers are able to use proxies as evidence to identify the place where these supplies take place. These proxies include: the location of the customer, the location of the IP address of the device used by the customer; the country of issuance or registration of the card, bank account or other method of payment used or the country code of the mobile phone´s SIM card being used. There is no registration threshold and foreign suppliers are in principle requested to register 30 days after the first sale to Mexican consumers. B2B supplies continue to be subject to a reverse charge mechanism if foreign suppliers are not registered for VAT in Mexico. Foreign suppliers are required to provide information to the tax administration quarterly on the number of services provided, classified by type of services and their price, as well as number of recipients and they to keep the appropriate records. When requested by their business customers in Mexico, foreign suppliers are required to issue proof of the payment made by these customer to the supplier with explicit and separate reference to the amount of VAT paid (to support these business customers' claim to input-VAT deduction).

European Union. Since 2003 (for non-EU suppliers) and 2015 (for intra-EU suppliers) foreign suppliers of B2C telecommunication, electronic and broadcasting (TBE) services are liable to account, collect and remit the VAT on those supplies in the Member State where the consumer has his residence. Under the VAT MOSS (Mini-One-Stop-Shop scheme), EU and non-EU businesses that are not established in the Member State where the consumer is resident can opt to register and account for the VAT due on those supplies in only one Member State. Whereas EU business have to choose their Member State of establishment, the non EU business can choose any Member State. This simplification measure avoids the need to register for VAT in all the Member States where the foreign supplier has B2C customers. From July 2021 onwards, this system will be adjusted. It will no longer be limited to TBE services and will become applicable to all B2C supplies of services and to cross border distance sales of goods. In addition, digital platforms ("marketplaces") will become liable to collect, report and remit the VAT on the inbound B2C supplies they facilitate. These platforms will have the possibility to register and account for VAT through the OSS.

Annex Table 2.A.9. VAT treatment of imports of low-value goods

Country	VAT treatment[1]	Exemption threshold		
		Currency	In local currency[2]	In USD[3]
Australia*	T	-	-	-
Austria	E	EUR	22	29
Belgium[4]	E	EUR	22	29
Canada*	E	CAD	20	17
Chile	E	USD	30	30
Colombia	T	USD	-	200
Czech Republic[4]	E	EUR	22	45
Denmark[4]	E	EUR	10	11
Estonia[5]	E	EUR	22	41
Finland[4]	E	EUR	22	26
France[4]*	T	EUR	(22)	(30)
Germany[4]	E	EUR	22	30
Greece[4]	E	EUR	22	39
Hungary[4]	E	EUR	22	51
Iceland*	E	ISK	2 000	15
Ireland[5]	E	EUR	22	28
Israel*	E	USD	75	75
Italy[5]	E	EUR	22	33
Japan	E	JPY	10 000	99
Korea*	E	USD	150	150
Latvia[5]	E	EUR	22	45
Lithuania[4]	E	EUR	22	49
Luxembourg[4]	E	EUR	22	26
Mexico*	E	USD	50	50
Netherlands[4]	E	EUR	22	28
New Zealand*	T	NZD	-	
Norway*	E	NOK	350	35
Poland[4]*	T	EUR	(22)	(54)
Portugal[4]	E	EUR	22	38
Slovak Republic[4]	E	EUR	22	43
Slovenia[4]	E	EUR	22	38
Spain[4]	E	EUR	22	35
Sweden[4]*	T	EUR	(22)	(27)
Switzerland*	E	CHF	65	57
Turkey	T	TRY	-	-
United Kingdom[4]*	E	GBP	15	22
European Union*	E	EUR	0-10-22	

Notes:

* See country notes

This table shows VAT collection thresholds below which the importation of goods dispatched by a foreign supplier to a buyer in the given country is exempt from VAT (exemption threshold). It does not cover other import scenarios such as imports of goods exchanged between private individuals or imports of goods in the personal luggage of travellers. Imports of excisable goods are generally excluded from the tax reliefs.

1. VAT treatment: this column shows situations where goods as described above are imported free of VAT (E) or taxed (T).

2. Amounts in local currency: for member states of the European Union, the threshold is mentioned in Euro (EUR) even for those that do not have the Euro as national currency (i.e. Czech Republic, Denmark, Hungary, Poland and Sweden), with the exception of the United Kingdom. The threshold applied in EU member countries is determined in EUR by common EU legislation (Directive 2009/132/EC). The amount in EUR is converted into USD (PPT) as follows: it is first converted into local currency at market exchange rate (Eurostat average 2015) and then into USD at PPP exchange rate. For Israel, Korea and Mexico, the threshold is not provided in local currency in national legislation but in USD. Except stated otherwise in the country notes, the amount reflects the intrinsic value of the goods (excluding freight, insurance and other costs and taxes).

3. Amounts are converted into USD at Purchase Parity Rates (PPPs) for GDP. PPPs are the rates of currency conversion that equalise the purchasing power of different countries by eliminating differences in price levels between countries. They show the specified number of monetary units needed in each country to buy the same representative basket of consumer goods and services, which costs USD 1 in the United States. The currency conversion rates used in Consumption Tax Trends are the PPP rates for GDP (see Annex A).
4. Members of the EU are bound by EU VAT and Customs legislation.
Source: National delegates; position as at 1 January 2020.

StatLink https://doi.org/10.1787/888934220154

Annex Box 2.A.5. Country notes to Table 2.A.9

Australia. From 1 July 2018, foreign suppliers shipping low-value goods (i.e. with a value of AUD 1 000 or less) to consumers in Australia are required to register, collect and remit the GST on those supplies if the volume of such supplies (and any other taxable supplies) exceeds the GST registration threshold of AUD 75 000 per annum. Digital platforms (Electronic Distribution Platforms) and "redeliverers" are liable to collect GST on such supplies made through them. Foreign suppliers/ Electronic Distribution Platforms/redeliverers can register for GST under the simplified "pay-only" registration procedure. B2B supplies follow the same principles as for services and intangibles. The GST is only collected by the customs authorities at the border for low-value goods where they are also subject to excise duties (i.e. alcohol and tobacco products) and for other goods with a value exceeding AUD 1 000.

Canada. From July 1, 2020, the threshold is CAD 40 for goods that are imported by courier from Mexico or the United States. The threshold is CAD 20 for all other courier and postal importations.

France. An exemption threshold of EUR 22 applies for imports of low-value goods that are imported outside the conditions of the distance sales (mail order).

Iceland. This exemption threshold applies only to the importation of goods via "express deliveries". An exemption threshold of ISK 1 500 applies to imports of goods by importers registered for VAT purposes in Iceland.

Israel. The threshold is given in USD in national legislation. The statistical data for Israel are supplied by and under the responsibility of the relevant Israeli authorities.

Korea. The threshold is given in USD in national legislation. Postal parcels and express consignments are exempt if their value does not exceed USD 150 and the quantity is such that the customs authorities recognise the goods as for personal use.

Mexico. The threshold is given in USD in national legislation. The threshold of USD 50 applies to imports by the postal service or by courier services.

New Zealand. From 1 December 2019, foreign suppliers shipping low-value goods (i.e. with a value of NZD 1 000 or less) to consumers in New Zealand are required to register, collect and remit the GST on those supplies if the volume of such supplies (and any other taxable supplies) exceeds the GST registration threshold of NZD 60 000 per annum. Digital platforms (online marketplaces and platforms) are liable to collect the GST on such supplies made through them. Foreign suppliers/online marketplaces and platforms can register for GST under the simplified "pay-only" registration scheme. For goods whose value exceeds NZD 1 000 the GST is collected by the customs authorities at the border.

Norway. From 1 April 2020, foreign suppliers of low-value goods (i.e. goods with a value below NOK 3 000) that are imported and delivered to consumers in Norway are required to register, collect and remit the VAT on those supplies in Norway, if the volume of such supplies exceeds the VAT registration threshold of NOK 50 000 per annum (the same threshold as for locally established traders). Foreign suppliers whose volume of relevant supplies exceeds the threshold must register and account for VAT from the first supply. Digital platforms (Marketplaces) are liable for collecting the VAT on such supplies made through them. Foreign suppliers/online marketplaces can register under a simplified "pay only" registration scheme (VOEC). Imports of goods with a value at or above NOK 3 000, foodstuffs, restricted goods, and goods subject to excise duties are outside the scope of the VOEC. These goods will be subject to collection of VAT at the border, along with applicable other duties (such as excise and customs duties).

Poland. The threshold does not apply to goods imported on mail order.

Sweden. The threshold does not apply to goods imported on mail order (including via digital platforms).

Switzerland. The importation of goods in Switzerland is exempt from VAT when the amount of the VAT due on such imports is CHF 5 or less per declaration. For ease of comparison, the equivalent threshold under the standard VAT rate is shown in the table above, i.e. CHF 65 x 7.7% VAT = CHF 5. For goods taxed under the reduced rate of 2.5 % (e.g. books) CHF 5 threshold is reached only for supplies of CHF 200 or above. However, anyone shipping such goods to consumers in Switzerland for an annual value of CHF 100 000 is considered as making taxable supplies of goods in Switzerland and must register, collect and remit the VAT on those supplies.

United Kingdom. There is no low value consignments relief on imports of goods into the UK from the Channel Islands purchased as part of a mail order/distance sale transaction. As a result of the UK's departure from the European Union, changes will be introduced from the end of December 2020 to remove low value consignment relief on imports of goods. Foreign suppliers and online marketplaces making supplies of goods not exceeding GBP135 in value imported and delivered to UK customers will be required to register, collect and remit the VAT.

European Union. From July 2021, the VAT exemption threshold for the importation of low-value goods will be removed. Foreign suppliers or digital platforms (marketplaces) selling low-value goods (i.e. goods with value below EUR 150) that are imported and delivered to consumers in the EU will be required to register, collect and remit VAT on those supplies. There will be no registration threshold and foreign suppliers will have to register and account for VAT from the first supply. Foreign suppliers/online marketplaces will be able to register under a simplified "pay only" registration scheme (One-Stop-Shop – OSS) in the Member State of their choice. This simplification measure avoids the need to register for VAT in all the Member States where the foreign supplier delivers low-value goods to customers. Imports of goods with value above EUR 150 and goods subject to excise duties are outside the scope of the OSS. These goods will be subject to border collection of VAT, excise and customs duties.

Annex Table 2.A.10. Availability of VAT relief or refund to foreign taxpayers

Country	Availability of VAT relief/refund mechanism to foreign businesses	Approach[2]	Reciprocity requirement	Availability of VAT deduction under the simplified registration and compliance regime[1]
Australia	Yes	Refund available for those registered other than as Limited Registration Entities	No	No ("pay-only" registration)
Austria	Yes	Refund available through direct refund mechanism (without registration or tax representative) or direct VAT registration: • Businesses established in the EU: refunds made under the terms of EU Directive 2008/9/EC; • Businesses established outside the EU: refunds made under the terms of the EU 13th Directive.	No	No ("pay-only" registration)
Belgium	Yes	Refund available through direct refund mechanism (without registration or tax representative) or direct VAT registration: • Businesses established in the EU: refunds made under the terms of EU Directive 2008/9/EC; • Businesses established outside the EU: refunds made under the terms of the EU 13th Directive.	No	No ("pay-only" registration)
Canada	Yes	Relief through zero-rating where appropriate. If not available, the following forms of relief may be available (facts and circumstances test): • No VAT to be charged to a foreign business on an otherwise taxable supply of goods in Canada provided the supplier to the foreign business receives a "drop shipment certificate" from a VAT registered person who is physically receiving the goods; • Allowing a foreign business to "flow through" VAT paid on the importation of goods into Canada or paid to a VAT registered person, to its VAT registered customer or supplier, who will in turn recover that VAT through its VAT return.	No	N/A
Chile	No	N/A	N/A	No ("pay-only" registration)
Colombia	No	N/A	N/A	No ("pay-only" registration)

Czech Republic	Yes	Refund available through direct refund mechanism (without registration or tax representative) or direct VAT registration: • Businesses established in the EU: refunds made under the terms of EU Directive 2008/9/EC; • Businesses established outside the EU: refunds made under the terms of the EU 13th Directive.	Yes: refunds are available only to businesses established in the EU and in countries that refund VAT to Czech businesses.	No ("pay-only" registration)
Denmark	Yes	Refund available through direct refund mechanism (without registration or tax representative) or direct VAT registration: • Businesses established in the EU: refunds made under the terms of EU Directive 2008/9/EC; • Businesses established outside the EU: refunds made under the terms of the EU 13th Directive.	No	No ("pay-only" registration)
Estonia	Yes	Refund available through direct refund mechanism (without registration or tax representative) or direct VAT registration: • Businesses established in the EU: refunds made under the terms of EU Directive 2008/9/EC; • Businesses established outside the EU: refunds made under the terms of the EU 13th Directive.	Yes: refunds are available only to businesses established in the EU and countries that refund VAT to Estonian businesses.	No ("pay-only" registration)
Finland	Yes	Refund available through direct refund mechanism (without registration or tax representative) or direct VAT registration: • Businesses established in the EU: refunds made under the terms of EU Directive 2008/9/EC; • Businesses established outside the EU: refunds made under the terms of the EU 13th Directive.	No	No ("pay-only" registration)
France	Yes	Refund available through direct refund mechanism (without registration or tax representative) or direct VAT registration: • Businesses established in the EU: refunds made under the terms of EU Directive 2008/9/EC; • Businesses established outside the EU: refunds made under the terms of the EU 13th Directive. •	No	No ("pay-only" registration)
Germany	Yes	Refund available through direct refund mechanism (without registration or tax representative) or direct VAT registration: • Businesses established in the EU: refunds made under the terms of EU Directive 2008/9/EC; • Businesses established outside the EU: refunds made under the terms of the EU 13th Directive.	Yes: refunds available only to businesses established in the EU, and in countries with which Germany has signed a reciprocity agreement.	No ("pay-only" registration)

Greece	Yes	Refund available through direct refund mechanism (without registration or tax representative) or direct VAT registration: • Businesses established in the EU: refunds made under the terms of EU Directive 2008/9/EC (electronic-based system); • Businesses established outside the EU: refunds made under the terms of the EU 13th Directive (paper-based system).	Yes refunds available only to businesses established in the EU, Norway and Switzerland.	No ("pay-only" registration)
Hungary	Yes	Refund available through direct refund mechanism (without registration or tax representative) or direct VAT registration: • Businesses established in the EU: refunds made under the terms of EU Directive 2008/9/EC; • Businesses established outside the EU: refunds made under the terms of the EU 13th Directive.	Yes: refunds available only to business established in the EU, Liechtenstein, Switzerland and Norway. Serbia and Turkey (for Turkey, only in respect of supply of fuel, road toll service, supplies in connection with the maintenance of vehicles acquired to carry out transportation of goods or persons; and supplies acquired to participate as an exhibitor on exhibitions, expositions and fairs).	
Iceland	Yes	Refund available through direct refund mechanism (without registration or tax representative).	No	N/A
Ireland	Yes	Refund available through direct refund mechanism (without registration or tax representative) or direct VAT registration: • Businesses established in the EU: refunds made under the terms of EU Directive 2008/9/EC; • Businesses established outside the EU: refunds made under the terms of the EU 13th Directive.	No	No ("pay-only" registration).
Israel	No	N/A	N/A	N/A
Italy	Yes	Refund available through direct refund mechanism (without registration or tax representative) or direct VAT registration: • Businesses established in the EU: refunds made under the terms of EU Directive 2008/9/EC; • Businesses established outside the EU: refunds made under the terms of the EU 13th Directive.	Yes: refunds available only to businesses established in the EU, Israel, Norway and Switzerland.	No ("pay-only" registration)
Japan	Yes	A non-established business must appoint a resident tax representative and elect to be treated as a taxable business.	No	No
Korea	Yes	Refund available through direct refund mechanism (without registration or tax representative).	Yes: refunds available only to foreign businesses on a reciprocal basis	No

Latvia	Yes	Refund available through direct refund mechanism (without registration or tax representative) or direct VAT registration: • Businesses established in the EU: refunds made under the terms of EU Directive 2008/9/EC; • Businesses established outside the EU: refunds made under the terms of the EU 13th Directive.	Yes: refunds available only to businesses established in the EU and in countries that refund VAT to Latvian businesses.	No ("pay-only" registration)
Lithuania	Yes	Refund available through direct refund mechanism (without registration or tax representative) or direct VAT registration: • Businesses established in the EU: refunds made under the terms of EU Directive 2008/9/EC; • Businesses established outside the EU: refunds made under the terms of the EU 13th Directive.	Yes: refunds are available only to businesses established in the EU and in countries that refund VAT to Lithuanian businesses. Refunds are available to businesses established in OECD member countries that do not operate a VAT or a similar tax.	No ("pay-only" registration)[2]
Luxembourg	Yes	Refund available through direct refund mechanism (without registration or tax representative) or direct VAT registration: • Businesses established in the EU: refunds made under the terms of EU Directive 2008/9/EC; • Businesses established outside the EU: refunds made under the terms of the EU 13th Directive.	No	No ("pay-only" registration)
Mexico	No	N/A	N/A	No ("pay-only" registration)
Netherlands	Yes	Refund available through direct refund mechanism (without registration or tax representative) or direct VAT registration: • Businesses established in the EU: refunds made under the terms of EU Directive 2008/9/EC; • Businesses established outside the EU: refunds made under the terms of the EU 13th Directive.	No	No ("pay-only" registration)
New Zealand	Yes	Most supplies to non-residents are zero-rated. However, non-resident businesses that do not make taxable supplies in New Zealand may register for GST to recover GST incurred in New Zealand under several conditions: (1) the non-resident business must be registered for GST or VAT in its own country; (2) the GST refund resulting from the first GST return must be more than NZD 500; (3) the GST input tax credits only arise when the non-resident has paid for the expenditure; (4) The non-resident cannot form a New Zealand GST group with New Zealand resident entities unless the non-resident is registered for GST under the ordinary rules; (5) the non-resident must not be making supplies of services that are likely to be received by a person in New Zealand who is not registered for GST; (6) the tax authority will not be legally obliged to refund the GST until 90 days after the GST return has been lodged.	No	No ("pay-only" registration). However, foreign suppliers may elect to register under the full registration regime allowing them to claim GST back on New Zealand-based costs.
Norway	Yes	Refund available through direct refund mechanism (without registration or tax representative).	No	No ("pay-only" registration)

Poland	Yes	Refund available through direct refund mechanism (without registration or tax representative) or direct VAT registration: • Businesses established in the EU: refunds made under the terms of EU Directive 2008/9/EC; • Businesses established outside the EU: refunds made under the terms of the EU 13th Directive.	Yes: refunds available only to businesses established in the EU and countries that refund VAT to Polish businesses.	No ("pay-only" registration)
Portugal	Yes	Refund available through direct refund mechanism: • Businesses established in the EU: refunds made under the terms of EU Directive 2008/9/EC; Businesses established outside the EU: refunds made under the terms of the EU 13th Directive through the appointment of a VAT representative in Portugal.	Yes: refunds available only to businesses established in the EU and countries that refund VAT to Portuguese businesses.	No ("pay-only" registration).
Slovak Republic	Yes	Refund available through direct refund mechanism (without registration or tax representative) or direct VAT registration: • Businesses established in the EU: refunds made under the terms of EU Directive 2008/9/EC; Businesses established outside the EU: refunds made under the terms of the EU 13th Directive.	Yes: refunds available only to businesses established in the EU and countries that refund VAT to Slovak businesses.	No ("pay-only" registration)
Slovenia	Yes	Refund available through direct refund mechanism (without registration or tax representative) or direct VAT registration: • Businesses established in the EU: refunds made under the terms of EU Directive 2008/9/EC; Businesses established outside the EU: refunds made under the terms of the EU 13th Directive.	Yes: refunds available only to businesses established in the EU and countries that refund VAT to Slovenian businesses.	No ("pay-only" registration)
Spain[3]	Yes	Refund available through direct refund mechanism (without registration or tax representative) or direct VAT registration: • Businesses established in the EU: refunds made under the terms of EU Directive 2008/9/EC; Businesses established outside the EU: refunds made under the terms of the EU 13th Directive.	Yes: refunds available only to businesses established in the EU, Canada, Israel, Japan, Monaco, Norway and Switzerland through appointment of a VAT representative in Spain.	No ("pay-only" registration)
Sweden	Yes	Refund available through direct refund mechanism (without registration or tax representative) or direct VAT registration: • Businesses established in the EU: refunds made under the terms of EU Directive 2008/9/EC; • Businesses established outside the EU: refunds made under the terms of the EU 13th Directive. Non-established businesses may claim relief of Swedish VAT to the same extent as VAT-registered businesses (effective as of 1 January 2010).	No	No ("pay-only" registration)

Switzerland	Yes	Switzerland refunds VAT incurred by businesses that are neither established nor registered for VAT in Switzerland or Liechtenstein and that have not made any supplies in Switzerland or Liechtenstein (subject to supplies that are exempt from the tax, services whose place of supply is the place of the recipient or supplies of electricity in cables, gas via the natural gas distribution network and district heating to persons liable to the tax on Swiss territory).	Yes: refunds are made on the condition of reciprocity	N/A
Turkey	Yes	Refund available through direct refund mechanism (without registration or tax representative) for certain transactions.	Yes (partially dependent on reciprocity)	Yes
United Kingdom	Yes	Refund available through direct refund mechanism (without registration or tax representative) or direct VAT registration: • Businesses established in the EU: refunds made under the terms of EU Directive 2008/9/EC; Businesses established outside the EU: refunds made under the terms of the EU 13th Directive.	No	No ("pay-only" registration)

Notes

The VAT relief or refund mechanisms presented in this table do not include the mechanisms associated with the exports of goods or tourists schemes.

1. The absence of input VAT relief for foreign suppliers under country's simplified registration and compliance regime generally does not prevent such foreign suppliers from exercising the right to obtain a relief of this input VAT under the standard procedure. For example, in the EU non-established suppliers registered under the MOSS can still apply for VAT refunds under the terms of the EU 13th Directive.

2. The terms "refund available" in this table does not mean that refunds are provided automatically. They may be subject to (manual) verification processes.

3. Spain: a direct VAT relief is provided on the purchase of moulds, designs and equipment for the manufacturing in Spain of goods to be dispatched out of the EU to a non-established business and for any service acquired for the assistance of commercial or professional fairs expositions or congresses organised in Spain.

Source: national delegations; position as at 1 January 2020

Annex Table 2.A.11. Electronic transaction reporting obligations[1]

Country	Electronic invoicing[2]	Mandatory electronic transaction reporting	Reporting format	Reporting provision	Reporting timing
Australia*	Paper invoices: allowed Digitised invoices: allowed E-invoices: allowed (with accredited service providers)	Transaction data: yes (1 January 2000) Electronic cash register: allowed (1 January 2000)	No specific format is required No specific format is required	On request (based on risk assessment) On request	- -
Austria*	Paper invoices: allowed Digitised invoices: allowed E-invoices: allowed (mandatory for B2G[4] supplies)	Transaction data: yes (1 January 2000) Electronic cash register: yes – offline (1 April 2017)	No specific format is required (SAF-T[3] is allowed since 2009) No specific format is required	On request Systematic (periodically) and on request	- Annual
Belgium*	Paper invoices: allowed Digitised invoices: allowed E-invoices: allowed	Transaction data : no Electronic cash register : yes (1 July 2016)	- Certified software	- On request	- -
Canada	Paper invoices: allowed Digitised invoices: allowed E-invoices: allowed	Transaction data : no Electronic cash register : no	- -	- -	- -
Chile*	Paper invoices: allowed for B2C Digitised invoices: not allowed for B2C E-invoices: mandatory for B2B and B2G supplies under XML format	Transaction data : yes (January 2003) Electronic cash register : optional (January 2014)	XML format determined by the tax authority Subject to approval by the tax authorities.	Systematic (real time direct automated access)	At the time the invoice is emitted (real time invoice reporting) Monthly
Colombia	Paper invoices: not allowed for B2C Digitised invoices: not allowed for B2C E-invoices: mandatory for B2B and B2G supplies under XML format	Transaction data : yes (January 2017) Electronic cash register : optional (January 2014)	XML format determined by the tax authority Subject to approval by the tax authorities.	Systematic (real time direct automated access)	At the time the invoice is emitted (real time invoice reporting) Monthly
Czech Republic	Paper invoices: allowed Digitised invoices: allowed E-invoices: allowed	Transaction data : yes Electronic cash register : yes - offline (1 January 2020)	Control Statement No specific format is required	Systematic (periodically) On request	At the same time as VAT return is lodged -

Denmark*	Paper invoices: allowed Digitised invoices: allowed E-invoices: allowed	Transaction data : yes (1 March 2015) Electronic cash register : no	No specific format is required -	On request -	- -
Estonia	Paper invoices: allowed Digitised invoices: allowed E-invoices: allowed	Transaction data : yes (2014) Electronic cash register : no	X-road XML, CSV -	Periodically -	At the time the VAT return is lodged -
Finland	Paper invoices: allowed Digitised invoices: allowed E-invoices: allowed	Transaction data : no Electronic cash register : no	- -	- -	- -
France	Paper invoices: allowed Digitised invoices: allowed E-invoices: allowed (mandatory for B2G[4] supplies)	Transaction data : yes (1 January 2014) Electronic cash register : yes - offline (1 January 2014)	SAF-T[3] No specific format is required	On request On request	- -
Germany	Paper invoices: allowed Digitised invoices: allowed E-invoices: allowed	Transaction data : yes (1 January 2014) Electronic cash register : no	No specific format is required -	On request -	- -
Greece*	Paper invoices: allowed Digitised invoices: allowed E-invoices: allowed	Transaction data : yes Electronic cash register : yes	Specific format is required Specific format is required	Systematic Systematic	
Hungary*	Paper invoices: allowed Digitised invoices: allowed E-invoices: allowed	Transaction data : yes Electronic cash register : yes	No specific format is required -	Systematic (real time) -	At the time the invoice is emitted (real time invoice reporting)
Iceland	Paper invoices: allowed Digitised invoices: allowed E-invoices: allowed	Transaction data : no Electronic cash register : no	- -	- -	- -
Ireland	Paper invoices: allowed Digitised invoices: allowed E-invoices: allowed	Transaction data : yes Electronic cash register : no	No specific format is required -	On request -	1 January 2014
Israel*	Paper invoices: allowed Digitised invoices: allowed E-invoices: allowed	Transaction data : yes (1 January 2010) Electronic cash register : yes	Specific format required: PCN874 No specific format is required	Systematic (periodically) Systematic (periodically)	Monthly Monthly

		(1 January 2010)			
Italy*	Paper invoices: not allowed Digitised invoices: not allowed E-invoices: mandatory for all transactions (with few exceptions)	Transaction data : yes (1 January 2019) Electronic cash register : yes	XML format -	Systematic (real time) -	At the same time the invoice is emitted (real time invoice reporting) 1 January 2020
Japan	Paper invoices: allowed Digitised invoices: allowed E-invoices: allowed	Transaction data : no Electronic cash register : no	- -	- -	- -
Korea*	Paper invoices: not allowed for B2B transactions Digitised invoices: not allowed for B2B transactions E-invoices: mandatory for B2B transactions	Transaction data : yes (1 January 2011) Electronic cash register : Yes (1 January 2005)	Electronic Tax Invoicing format No specific format is required	Systematic (near real time) Systematic	One day after the invoice is emitted Daily
Latvia*	Paper invoices: allowed Digitised invoices: allowed E-invoices: allowed	Transaction data : yes (26 October 2011) Electronic cash register : yes (1 July 2017)	No specific format is required No specific format is required	On request On request	- -
Lithuania	Paper invoices: allowed Digitised invoices: allowed E-invoices: allowed	Transaction data : yes (1 October 2016) Electronic cash register : optional	SAF-T[3] Certified software	Systematic On request	Monthly
Luxembourg*	Paper invoices: allowed Digitised invoices: allowed E-invoices: allowed	Transaction data : yes Electronic cash register : no	SAF-T[3] -	On request -	- -
Mexico*	Paper invoices: not allowed for B2B and B2G transactions Digitised invoices: not allowed for B2B and B2G transactions E-invoices: mandatory for B2B and B2G transactions	Transaction data : yes (1 January 2015) Electronic cash register : no	XML format -	Systematic (automated, periodic and on request) -	E-invoices: at the same time the invoice is emitted (real time invoice reporting) Transaction data: monthly
Netherlands	Paper invoices: allowed Digitised invoices: allowed E-invoices: allowed	Transaction data : yes (1 January 2000) Electronic cash register : no	SAFT[3] -	On request –	- -

New Zealand	Paper invoices: allowed Digitised invoices: allowed E-invoices: allowed	Transaction data : yes (1 January 2000) Electronic cash register : no	No specific format is required -	On request -	- -
Norway*	Paper invoices: not allowed for B2B and B2G[4] transactions Digitised invoices: not allowed for B2B and B2G transactions E-invoices: mandatory for B2B and B2G[4] transactions	Transaction data : yes (1 January 2020) Electronic cash register : Yes (1 January 2019)	SAF-T[3] Software approved by the tax administration	On request On request	- -
Poland	Paper invoices: allowed Digitised invoices: allowed E-invoices: allowed	Transaction data : yes (1 January 2018) Electronic cash register : yes	SAF-T[3] Certified software	Systematic and on request On request	Monthly - -
Portugal	Paper invoices: allowed Digitised invoices: allowed E-invoices: mandatory for B2G[4] transactions	Invoicing data : yes (1 January 2013) Electronic cash register : optional	Web-service format (real time) or Structured file based on SAF-T[3]/Direct upload on the tax administration (monthly) Mandatory invoice software certification (1 January 2011) Certified software	Systematic (until the 12th day following each month On request for audit purposes	Real time / Monthly -
Slovak Republic	Paper invoices: allowed Digitised invoices: allowed E-invoices: allowed	Transaction data : yes (1 January 2014) Electronic cash register : yes (1 January 2012)	Specific software is required Certified software	Systematic (in the same time as VAT return) Systematic	Monthly/quarterly In real time
Slovenia	Paper invoices: allowed Digitised invoices: allowed E-invoices: allowed	Transaction data : yes Electronic cash register : yes	SAF-T[3] Certified software	On request Systematic	- In real time
Spain*	Paper invoices: allowed Digitised invoices: allowed E-invoices: allowed	Transaction data : yes Electronic cash register : no	XML -	Systematic (near real time) -	Within four days of issuance of the invoice (near real time)
Sweden*	Paper invoices: allowed Digitised invoices: allowed E-invoices: allowed	Transaction data : yes Electronic cash register : yes	No specific format is required Certified software	On request On request	- -
Switzerland*		Transaction data : yes Electronic cash register	No specific format is required	On request	-

		: no			
Turkey	Paper invoices: allowed for B2C Digitised invoices: not allowed for B2C E-invoices: mandatory for B2B and B2G supplies under XML format	Transaction data : yes (January 2020) Electronic cash register : no	XML format determined by the tax authority -	Systematic (real time)	Daily -
United Kingdom	Paper invoices: allowed Digitised invoices: allowed E-invoices: allowed	Transaction data : yes Electronic cash register : no	Functional compatible software	On request	-

Notes

1. For the purpose of this table, electronic transaction reporting means the transmission by registered businesses of detailed information under electronic format concerning individual taxable transactions, including accounting information, invoicing information or any other information allowing tax authorities to obtain information on each taxable supply made or received by a taxpayer. This does *not* include the electronic provision of bulk data such as total sales/turnover or deductible amounts e.g. in periodic returns or statements.

2. For the purpose of this table, "electronic invoice" or "e-invoice" means the automated exchange of invoice information directly between accounting systems of parties to a transaction; "digitised invoice" means a copy of an invoice (e.g. in pdf format) sent by electronic means (e.g. by email) between parties to a transaction.

3. SAF-T stands for Standard Audit File for Tax, a mechanism that was developed by the OECD Forum on Tax Administration. It involves the use of accounting software to create an electronic file (the SAF-T) containing accounting data. The SAF-T enables the transfer of data from the taxpayer to the tax authorities in a standardised, electronic format. (Guidance for Developers of Business and Accounting Software Concerning Tax Audit Requirements available here http://www.oecd.org/tax/administration/guidancenote-guidancefordevelopersofbusinessandaccountingsoftwareconcerningtaxauditrequirements.htm). In most cases, a local version of the SAF-T is created to respond to local needs.

4. B2G means supplies made by VAT registered businesses to government or public authorities or agencies

Source: National delegations; position as at 1 January 2020

Annex Box 2.A.6. Country notes to Table 2.A.11

Australia. ***Electronic transaction information*** may be required from the taxpayer only when a risk assessment of activities reveals a need for further information. This may be simply a copy of invoices (possibly in pdf format), other substantiating document, or an electronic spreadsheet of transactions. It is rare for the Australian Tax Administration to access the actual electronic records within the business system.

Austria. ***Electronic transaction information***: from 2000, there is an obligation to provide transaction data on data carriers at the request of tax authorities (in the course of an audit). From 2009 data transmission under the SAF-T format is allowed. ***Electronic cash registers***: the use of electronic cash registers is mandatory for taxpayers with a net annual turnover of EUR 15 000 or more, provided that the cash turnover exceeds EUR 7 500 per year. The applicable annual turnover is of EUR 30 000 for businesses in the following areas: outdoor sales; sales of alpine – mountain ski and refuge hunts; sales in specific kinds of wine taverns ("Buschenschank"); sales in canteens of non-profit organisations. General exemption from the cash register obligation applies to non-profit organisations, charitable and ecclesiastic bodies; self-service automates with single sales of less than EUR 20. As from 1 January 2020, a special reporting obligation applies to platforms, in respect of goods and services of other suppliers facilitated by the platform.

Belgium. ***Electronic cash registers***: the obligation to issue cash receipts delivered by a cash registered system (CRS) is imposed on taxpayers supplying meals or catering services on a regular basis when their annual turnover, excluding VAT, related to the restaurant and catering services, exclusive of the supply of drinks, exceeds EUR 25 000. If the threshold is exceeded, CRS cash receipts must be issued for all their supplies relating to the provision of meals and drinks (supplied during the meal or not), including all sales of food and drinks.

Chile. The obligation to use ***electronic invoicing*** and to provide B2B ***transaction information electronically*** to tax authorities started in 2003. In 2017, this obligation was extended to the provision of other accounting data to an electronic record kept by the tax authority. Transaction data must be transmitted to tax authorities in real time. Invoicing data must be cleared by tax authorities to be considered as a valid accounting document (incl. for the right to deduct input VAT). This obligation is imposed on all taxpayers. Cash registers can be used by any VAT taxpayer. Prior authorization of the tax authority is required when vouchers replace non-electronic VAT receipts. In this case, the tax authority requires the model of the cash register to be certified according to certain criteria. Authorization is issued on a per-case basis, upon request of the taxpayer. As from January 2021, the Law 21210 (as modified by Law 21256) has introduced the obligation to issue B2C ***invoices electronically***. The electronic invoice can be sent through any electronic method (cell phone, email, etc.) provided that it is accessible to the consumer and the business. Some minor exceptions may apply where no internet connection neither electricity exist, but an authorization by the tax authority is needed.

Denmark. Legislation has been passed to require taxpayers to use electronic cash registers when they belong to a category considered at risk. The implementation date is still to be decided.

Estonia. Transaction data must be systematically transmitted to the tax authority at the time the VAT return is lodged for all transactions above EUR 1000 per business partner (below the threshold, transactions data can be reported as an aggregate amount). Reporting format: X-road by sending a VAT return directly from the business software; in online self-service environment using formats XML, CSV.

France. ***Electronic invoicing*** is not mandatory, except for B2G supplies. Electronic invoicing should become mandatory for all B2B supplies by 2025 at the latest. ***Electronic transaction information***: taxpayers keeping electronic accounts must provide them in the form of digital files upon request by tax administration for control purposes (these files should meet specific standards). ***Electronic cash registers***: VAT registered taxpayers making sales to final consumers, which record payments using electronic cash registers must use certified software meeting several technical conditions (inalterability, security, preservation) for tax control purposes. However, the use of electronic cash registers is not mandatory.

Greece. Issuance of retail receipts through ***electronic cash registers*** ("tax machines") is mandatory, except for those listed by the tax administration regulation (e.g. solicitors, accountants, farmers, etc.). All entities subject to the provisions of the Greek Accounting Standards have to ***digitally transmit*** to the tax administration's e-books platform named myDATA (my Digital Accounting & Tax Application): (1) a summary of issued and received sales documents (invoices, retail receipts etc.); (2) the characterisation of the transactions covered by these sales documents classifying them to revenue and expenses categories; (3) data of the additional adjustment accounting entries (e.g. payroll, depreciation) that form their accounting/tax base for the export of the accounting/tax result of each fiscal year. Such data shall be transmitted through: an interoperable accounting/commercial software, special Data Entry Form, ***connected Electronic Tax Register Machines*** (ETRMs) for retail sale transactions (Online Cash Registers, OCR) or Electronic Invoicing through Licensed Providers. Furthermore, apart from the above-mentioned obligation, businesses-petrol stations have to report on-line each purchase/sale regarding fuel (petrol, oil).

Hungary. ***Invoicing information*** for invoices emitted by an invoicing programme (for invoices from HUF 100 000) must be transmitted to the tax authorities at the same time the invoice is emitted by the taxpayer (***real time reporting***). Information on 'paper invoices' must be provided to the tax authorities within a 1 or 5 days deadline (depending on whether the value of VAT figuring in the invoice surpasses – respectively – HUF 500 000 or HUF 100 000). The customer who wishes to deduct VAT has certain reporting obligations too. Further reporting obligations apply for the modification or cancellation of invoices, as well. As of 1 July 2020, the HUF 100 000 threshold is eliminated and information must be provided concerning all invoices emitted in respect of domestic supplies to taxable persons registered in Hungary (B2B). Such reporting must be either real time (invoicing programme) or must be accomplished within a 1 or 4 days deadline ('paper invoices', depending on the value of VAT figuring in the invoice). Detailed rules apply for the modification or cancellation of invoices and for the reporting obligation of the customer, as well. These reporting rules do not apply to invoices emitted in relation to exempt Intra-Community (i.e. within the EU) supply of goods.

Israel. ***Transaction data transmission***: taxpayers ("licenced dealers") whose turnover exceeds ILS 2 500 000 or that are obliged to implement the double-entry bookkeeping system; or those whose turnover exceed ILS 1 500 000 and are required by law to prepare balance sheets and to appoint an auditor must transmit invoicing information every month (i.e. by the 23rd of the following month) to the tax administration under the prescribed format (PCN874). Certified electronic cash registers: the obligation to use certified electronic cash registers is imposed on/available to certain taxpayers depending on their activity and turnover. For example, all retailers must use ***certified electronic cash registers*** (no threshold applies but under ILS 350 000 annual turnover, the retailer can choose to use sales book instead). Wholesalers with turnover up to ILS 10 100 000 can use certified electronic cash registers as an option for cash transaction up to ILS 710 instead of invoices. Transportation service providers can use certified electronic cash registers (no threshold). For other services, electronic cash registers can be used (no threshold); if a transaction is recorded with a receipt, the receipt replaces the electronic cash registers.

Italy. All VAT-registered businesses established in Italy are obliged to accept and issue ***invoices in electronic format*** through the Italian Revenue Agency's e-invoicing platform, Sistema di Interscambio (SdI), for the operations that take place between taxable persons established on the Italian territory, excluding those carried out by taxable persons subject to VAT exemption regimes. For businesses engaged in the retail trade and similar activities, the issuance of the invoice is not mandatory if it is not requested by the customer no later than at the time of the supply. With regard to these taxpayers, from 1 January 2020 and with a few exceptions, taxpayers engaged in the retail trade and similar activities must register their supplies electronically and transmit them to the Italian Revenue Agency, regardless of their turnover.

Korea. *Transaction data transmission*: all business operators and individual businesses whose total value of supplies of goods and services for the immediately preceding taxable year is at least KRW 300 million are required to issue electronic invoices under a prescribed format for all B2B supplies. The tax administration must have a direct automated access to invoicing information (only) 1 day after the invoice is emitted through the Electronic Tax Invoicing System. The invoicing information must be available to the tax administration for clearance before it can be considered as a valid accounting document, including as a supporting evidence for deduction of input VAT. ***Electronic cash receipts***: individual businesses who supply goods or services mainly to final consumers must issue electronic cash receipts and transaction data must be transmitted daily to the tax authority.

Latvia. *Transaction data transmission*: if a taxpayer maintains accounting registers in electronic form, it must, at the request of the tax administration, provide access to any information related to its economic activities, stored in electronic form. The accounting computer programme shall ensure the recording of accounting data in such formats: MS Excel, dBase/FoxPro, Text Report files, Flat files, Excel, Access, PDF, Adobe PDF, XML or ODBC data sources. ***Electronic cash receipts:*** in street trading venues, taxpayers shall use a cash register stipulated by law if the combined value of its supplies of goods and services does reach EUR 150 000 within the period of previous 12 months. For passenger transport activities, taxpayers shall use cash-register systems stipulated by law if the combined value of transactions performed in a particular structural unit or passenger transport vehicle exceeds EUR 1 500 000 during the period of previous 12 months. The use a cash register stipulated by law is mandatory for taxpayers registered with the Value Added Tax Payers Register of the State Revenue Service, petrol stations and taxi.

Luxembourg. *The transaction information transmission obligation* was implemented for the fiscal year 2011. The requirement to make transaction information available to the tax administration under the SAF-T format is not imposed on taxpayers who: are not liable to the plan comptable normalisé (standardised chart account); or benefit from the simplified regime; or whose turnover is below EUR 112 000; or having no reasonable volume of booking transactions (under +/- 500).

Mexico. *Electronic invoicing* is mandatory since 1 January 2014. The ***transmission of transaction data*** to the tax authority is mandatory since 1 January 2015. Invoicing information must transmitted to tax authorities at the time the invoice is emitted (real time transmission). This obligation applies to all taxpayers and covers the domestic supplies of goods and services for both B2B and B2C transactions. Periodic transmission of transaction information is also imposed to all taxpayers. Federative entities, municipalities, trade unions and entities of the parastatal public administration; certain small taxpayers and non-profit legal persons are relieved from that obligation.

Norway. *Transaction data transmission*: the Norwegian Bookkeeping Regulation includes a requirement to disclose accounting data in the SAF-T format for all businesses with annual turnover of NOK 5 million or more. This requirement also applies to businesses with an annual turnover of less than NOK 5 million if they have bookkeeping information available electronically. The companies subject to bookkeeping obligations are only obliged to submit accounting information in SAF-T format on request by the tax authorities. ***Cash registers***: from 1 January 2017, cash register systems must meet the requirements laid down in the Norwegian Cash Register Systems Act and regulations. Suppliers must declare the systems to be in compliance with the new rules. Companies subject to a bookkeeping obligation must start using new cash register systems from 1 January 2019.

Poland. ***Transaction data provision***: taxable persons must provide transaction data to the tax authorities under the SAF-T format on a monthly basis. Taxable persons carrying out only supplies exempt from VAT or those benefiting from the VAT exemption for the small enterprises whose annual turnover does not exceed PLN 200 000 (the registration threshold), are exempt from this obligation. The tax authority can also obtain electronic transaction information on request only from taxpayers who keep accounting books using computer programs. This obligation also applies to stock movement, invoicing and bank statement programs. As of 1 October 2020 the SAF-T contains new fields to include VAT return data previously submitted in different separate files. ***Electronic cash registers:*** taxable persons whose annual turnover on B2C supplies, exclusive of VAT, does not in the current tax year exceed PLN 20 000 and did not do so in the course of the preceding tax year are exempt from the obligation to use certified electronic cash registers (the exemption does not apply to certain categories of goods /services). Are also exempt certain categories of supplies e.g. when an invoice is emitted and/or the payment is made by bank transfer. ***Online cash registers*** have been gradually introduced for industries recognised as particularly vulnerable to fraud and non-compliance: for fuel suppliers, car repair services as of 1 January 2020; restaurants and catering services, supplies of coal, short-term accommodation services as of 1 January 2021; hair and beauty salons, construction services, private medical practice, legal services, fitness clubs and gyms as of 1 July 2021. ***Cash registers in the form of software*** (the so called virtual cash registers) are a type of online cash registers not requiring hardware equipment or any external devices and they are available for taxpayers conducting activity in specified sectors (e.g. transportation).

Portugal. ***Transaction data transmission***: taxpayers with a permanent establishment in Portugal providing supplies subject to VAT must systematically (at the latest 12 days after the end of each month) transmit invoicing data to the tax administration. This can be done in real time (via web-service) or on a monthly basis through a structured file based on the SAF-T format or by filing it directly in the Tax Authority Web portal. The tax administration can request a SAF-T file for audit purposes, which includes accounting and invoicing data. Taxpayers with a turnover above EUR 50 000 during the previous taxation period are required to use, exclusively, computer invoicing programs previously certified by the Tax and Customs Authority (AT). ***Common Simplified Report*** (IES): accounting and financial reporting information to different government bodies is provided through one single common declaration. ***Electronic cash registers***: the use of certified ECR it's not mandatory but given the obligation to issue an invoice for any transaction and the obligation for taxpayers to use certified invoicing programs, most taxpayers use certified invoicing software instead of electronic cash registers.

Slovak Republic. ***Transaction data provision:*** all taxable persons registered for VAT purposes in the Slovak Republic are obliged to submit a special VAT Control Statement, together with their VAT returns to the Financial Administration (FA). VAT listings are submitted separately and are not dependant on the VAT return. Some crosschecking between VAT listings and VAT returns are built into the analytical system. ***Electronic cash registers***: the use of certified cash registers is mandatory for all suppliers that receives payments in cash or by other payment methods replacing cash at the point of sale and those providing sole services listed in the law. Data from these electronic cash registers must be transmitted to the tax authorities in real time.

Spain. ***Transaction data provision***: taxpayers registered in the monthly VAT refund register; those whose annual turnover exceed EUR 6 million and company groups for VAT purposes are required to provide the tax administration with invoicing data in XML format within four calendar days after the invoice is issued or received (Immediate Supply of Information – SII). Information on investment goods should also be provided within the submission deadline of the last settlement period of the year.

Sweden. ***Electronic cash registers*****:** the use of certified electronic cash registers is mandatory for taxpayers above the annual turnover threshold of SEK 182 000. It is not imposed on certain taxpayers such as taxi drivers and sales from vending machines. Taxpayers can apply for an exemption of the obligation to use certified electronic cash registers.

Switzerland. ***Electronic cash registers:*** data on individual transactions must be transmitted to the tax administration on request or during an audit.

Turkey. From 1 January 2020 paper invoices are no longer legally valid. All invoices must be sent under ***electronic format*** via the e-arşiv fatura system. Every time an electronic invoice is issued, the recipient receives a notification by email. All businesses must file a daily statement with a summary list with all the e-arşiv fatura and send it to the tax administration.

United Kingdom. Under the Making Tax Digital initiative, VAT registered businesses with taxable turnover above the VAT registration threshold need to ***keep digital records*** and submit VAT Returns to HMRC using functional compatible software.

Annex Table 2.A.12. Application of domestic reverse charge and split payment mechanisms

Country	Domestic reverse charge system	Domestic split payment mechanism
Australia		Recipients of new residential premises are required to remit GST directly to the tax authorities. This payment is reconciled against GST amounts reported by the supplier in respect of these supplies.
Austria	Supply of laptops, tablets, PCs, game consoles, mobile phones and integrated circuit devices if the amount of the invoice is at least EUR 5,000; Supply of gas and electric energy to taxable dealers; Supply of gas and electric energy certificates; Supply of CO_2 emission allowances; Supply of certain metals and of taxable investment gold; Supply of scrap and industrial and non-industrial waste and recyclable waste; Construction services if the recipient is acting as general contractor or if he usually is rendering construction services; Supplies of staff engaged in the construction sector; Supply of goods provided as security by a VAT taxable person to another person in execution of that security; Supply of goods following the cession of the reservation of ownership to an assignee and the exercising of this right by the assignee; Supply of immovable property sold by the judgment debtor in a compulsory sale procedure to another person.	
Belgium	Some supplies of investment gold and of gold products of a purity of at least 325 thousands; Supply of work on immovable property under several conditions; Supplies of staff engaged in the construction sector; Supply of CO_2 emissions allowances.	
Canada	Certain purchasers of real property are required to self-assess (e.g. when the supplier is a non-resident; or when the purchaser is registered for GST/HST and, if he is an individual, the property is not a residential complex); Self-assessment is generally required with respect to supplies of carbon emission allowances; In certain circumstances, persons may be required to self-assess the provincial part of the HST when certain property or services are moved from one province to another.	
Chile	Supplies of rice, construction works, waste, marine species, livestock, vegetables, wood, wild products, wheat and berries.	
Colombia	-	
Czech Republic	Supply of taxable investment gold and gold material of purity equal to or greater than 333 thousandths; Supply of designated categories of scrap and waste; Supply of CO^2 emission allowances; Supply of construction and assembly services provided between taxable persons registered for Czech VAT; Supply of mobile phones, integrated circuit devices, notebooks, tablets and videogame consoles; Supply of certain metals and basic products from metals; Supply of cereals and industrial crops, including oil seeds and sugar beet; Supply of immovable property under the option for taxation; Supply of gas and electric energy to taxable dealers; Supply of gas and electric energy certificates; Supply of goods following the cession of a reservation of ownership to an assignee and the exercising of this right by the assignee; Supply of immovable property sold by a judgment debtor in a compulsory sale procedure; Supply of staff engaged in construction and assembly services;	A special method for securing the payment of VAT can be used by customers of taxable supplies that wish to avoid joint and several liability for the supplier's unpaid taxes. Similarly to the split payment mechanism, the customer then pays the VAT due directly to the account of the supplier's tax office.

	Supply of certain telecommunication services.	
Denmark	Supply of CO_2 emission allowances; Supply of scrap metals; Supply of investment gold; Supply of mobile phones, integrated circuit devices, games consoles, tablets PCs and laptops.	
Estonia	Supply of immovable property and investment gold, where the supplier has opted for taxation; Supply of gold material, including semi-finished gold products (purity of at least 325 thousandths); Supply of scrap metal and precious metals.	
Finland	Supply of taxable investment gold as well as gold material and semi-manufactured gold products of purity equal to or greater than 325 thousandths; Supply of CO_2 emission allowances; Supply of scrap metal and waste; Construction services, including supply of staff engaged in the construction sector.	
France	Supply of CO_2 emission allowances; Supply of used materials, scrap and waste; Supply of investment gold and gold products of a purity of at least 325 thousandths; Construction services (limited to certain services provided on a building when performed by a subcontractor on behalf of a taxable person); Supply of gas and electric energy to taxable dealers; Supply of certain telecommunication services. Supply of certificates/guarantees of origin of electricity from renewable energy sources; Supply of certificate of performance guarantee of the public power transport system operator.	
Germany	Supplies of pledged assets by the guarantor to the recipient of the security outside the framework of judicial liquidation; Supplies covered by the Real Property Transfer Tax Law (in particular transfers of real estate); If the customer is an entrepreneur: supplies of work or other services serving the construction, repair, maintenance, alteration or removal of structures (except for planning, engineering and supervision) and cleaning of buildings when the customer himself supplies such services; Supply of gold (unwrought or semi-finished of a purity of at least 325 thousandths); Supply of CO_2 emissions allowances; Supply of industrial scrap, ferrous and non-ferrous waste and other waste; Supply of mobile devices, integrated circuit devices, game consoles and tablet PC if the transaction value is or exceeds EUR 5 000; Supply of electricity (generally applicable only if supplier and recipient are both treated as resellers) and supply of gas (generally applicable only if the recipient is to be treated as reseller); Transfer of gas and electricity certificates; Supply of precious metals as well as certain ignoble metals (e.g. copper, nickel, aluminum, lead, zinc), unwrought or semi-manufactured, if the transaction value is or exceeds EUR 5 000.	
Greece	Construction work on immovable property assigned to contractors of public works by public authorities (that are not necessarily public law entities), when these public authorities are owners of these works and are taxable persons with the right to input VAT deduction. Major projects as defined by EU Regulations are exempt from the reverse charge system. Provided the supply is intended for recycling, the following supplies of recyclable waste: Supply of ferrous and non-ferrous waste metals, scrap(clippings) and	

	other used materials Supply of semi-finished products made of ferrous and non-ferrous metals, Supply of residues and other recyclable materials consisting of ferrous and non-ferrous metals, alloys, slag, scales or ash and industrial residues containing metals or metal alloys; Supply of scrapings and scrap (clippings), waste and used recyclable material consisting of glass fragments, glass, paper, cardboard, rags, bone, leather (natural or artificial), diphtheria, raw hides and skins, tendons and sinews, twine, rope and head rope , cables, rubber and plastic materials; Supply of scrap (clippings) and waste from the working of base materials Supply of the aforementioned materials after cleaning, polishing, selection, cutting, fragmenting and pressing; Supply of greenhouse gas emissions allowances according to EU Directive 2003/87/EC; Supply of mobile phones, videogame consoles, tablets and laptops provided the acquirer is a taxable person entitled to input tax deduction (that is if registered under the normal VAT scheme).	
Hungary	Supply of construction works regarded as a supply of goods; Construction or other alteration or repair activity qualifying as service, directed at the construction, expansion, rearrangement or other modification (including demolition) of immovable property and subject to acquiescence or authorisation by the building authority; Hiring-out of employees and the supply of staff; Supply of scrap and waste products; Supply of a building and the land on which it stands or of an inbuilt plot of land (with certain exceptions) if the supplier opted for taxation; In relation with debtors and creditors, the supply of goods that were pledged as collateral security to cover an overdue claim in execution of that security; Supply of goods with an open market value of more than HUF 100,000 (EUR 334) used by the taxable person for the purposes of his business if the supplier is adjudicated in liquidation proceedings or any similar insolvency proceedings; Supply of CO_2 emissions allowances; Supply of certain specific agricultural products such as wheat and meslin, rye, barley, oats, maize, triticale, soya beans whether or not broken; rape and colza seeds whether or not broken; sunflower seeds whether or not broken. Supply of certain iron and non-alloy steel products such as flat-rolled products of iron or non-alloy steel, bars and rods of iron or non-alloy steel, angles, shapes and sections of iron or non-alloy steel, wire of iron or non-alloy steel, tubes, pipes and hollow profiles of iron or non-alloy steel.	
Iceland	-	
Ireland	Supply of construction services supplied by sub-contractors to principal contractors; Supply of immovable property under the option for taxation (including sale by receiver, liquidator or mortgagee in possession; Supply of used material and scrap metal; Supply of CO_2 emissions allowances; Supply of gas and electricity by a business in Ireland to a taxable dealer carrying on business in Ireland; Supply of gas certificates or electricity certificates by a business in Ireland to another business in Ireland.	
Israel	A person not liable for payment of the tax may, with the Director's consent and on conditions prescribed by him, take the payment upon himself, and after the date of that consent be treated as the person liable for its payment; The tax levied on a buyer, if the buyer is a dealer, a non-profit	

	organisation or a financial institution and has committed a real estate sale which is an occasional transaction; Sale of metal debris; Services of the types specified below acquired by a dealer, a non-profit organisation or a financial institution from a person, whose main income is from wage, benefit or pension, shall pay the tax in respect of that service, unless a tax invoice was received from the person rendering the service: Artistic performance; construction or preparation of stage sets; preparation, checking, conducting and supervising exams; lectures etc. Services of the following professionals: agronomist, architect, ; practical engineer; private investigator; rabbinical pleader; technician; dental technician; organizational, management, scientific or tax consultant; economist; engineer etc.	
Italy	Supplies carried out by subcontractors in the building sector; Supply of staff engaged in the construction sector; Supply of immovable property under the option for taxation; Supply of used materials, scrap, waste and specific services; Supply of investment gold, including supply of semi-finished products and of gold of a purity of at least 325 thousandths(so called industrial gold); Supply of scrap iron; Supply of mobile phones, tablets, personal computers and integrated circuit devices under certain conditions; Supply of CO_2 emission allowances; Supply of gas and electric energy to taxable dealers; Supply of gas and electric energy certificates.	Supplies of goods and services made to public authorities or government bodies, public owned companies, companies listed on the Italian Stock Market (FITSE-MIB)
Japan		
Korea	-	For supplies of gold bullion (99.5% or higher purity) and second hand gold products (with 58.5% or higher purity), copper, gold and iron scrap, the supplier must open a bank account designated for the gold or scrap transactions and the purchase price (without VAT) must be transferred to the supplier using the designated bank account. At the same time, the recipient must also deposit the relevant VAT amount into an account designated by the Director of the National Tax Services.
Latvia	Supply of timber and services related to the supply of timber; Supply of construction services; Supply of scrap metals and services related to the supply of scrap metals Supply of mobile telephones, integrated circuit devices, tablet PC's and laptops; Supply of cereals and industrial crops (including oil seeds), including mixtures of these goods, that are not normally used in the unaltered state for final consumption; Supply of raw and semi-finished precious metals, where they are not covered by special scheme for investment gold, raw and semi-finished precious metal alloys and precious metal clad, as well as precious metal or precious metal clad scrap and debris; Supply of game consoles; Supply of ferrous and non-ferrous semi-finished metals.	
Lithuania	Supply of timber; Supply of construction services; Supply of ferrous waste and scrap, residues and other recyclable materials consisting of ferrous and non-ferrous metals; Supplies by a taxable person under insolvency procedure; Supply of essential (material) improvement to the owner of the building; VAT calculated on assets taken over as a contribution in kind or due to reorganisation of another person registered for VAT purposes.	

Luxembourg	Supply of CO_2 emission allowances; supply of gas and electricity certificates.	
Mexico	Domestic reverse charge applies to: Corporations that receive independent personal services from individuals or rent goods from them; acquire waste to be used for commercial or industrial activities; receive services rendered by commissionaires who are individuals; and receive land motor transportation services of goods lent to both individuals and corporations; Credit institutions acquiring assets through payments in kind or through legal or trust adjudication; Individuals or entities acquiring or having temporary use or enjoyment of tangible assets transferred or granted by foreign residents who do not have a permanent establishment in Mexico; and Individuals or corporations who receive services through which personnel are made available directly to the contractor to carried out their duties at their facilities, regardless of the name given to the contractual obligation.	
Netherlands	Supply of construction work (including shipbuilding), including repair, cleaning, maintenance, alteration and demolition services in relation to immovable property, including the handing over of construction works; Supply of staff engaged in the construction sector; Supply of immovable property under the option for taxation; Supply of used materials, scrap, waste and specific services; Supply of goods provided as security by one taxable person to another in execution of that security; Supply of immovable property sold by a judgement debtor in a compulsory sale procedure; Supply of CO_2 emission allowances; Supply of mobile phones, integrated circuit devices, laptops, game consoles and tablet pc's provided that the value of the transactions exceeds EUR 10,000. Supply of gas and electricity certificates (e.g. green certificates, guarantees of origin)	
New Zealand	If the supply of land has been incorrectly zero-rated and the incorrect treatment is discovered after settlement, the recipient of the supply is made responsible for paying the GST.	
Norway	Supply of CO_2 emission allowances; Supply of investment gold (with purity equal to or greater than 325 thousandths).	
Poland	As of November 2019 the domestic reverse charge mechanism was replaced by a mandatory split payment mechanism. As of that date, supplies previously covered by the domestic reverse charge are now subject to the mandatory split payment.	As of November 2019 the mandatory split payment mechanism is applicable to the following B2B supplies, which previously were generally covered by the joint and several liability and domestic reverse charge, if the invoiced gross amount exceeds PLN 15 000: Supply of scrap metal, metal waste and metal materials; Supply of CO2 emission allowances; Supply of mobile phones (including smart phones), video game consoles, tablets, notebooks, and laptops; Supply of microprocessors; Construction services supplied by subcontractors; Supply of unwrought non-ferrous metals (aluminum, lead, zinc, tin, nickel); Supply of raw and semi-finished metals, including gold materials and intermediate products containing gold, investment gold and selected steel products. Upon decision of the customer, an optional split payment mechanism can be applied to B2B

		supplies which are not covered by the mandatory split payment (all taxpayers have automatically a VAT account associated with their bank account separating the VAT from the net amount of the transaction).
Portugal	Supply of used material, scrap metal, waste and specific services; Supply of immovable property under the option for taxation; Work on immovable property (such as repair, cleaning, maintenance, alteration and demolition services, including the handing over of construction works); Supply of taxable investment gold and gold material of purity equal to or greater than 325 thousandths; Supplies of CO_2 emission allowances; Supplies of cork, wood, pine cones and pine kernels in their shell.	
Slovak Republic	Supply of certain construction works including supply of building services and the supply of certain goods requiring installation or assembly; Supply of immovable property under the option for taxation; Supply of goods which are pledged as a security of a receivable of a creditor within the enforcement of such pledge; Supply of a building or a part of a building in the Slovak Republic which the supplier as a debtor recognised by a court or another relevant state authority sold within the statutory enforcement proceedings; Supply of goods following the cession of a reservation of ownership to an assignee and the exercising of this right by the assignee; Supply of investment gold and of gold material or semi-manufactured products of gold of a purity of at least 325 thousandths between taxable persons; Supply of metal scrap and metal waste; Supply of CO_2 emission allowances; Supply of cereals and oil seeds, grains, straw and fodder crops, which are not typically intended in the unaltered state for final consumption; Supplies of iron and steel; Supply of mobile phones, being devices made or adapted for use in connection with a licensed network and operated on specified frequencies, whether or not they have any other use, if the taxable amount in the invoice for the supply of mobile telephones is EUR 5 000 and more; Supply of integrated circuit devices such as microprocessors and central processing units in a state prior to integration into end user products, if the taxable amount in the invoice for the supply is EUR 5 000 and more; Supply of construction work, including repair, cleaning, maintenance, alteration and demolition services in relation to immovable property as well as the handing over of construction works regarded as a supply of goods.	
Slovenia	Supply of construction work (including repair, cleaning, maintenance, alteration and demolition services in relation to immovable property); Supply of staff engaged in the mentioned activities; Supply of certain immovable property, where the supplier has opted for taxation of the supply; Supply of certain waste, scrap, used material and services; Supply of allowances to emit greenhouse gases.	
Spain	Construction works, including the supply of staff for its performance, in the framework of development, construction or renovation of immovable property; Supply of CO_2 emission allowances; Supply of metal scrap and metal waste; Supply of investment gold and supply of gold material or semi-finished products of a purity of at least 325 thousandths; Supply of buildings in certain situations; Supply of immovable property within bankruptcy proceedings;	

	Supply of immovable property made under enforcement of a security or with the obligation for the acquirer to settle the securitized debt; Supply of mobile phones, videogame consoles, laptop and tablet PCs, only where the customer is a reseller of the goods (traders habitually engaging in the resale of these goods) or, otherwise, where the total amount of supplies to one trader exceeds EUR 10,000; Supply of silver, platinum and palladium.	
Sweden	Supply of construction work, including repair, cleaning, maintenance, alteration and demolition services in relation to immovable property, including the handing over of construction works; Supply of staff engaged in the construction sector; Supply of CO_2 emissions allowances; Supply of used materials, scrap, waste and specific services; Supply of investment gold and gold products of a purity of at least 325 thousandths.	
Switzerland	-	-
Turkey	Supply of lease of movable property by non-taxable persons to taxable persons; Supply of scientific, artistic and literary works provided to taxable persons. Supply of advertisement services provided by non-taxable persons to taxable persons.	Certain recipients of a number of specified services are required to withhold a percentage of the VAT charged to them by the service provider and remit it directly to the tax authorities (*partial withholding*). Among others, these services are (a) supervisory services for building construction, (b) scrap metal, glass, plastic and paper (in cases where the supplier waives the VAT exemption), (c) advisory, supervisory and audit services maintenance and (d) repair services for machinery, equipment and other fixed assets.
United Kingdom	Supply of investment gold and of gold products of a purity of at least 325 thousandths; Supply of CO_2 emissions allowances; Supply of mobile phones and integrated circuit devices if the value of the goods supplied exceeds GBP 5,000 (VAT inclusive). The value limit does not apply to services; Supply of gas through a natural gas system situated in the United Kingdom or any network connected to such a system and to electricity; Wholesale supply of electronic communication services; Supply of renewable energy certificates.	

Notes

1. For the purpose of this table, are considered as a "domestic reverse charge" regime, regimes whereby the customer rather than the supplier of goods, services or intangibles is liable to remit the VAT to the tax authorities on a domestic supply (i.e. a supply where both the supplier and the customer are established in the same jurisdiction, where the supply takes place). The supplier does not charge the VAT to the customer.

2. For the purpose of this table, a "domestic split payment mechanism" is a mechanism whereby, on a domestic supply of goods, services or intangibles, the supplier remains liable to charge the VAT to the customer, but where (part of) this VAT is directly transferred to the tax authorities or to a specific (blocked) "VAT account" that may belong to the supplier or customer.

Source: national delegates; position as at 1 January 2020

References

Australian Taxation Office (2020), *Goods and Services Tax Gap 2020 Report*, Australian Taxation Office. [20]

Bartosz Gryziak (2020), "Split Payment across the European Union – Review and Analysis", *International VAT Monitor*, Vol. 31/1. [29]

Bird, R. and P. Gendron (2007), *The VAT in Developing and Transitional Countries*, Cambridge University Press, Cambridge, http://dx.doi.org/10.1017/cbo9780511619366. [6]

C. Evans; R. Highfield; B. Tran-Nam; M. Walpole (2020), "Diagnosing the VAT Compliance Burden: A Cross-Country Assessment", *International VAT Monitor*, Vol. 31/2. [4]

CASE – Center for Social and Economic Research (2020), *Study and Reports on the VAT Gap in the EU-28 Member States 2020 Final report*, European Commission, Brussels. [19]

CEPAL (2020), *Panorama Fiscal de América Latina y el Caribe*, United Nations, https://repositorio.cepal.org/bitstream/handle/11362/45730/5/S2000154_es.pdf (accessed on 6 November 2020). [24]

Court Auditors, E. (2015), *Tackling intra-Community VAT fraud: More action needed*, http://dx.doi.org/10.2865/623638. [33]

CRA (2016), *Estimating and Analyzing the Tax Gap related to GST/HST in Canada*, https://www.canada.ca/content/dam/cra-arc/migration/cra-arc/formspubs/pbs/GST-report-eng.pdf. [23]

de la Feria, R. (n.d.), "EU VAT rate structure: towards unilateral convergence?", in *La réorientation européenne de la TVA à la suite du renoncement au régime définitif*, Presses de l'Université Toulouse 1 Capitole, http://dx.doi.org/10.4000/books.putc.1430. [7]

Ebrill, L. et al. (2001), *The Modern VAT*, http://www.imf.org. [14]

Eric Hutton (2017), *The Revenue Administration—Gap Analysis Program: Model and Methodology for Value-Added Tax Gap Estimation*, IMF. [21]

European Commission (2013), *Results of the public consultation on the TOP10 most burdensome legislative acts for SMEs*. [9]

European Commission (2011), *European Commission (2011) Green paper on the future of VAT COM(2010)695 final*. [8]

Europex – Association of European Energy Exchanges (2018), *Europex Common energy sector statement on VAT fraud*, https://eur-lex.europa.eu/legal-content/EN/TXT/?uri=celex%3A32013L0043. [26]

EUROPOL (2020), *Enterprising criminals*, EUROPOL. [25]

Evans, C. et al. (2018), "The Development and Testing of a Diagnostic Tool for Assessing VAT Compliance Costs Draft Report of Pilot Study Findings [ATAX version]", https://www.business.unsw.edu.au/About-Site/Schools-Site/Taxation-Business-Law-Site/Documents/ime-Highfield,-Walpole-Evans-VAT-Diagnostic-Tool-paper.pdf. [10]

HMRC (2020), *Preliminary estimate of the VAT gap for 2018-19*, HM Revenue and Customs, London. [22]

Institute for Advanced Studies (2015), *Study and Reports on the VAT Gap in the EU-28 Member States: 2018 Final Report*, https://ec.europa.eu/taxation_customs/sites/taxation/files/2018_vat_gap_report_en.pdf. [18]

Jens Matthias Arnold, B. (2011), "TAX POLICY FOR ECONOMIC RECOVERY AND GROWTH", *The Economic Journal* 121. [1]

Li Liu, B. (2019), *VAT Notches, Voluntary Registration, and Bunching: Theory and UK Evidence*, IMF. [12]

OECD (2020), *Revenue Statistics 2020*, OECD Publishing, Paris, https://dx.doi.org/10.1787/8625f8e5-en. [16]

OECD (2020), *Tax and fiscal policy in response to the Coronavirus crisis: Strengthening confidence and resilience*, http://www.oecd.org/coronavirus/policy-responses/tax-and-fiscal-policy-in-response-to-the-coronavirus-crisis-strengthening-confidence-and-resilience-60f640a8/ (accessed on 24 June 2020). [38]

OECD (2020), *Tax and Fiscal Policy in Response to the Coronavirus Crisis: Strengthening Confidence and Resilience*, OECD. [37]

OECD (2020), *Tax Policy Reforms 2020: OECD and Selected Partner Economies*, OECD Publishing, Paris, https://dx.doi.org/10.1787/7af51916-en. [36]

OECD (2018), *Tax Policy Reforms 2018: OECD and Selected Partner Economies*, OECD Publishing, Paris, https://dx.doi.org/10.1787/9789264304468-en. [5]

OECD (2017), *Mechanisms for the Effective Collection of VAT/GST where the supplier is not located in the jurisdiction of taxation*, OECD, Paris, http://www.oecd.org/tax/consumption/mechanisms-for-the-effective-collection-of-vat-gst.htm. [13]

OECD (2016), *Consumption Tax Trends 2016: VAT/GST and excise rates, trends and policy issues*, OECD Publishing, Paris, https://dx.doi.org/10.1787/ctt-2016-en. [17]

OECD (2015), *Addressing the Tax Challenges of the Digital Economy, Action 1 - 2015 Final Report*, OECD/G20 Base Erosion and Profit Shifting Project, OECD Publishing, Paris, https://dx.doi.org/10.1787/9789264241046-en. [28]

OECD (2015), *Addressing the Tax Challenges of the Digital Economy, Action 1 - 2015 Final Report*, OECD/G20 Base Erosion and Profit Shifting Project, OECD Publishing, Paris, https://dx.doi.org/10.1787/9789264241046-en. [34]

OECD (2015), *Tax Administration 2015: Comparative Information on OECD and Other Advanced and Emerging Economies*, OECD Publishing, Paris, https://dx.doi.org/10.1787/tax_admin-2015-en. [30]

OECD (2015), *Taxation of SMEs in OECD and G20 Countries*, OECD Tax Policy Studies, No. 23, OECD Publishing, Paris, https://dx.doi.org/10.1787/9789264243507-en. [11]

OECD (2013), *Electronic Sales Suppression: A threat to tax revenues - OECD*, http://www.oecd.org/ctp/crime/electronic-sales-suppression-a-threat-to-tax-revenues.htm. [27]

OECD (2012), *Keeping It Safe*, OECD. [32]

OECD (2010), *Choosing a Broad Base - Low Rate Approach to Taxation*, OECD Tax Policy Studies, No. 19, OECD Publishing, Paris, https://dx.doi.org/10.1787/9789264091320-en. [15]

OECD (2005), "Guidance on Tax Compliance for Business and Accounting Software", https://www.oecd.org/tax/forum-on-tax-administration/publications-and-products/hnwi/34910263.pdf. [31]

OECD/Council of Europe (2011), *The Multilateral Convention on Mutual Administrative Assistance in Tax Matters: Amended by the 2010 Protocol*, OECD Publishing, Paris, https://dx.doi.org/10.1787/9789264115606-en. [35]

OECD/KIPF (2014), *The Distributional Effects of Consumption Taxes in OECD Countries*, OECD Tax Policy Studies, No. 22, OECD Publishing, Paris, https://dx.doi.org/10.1787/9789264224520-en. [2]

Thomas, A. (2020), "Reassessing the regressivity of the VAT", *OECD Taxation Working Papers*, No. 49, OECD Publishing, Paris, https://dx.doi.org/10.1787/b76ced82-en. [3]

3 Selected Excise Duties in OECD Countries

3.1. Introduction

Although excise may be levied on a broad range of products, excise taxes on alcohol, tobacco and hydrocarbon oils in particular raise significant revenues for governments in all OECD countries. In recent decades, governments have increasingly used these taxes not only to raise revenue but also to influence customer behaviour where consumption of certain products is considered harmful to health or to the environment.

This chapter presents an overview of the key characteristics of excise duties and the evolution in their use by governments in selected areas (Section 3.2). It then looks in some further detail at the excise rates structure for three main categories of products: alcoholic beverages (Section 3.3), tobacco products (Section 3.4) and mineral oil products (Section 3.5). This is followed by a brief description of the impact of differences in excise rates between countries on cross-border trade (Section 3.6) and on their distributional effects (Section 3.7). A more detailed analysis of the impact of excise duties on motor vehicle and aviation fuels is provided in Chapter 4.

3.2. Key characteristics and revenue trends

3.2.1. Key characteristics of excise taxes

Excise, unlike other general consumption taxes (incl. value added taxes - VAT[1]) is levied only on specific goods. Although many products can be subject to excise, such as chocolate, coffee and orange juice, this chapter focuses on three principal product groups that are subject to excise in all OECD countries: alcoholic beverages, mineral oils and tobacco products.

Before looking at the key characteristics of these three groups and their comparative treatment in different countries, it is useful to recall the following general characteristics of excise duties:

- Excise duties are generally calculated by reference to the weight, volume, strength, or quantity of the product, combined in some cases with the value, but sometimes on a value basis only.
- Excise duties normally become payable when the goods enter free circulation. Transfers of ownership of excisable goods can take place within a controlled warehousing environment or between registered operators without creating an excise charge.
- The excise system is characterised by small numbers of taxpayers that are active in the manufacturing, wholesale stage or importation of the three main product groups.

Unlike VAT, which is collected through a staged collection process by all the stakeholders in the value chain until the final consumer (see Chapter 2), excise duties are normally collected only once, from a registered operator, at the time the goods are released for consumption. In the European Union, the movement of excisable products between Member States takes place under a duty-suspension arrangement until the moment these products are released for free circulation. In the United States, excise duties are levied by the federal government and by many states and local governments. Federal excise taxes are collected by the Internal Revenue Service while states may impose the tax according to their own rules and rates.

The level of revenues raised by excise duties and the economic impact of these taxes depends on their structure. There are two main ways for levying excise duties on excisable products: *ad valorem* and *ad quantum*. Under an *ad quantum* excise (also referred to as a "specific" excise), a fixed amount of tax is levied per unit of the product (e.g. USD 1 per litre), which means that this is a tax on the volume of sales. Under an *ad valorem* excise, the tax is levied as a proportion of the product price (e.g. 20% of the selling price), and it is thus a tax on the value of sales. In a number of instances (e.g. tobacco taxes as presented in Annex Table 3.A.4) excise duties can be levied on the basis of a mix of *ad valorem* and *ad quantum* taxes. *Ad quantum* taxes requires a precise definition of the nature and characteristics of the tax base (e.g. a litre of unleaded gasoline with 94 RON) while an *ad valorem* tax is simply based on the price of the excisable good.

Most excisable products naturally present a bundle of different characteristics (volume, weight, strength, octane, alcoholic or carbon content, etc.). *Ad quantum* taxes remain unaffected by changes in the product characteristics that have not been defined as being relevant for the tax base, whereas *ad valorem* taxes bear on all the characteristics of the product that are reflected in the price. Depending on the structure of the excise, its impact on production and consumption is different. For example, a specific ad quantum excise on beer (per % absolute alcohol in volume) may encourage brewers to develop varieties of beer, including more luxurious products that could be offered at higher prices while remaining subject to the same level of excise as the cheaper product. On the other hand, ad valorem taxes may discourage costly improvements in product quality or encourage consumers to switch to low-cost products. An *ad quantum* excise may be easier to administer, because it requires only the determination of the physical quantity of the product taxed.

The tax revenue raised from excise duties and the revenue impact of changes of the design of these taxes are influenced by a wide range of factors. When assessing the impact of change to excise duty regimes, it is important to note that excise is normally part of the VAT base, i.e. VAT is usually levied on the duty-paid value of the excise products. The revenue impact of any changes in an excise tax will thus also be influenced by the level of the VAT rate on a given excisable product. Elasticity of the demand for the taxed products is a key factor in determining the revenue impact of excise duty reforms. The more elastic the demand is, the higher the likelihood that an increase in the price from an increase in excise will lead to a lower demand and thus to lower tax revenue. A price increase from higher excises may induce households to shift to other, more lightly taxed products so that the revenue impact will also depend on the tax rates levied on close substitutes. The impact of these various factors will ultimately depend on the extent in which any tax increase is passed onto consumers in the form of higher after-tax prices. If producers reduce the before-tax price in response to a tax increase, this increase will not be (fully) reflected in the consumer price as producers absorb it (partially or fully) through a reduction in their profit margin. It is also noteworthy in this context that empirical experience suggests that *ad quantum* tax increases tend to be more than fully passed through to consumers (prices rise by more than the tax increase), whereas *ad valorem* tax increases tend to be less than fully passed through (Sassi, Belloni and Capobianco, 2013[1]). In general, *ad quantum* taxes produce a more predictable revenue stream than ad valorem taxes, as revenue does not vary with the price of the product. On the other hand, *ad valorem* taxes may keep pace with inflation better than ad quantum taxes (although it is possible to adjust *ad quantum* taxes for inflation).

From a distributional perspective, there may be a case for *ad valorem* rather than *ad quantum* taxation. If one assumes that high-income taxpayers purchase more expensive products than low-income consumers, then an *ad valorem* tax could be assumed to impose a higher tax burden on high-income taxpayers relative to low-income consumers. However, this is not entirely straightforward: the exact distributional impact will depend on consumption patterns, and even with an *ad valorem* tax, high-income taxpayers may still end up paying less tax relative to their income than low-income households. Addressing redistributive goals is likely to be better achieved through a progressive personal income tax which directly links taxes paid to income (Brys et al., 2016[2])(see also Section 3.4 below).

There may be a case for a combination of *ad quantum* and *ad valorem* taxes if the tax is aimed at discouraging consumption of, or maximising revenue from, both high and low value products. Where there are large differences in prices of a product, an *ad quantum* tax will be less likely to reduce demand for the high value product, and will raise less revenue from it than an *ad valorem* tax. Additionally, higher income consumers who are more likely to consume high value products may be less responsive than low-income groups to the imposition of a given tax (although *ad quantum* taxes may reduce the price differentials). Imposing a higher aggregate tax on these expensive products will therefore be needed to affect behaviour. To achieve this, an *ad valorem* tax can be combined with an *ad quantum* tax, which is common in tobacco taxation (see Section 3.3 below). Setting the "optimal" balance between *ad quantum* and *ad valorem* components of excise will depend of the products concerned, the market structure and the government's objective, hence there is no optimal balance between the two taxes in absolute (KEEN, 1998[3])

Finally, illicit trade and opportunities for cross border shopping are other factors that might influence the revenue potential and the impact on consumption of excisable products.

All these factors need to be taken into account by governments depending on their policy objectives i.e. to reduce consumption of products considered harmful to health or increase revenue or both.

3.2.2. Excise revenue trends in OECD countries

In the OECD countries, the relative share of excise duties in total tax revenue has seen a long decline between 1975, when they accounted for 10.5% on average, and 2018 when these taxes represented 7.2% of total tax revenue on average (see Annex Table 1.A.5). Although some large differences between countries can be observed, with excise accounting for 2.6% of total tax revenue in New Zealand and 14.9% in Turkey, the weight of excise duties is between 5% and 10% of total tax revenue in the majority of OECD countries (26 out of 37). These taxes account for less than 5% of total taxes in eight OECD countries (Australia, Canada, Israel, Japan, New Zealand, Sweden, Switzerland and the United States). They account for more than 10% of total tax revenue in 5 OECD countries (Estonia, Latvia, Lithuania, Poland and Turkey), down from twelve OECD countries in 2010.

The main characteristics of excise duties and their policy objectives as revenue raisers and tools to influence consumer behaviour are largely shared amongst OECD countries. However, their rates and structure differ significantly and showing the order of magnitude of the total tax burden on specific excisable goods is therefore not straightforward. For example, standard excise rates on beer may be tempered by the application of reduced rates on small breweries. For tobacco products, different duty rates applicable to substitutes (cigarettes and rolling tobacco) may also blur the picture. Similarly, excise duties on road fuels show only a part of automotive taxation policy that also includes road tolls, taxes on registration and use of vehicles, taxes on insurance, etc.

The following sections provide some more detail on the main differences in the structure of excise duties and on their increasing use as an instrument to influence behaviour.

3.3. Alcoholic beverages

Alcoholic beverages exist in a wide variety across the world and are produced from a wide range of fermented or distilled ingredients (grapes, apples, malt, rice, etc.). The Customs Combined Nomenclature Code (CN) provides a classification of alcoholic beverages with which excise categories are intrinsically linked. The CN includes six main categories of alcoholic beverages: beer made from malt (code 22.03); wine of fresh grapes, including fortified wines (code 22.04); vermouth and other wine of fresh grapes flavoured with plants or aromatic substances (code 22.05); other fermented beverages (for example, cider, perry, mead), mixtures of fermented beverages and mixtures of fermented beverages and non-alcoholic beverages (code 22.06); undenatured ethyl alcohol of an alcoholic strength of 80 % pure alcohol by volume (abv) or higher (code 22.07) and undenatured ethyl alcohol of an alcoholic strength of less than 80 % abv (code 22.08). There are inevitably subdivisions within each of these broad categories but the use of the internationally accepted nomenclature enhances consistency and helps to avoid contradictory definitions in applying rates. Member States of the European Union apply a harmonised structure for excise duties on alcohol and alcoholic beverages (Council Directive 92/83/EEC). Except otherwise mentioned in country notes, Annex Table 3.A.1 and Annex Table 3.A.1 cover products under CN codes 22.03 and 22.04. Annex Table 3.A.3 covers products not included in Annex Table 3.A.1 and Annex Table 3.A.2.

Given the long history of alcohol taxation, several methods and measures have been developed over time for assessing the alcoholic content of a product. The alcohol by volume (abv) is now the standard measure of the level of alcohol contained in an alcoholic beverage. It is defined as the number of litres of pure ethanol present in 100 litres of solution at 20 °C, expressed as a percentage of the total volume. Annex Table 3.A.1 and Annex Table 3.A.2 provide an overview of excise taxation of beer and wine, whereby the alcoholic content is expressed in % abv. In some countries, the excise taxation of beer calculates the alcoholic content in degree Plato (measuring the density of beer wort in terms of percentage of extract by weight). To allow cross-country comparison, Annex Table 3.A.1 shows the estimated amounts of tax per % abv for these countries based on a conversion from the amounts of tax per degree Plato. There is no precise method to convert from degrees Plato and alcohol per volume but for tax purposes it is assumed that 1% abv is equivalent to 2.5 degrees Plato. The tax amounts per degree Plato have thus been multiplied by 2.5 to obtain the rates in degree abv for the relevant countries in Annex Table 3.A.1.

Excise can be applied to alcoholic beverages in two main ways. The duty can be either *ad quantum* in relation to the alcoholic content of the product or *ad valorem* calculated according to the value of the product. The two methods are generally combined to include both the volume (based on alcohol content) and value. One exception is Mexico where the rate of tax on alcoholic beverages is calculated exclusively on the value of the product, with a graduated rate for beer that takes into account the alcoholic content of the product.

Annex Table 3.A.1, Annex Table 3.A.2, and Annex Table 3.A.3 in respect of excise duties on beer, wine and other alcoholic beverages illustrate the complexity of the computation of excise duties in many instances. The existence of differing subcategories and specific rates (e.g. for low-alcohol products and for small breweries) and calculations based on both the value and the nature of the product, make it difficult to show an exact estimate of the precise excise tax burden at the consumer level. Nevertheless, Annex Table 3.A.1, Annex Table 3.A.2, and Annex Table 3.A.3 show the large differences of taxation levels between countries. Excise on beer (Annex Table 3.A.1), for instance, varies from less than USD 5 per hectolitre per % abv (Czech Republic, Germany, Luxembourg, Slovak Republic and Turkey) up to more than USD 20 (Finland, Ireland, New Zealand, Sweden and United Kingdom) with the highest levels observed in Finland (USD 41.01) and Israel (USD 66.01). Three quarters of OECD countries (29 out of 36) apply reduced rates to small breweries, with a progressive increase in the tax rate according to their annual production in many cases. Country notes to Table 3.A.1 illustrate the wide diversity of these tax regimes.

Excise rates on still wine (Annex Table 3.A.2) also vary widely across OECD countries from zero (Austria, Czech Republic, Germany, Greece, Hungary, Israel, Italy, Luxemburg, Portugal, Slovak Republic, Slovenia, Spain and Switzerland) to more than USD 4 per litre in Finland and Ireland and more than USD 6 per litre in Norway. In addition, if almost all OECD countries apply the standard VAT rate to alcoholic beverages, Colombia and Luxembourg apply a reduced VAT of respectively 5% and 14% to still wine. Four OECD countries do not apply any *ad quantum* excise to wine but only *ad valorem* taxes (Australia, Chile, Korea and Mexico).

For other alcoholic beverages (Annex Table 3.A.3), the excise duty rates also vary across OECD countries, but to a lesser extent than for wine and beer, as there are no zero-rates or reduced rates for small producers. These range from less than USD 15 per litre of absolute alcohol (Hungary, Germany, Czech Republic) up to about USD 90 per litre of absolute alcohol in Norway and USD 126 in Iceland. The only country to apply a reduced VAT rate (5%) to alcoholic beverages is Colombia.

3.4. Tobacco products

Historically, as for alcohol taxation, the primary motivation for tobacco taxation was the raising of government revenue. Nearly all OECD countries have taxed tobacco products for many decades and even for centuries in some cases. The significant tobacco consumption and the relatively low elasticity of demand for tobacco products (i.e. the less than proportionate response of tobacco product consumption to a moderate price increase) along with the small number of producers made these products a particularly attractive target for excise and other taxation. Overtime, the clear evidence of the negative health consequences of tobacco use have turned tobacco taxation increasingly into a tool reduce tobacco consumption. The World Health Organisation provides economic evidence of the effectiveness of increased tobacco taxation and pricing in reducing tobacco use. It shows that tobacco taxation is highly cost-effective, combining the potential for massive impact with a low implementation cost as returns and economic benefits from tobacco taxation have proven to be several times higher than the cost of this measure (WHO, 2019[4]).

As with alcohol and mineral oils, tobacco products are subdivided into a number of categories i.e. cigarettes, cigars, cigarette rolling tobacco and pipe tobacco. New tobacco products have also emerged in recent years such as Heated Tobacco Products (HTP), and Electronic Nicotine Delivery Systems (ENDS), which may be subject to specific tax rates.

Unlike excises on alcoholic beverages and mineral oils, which are almost exclusively *ad quantum*, the majority of countries use a combination of *ad quantum* and *ad valorem* elements to calculate excise on tobacco products.

Annex Table 3.A.4 and Annex Table 3.A.5 show large differences in tax rates between countries. Difference in tax levels can also exist within a jurisdiction that allows excises to be levied at the sub-national level such as in the United States where, for instance, local excise rates on cigarettes (on the top of the federal tax) range from USD 0.17 in Missouri and USD 0.30 in Virginia to USD 4.50 in the District of Columbia and USD 4.35 in New York per pack of 20 cigarettes (Federation of Tax Administrators, 2020[5])

It should be noted that the individual rates or amounts of tax (*ad valorem/ad quantum* excise, VAT, duties, etc.) per type of tobacco product as shown in Annex Table 3.A.4 are not sufficient to assess the overall tax burden on those products. Indeed, a high *ad valorem* tax on a given product group can be balanced with a low *ad quantum* excise (or vice versa) when excise is levied on the basis of a mix of both *ad valorem* and *ad quantum* taxes for this product group. *Ad valorem* excises can be assessed on a range of different bases (producer price, import price, retail price). The combined effect of the VAT rate with excise duties needs to be assessed etc.

A better understanding of the relative taxation levels may therefore be gained by calculating the total tax burden (TTB) as a share of the total retail selling price (RSP) of a given product to the final consumer. To illustrate this, Annex Table 3.A.5 shows the total tax burden (*ad quantum* excise + *ad valorem* excise + VAT) for cigarettes as a share of the retail selling price (RSP) of a pack of 20 cigarettes in OECD countries. This table shows that the total tax burden for a pack of 20 cigarettes varies widely between countries, from 39.47% of the RSP in the United States (national average estimate of federal and local taxes) and 55.49% in Iceland to 82.69% in the Czech Republic and 87.41% in Finland. The tax burden is above 60% of the

RSP in all the OECD countries, except Iceland and the United States; and above 75% (as recommended by the WHO) in 21 OECD countries.

Annex Table 3.A.5 also shows that there may be substantial differences in the pre-tax prices, depending on the structure of the market, the geographic location (in particular with respect to cross-border shopping) and the relevant tax structure.

Determining the rate for tobacco taxation depends on the policy objectives of the tax. If the tax is primarily intended to raise revenue, then the tax rate will be determined in light of the revenue targets and the elasticity of the demand for the taxed products. A moderate rate may be sufficient to generate stable revenue without creating significant political economy difficulties. If the tax is intended to have a significant impact on customer behaviour, then a higher tax rate is likely to be required to achieve the desired health outcomes. In the specific case of tobacco, research (Goodchild, Perucic and Nargis, 2016[6])has shown that higher taxes and prices on tobacco reduce both prevalence (i.e. users quitting) and intensity of tobacco use (i.e. users consuming less), in particular for vulnerable populations (young people and low-income households). The monetary burden of higher tobacco taxes also appears to fall more heavily on the wealthiest users, whose tobacco use declines less, while most of the health and economic benefits from reductions in tobacco consumption accrue to the most disadvantaged populations, whose tobacco use declines more when taxes increase (Belinda Loring, 2014[7]). Political economy factors (e.g., industry lobbying, public opposition) may make imposing a higher rate difficult to achieve. Earmarking (part of) the revenue from the taxes for specific health related purposes such as funding health programmes and/or tobacco control activities may increase public support, although it reduces the flexibility in government budgeting. It may also provide a regular source of funding for health care and health promotion programmes that is not subject to annual budgetary review (World Health Organisation, 2016[8]). Concerns about cross-border trade and bootlegging between countries with high price differentials may make it difficult to impose a high tax rate in some countries in the absence of efficient regional co-operation.

3.5. Heating fuel

Mineral oils are usually sub divided into product categories on the basis of technical specifications. The main product categories for excise duty purposes are unleaded gasoline, diesel oil, and heavy fuel oil. Some OECD countries also tax other energy products such as natural gas, electricity and coal through excises or specific taxes on energy products, such as carbon taxes. This publication only considers VAT and excise taxes, or taxes considered as such or included in the excise amount. These taxes are set *ad valorem* or *ad quantum* rather than by energy or CO_2 content of the fuel.

In most OECD countries, heating oil is taxed at lower rates than motor fuels. In the European Union, a minimum rate is established by the Energy Tax Directive for heating fuel (EUR 0.021/litre), which is much lower than the one for motor fuel (EUR 0.3/litre of diesel). Only a few member countries (Czech Republic, Hungary and the Netherlands) apply practically the same excise duty rates for heating oil and diesel oil. Ireland, Luxembourg and the UK also apply a reduced VAT rate for heating oil, while none of the OECD countries reported reduced VAT rates for diesel or gasoline for cars.

The large differences in the excise duty rates are reflected in the wide variation in heating oil prices across the OECD, ranging from USD 0.705/litre in Luxembourg and 0.751/litre in Belgium (which have also the lowest excise rates) to USD 1.509/litre in Denmark and USD 1.877/litre in Israel.

3.6. Impact on cross-border trade

Differences in excise rates between countries often result from national traditions, social, environmental and health policy, local production and government financing needs. Such differences are not without impact on the cross-border movement of goods. The development of integrated markets (e.g. the European Union) and elimination of border controls at frontiers have shed light on the sometime considerable difference in excise between neighbouring countries to the extent that market forces are affected. In such circumstances, the effects of cross border shopping can have a significant economic impact on businesses and put pressure on the relevant tax authorities to seek closer approximation of excise duty rates with their neighbours. Differences between certain neighbouring countries may also encourage cross-border "bootlegging" activities (McKee Laura MacLehose Ellen Nolte et al., 2004[9]). Although some would argue that market forces should encourage a move towards convergence of rates, this is contradictory with other policy factors when issues such as health are taken into account in setting the rates.

3.7. Distributional impact of excise

While excise taxes can reduce the demand for the taxed goods that are considered harmful and thus the money that households spend on them over time, they can increase immediate budgetary pressure for lower income households if introduced without further support measures. It is thus important to understand the likely distributional impact of excise tax policy and to complement excise tax increases with compensatory measures, ideally through the social transfer and benefit system, to reduce adverse distributional consequences where appropriate. Flues and Van Dender (Flues and van Dender, 2017[10]) notably show that just one-third of the additional revenues raised from stronger excise taxes on energy may be sufficient to not only fully compensate lower income households for the tax increase but to even reduce their energy bill through cash transfers.

The distributional impact of excise taxes varies across the products on which they are imposed. A study by the OECD for 20 mainly European OECD countries showed that the combined impact of excise taxes on alcohol, tobacco and transport fuels tends to be regressive both when measured as a percentage of income and expenditure (OECD/KIPF, 2014[11]). These results imply that as households earn more they spend a smaller proportion of their income and total expenditure on these products. Exact burdens can vary depending on tax design. For example, if richer households consume more expensive alcohol and tobacco than poorer households, richer households will face relatively higher tax burdens with an *ad valorem* tax that taxes the value of the product compared to an *ad quantum* tax that taxes the quantity consumed.

For the tables in annex, references to the 'European Union and its Member States' includes the UK as a Member State for January 2020 and as an addition to the Member States ('Member States and the UK') for the period 1 February 2020 until the end of December 2020.

References

Belinda Loring (2014), *Tobacco and inequities*, World Health Organisation; European Union. [7]

Brys, B. et al. (2016), "Tax Design for Inclusive Economic Growth", *OECD Taxation Working Papers*, No. 26, OECD Publishing, Paris, https://dx.doi.org/10.1787/5jlv74ggk0g7-en. [2]

Federation of Tax Administrators (2020), *State Excise Tax Rates on Cigarettes*, FEDERATION OF TAX ADMINISTRATORS, https://www.taxadmin.org/assets/docs/Research/Rates/cigarette.pdf (accessed on 12 November 2020). [5]

Flues, F. and K. van Dender (2017), "The impact of energy taxes on the affordability of domestic energy", *OECD Taxation Working Papers*, No. 30, OECD Publishing, Paris, https://dx.doi.org/10.1787/08705547-en. [10]

Goodchild, M., A. Perucic and N. Nargis (2016), "Modelling the impact of raising tobacco taxes on public health and finance", *Bulletin of the World Health Organization*, Vol. 94/4, pp. 250-257, http://dx.doi.org/10.2471/blt.15.164707. [6]

KEEN, M. (1998), "The Balance between Specific and Ad Valorem Taxation", *Fiscal Studies*, Vol. 19/1, pp. 1-37, http://dx.doi.org/10.1111/j.1475-5890.1998.tb00274.x. [3]

McKee Laura MacLehose Ellen Nolte, M. et al. (2004), *Health policy and European Union enlargement*, http://www.openup.co.uk. [9]

OECD/KIPF (2014), *The Distributional Effects of Consumption Taxes in OECD Countries*, OECD Tax Policy Studies, No. 22, OECD Publishing, Paris, https://dx.doi.org/10.1787/9789264224520-en. [11]

Sassi, F., A. Belloni and C. Capobianco (2013), "The Role of Fiscal Policies in Health Promotion", *OECD Health Working Papers*, No. 66, OECD Publishing, Paris, https://dx.doi.org/10.1787/5k3twr94kvzx-en. [1]

WHO (2019), *WHO report on the global tobacco epidemic 2019: offer help to quit tobacco use*, WHO. [4]

World Health Organisation (2016), *Earmarked Tobacco Taxes - Experience from nine countries*. [8]

Annex 3.A. Excise duties

Annex Table 3.A.1. Taxation of beer

Country	Currency	Specific excise per hectoliter per % abv[1]		Lower excise for small independent breweries			Excise duty on low alcohol beer Excise on hectoliter of product		VAT rate	Excise rate progressive by strength
		National currency	USD	Annual production (hl)	National currency	USD	National currency	USD	%	
Australia*	AUD	Country note		Country note			Country note		10.0	Yes
Austria	EUR	5.00	5.62	≤ 12 500	3	3.37	–	–	20.0	No
				≤ 25 000	3.5	3.93			20.0	
				≤ 37 500	4	4.49			20.0	
				≤ 50 000	4.5	5.06			20.0	
Belgium	EUR	5.01	5.63	≤ 12 500	4.36	4.90	–	–	21.0	No
				≤ 25 000	4.50	5.06			21.0	
				≤ 50 000	4.65	5.22			21.0	
				≤ 75 000	4.79	5.38			21.0	
				≤ 200 000	4.94	5.55			21.0	
Canada*	CAD	Country note		Country note	Country note		Country note		5.0/13.0 15.0	Yes
Chile*	CLP	Country note		Country note			Country note		19.0	No
Colombia		Country note		Country note			Country note		19.0	
Czech Republic	CZK	80.00	3.42	≤ 10 000	40.00	1.71	–	–	21.0	No
				≤ 50 000	48.00	2.06			21.0	
				≤ 100 000	56.00	2.39			21.0	
				≤ 150 000	64.00	2.74			21.0	
				≤ 200 000	72.00	3.08			21.0	
Denmark*	DKK	48.74	7.31	≤ 3 700	Country note		0.00	0.00	25.0	No
				≤ 20 000	Country note				25.0	
				≤ 200 000	Country note				25.0	
Estonia	EUR	12.70	14.27	≤ 15 000	6.35	7.15	–	–	20.0	No
Finland*	EUR	36.50	41.01	≤ 5 000	18.25	20.51	11.40	8.88	24.0	No
				≤ 30 000	25.55	28.71			24.0	
				≤ 55 000	29.2028.44	32.81			24.0	
				≤ 100 000	32.85	36.85			24.0	
France*	EUR	7.49	8.42	≤ 200 000	3.75	4.21	3.75	4.21	20.0	No
Germany*	EUR	1.97	2.21	≤ 5 000	1.10	1.24	–	–	19.0	No
				≤ 10 000	1.32	1.48			19.0	
				≤ 20 000	1.54	1.73			19.0	
				≤ 40 000	1.65	1.85			19.0	
Greece	EUR	12.50	14.04	≤ 200 000	6.25	7.02	–	–	24.0	No

Hungary	HUF	1620.00	5.90	≤ 200 000	810.00	2.95	-	-	27.0	No
Iceland*	ISK	Country note		–	–	–	Country note	–	11.0	Yes
Ireland*	EUR	22.55	25.34	≤ 50 000	Country note		Country note		23.0	No
Israel*	ILS	235.00	66.01	–	–	–	Country note		17.0	No
Italy*	EUR	7.48	8.40	≤ 10 000	4.67	5.04	Country note	–	22.0	No
Japan*	JPY	Country note		≤ 100 000	Country note		–	–	10.0	No
Korea*	KRW	Country note					Country note		10.0	No
Latvia*	EUR	7.40	8.31	≤ 10 000	3.70	4.16	-	-	21.0	No
Lithuania	EUR	7.11	7.99	-	-	-	-	-	21.0	No
Luxembourg*	EUR	1.98	2.22	≤ 50 000	0.98	1.10	–	–	17.0	No
				≤ 200 000	1.12	1.26	–	–	17.0	
Mexico*	MXN	26.50%					–	–	16.0	Yes
Netherlands*	EUR	Country note		≤ 200 000	Country note	–	–	–	21.0	Yes
New Zealand*	NZD	29.05	20.61				Country note		15.0	No
Norway*	NOK	See note					Country note		25.0	Yes
Poland*	PLN	21.43	5.64	≤ 200 000	Country note		–	–	23.0	No
Portugal*	EUR	See note		≤ 200 000	Country note		Country note		23.0	No
Slovak Republic	EUR	3.59	4.03	≤ 200 000	2.65	2.98	–	–	20.0	No
Slovenia*	EUR	12.10	13.60	≤ 20 000	6.05	6.80	–	–	22.0	No
Spain*	EUR	Country note		–	–	–	Country note		21.0	No
Sweden	SEK	202.00	23.63	–	–	–	–	–	25.0	No
Switzerland*	CHF	Country note		≤ 55 000	Country note		Country note		7.7	Yes
Turkey*	TRY	204.42	3.59	–	–	–	–	–	18.0	No
United Kingdom*	GBP	19.08	24.46	≤ 60 000	Country note		8.42	10.79	20.0	No
United States*	USD	Country note		≤ 2 347 000	Country note		–	–		No

Notes

*See Country notes

Conversion of national currency in USD: conversion rates are average market rates (2019) published in OECD Monthly Monetary Statistics (*stats.oecd.org*).

1. % abv = percentage of pure alcohol by volume at 20°C. In some countries, the excise rate on beer is calculated per hectolitre per degree Plato. For ease of reading, all amounts have been converted in % abv. There is no precise conversion between degrees Plato and % abv but for tax purposes it is often assumed that 1% abv is equivalent to 2.5 degrees Plato. As a result, tax rates expressed in degree Plato have been multiplied by 2.5 to obtain the % abv.

Source: national delegates; position as at 1 January 2020.

StatLink https://doi.org/10.1787/888934220173

Annex Box 3.A.1. Country notes to Table 3.A.1.

Australia. The excise rates for beer in individual containers of less than 8 litres; or individual containers of at least 8 litres but not exceeding 48 litres and not designed to connect to a pressurised gas delivery system or pump delivery system are: AUD 43.53 per litre of alcohol where the alcohol volume does not exceed 3%, AUD 50.70 where the alcohol volume exceeds 3% but does not exceed 3.5%, and AUD 50.70 where the alcohol volume exceeds 3.5%. The excise rates for beer in individual containers exceeding 48 litres; or individual containers of at least 8 litres but not exceeding 48 litres and designed to connect to a pressurised gas delivery system or pump delivery system are: AUD 8.71 per litre of alcohol where the alcohol volume does not exceed 3%, AUD 27.26 where the alcohol volume exceeds 3% but does not exceed 3.5%, and AUD 35.71 where the alcohol volume exceeds 3.5%. Lower rates also apply for beer produced for non-commercial purposes using commercial facilities or equipment, being AUD 3.06 per litre of alcohol for beer where the alcohol volume does not exceed 3% and 3.53 per litre of alcohol for beer where the alcohol volume is 3% or more. Excise duty on beer is calculated on the amount by which the alcohol content exceeds 1.15% by volume of alcohol. Beer that does not contain more than 1.15% by volume of alcohol is not subject to excise duty. These rates are indexed to inflation in February and August each year. Eligible manufacturers can receive a refund of 60% of the excise duty paid up to a maximum of AUD 100 000 per financial year.

Canada. Excise duty rates for beer are imposed per hectolitre of product (not per hectolitre per degree alcohol). Provincial and territorial governments also charge taxes and mark-ups on beer. Federal excise duty rates, on all beer or malt liquor containing: (1) more than 2.5% abv, CAD 33.03 per hectolitre; (2) more than 1.2% abv but not more than 2.5% abv, CAD 16.52 per hectolitre; (3) not more than 1.2% abv, CAD 2.742 per hectolitre. Reduced rates of excise duty apply on the first 75 000 hectolitres of beer and malt liquor brewed in Canada per year by licensed brewers: the aforementioned rates are reduced by (1) 90%, on the first 2 000 hectolitres, (2) 80%, on the next 3 000 hectolitres, (3) 60%, on the next 10 000 hectolitres, (4) 30%, on the next 35 000 hectolitres, and (4) 15%, on the next 25 000 hectolitres. Automatic inflationary adjustments on duty rates for beer occur annually on April 1.

Chile. The sale of alcoholic beverages (including wine, beer, distilled alcoholic beverages and other alcoholic beverages) is subject to 19% VAT and also to a surtax on the sale or import of alcoholic beverages. The rate applied to beer is of 20.5% and does not depend upon the degree of alcohol that the beer contains. The tax is applied to the VAT base, that is the sale`s price (excluding VAT itself) and levies sales made between wholesale dealers. For sales between wholesalers, the tax paid to the vendor is creditable against the tax applied on sales at each stage of the value chain (including imports) until the last sale to the final retailer. The sale from the retailer to the final consumer is not subject to the surtax and the retailer cannot deduct the input tax.

Colombia. The sale of beer is subject to an excise tax of 48% for beers produced in Colombia and an additional VAT of 19% after reducing the taxable base with the excise tax. Regarding foreign produced beers, the excise tax is determined by the Ministry of Finance on a semester basis.

Denmark. Lower rates on small independent breweries: production ≤ 3 700 hl receives a tax reduction of DKK 77.08 per hl; production ≤ 20 000 (X) receives a tax reduction of DKK 259.81/X + 6.83 per hl; production < 200 000 hl receives a tax reduction of DKK 22.02 - X/9083 per hl. An additional duty is placed on products which contain a mixture of beer and non-alcoholic drinks. Rates: DKK 9.38/l. of mixture with alcohol content ≤ 10% vol. in the final product and DKK 16.39/l. of mixture with alcohol content >10% vol. in the final product. Beer with alcohol content less than 2.8% vol. is free of excise tax.

Finland. Beer with an alcoholic content less than 0.5 % vol. is free of excise.

France. Beer with alcoholic content above 18% support an additional taxation for social budget : EUR 3.05/degree of alcohol/hectolitre

Germany. From 1 July to 31 December 2020 the VAT rate is reduced from 19% to 16% to offset the economic impact of the Covid-19 pandemic.

Iceland. The duty in Iceland is ISK 125.65 per centilitre of alcohol per litre minus 2.25 centilitres. For example, one litre of beer that has 6% abv has 6 centilitres alcohol per litre. Therefore, the duty for one litre of beer that contains 6% abv would be as follows: (6-2.25) * 125.65 = ISK 472.2 per litre. As a result of this formula, beer with less than 2.25% abv is not taxed.

Ireland. There is remission or repayment of 50% alcohol products tax (excise duty) on beer brewed in independent small breweries producing up to 50 000 hl a year. Budget 2020 increased the qualifying production level from 40 000 to 50 000 hectolitres but maintained the current 30 000 hectolitre limit for remission/repayment of APT. For low alcohol beer, the rate is 0.00 (beer ≤ 1.2% abv) and EUR 11.27 (beer > 1.2% abv up to 2.8% abv).

Israel. The duty was set as ILS 235 on 1 January 2020. The amount is updated each year according to the change in the Consumer Price Index (CPI). There is no duty on beer under 2% alcohol (or under 3.8% alcohol if marketed in reusable bottles).

Italy. Beer with volume of alcohol does not exceed 0.5 percent is not taxed. For small breweries with an annual production of no more than 10 000 hectolitres, the excise duty rate for beer is reduced by 40 percent.

Japan. Excise rates are JPY 22 000 per hl of product. Reduced rates for small brewers (annual production of liquor up to 100 000 hl) apply for the first 2 000 hl of beer per year at the following rates: (a) if annual production of beer is less than or equal to 10 000 hl JPY 18 700/hl; (b) if annual production of beer is more than 10 000 hl or less than or equal to 13 000 hl, JPY 20 350/hl (temporary measure). Reference information (FY2017 Liquor tax reform). From 1 October 2020, the excise rates for liquor were changed in order to restore fairness in tax burden between different types of beer. Specifically, the excise rates for beer and beer-like liquors will be unified at JPY 15 500 per hl in October 2026 (the revision will be implemented in three stages).

Korea. The tax rate of beer is KRW 830.300 per kilolitre (as for beer sold in the container sized 8 litre or bigger that uses a separate dispensing tap before December 31, 2021, KRW 664.200 of tax rate applied). Each year, the beer tax rate is determined in accordance with the changes in consumer price index.

Latvia. Starting from 1 March 2020 the excise per hectolitre per % abv is EUR 7.8; excise per hectolitre per % abv for small independent breweries is EUR 3.9 (not less than EUR 14.4 per hectolitre of beer). The reduced rate for small independent breweries (annual production up to 50 000 hl) is applied for the first produced 10 000 hl of beer.

Lithuania. Beer with an alcoholic content of less than 0.5% vol. is free of excise.

Luxembourg. Rates for small breweries (annual production up to 200 000 hl) range from EUR 0.40 to EUR 0.45. Additional rate for alcopops: EUR 600 per hectolitre.

Mexico. The rates apply to the value of the goods as follows: 26.5% for beer and other alcoholic beverages up to 14° Gay-Lussac (GL); 30% for beverages above 14° G.L. and up to 20° G.L.; 53% for beverages above 20° G.L.

Netherlands. Excise duty rates are as follows per hectolitre of product: a) Up to 7° Plato EUR 8.83; b) 7°-11° Plato EUR 28.49; c) 11°-15° Plato EUR 37.96; d) 15 or more degrees Plato EUR 47.48. Rates for small breweries (annual production up to 200 000 hl) are as follows: a) up to 7° Plato the above mentioned rate; b) 7°-11° Plato EUR 26.35; c) 11-15 degrees Plato EUR 35.11; d) 15 or more degrees Plato EUR 43.92. For beer with a maximum alcohol content of 0.5% a consumer tax of EUR 8.83 per hectolitre is applicable and a VAT rate of 9%.

New Zealand. The excise rate for beer containing more than 2.5% abv is NZD 29.054 per litre of alcohol in finished product. The rate for beer containing more than 1.15% abv but not more than 2.5% abv is NZD 0.43573 per litre of product. There is no excise duty on beer containing less than 1.15% abv.

Norway. Excise rates are as follows per hectolitre of product: a) 0.0-0.7% abv: NOK 0; b) 0.7-2.7% abv: NOK 351; c) 2.7-3.7% abv: NOK 1 318; d) 3.7-4.7% abv: NOK 2 283. The excise rate for beer with an alcoholic content of more than 4.7% abv is NOK 511 per degree of alcohol and hectolitre.

Poland. Exemptions from excise for small breweries: 1) production ≤ 200 000 hl a year – 50% of the amount of excise duty calculated with the standard rate of excise duty on beer; if producers produce more than 200 000 hl a year – to all beer produced in a year is applied the standard rate of excise duty on beer with no possibility of excise tax exemption; the above rules also apply to producers who cooperate with each other; 2) intra-Community purchase or import of beer by entities that meet the conditions specified in law – 50% of the amount of excise duty calculated with the standard rate of excise duty on beer.

Portugal. Excise rates for beer are as follows per hectolitre of product: (a) >0.5. ≤ 1.2% abv EUR 8.34; (b) >1.2 ≤2.8% abv EUR 10.44; (c) > 2.8 ≤ 4.4% abv EUR 16.70; (d) > 4.4 ≤ 5.2% abv EUR 20.89; (e) > 5.2 ≤ 6% abv EUR 25.06; (f) >6% abv EUR 29.30 (rates as at 01 January 2020). Rates for small breweries (annual production up to 200 000 hl) are 50% of the normal rates.

Slovenia. Reduced rate for small breweries (yearly production ≤ 20 000 hl): EUR 6.05 per hl per % abv. Exemption for natural person use of beer if yearly production is less than 500 l. Reduced rate for small breweries (yearly production ≤ 20 000 hl) is 50% of the standard rate of excise duty for beer: EUR 6.05.

Spain. Excise rate according to strength is: beer < 1.2% abv is free of excise; beer between 1.2% and 2.8% abv is EUR 2.75/hl; beer between 2.8% abv and 11° Plato is EUR 7.48/hl; beer with a degree Plato > 11 and not > 15 = EUR 9.96/hl; beer with a degree Plato > 15 and not > 19 = EUR 13.56/hl; beer with a degree Plato > 19 = EUR 0.91/hl and per degree Plato. There is no tax on Beer in Ceuta and Melilla (Spanish cities situated in the North of Africa).

Sweden. The excise duty for beer with an alcoholic content below 2.8 % abv is SEK 0.

Switzerland. Rates per hectolitre: light beer (up to 10.0° Plato): CHF 16.88, regular and special beer (10.1 to 14.0° Plato): CHF 25.32, strong beer (from 14.1° Plato): CHF 33.76. For small breweries producing less than 55 000hl per year the tax rate is progressively reduced according to the volume of production up to 40 % reduction (annual production of max. 15 000 hl). Beer with more than 15 % vol. is taxed as an alcoholic beverage (CHF 2900 per hectolitre of absolute alcohol).

Turkey. The minimum tax amount is TL 134.98 per hectolitre/degree. If the amount computed according to the tax rate (63%) is lower than the minimum tax amount, the minimum tax amount is paid.

United Kingdom. Beer with an alcoholic content below 1.2% abv is free of excise duty. Lower strength beer duty applies to beer with a strength between 1.2% to 2.8% abv. High strength beer duty was introduced on 1 October 2011 and is a duty applied to all beer exceeding 7.5% abv. It is charged in addition to general beer duty.

Reduced duty rates apply for independent breweries making ‘Small Brewery Beer’. The rates are as follows;

- producing no more than 5 000 hl: 50% of the standard duty rate of duty
- producing more than 5 000 hl but no more than 30 000 hl – duty is calculated using the formula: Annual production minus 2500 /annual production x standard rate of duty
- producing more than 30 000 hl but no more than 60 000 hl – duty is calculated using the formula: Annual production minus (2500 minus 8.33% of annual production in excess of 30 000 hl)/annual production x standard rate of duty

Breweries making ‘Small Brewery Beer’ cannot claim a reduction in the rate of lower strength beer duty’.

United States. The weighted average Federal and State excise tax rate is USD 20 per hectolitre of product. The Federal tax is USD 16.00 per barrel (31 gallons) for the first 6 million barrels of beer and then USD 18.00 per barrel for each barrel after. 1 barrel = 1.1735 hectolitres. Small domestic brewers who produce less than 2 million barrels of beer per calendar year pay USD 3.50 in federal tax per barrel on the first 60 000 barrels and then USD 16.00 for each barrel over 60 000. There is no progressive rate structure based on alcohol content and no Federal VAT.

European Union. According to Directive 92/83/EEC, beer with an alcoholic content less than 0.5% abv. is not a beer and is not taxed in the EU.

Annex Table 3.A.2. Taxation of wine

Country	Currency	Still wine			Sparkling wine			Low-alcohol wine (< 8.5% abv)		
		Excise per hectolitre of product		VAT	Excise per hectolitre of product		VAT	Excise per hectolitre of product		VAT
		National currency	USD	%	National currency	USD	%	National currency	USD	%
Australia*	AUD	Country note	-	10.00	Country note	-	10.00	Country note	-	10.00
Austria	EUR	0.00	0.00	20.00	100.00	112.36	20.00	0.00	0.00	20.00
Belgium	EUR	74.91	84.17	21.00	256.32	288.40	21.00	23.91	26.87	21.00
Canada*	CAD	65.30	49.10	5.0/13.0 15.0	65.30	49.10	5.0/13.0 15.0	Country note	-	5.0/13.0 15.0
Chile*	CLP	Country note	-	19.00	Country note	-	19.00	Country note	-	19.00
Colombia	COP	Country note		5.0	Country note		5.0	Country note		5.0
Czech Republic	CZK	0.00	0.00	21.00	2340.00	100.04	21.00	0.00	0.00	21.00
Denmark*	DKK	1126.00	168.82	25.00	1461.00	219.04	25.00	518.00	77.66	25.00
Estonia*	EUR	147.82	166.09	20.00	147.82	166.09	20.00	63.35	71.18	20.00
Finland*	EUR	397.00	446.07	24.00	397.00	446.07	24.00	Country note	-	24.00
France*	EUR	3.82	4.29	20.00	9.44	10.61	20.00	3.82	4.29	20.00
Germany*	EUR	0.00	0.00	19.00	136.00	152.81	19.00	0.00	0.00	19.00
Greece	EUR	0.00	0.00	24.00	0.00	-	24.00	0.00	0.00	24.00
Hungary*	HUF	0.00	0.00	27.00	16460.00	59.97	27.00	0.00	0.00	27.00
Iceland*	ISK	Country note	-	11.00	Country note	-	11.00	Country note	-	11.00
Ireland*	EUR	424.84	477.35	23.00	849.68	954.70	23.00	141.57	159.07	23.00
Israel	ILS	0.00	0.00	17.00	See note	-	17.00	0.00	0.00	17.00
Italy	EUR	0.00	0.00	22.00	0.00	0.00	22.00	0.00	0.00	22.00
Japan	JPY	8000.00	73.33	10.00	8000.00	73.33	10.00	8000.00	73.33	10.00
Korea*	KRW	Country note	-	10.00	Country note	-	10.00	Country note	-	10.00
Latvia*	EUR	101.00	113.48	21.00	101.00	113.48	21.00	Country note		21.00
Lithuania*	EUR	164.67	185.02	21.00	164.67	185.02	21.00	65.46	73.55	21.00
Luxembourg*	EUR	0.00	0.00	14 or 17	0.00	0.00	17.00	0.00	0.00	14.00
Mexico*	MXN	26.5%/30%	-	16.00	26.5%/30%	-	16.00	26.5%	-	16.00
Netherlands*	EUR	88.30	99.21	21.00	88.30	99.21	21.00	44.24	49.71	21.00
New Zealand*	NZD	290,54	191.14	15.00	290,54	191.14	15.00	290,54	191.14	15.00
Norway*	NOK	6132.00	696.82	25.00	6132.00	696.82	25.00	Country note	-	25.00
Poland	PLN	174.00	45.31	23.00	174.00	45.31	23.00	174.00	45.31	23.00
Portugal	EUR	0.00	0.00	13.00	0.00	0.00	23.00	0.00	0.00	23.00
Slovak Republic*	EUR	0.00	0.00	20.00	79.65	89.49	20.00	0.00	0.00	20.00
Slovenia	EUR	0.00	0.00	22.00	0.00	0.00	22.00	0.00	0.00	22.00
Spain*	EUR	0.00	0.00	21.00	0.00	0.00	21.00	0.00	0.00	21.00
Sweden*	SEK	Country note	-	25.00	Country note	-	25.00	Country note	-	25.00
Switzerland*	CHF	0.00	0.00	7.70	0.00	0.00	7.70	0.00	0.00	7.70
Turkey*	TRY	1005.11	177.27	18.00	6790.74	1197.66	18.00	1005.11	177.27	18.00

United Kingdom*	GBP	288.65	370.06	20.00	369.72	474.00	20.00	88.93	114.01	20.00
United States*	USD	37.00	37.00	-	110.00	110.00	-	Country note	-	-

Notes
* See Country notes
Conversion of national currency in USD: conversion rates are average market rates (2019) published in OECD Monthly Monetary Statistics (*stats.oecd.org*).
Source: National delegates; position as at 1 January 2020

StatLink https://doi.org/10.1787/888934220192

Annex Box 3.A.2. Country notes to Table 3.A.2.

Australia. All wine (which includes grape wine, grape wine products, fruit or vegetable wine, cider or perry, mead and sake – subject to specific definitions) is generally subject to the wine equalisation tax (WET). WET applies at 29% of the wholesale value of the wine, and generally only applies when an entity is registered or required to be registered for goods and services tax (GST). The WET producer rebate, calculated as the amount of WET paid, or the amount of WET that would have been paid had the purchaser not quoted, applies to eligible producers in certain circumstances, up to a maximum of AUD 350 000 per financial year.

Canada. (1) A rate of CAD 0.653 per litre applies to wine with more than 7% abv. The rate is CAD 0.313 per litre on wine of more than 1.2% abv, but not more than 7%abv; and for all wine with 1.2% abv or less the rate is CAD 0.021 per litre. (2) Fortified wine in excess of 22.9% abv would not be included in the definition of "wine" (and, therefore, fall within the definition of "spirits"). Provincial and territorial governments also charge taxes and mark-ups on wine. Automatic inflationary adjustments on duty rates for wine occur annually on April 1.

Chile. The sale of alcoholic beverages is subject to a surtax of 20.5% on the sale or import of wine, sparkling wine, champagne, cider and other alcoholic beverages (among others). The tax is applied to the VAT base, that is the sale`s price (excluding VAT itself), and levies sales made between wholesale dealers. For sales between wholesalers, the tax paid to the vendor is creditable against the tax applied on sales at each stage of the value chain (including imports) until the last sale to the final retailer. The sale from the retailer to the final consumer is not subject to this surtax and the retailer cannot deduct the input tax nor is levied with this tax the sale of wine in bulk made by producers to a taxpayer seller subject to this surtax.

Colombia. The sale of wines is subject to a VAT of 5%, an ad valorem tax of 20% and a consumption tax of COP 150 per for each degree of alcohol (abv).

Denmark. The rate for high-alcohol wine > 15 % abv – maximum 22 % abv is DKK 1 508 per hectolitre. Medium-alcohol wine < 6% abv – maximum 15 % abv is DKK 1 126 per hectolitre. Low-alcohol wine < 1.2 % abv – maximum 6 % abv is DKK 518 per hectolitre. The rates for sparkling wine correspond to the rates for still wine plus DKK 335 per hectolitre. An additional duty is placed on products that contain a mixture of wine and non-alcoholic drinks. Rates: DKK 7.13 per litre of mixture with alcohol content ≤10 % abv in the final product and DKK 11.50 per litre of mixture with alcohol content > 10 % abv in the final product.

Estonia. Low alcohol wine means wine with alcohol content up to 6% abv.

Finland. Excise rates for low alcohol wine are as follows: a) over 1.2% abv and up to 2.8% abv EUR 32.00; b) over 2.8% abv and up to 5.5% abv EUR 191.00; c) over 5.5% abv and up to 8.0% abv EUR 275.00.

France. A reduced rate of EUR 1.34/hl applies to the following categories of low-alcohol wine: cider, perry, mead, grapes juice lightly sparking.

Germany. Excise rate for low alcohol sparkling wine < 6 % abv is EUR 51.00. Intermediate products with a volume of alcoholic degree between 1.2 % and 22 % abv are taxed according to the following rates: > 15 % abv - 22 % abv = EUR 153/hl; <= 15 % abv = EUR 102/hl; <= 15 % abv and sparkling = EUR 136/hl. Wine is not subject to an excise duty. Nevertheless, wine is subject to excise duty supervision in the German tax territory. *From 1 July to 31 December 2020 the VAT rate is reduced from 19% to 16% to offset the economic impact of the Covid-19 pandemic.*

Hungary. The rates for other fermented beverages (mostly fruit wines) are as follows: a) still: HUF 9870 per hectolitre of product, b) sparkling: HUF 16460 per hectolitre of product. c) low alcohol: HUF 0 per hectolitre of still blend of more than 50% wine and sparkling mineral water without added flavouring and not exceeding 8.5% vol. The rate for intermediate products is HUF 25520 per hectolitre of product.

Iceland. The duty rate is ISK 114.45 per centilitre of alcohol per litre minus 2.25 centilitres for wine up to 15% abv. For example, one litre of wine that has 15% abv has 15 centilitres alcohol per litre. So the duty for one litre of wine that contains 15% abv would be as follows: (15-2.25) * 114.45 = ISK 1459.2 per litre.

Ireland. The rate for low alcohol wine applies to wine with an alcoholic content not exceeding 5.5% abv. The rate for still wine with alcoholic content > 15% abv is EUR 616.45. The rate for still wine exceeding 5.5% vol but not exceeding 15% volume is EUR 424.84.

Japan. From 1 October 2020, the excise rate is JPY 9000 per hl.

Korea. The rate of liquor tax on wine is 30% on the manufacturer's price (or imported price). In addition, Education Tax (10% of the amount of Liquor tax levied) is also levied. These rates are applicable to both still and sparkling wine regardless of alcohol content.

Latvia. Starting from 1 March 2020 the excise for wine (still and sparkling) is EUR 106 per hectolitre. There is no specific rate for low-alcohol (still) wine (<8.5% abv).

Lithuania. Low-alcohol wine covers still and sparkling wine < 8.5% abv.

Luxembourg. The reduced VAT rate (14%) applies to still wine with alcoholic content ≤ 13% abv. Additional rate for alcopops: EUR 600 per hectolitre.

Mexico. All rates apply to the value of the goods, and not per hectolitre of product, as follows: 26.5% for beer and other alcoholic beverages up to 14° Gay-Lussac (GL); 30% for beverages above 14° G.L. and up to 20° G.L.; 53% for beverages above 20° G.L.

Netherlands. For low alcohol wine < 1.2% abv the VAT rate is 9%.

Norway. The rate shown in the table is the rate for wine with an alcoholic content of 12% abv. Excise rates for wine with an alcoholic content of 4.7%-22% abv = NOK 511 per vol. pct. alcohol and per hectolitre.

Slovak Republic. The rate of EUR 54.16/hl applies to sparkling fermented beverages with an alcoholic strength by volume not exceeding 8.5 % abv. The rate for intermediate products is EUR 84.24/hl.

Spain. Intermediate products - products to which distilled alcohol has been added - and with a volume of alcoholic degree between 1.2% abv and less than 22% abv are taxed according to the following rates: alcoholic degree > 1.2% abv and less than 15% abv = EUR 338.48/hl. Others = EUR 64.13/hl (in the Canary Islands rates are 30.14% and 50.21% respectively).

Sweden. Excise rates for alcohol wine (still and sparkling) are as follows: a) < 2.25%abv SEK 0; b) 2.25%-4.5% abv SEK 919; c) 4.5%-7% abv SEK 1358; d) 7%-8.5% abv SEK 1869; e) 8,5-15% abv SEK 2618; f) 15,0-18,0% abv SEK 5479.

Switzerland. In general natural wines made from fresh grapes with more than 18% abv and other wines with more than 15% abv are taxed as an alcoholic beverage (CHF 1 450 per hectolitre of absolute alcohol). All wines with more than 22% abv are taxed as an alcoholic beverage (CHF 2 900 per hectolitre of absolute alcohol).

Turkey. The excise rate is 0%.

United Kingdom. Reduced Rates for lower strength drinks (wine categories) are as follows: exceeding 1.2% but not exceeding 4% abv = GBP 88.93; (b) exceeding 4% but not exceeding 5.5% abv = GBP

122.30; (c) low strength sparkling wine exceeding 5.5% but less than 8.5% abv = GBP 279.46; (d) sparkling wine and made wine at least 8.5% abv but not exceeding 15% abv = GBP 369.72. Rate for the band exceeding 15% abv but not exceeding 22% abv = GBP 384.82. The duty rates on wine changed on 13 March 2017 to excise duty rate on still wine 288.65, reduced rate for lower strength drinks (wine categories) (a) exceeding 1.2% but not exceeding 4% abv = GBP 88.93 (b)exceeding 4% but not exceeding 5.5% abv = GBP 122.30 and (c) low strength sparkling wine exceeding 5.5% but less than 8.5% abv = 279.46 (d) sparkling wine and made wine at least 8.5% abv but not exceeding 15% abv = 369.72. Rate in the band exceeding 15% abv but not exceeding 22% abv = GBP 384.82.

United States. The weighted average Federal and State excise tax rate is USD 37 per hectolitre of product for still wine up to 16% abv and USD 110 for sparkling wine. The Federal excise rates are as follows: a) up to 16% abv: USD 0.07 per gallon for the first 30 000 wine gallons, USD 0.17 for each wine gallon over 30 000 up to 130 000, USD 0.535 for each wine gallon over 130 000 up to 750 000, and USD 1.07 per gallon over 750 000 gallons; b) 16%-21% abv: USD 0.57 per gallon for the first 30 000 wine gallons, USD 0.67 for each wine gallon over 30 000 up to 130 000, USD 1.035 for each wine gallon over 130 000 up to 750 000 gallons, and USD 1.57 per gallon over 750 000 gallons; c) 21%-24% abv: USD 2.15 for the first 30 000 wine gallons, USD 2.25 for each wine gallon over 30 000 up to 130 000, USD 2.615 for each wine gallon over 130 000 up to 750 000, and USD 3.15 per gallon over 750 000 gallons; d) artificially carbonated wine: USD 2.30 for the first 30 000 gallons, USD 2.40 for each gallon over 30 000 up to 130 000, USD 2.765 for each gallon over 130 000 up to 750 000, and USD 3.30 per gallon over 750 000 gallons; and e) sparkling wine: USD 2.40 for the first 30 000 gallons, USD 2.50 for each gallon over 30 000 up to 130 000, USD 2.865 for each gallon over 130 000 up to 750 000, and USD 3.40 per gallon over 750 000 gallons. 26.42 US gallons = 1 hectolitre. There is no Federal VAT.

Annex Table 3.A.3. Taxation of alcoholic beverages

Country	Currency	Tax per hectolitre of absolute alcohol			
		Excise		VAT rate	Small distillery rate
		National currency	USD	%	
Australia*	AUD	8587.00	5628.47	10.00	No
Austria*	EUR	1200.00	1348.31	20.00	Yes
Belgium	EUR	2992.79	3362.69	21.00	No
Canada*	CAD	1237.50	930.45	5.0/13.0/15.0	No
Chile*	CLP	Country note	-	19.00	No
Colombia	COP	Country note		5.00	No
Czech Republic	CZK	32250.00	1406.45	21.00	No
Denmark*	DKK	15000.00	2272.73	25.00	No
Estonia	EUR	1881	2113.48	20.00	No
Finland*	EUR	4880.00	5483.15	24.00	No
France*	EUR	1758.54	1975.89	20.00	No
Germany*	EUR	1303.00	1464.04	19.00	Yes
Greece*	EUR	2450.00	2752.81	24.00	No
Hungary*	HUF	333385.00	1214.61	27.00	Yes
Iceland*	ISK	1549000.00	12633.55	11.00	No
Ireland*	EUR	4257.00	4783.15	23.00	No
Israel	ILS	8551.00	2340.00	17.00	No
Italy*	EUR	1035.52	1160.13	22.00	No
Japan*	JPY	Country note	-	10.00	No
Korea*	KRW	See note	-	10.00	No
Latvia*	EUR	1564.00	1757.30	21.00	Yes
Lithuania*	EUR	1832.00	2401.97	21.00	No
Luxembourg	EUR	1041.15	1169.83	17.00	No
Mexico*	MXN	53%	-	16.00	No
Netherlands*	EUR	1686.00	1894.38	9.0/21.0	No
New Zealand*	NZD	Country note	-	15.00	No
Norway	NOK	78400.00	8909.09	25.00	No
Poland	PLN	6275.00	1634.11	23.00	No
Portugal*	EUR	1386.93	1558.35	23.00	Yes
Slovak Republic*	EUR	1080.00	1213.48	20.00	No
Slovenia*	EUR	1320.00	1483.15	22.00	Yes
Spain*	EUR	958.94	1077.46	21.00	Yes
Sweden	SEK	51659.00	6031.46	25.00	No
Switzerland*	CHF	2900.00	2929.29	7.70	Yes
Turkey*	TRY	27929.02	4925.75	18.00	No
United Kingdom*	GBP	2874.00	3684.62	20.00	No
United States*	USD	909.00	909.00	-	No

Notes
* See Country notes
Conversion of national currency in USD: conversion rates are average market rates (2019) published in OECD Monthly Monetary Statistics (*stats.oecd.org*).
Source: national delegates. Position as at 1 January 2020.

StatLink https://doi.org/10.1787/888934220211

Annex Box 3.A.3. Country notes to Table 3.A.3.

Australia. The excise duty of AUD 85.87 per litre of alcohol applies to spirits and other excisable beverages (except beer). A lower rate of AUD 80.20 per litre of alcohol applies to brandy (distilled from grape wine). These rates apply as of 1 August 2019 and are indexed to inflation in February and August of each year. Independent distillers receive an excise refund of 60% of the excise paid up to a maximum of AUD 100 000 per financial year.

Austria. For small distilleries producing not more than 4hl pure alcohol per year the rate is EUR 648.(54% of the standard rate).

Canada. (1) Spirits are subject to excise duty at the rate of CAD 12.375 per litre abv. Spirits containing not more than 7% abv are subject to excise duty at the rate of CAD 0.313 per litre. (2) Beer with an alcoholic strength in excess of 11.9% abv and fortified wine with an alcoholic strength in excess of 22.9% abv are deemed to be Spirits. Provincial and territorial governments also charge taxes and mark-ups on spirits. Automatic inflationary adjustments on duty rates for alcoholic beverages occur annually on April 1.

Chile. Alcoholic beverages are subject to a surtax on the sale or import. The rates applied are the following: 31.5% on liquors, brandy, vermouth, pisco, whiskey and other distilled alcoholic beverages; 20.5% on beer, wine, sparkling wine, champagne, cider and other alcoholic beverages. The tax is applied to the VAT base, that is the sale`s price (excluding VAT itself) and levies sales made between wholesale dealers. For sales between wholesalers, the tax paid to the vendor is creditable against the tax applied on sales at each stage of the value chain (including imports) until the last sale to the final retailer. The sale from this retailer to the final consumer is not subject to the surtax and the retailer cannot deduct the input tax nor is levied with this tax the sale of wine in bulk made by producers to a taxpayer seller subject to this surtax.

Colombia. Alcoholic beverages are subject to a 5% VAT, and ad valorem tax of 25% and a consumption tax of COP 236 for each degree of alcohol.

Czech Republic. The reduced rate of CZK 16 200 per hectolitre of pure alcohol applies for small fruit grower's distilleries producing no more than 30 litres of fruit spirit per year per household. The excise duty of CZK 2 340 per hectolitre of product is applicable for intermediate products.

Denmark. An additional duty is placed on products which contain a mixture of spirits and non-alcoholic drinks, Rates: DKK 4.21 per litre of mixture.

Finland. Excise rates are as follows: (a) CN - code 2208 alcoholic content between 1.2% abv and 2.8% abv. EUR 1140; (b) Other products EUR 4 880.

France. Additional taxation for social budget: EUR 573.64 per hectolitre of absolute alcohol.

Germany. The rates for small distilleries are EUR 730 or EUR 1 022. Additional rate for alcopops: EUR 5 550 per hectolitre of absolute alcohol. From 1 July to 31 December 2020 the VAT rate is reduced from 19% to 16% to offset the economic impact of the Covid-19 pandemic.

Greece. The rate for ouzo is EUR 1 225 per hectolitre of pure alcohol.

Hungary. A reduced rate of 50% applies to ethyl-alcohol produced by fruit growers' distilleries from fruit supplied to them by private fruit growers. The application of reduced rate is limited to 43 litres of pure alcohol for private consumption per fruit grower household per year.

Iceland. Excise rate shown in the table is the rate for other alcohol than beer or wine up to 15% abv. The rate is ISK 154.9 per each centilitre of alcohol.

Ireland. This table illustrates the tax per hectolitre of absolute alcohol for spirits. However, other fermented beverages and intermediate beverages are taxed as follows: other fermented beverages (cider and perry) still and sparkling ≤ 2.8% abv EUR 47.23/hl; still and sparkling > 2.8% avb but not exceeding 6.0% avb EUR 94.46/hl; still and sparkling >6.0% avb but not exceeding 8.5% avb EUR 218.44/hl; still >8.5% avb EUR 309.84/hl and sparkling >8.5% avb EUR 619.70/hl. Other fermented beverages (other than cider and perry) still and sparkling ≤ 5.5% abv EUR 141.57/hl; still >5.5% avb EUR 424.84/hl and sparkling >5.5% avb EUR 849.68/hl. Intermediate beverages: still ≤ 15% abv EUR 424.84/hl; still >15% avb EUR 616.45/hl; sparkling EUR 849.68/hl.

Italy. Taxation applies for beverages of alcoholic strength exceeding 1.2% abv. The rate of EUR 88.67 per hectolitre applies to intermediate products.

Japan. Excise rates are as follows (per hectolitre): a) Whiskey and brandy (40% abv) JPY 40 000; b) Spirits (37% abv) JPY 37 000; c) Shochu Group A and B (25% abv) JPY 25 000.

Korea. As Excise Tax for liquor is based on the value of the product, the rate does not vary with alcohol content. For whiskey, brandy, general distilled spirits, liquor, diluted soju and distilled soju, the Liquor tax is 72% and the Education tax is 30%.

Latvia. Starting from 1 March 2020 the excise rate is EUR 1642 per hectolitre of absolute alcohol. The reduced excise rate for ethyl alcohol produced by small distillery (not more than 10 hl of absolute alcohol) is applied since 1 March 2019. Starting from 1 March 2020 the reduced rate is EUR 821 per hectolitre of absolute alcohol.

Lithuania. Intermediate products below 15% abv are taxed at 185.82 per hectolitre of product; intermediate products above 15% abv are taxed at 264.52 per hectolitre of product. Ethyl alcohol is taxed at EUR 2025.00 per hectolitre of product at 1 March 2020.

Luxembourg. Additional rate for alcopops: EUR 600 per hectolitre.

Mexico. The excise tax is set at an ad valorem rate and not per hectolitre of product. The rates for alcoholic beverages apply to the value of the goods as follows: 26.5% up to 14° Gay-Lussac (G.L.); 30% above 14° G.L. and up to 20° G.L.; 53% above 20° G.L.

Netherlands. For low alcohol spirits with an alcoholic content <1.2% the VAT rate is 9%.

New Zealand. For alcoholic beverages with 9-14% abv, the excise rate is NZD 2.9054 per litre. For alcoholic beverages above 14% abv, the excise rate is NZD 52.916 per litre of absolute alcohol (with the exception of unfortified wine and vermouth which has the rate of NZD 2.7870 per litre of product).

Portugal. Intermediate products are taxed at EUR 76,10/hl; Ethyl alcohol/spirits: EUR 1 386,93/hl (rates as at 01 January 2020). A reduced rate of 50% applies to small distilleries.

Slovak Republic. A reduced rate of 50 % of the national rate of excise duty on ethyl alcohol, applies to ethyl alcohol produced by fruit growers´ distilleries. The application of the reduced rate is limited to 43 litres of ethyl alcohol for personal consumption of the fruit growers´ household per year.

Slovenia. Tax per hectolitre of absolute alcohol is EUR 1 320. For small producers not producing more than 150 litres of pure alcohol per year, the rate is EUR 660 per hl.

Spain. The excise rate in the Canary Islands is EUR 750.36 per hl of pure alcohol. There is a special regime for small distilleries for which the rate is EUR 839.15 per hl (or EUR 653.34 in the Canary Islands).

Sweden. Excise rates for alcoholic beverages (other than beer and wine) are as follow: a) <2.25% abv SEK 0; b) 2.25%-4.5% abv SEK 919; c) 4.5%-7% abv SEK 1358; d) 7%-8.5% abv SEK 1869; e) 8.5%-

15% abv SEK 2618. Intermediate products, a) 1.2%-15% abv SEK 3299; b) 15%-22% abv SEK 5479. Ethyl alcohol, 100 % abv SEK 51659.

Switzerland. Under certain conditions farmers do not pay tax on the alcohol produced for their personal consumption. A reduced rate of 30 % is applied to the first 30 litres of pure alcohol produced per year by small producers. Normal rate: CHF 2900 per hectolitre. Special rate for certain types of wines: CHF 1450 per hectolitre. Special rate for alcopops: CHF 11 600 per hectolitre (Alcopop -also called ready to drink (RTD) or designer drink) is a mix of alcohol and soda.

Turkey. The excise rate is 0%. If the tax amount computed according to the tax rate is lower than the minimum tax amount specified in the table, then the minimum tax amount is paid.

United Kingdom. All drinks over 22% are taxed as spirits. Most other mixtures of spirits with other types of alcohol are also taxed as spirits. The duty rates for cider and perry are: still cider and perry exceeding 1.2% but not exceeding 7.5% abv =GBP 40.38; still cider and perry exceeding 7.5% but less than 8.5% abv = GBP 61.04; sparkling cider and perry exceeding 1.2% abv but not exceeding 5.5% abv = GBP 279.46; sparkling cider and perry exceeding 5.5% but not exceeding 8.5% abv = GBP 279.46.

United States. The weighted average Federal and State excise tax rate is USD 909 per hectolitre. The Federal excise rate is USD 2.70 per proof gallon for the first 100 000 proof gallons, USD 13.34 on the next 22 130 000 proof gallons, and USD 13.50 for every proof gallon over 22 230 000. A proof gallon is a US gallon (3.785 litres) containing 50% alcohol. There is no Federal VAT.

Annex Table 3.A.4. Taxation of tobacco

Country	Currency	Cigarettes			Cigars[2]			Rolling tobacco for cigarettes			VAT
		Specific excise per 1 000		Excise on value	Specific excise per 1 000		Excise on value	Specific excise per 1 000 grams		Excise on value	
		National currency	USD	% of RSP[1]	National currency	USD	% of RSP[1]	National currency	USD	% of RSP[1]	%
Australia*	AUD	936.53	650.37	0.00	Country note	-	0.00	1291.77	897.06	0.00	10.00
Austria*	EUR	58.00	65.17	37.50	0.00	0.00	13.00	0.00	0.00	56.00	20.00
Belgium	EUR	66.47	72.58	40.04	0.00	0.00	10.00	48.31	47.58	31.50	21.00
Canada*	CAD	121.89	91.65	00.00	Country note	-	Country note	152.36	114.56	00.00	5.0/13.0/15.0
Chile*	CLP	46323.00	71.41	30.00	0.00	0.00	52.60	0.00	0.00	59.70	19.00
Colombia	COP	121 500.00	37.03	10.00	121 500.00	37.03	10.00	193 000.00	58.83	10.00	19.00
Czech Republic	CZK	1610.00	70.21	30.00	1880.00	81.99	-	2460.00	107.28	-	21.00
Denmark*	DKK	1737.90	260.55	1.00	500.00	75.76	10.00	1350.90	202.53	0.00	25.00
Estonia*	EUR	81.95	92.08	30.00	151.00	169.66	10.00	89.63	100.71	0.00	20.00
Finland*	EUR	69.75	78.37	52.00	30.00	33.71	34.00	46.50	52.25	52.00	24.00
France	EUR	62.00	69.66	52.70	35.30	39.66	32.30	76.20	85.62	46.70	20.00
Germany*	EUR	98.20	110.34	21.69	14.00	15.73	1.47	48.49	54.48	14.76	19.00
Greece	EUR	82.50	92.70	26.00	0.00	0.00	35.00	170.00	191.01	0.00	24.00
Hungary*	HUF	20 500.00	70.53	23.00	0.00	0.00	14.00	20 100.00	69.15	0.00	27.00
Iceland*	ISK	257.97.50	210.40	0.00	Country note	-	0.00	28700.00	234.08	0.00	24.00
Ireland*	EUR	346.04	388.81	8.91	Country note	-	0.00	379.83	426.78	0.00	23.00
Israel*	ILS	400.94	112.62	Country note	0.00	0.00	Country note	1138.04	319.67	0.00	17.00
Italy	EUR	19.36	21.75	59.10	0.00	0.00	23.00	0.00	0.00	58.50	22.00
Japan*	JPY	13244.00	121.49	0.00	13244.00	121.49	0.00	13244.00	112.32	0.00	10.00
Korea*	KRW	145 720.00	125.03	64.76	Country note	-	0.00	103200.00	88.55	0.00	10.00
Latvia*	EUR	78.70	88.43	20.00	95.20	106.97	-	75.00	88.55	-	21.00
Lithuania*	EUR	62.25	69.94	25.00	42.00	47.19	-	68.60	84.27	-	21.00
Luxembourg	EUR	18.89	21.22	46.65	0.00	0.00	10.00	16.50	18.54	33.15	17.00
Mexico*	MXN	494.4	25.67	39.07	Country note	-	Country note	Country note	-	Country note	16.00
Netherlands	EUR	219.25	246.35	5.00	0.00	0.00	8.00	155.97	175.25	0.00	21.00
New Zealand*	NZD	Country note	-	0.00	Country note	-	0.00	Country note	-	0.00	15.00
Norway	NOK	2680.00	304.55	0.00	2680.00	304.55	0.00	2680.00	304.55	0.00	25.00

Poland*	PLN	228.10	59.40	32.05	433.00	112.76	-	155.70	40.55	32.05	23.00
Portugal*	EUR	96.12	108.00	15.00	0.00	0.00	25.00	81.00	91.01	15.00	23.00
Slovak Republic*	EUR	64.10	72.02	23.00	76.70	86.18	-	76.70	86.18	0.00	20.00
Slovenia*	EUR	73.64	82.74	21.88	0.00	0.00	6.30	43.00	46.62	37.00	22.00
Spain	EUR	24.70	27.75	51.00	0.00	0.00	15.80	23.50	26.40	41.50	21.00
Sweden	SEK	1600.00	169.13	1.00	1410.00	149.05	0.00	1957.00	206.87	0.00	25.00
Switzerland*	CHF	118.32	119.52	25.00	5.60	5.66	1.00	38.00	38.38	25.00	7.70
Turkey*	TRY	485.1	85.56	67.00	500.80	88.32	80.00	485.10	85.56	40	18.00
United Kingdom*	GBP	228.29	292.68	16.50	284.76	365.08	0.00	234.65	300.83	0.00	20.00
United States*	USD	141.00	141.00	Country note	Country note	-	-	Country note	-	-	-

Notes
* See Country notes
Conversion of national currency in USD: conversion rates are average market rates (2019) published in OECD Monthly Monetary Statistics (*stats.oecd.org*).
1. RSP. Retail selling price.
2. Cigars. Denmark and Japan tax cigars at a rate per 1 000 pieces and not according to weight. In Denmark it is assumed that a cigar weighs 3 grams and in Japan 1 gram.
Source: national delegates. Position as at 1 January 2020

StatLink https://doi.org/10.1787/888934220230

Annex Box 3.A.4. Country notes to Table 3.A.4.

Australia. The excise rate of AUD 0.93653 per stick applies to cigarettes or cigars (in stick form) not exceeding in weight 0.8 grams per stick actual tobacco content. Other tobacco products are subject to an excise rate of AUD 1291.77 per kilogram of tobacco content. These rates apply from 1 January 2020.

Austria. The excise duty on cigars is 13% of RSP, at least EUR 100 for 1 000 pieces. Minimum excise duty on rolling tobacco for cigarettes is EUR 100 per kg. The minimum excise duty on cigarettes is 98% of the total excise duty burden on cigarettes falling under the WAP.

Canada. The excise duty on cigars is CAD 26.5294 per 1 000 cigars plus an additional excise duty based on the greater of CAD 0.09536 per cigar and 88% of the sale price. Each province and territory also levies a tobacco tax at varying rates on all tobacco products. Retail sales prices are subject to GST/HST and, in some cases, when the HST is not applicable, to a provincial sales tax. Automatic inflationary adjustments on tobacco duty rates occur annually on April 1.

Chile. The sale of tobacco products is subject to 19% VAT. There is also a tax levied on the sale or import of processed tobacco, cigarettes and cigars. The tax rate applied on the sale price of processed tobacco is 59.7%. Cigars are taxed at a rate of 52.6%. Cigarettes are taxed at a rate of 30% on the pack's sale price and an additional rate of 0,0010304240 is levied on a Monthly Tax Unit for each cigarette in a cigarette's pack (Monthly Tax Unit: CLP 47 019 or USD 76.48 approx.). The tax base of the excise tax considers the sale price to the final consumer, the VAT and the tax levied on tobacco, cigarettes and cigars.

Denmark. The excise tax for other smoking tobaccos is DKK 1300.90 / 1 000 g. for coarse-cut tobacco

Estonia. For cigarettes, the minimal excise amount to be paid is EUR 138.65 per 1000 items. For cigars and cigarillos, the minimal excise amount to be paid is EUR 211 per 1000 items.

Finland. Excise rates shown as of 1 January 2020. Cigarette paper: excise 60% of RSP. Other smoking tobacco: EUR 65.00 /kg and 48 % of RSP. Minimum excise tax for cigarettes is EUR 282.75 per 1000 pieces and EUR 173.50 /kg for fine cut rolling tobacco for cigarettes.

France. The minimal excise amounts to be paid are EUR 297 per 1000 items for cigarettes, EUR 205 per 1000 items for cigars and EUR 260 per 1000g for rolling tobacco for cigarettes.

Germany. Minimum excise duty is EUR 163.6 per 1 000 cigarettes. Minimum excise duty is EUR 70.97 /kg of rolling tobacco for cigarettes. Other smoking tobacco is subject to excise duty at a rate of EUR 15.66/kg and 13.13% of RSP. Minimum excise duty is EUR 22/kg for other smoking tobacco. *From 1 July to 31 December 2020 the VAT rate is reduced from 19% to 16% to offset the economic impact of the Covid-19 pandemic.*

Hungary. Minimum excise tax is HUF 33 500 per 1000 pieces for cigarettes, HUF 4 180 per 1000 pieces for cigar and cigarillo. VAT as % of tax included retail selling price is 21.26%.

Iceland. There is no specific excise rate for a piece of cigar. The rate is ISK 28 700 per 1000 grams of cigars (i.e. the same rate as for rolling tobacco).

Ireland. The rate of excise duty on cigarettes is EUR 346.04 per 1000 cigarettes together with an amount equal to 8.91% of the price at which the cigarettes are sold by retail or EUR 395.05 per 1000 cigarettes, whichever is the greater. The rate of excise duty on cigars is EUR 394.811 per kilogram. The rate of excise duty on fine-cut tobacco for the rolling of cigarettes is EUR 379.831 per kilogram. Other smoking tobacco is subject to excise duty at a rate of EUR 273.903 per kilogram.

Israel. Excises on value for cigarettes are 270% of the wholesale price plus ILS 400.94 per 1000 cigarettes and for cigars the excise is 90% of the wholesale price.

Japan. The tax consists of a national element, a prefectural element and a municipal element. From 1 October 2020, the excise rate is JPY 14 244 per 1 000 pieces (cigarettes, cigars) or per 1 000 grams (rolling tobacco for cigarettes).

Korea. The excise tax on cigars is KRW 294800/1000g. National tax (Individual Consumption Tax) levies on tobacco since 2015.

Latvia. Starting from 1 July 2019 minimum excise is EUR 114.70 per 1000 cigarettes.

Lithuania. Minimum excise for cigarettes is EUR 102.00 per 1000 pieces from 1 March 2019. Starting from 1 March 2020 the specific excise for cigarettes is EUR 65.70 per 1000 pieces; minimum excise is EUR 108.50 per 1000 cigarettes. The excise rate for cigars and cigarillos is set per kilogram. Starting from 1 March 2020 excise for cigars and cigarillos is EUR 48.00 per kilogram. For smoking tobacco (rolling tobacco for cigarettes and other smoking tobacco) the excise is EUR 78.50 per kilogram. From 1 March 2019 liquids for e-cigarettes are subject to excise duty and the excise duty rate for them is EUR 0.12 per ml of the product. From 1 March 2019 heated tobacco products are subject to excise duty as a separate category at a rate of EUR 68.60 per kilogram. From 1 March 2020, this rate is increased to EUR 113.2 per kilogram. Until 28 February 2019, the rate of smoking tobacco was applied for heated tobacco products.

Luxembourg. Change of excise duties on tobacco products is generally applicable starting 1st February. Minimum excise duty is EUR 116 per 1 000 cigarettes. Minimum excise duty is EUR 50 per kilo of rolling tobacco for cigarettes. Minimum excise duty for cigars is EUR 23.50 per 1 000.

Mexico. An ad-valorem rate of 160% on the producer or importer price applies for all categories. A reduced rate of 30.4% applies for cigars or rolling tobacco as long as these products are fully handmade. The ad-valorem tax applies at the stage of the producer or importer but on the retail price. In addition a charge of MXN 0.4944 should be paid for each sold or imported cigarette. This charge also applies for cigars and other tobacco (MXN 0.4944 per each 0.75 grams), with the exemption of those that are fully handmade.

New Zealand. The excise rate for 1 000 cigarettes with actual tobacco content not exceeding in weight of 0.8 kg is NZD1 030,90 per kilo tobacco content. The excise rate for cigarettes exceeding 0.8 kg in actual tobacco content per 1 000 cigarettes and for rolling tobacco for cigarettes is NZD 1 469,03 per kilo tobacco content. The excise rate for other tobacco products, such as snuff, cigars, cheroots and cigarillos is NZD 1 288,59 per kilo of tobacco content.

Poland. Since 1 January 2015 the excise duty rate for cigars is calculated on per kilogramme basis.

Portugal. Rates applicable on 1 January 2020. Excise tax on cigarettes is reduced to (1) EUR 34.00 and 42% for cigarettes sold in Azores Islands and made by small producers from the Azores and Madeira Islands; (2) 78.37 and 20% for cigarettes sold in Madeira Island and made by small producers from the Azores and Madeira Islands. Since 1 April 2020, tax rates are as follows: Cigarettes: Specific excise per 1000 – EUR 101.00; Excise on value % - 14.00. Cigars: Excise on value % - 25.00. Rolling tobacco for cigarettes: Specific excise per 1000 grams – EUR 81.00; Excise on value % - 15.00. VAT % - 23.00. Excise tax on cigarettes is reduced to (1) EUR 34.00 and 42% for cigarettes sold in Azores Islands and made by small producers from the Azores and Madeira Islands; (2) 82.34 and 18% for cigarettes sold in Madeira Island and made by small producers from the Azores and Madeira Islands.

Slovak Republic. Tax on rolling tobacco for cigarettes includes other smoking tobacco. The excise for cigars is EUR 73.90/kg.

Slovenia. Minimum excise duty is EUR 114 per 1 000 cigarettes. Minimum excise duty is EUR 94 per kilo of rolling tobacco for cigarettes. Minimum excise duty for cigars is EUR 43 per kilo.

Sweden. Cigarettes with a length over 8 cm up to 11 cm should be taxed as two cigarettes. If the cigarette is longer than 11 cm every started additional 3 cm is considered a cigarette.

Switzerland. If the Retail Selling Price for 1 000 cigarettes is CHF 375.00 or less, minimum excise duty (specific + on value) yields CHF 212.10 for 1 000 pieces. Specific excise per 1 000 grams of rolling tobacco for cigarettes: the minimum excise duty (specific + on value) yields CHF 80.00 per 1 000 grams.

Turkey. Minimum tax amount per 1000 cigarettes is TL 488.30. Specific tax amount is TL 0.4851 for 1 pack of cigarettes. Tax on cigarettes and other tobacco products computed according to the tax rate cannot be less than the minimum tax amount. After calculating the tax according to minimum tax amount system, specific tax amount is added to the tax for 1 pack of cigarettes.

United Kingdom. Specific excise rate for cigars is given per kilogramme and not for 1 000 units. Specific rates exist for "other smoking tobacco and chewing tobacco" and "tobacco for heating" which at 1 January 2020 were set at GBP 125.20 and GBP 234.65 per kilo respectively.

United States. State taxes vary widely. The weighted average of Federal and State taxes per thousand cigarettes is USD 141.00. Federal specific excise tax rates on tobacco are: USD 50.33 per thousand for small cigarettes (no more than 3 pounds per thousand); USD 105.69 per thousand for large cigarettes; USD 50.33 per thousand for small cigars weighing no more than 3 pounds per thousand; 52.75% of the manufacturers price but not more than USD 402.60 per thousand for large cigars; and USD 24.78 per pound (54.63 per kg) for roll-your-own tobacco. Some states also tax on an ad valorem basis.

Annex Table 3.A.5. Tax burden as a share of total price for cigarettes (2018)

Country	Ex-tax price (USD)[1]	Specific excise % RSP[2]	Excise on value % RSP[3]	VAT/GST/RST % RSP[4]	Total tax share % RSP	Price of a 20 cigarettes pack[5]		
						Currency	Price (RSP in local currency)	Price (RSP in USD)[6]
Australia	3.36	68.43	0.00	9.09	77.52	AUD	20.75	14.93
Austria	1.60	21.09	37.50	16.67	75.26	EUR	5.50	6.47
Belgium	1.79	19.58	40.04	17.36	76.98	EUR	6.60	7.76
Canada*	3.20	55.65	0.00	8.40	64.05	CAD	11.57	8.90
Chile	0.74	36.39	30.00	15.97	82.36	CLP	2700.00	4.21
Colombia	0.29	52.46	10.00	15.97	78.43	COP	4003.00	1.35
Czech Republic	0.73	35.31	30.00	17.36	82.69	CZK	91.2	4.20
Denmark	1.82	53.15	1.00	20.00	74.15	DKK	44.50	7.04
Estonia	1.03	32.71	30.00	16.67	79.38	EUR	4.25	5.00
Finland*	1.07	16.06	52.00	19.35	87.41	EUR	7.22	8.49
France	1.65	14.98	50.80	16.67	82.45	EUR	8.00	9.41
Germany	2.16	32.27	21.69	15.97	69.92	EUR	6.09	7.16
Greece	1.02	35.87	26.00	19.35	81.22	EUR	4.60	5.41
Hungary	1.28	26.02	25.00	21.26	72.28	HUF	1245.00	4.61
Iceland	5.59	36.13	0.00	19.35	55.49	ISK	1359.00	12.55
Ireland	3.10	50.66	9.04	18.70	78.40	EUR	12.20	14.35
Israel	1.98	23.20	41.30	14.53	79.10	ILS	34.00	9.47
Italy	1.55	7.01	51.00	18.03	76.04	EUR	5.50	6.47
Japan	1.47	55.65	0.00	7.41	63.06	JPY	440.00	3.98
Korea	1.07	64.76	0.00	9.09	73.85	KRW	4500.00	4.09
Latvia	0.82	42.63	20.00	17.36	79.99	EUR	3.59	4.22
Lithuania	1.15	31.47	25.00	17.36	73.83	EUR	3.75	4.41
Luxembourg	1.98	7.13	46.65	14.53	68.31	EUR	5.30	6.24
Mexico	1.03	15.69	39.07	13.79	68.55	MXN	63.02	3.27
Netherlands	2.32	49.46	5.00	17.36	71.81	EUR	7.00	8.24
New Zealand*	2.93	69.17	0.00	13.04	82.21	NZD	23.90	16.48
Norway	5.22	43.97	0.00	20.00	63.97	NOK	117.80	14.49
Poland	1.00	26.68	31.41	18.70	76.79	PLN	15.50	4.29
Portugal	1.67	37.96	15.00	18.70	71.66	EUR	5.00	5.88
Slovak Republic	0.90	37.23	23.00	16.67	76.90	EUR	3.32	3.91
Slovenia	0.91	38.55	22.61	18.03	79.19	EUR	3.70	4.35
Spain	1.28	9.88	51.00	17.36	78.24	EUR	5.00	5.88
Sweden	2.37	47.38	1.00	20.00	68.38	SEK	65.00	7.48
Switzerland	3.49	27.51	25.00	7.15	60.27	CHF	8.60	8.78
Turkey	0.52	3.11	63.00	15.25	81.37	TRY	13.50	2.80
United Kingdom	2.58	46.22	16.50	16.67	79.39	GBP	9.40	12.53
United States*	4.14	36.12	0.00	5.52	39.47	USD	6.90	6.90

Notes

* Canada and the United States, national average estimates calculated for prices and taxes reflect the fact that different rates are applied by state/province over and above the applicable federal tax.
* Finland: the MSB is not available. The Weighted Average Price (WAP) is used.

The share of taxes are presented as a % of Retail Selling Price (RSP) for a pack of 20 cigarettes. The RSP is defined as the average price of the most sold brand of cigarettes on the market (MSB - see Annex C). This table reflects the situation in 2018 since it is based on annual average prices and taxes that are not available for the year 2019 at the time of this publication.

1. The pre-tax price includes the producer and distributor margins. It is estimated by the deduction of the total tax share from the RSP.

2. Specific excise: a specific excise tax is a tax on a specific good produced or imported in a country charged as a fixed amount per unit of the product. The amount shown in this table is as a percentage of RSP.
3. Excise on value: an excise on value or ad valorem is a tax on a product produced or imported in a country charged as a percentage of the value of a transaction. Example: 50% of the RSP.
4. VAT/GST: Value added tax or Goods and services tax (see Chapter 1). RST: retail sales taxes for Canada (in some provinces) and the United States. The amount is shown as a percentage of RSP.
5. Price of a 20 cigarettes pack of the Most Sold Brand (see Annex D).
6. In this table, amounts in local currency are converted in USD using the average market exchange rate 2019 published in OECD Monthly Monetary Statistics (*stats.oecd.org*).
Source: WHO Report on the Global Tobacco Epidemic, 2019 and national delegates. Situation for the year 2018

StatLink https://doi.org/10.1787/888934220249

Annex Table 3.A.6. Taxation of fuel oil for households (per litre, 2019)

Country		Ex-tax price[1]		Excise[2]	VAT rate[3]	VAT amount	Total tax	Total price		Total tax as % of total price
	Currency	National currency	USD	National currency	%	National currency	National currency	National currency	USD	
Australia*	AUD	See note			10.00					
Austria*	EUR	0.551	0.617	0.109	20.00	0.132	0.241	0.792	0.887	30.4
Belgium	EUR	0.536	0.600	0.019	21.00	0.116	0.135	0.671	0.751	20.1
Canada*	CAD	1.127	0.849	0.000	9.93	0.112	0.112	1.239	0.934	9.0
Chile*	CLP	560.406	0.797	0.000	19.00	106.477	106.477	666.883	0.948	16.0
Colombia	COP	See note								
Czech Republic*	CZK	13.549	0.591	0.660	21.00	5.145	5.805	19.354	0.844	30.0
Denmark*	DKK	5.063	0.759	2.988	25.00	2.013	5.000	10.064	1.509	49.7
Estonia	EUR	0.678	0.759	0.058	20.00	0.147	0.205	0.883	0.989	23.2
Finland*	EUR	0.542	0.607	0.249	24.00	0.190	0.439	0.981	1.099	44.8
France	EUR	0.619	0.693	0.156	20.00	0.155	0.311	0.930	1.041	33.4
Germany*	EUR	0.507	0.568	0.061	19.00	0.108	0.169	0.676	0.757	25.0
Greece*	EUR	0.515	0.577	0.280	24.00	0.191	0.471	0.986	1.104	47.8
Hungary*	HUF	212.925	0.733	122.855	27.00	87.961	200.816	413.741	1.424	48.5
Iceland*	ISK	See note			24.00					
Ireland*	EUR	0.527	0.594	0.102	13.50	0.085	0.187	0.714	0.805	26.2
Israel	ILS	2.773	0.778	2.945	17.00	0.972	3.917	6.690	1.877	58.6
Italy	EUR	0.668	0.748	0.403	22.00	0.236	0.639	1.306	1.462	48.9
Japan*	JPY	80.988	0.743	2.800	10.00	8.379	11.179	92.167	0.845	12.1
Korea*	KRW	801.786	0.688	72.450	10.00	87.424	159.874	961.660	0.825	16.6
Latvia	EUR	0.607	0.680	0.057	21.00	0.139	0.196	0.803	0.899	24.4
Lithuania	EUR	0.397	0.498	0.021	21.00	0.088	0.109	0.506	0.567	21.5
Luxembourg*	EUR	0.542	0.607	0.010	14.00	0.077	0.087	0.629	0.705	13.9
Mexico*	MXN	See note								
Netherlands	EUR	0.406	0.455	0.788	21.00	0.251	1.039	1.445	1.618	71.9
New Zealand*	NZD	See note								
Norway	NOK	6.576	0.747	3.000	25.00	2.394	5.394	11.970	1.360	45.1
Poland	PLN	2.507	0.653	0.232	23.00	0.630	0.862	3.369	0.878	25.6
Portugal	EUR	0.606	0.679	0.362	13.0	0.126	0.488	1.194	1.225	44.6
Slovak Republic*	EUR	see note								
Slovenia	EUR	0.549	0.615	0.222	22.00	0.170	0.392	0.941	1.053	41.6
Spain*	EUR	0.540	0.605	0.097	21.00	0.134	0.231	0.771	0.863	29.9
Sweden*	SEK	4.910	0.519	4.247	25.00	2.289	6.536	11.446	1.210	57.1
Switzerland	CHF	0.581	0.585	0.259	7.70	0.065	0.324	0.905	0.910	35.8
Turkey	TRY	3.564	0.628	1.137	18.00	0.846	1.983	5.547	0.977	35.8
United Kingdom	GBP	0.449	0.573	0.111	5.00	0.028	0.139	0.588	0.750	23.6
United States*	USD	0.793	0.793	0.035	0.00	0.000	0.035	0.828	0.828	4.2

Notes

* See country notes.

Conversion of national currency in USD: conversion rates are average market rates (2019) published in OECD Monthly Monetary Statistics (stats.oecd.org). See also Annex B.

Prices are average prices for the year 2019. Tax rates are those applicable as at 1 October 2019.

1. Ex-tax price is the price excluding VAT and excise.

2. Excise taxes are expressed in local currency per litre. They include all non-VAT taxes levied on the product. For the purposes of this table, payments made to specific bodies that use all the amounts collected to accomplish specific missions (e.g. some emergency stock fees) are not considered as "taxes" and are included in the ex-tax price. When different rates apply to the same product depending e.g. on its biofuel or sulphur content, the rate shown is the one applicable to the most commonly used fuel in the country.
3. GST for Australia, and New Zealand; volume-weighted GST-HST/retail sales taxes for Canada; sales taxes for the United States and Consumption Tax for Japan. VAT for all other countries.
Source: International Energy Agency, IEA Energy Prices, 2020 edition https://www.iea.org/reports/world-energy-prices-2020 and country delegates.

StatLink https://doi.org/10.1787/888934220268

Annex Box 3.A.5. Country notes to Table 3.A.6.

Australia. No data is available.

Austria. Tax amount of EUR 0.098/l applies to light fuel oil with sulphur content ≤ 10mg/kg. Otherwise the excise duty is EUR 0.128/l.

Canada. Fuel oil is assumed to be heating oil. There is no federal or provincial fuel tax on heating oil. The federal GST rate is 5%. Most provinces do not apply their provincial GST/retail sales tax on heating oil. The volume weighted GST/sales tax rate was 9.93%. Municipal taxes and carbon pollution pricing are not included in the excise taxes.

Chile. Domestic Kerosene is covered by the Oil Price Stabilisation Fund (*Fondo de Estabilización de Precios del Petróleo* or FEPP, Law 19.030) which applies as a tax or as a fiscal credit/subsidy weekly, and it is measured in USD per m3. This tax cannot be included in the VAT base at any stage of the value chain (import, production, refining, distribution or sale to the consumer). On the contrary, the fiscal credit may be deducted from the taxable base either on the first sale or importation.

Colombia. Data is not available for this edition.

Czech Republic. Fuel oil marked in accordance with Directive 95/60/EC is subject to reimbursement of an excise duty amount of CZK 10 290/1000 l when it has been duly proved that the fuel oil has been used for heating purposes. The excise amount shown in the table includes the reimbursement. However the VAT amount is calculated on the full excise value.

Denmark. The amount of DKK 2.406/l includes the Excise tax of DKK 1.955/l; the Environment tax of DKK 0.455/l and the NOx tax of DKK 0.0009/l.

Finland. The excise amount of EUR 0.2488/l includes the energy content tax EUR 0.0763, CO2 tax EUR 0.1690 and the strategic stockpile fee (EUR 0.0035).

Germany. The excise amount is for properly marked gas oil with a sulphur content ≤ 50mg/kg. Otherwise the excise amount is EUR 0.0764/l. *From 1 July to 31* December *2020 the VAT rate is reduced from 19% to 16% to offset the economic impact of the Covid-19 pandemic.*

Greece. The excise of EUR 0.280/l for heating oil for households applies during the winter season (15 October - 30 April). Otherwise the excise is 0.410/l.

Hungary. Excise amount depends on the world market price of crude oil. If the world market price of crude oil is higher than 50 USD/barrel the excise amount is HUF 112.855/l (including the excise duty of HUF 110.35/l and the strategic stock fee of HUF 2.505/l). If the world market price of crude oil is 50 USD/barrel or less the excise amount is HUF 112.855 (including the excise duty of HUF 120.35/l and the strategic stock fee of HUF 2.505/l).

Iceland. No data is available

Ireland. The 'Ex-tax price' includes a National Oil Reserves Agency (NORA) levy which is charged at a rate of EUR 0.02 per litre. The "Excise" rate of EUR 0.102 per litre applies to marked gas oil (marked diesel). Marked kerosene is also widely used for heating (including domestic heating) and the rate for that is EUR 0.05073per litre. From 1 May 2020 the "Excise" rate for marked gas oil increased to EUR 0.117 per litre and marked kerosene increased to EUR 0.06574 per litre.

Japan. Kerosene for households.

Korea. Kerosene for households

Latvia. Excise tax of EUR 0.021/litre for marked fuel for heating purposes applies if it contains at least 5% biodiesel of total volume of product.

Luxembourg. A reduced VAT rate of 14% applies to heating gas oil.

Mexico. Fuel oil as heating oil for households is only used in small areas in northern Mexico and no sales have been registered since 2016. Fuel oil as residual oil (combustoleo) is not used by households but is taxed with an excise equal to MXN 16.99 cents per litre. Other fossil fuels that are used for heating are propane (MXN 7.48 cents per litre), butane (MXN 9.68 cents per litre), kerosene (MXN 15.67 cents per litre), diesel (MXN 15.92 cents per litre) and coal (MXN 34.81 pesos per ton).

Netherlands. For gasoline a stockpiling tax of 0.008/l applies, this is not included in the mentioned excise rate.

New Zealand. No data is provided because the product is not consumed in significant quantities.

Norway. The amount of NOK 3.0/l includes base tax of NOK 1.65/l and CO_2 tax of NOK 1.35/l.

Slovak Republic. No data is provided because the product is not consumed in significant quantities.

Slovenia. The amount of EUR 222 per 1 000 litres includes the excise duty of EUR 157.50, EUR 8.00 surcharge on energy end-use efficiency on gasoil used for heating purposes, EUR 9.90 surcharge for the promotion of electricity generation from renewable energy sources and high-efficiency cogeneration on gasoil used for heating purposes, and EUR 46.71 CO_2-tax.

Spain. The excise amount of EUR 0.088/l includes the Excise tax (EUR 0.085/l) and the average Regional authorities' tax (EUR 0.003/l).

Sweden. Price data are not available in IEA statistics. Price data is extracted from economic information available on ec.europa.eu/energy/observatory/reports. Excise tax includes the Energy Tax (SEK 0.887/l) and CO_2 Tax (SEK 3.360/l).

Turkey. Kerosene for households.

United States. Average federal and state taxes - there is no VAT

European Union. Directive 2003/96/EC sets minimal excise rates for energy products and electricity.

Notes

[1] VAT may also be referred to as Goods and Services Tax (GST). For ease of reading, all value added taxes will be referred to as VAT in this chapter.

4 Taxing Vehicle Use

4.1. Introduction

Taxes related to the ownership and usage of vehicles were introduced in most OECD countries in the first half of the 20th century and have become an important source of tax revenue for many governments. All member countries rely on a range of tax instruments to ensure significant revenue from both private and commercial vehicle owners and road users. Vehicle and vehicle usage taxation in its widest definition represents a prime example of the use of the whole spectrum of consumption taxes for taxing vehicles and their use, including VAT as well as *ad quantum* or *ad valorem* taxes (see definitions in Chapter 3). These taxes have progressively been adapted to influence consumer behaviour and curb transport externalities, in particular environmental externalities.

Taxes and charges on vehicles include:

- Taxes (including VAT and retail sales taxes) on the purchase and registration of motor vehicles, payable once at the time of acquisition and/or first putting into service of a vehicle (see Annex Table 4.A.1).
- Periodic taxes payable in connection with the ownership or use of the vehicles (see Annex Table 4.A.2).
- Taxes on road fuels (see Annex Table 4.A.3 and Annex Table 4.A.4).

Taxes on aviation fuels (see Annex Table 4.A.5

- Annex Table 4.A.5).
- Any other taxes and charges that are directly or indirectly connected with the use or ownership of vehicles, such as import duties, insurance taxes, road tolls, distance charges, congestion charges, company car taxation, passenger transport taxes, etc. (these taxes are not covered in this publication).

4.2. Taxation of motor vehicles

The sale and use of motor vehicles generate considerable VAT or retail sales tax revenues. These taxes are levied on the import and sale of vehicles (in the latter case by application to the full selling price or, for used cars, to the margin between the buying and the selling price). VAT or retail sales tax will generally also apply to general maintenance and running costs. In addition, they are levied in most cases on the final duty-paid value (e.g. VAT on fuel is levied on the excise-inclusive price - see Annex Tables 3.A.3 and 3.A.4 in Chapter 3).

Taxes on vehicles reflect a variety of influences beyond the obvious need to raise revenue. Geographic, industrial, social, energy, transport, urban and environmental policy considerations have all had an influence on the level and structure of taxation. Many taxes on vehicles were instituted in a time when cars were considered luxury items. Wider ownership of cars in recent decades has reduced the progressivity of those taxes (many low-income households have at least one car today). Currently, taxation schemes are increasingly used to influence consumer or business behaviour. Energy and environmental considerations have led to an adjustment of taxation according to the fuel efficiency of vehicles, CO_2 and polluting emissions. Taxes on road use have also been introduced to manage the external cost of transport and raise additional revenue.

In most countries total taxes on vehicles result from a combination of one-off (on purchase or import) and recurrent (on ownership or use) taxes as well as from a mix between *ad valorem* (on the price) and *ad quantum* taxes (taking into account polluting emissions, weight, engine power, number of axles, age, fuel efficiency, equipment, suspension, cylinder capacity, number of seats, type of fuel, electric propulsion and distance covered).

Taxes on the sale/registration and use of motor vehicles (Annex Table 4.A.1 and Annex Table 4.A.2) cannot be considered in isolation from other tax bases and rates. A number of other elements should also be taken into account when considering the taxation of vehicles such as insurance premium taxes, specific road tolls (bridge or motorway tolls, congestion charges, distance charges), fuel taxes, energy taxes and a number of direct tax components such as the personal tax treatment of company cars (Harding, 2014[1]).

4.2.1. The nature and level of taxes on motor vehicles vary widely between OECD countries

Taxes on purchase and registration

All OECD countries levy taxes on purchase and/or registration of motor vehicles. These taxes may include VAT, sales taxes, excise duties and other fees and charges associated with the registration of a vehicle. These taxes may vary considerably from one country to another (see Annex Table 4.A.1). They are based on a large diversity of criteria or on a combination of these criteria. There are five main criteria against which the tax can be assessed:

- The price or value of the vehicle;
- The engine power or cylinder capacity;
- Environmental impact, incl. polluting emissions, CO_2 emissions and the type of fuel used;

- Social considerations incl. preferential treatment of emergency vehicles, ambulances, vehicles for disabled people, vehicles for public transport, etc.;
- The use of the vehicle including specific criteria applying to commercial vehicles such as number of axles, cargo room, number of seats, etc.

A number of specific elements can further be taken in consideration for determining the tax burden, such as weight, presence of safety equipment, air conditioning, etc. A specific tax applies to tyres in the United States. Taxation depends on the age of the vehicle in several countries.

The burden of these taxes varies considerably from one country to another and may differ between states, provinces, cities or regions within a country. For example, a VAT rate of 10% and a 3% acquisition tax apply in Japan whereas a 25% VAT and a registration tax up to 150% is applied in Denmark. However, these amounts are most often adjusted according to the environmental performance of the vehicles (see Section 4.4 below).

The international differences in taxation of sales and registration of motor vehicles do not give rise to considerable cross-border shopping as motor vehicles need to be registered with a unique identification number in the principal country of use. Similarly VAT levied on the importation of a vehicle (or on its "acquisition" for cross-border sales within the EU) will generally be due in the country of registration. Even in the integrated market of the EU there has been no harmonisation or even approximation of taxes or tax rates on motor vehicles.

Nevertheless, motor vehicle taxation can affect the functioning of the motor vehicle market. This may notably be the case for registration taxes. Generally, registration tax paid in the country of first registration is not paid back when a car is transferred from one country to another (e.g. when the owner moves from one country to another). When registration tax has to be paid (again) in the country of destination where the car is to remain permanently, double taxation occurs. In addition, large differences in tax systems reinforce car market fragmentation. Cars marketed in one country with specifications designed to meet the national tax structure (e.g. brackets of fiscal horsepower, tax policy regarding diesel) are imperfect substitutes and may not effectively compete with cars sold in another country with different tax requirements. Also pre-tax prices appear to be influenced by tax considerations. Significant tax differentials may encourage consumers in some cases to buy cars in countries where registration taxes are very high and where car manufacturers tend to offer lower prices net of taxes by compensation and import and register them in their own country. This may undermine the benefits that should derive from a competitive market for both consumers and industry.

Periodic taxes on ownership or use

All OECD countries levy taxes on ownership or use of motor vehicles, or both. These taxes include recurring charges levied on the right to drive on public roads, usually in the form of an annual motor tax (see Annex Table 4.A.2). Taxes on the operation of motor vehicles also include excise duties on fuel (see Section 4.3 below) and motorway charges or other road user tolls and motor fuel taxation (see Section 4.4. below). Recurring taxes on the ownership of motor vehicles can take many forms. The main elements used to assess these kinds of taxes are very similar to those used for assessing taxes on sale and registration such as use (commercial or not), vehicle type, type of fuel, engine size, age, emissions of pollutants and fuel efficiency.

As for taxes on sale and registration of motor vehicles, the level of taxes on the ownership or use of motor vehicles varies widely between OECD countries. In about one third of these countries (13 out of 37 i.e. Australia, Belgium, Canada, Chile, Colombia, Japan, Mexico, Netherlands, Poland, Portugal, Spain, Switzerland and the United States) local taxes are levied on ownership or use of motor vehicles. Preferential treatment is given in many countries to emergency vehicles, ambulances, vehicles for disabled people, vehicles for public transport or use by public authorities, diplomats, etc. Rebates and exemptions based on environmental criteria are provided in two thirds of OECD countries (see Section 4.4. below).

4.3. Taxation of motor fuels

4.3.1. Taxation of road fuels

The revenues raised from these taxes are significant in OECD countries, as a result of the considerable level of consumption and high tax rates in many of these countries. Although there are large differences between countries, the level of taxation for fuel relative to the base is very high compared to other taxes within the overall economy. For premium unleaded gasoline, for instance, the total tax burden (mainly excise plus VAT) exceeds 100% of pre-tax prices in all the OECD countries, except Australia, Canada, Colombia, Chile, Japan, Mexico, New Zealand and the United States (Annex Table 4.A.3). The lowest percentage of taxes in the consumer price for unleaded gasoline are recorded in Mexico (13.8%), the United States (18.6%) and Colombia (22%). The highest rates are recorded in Finland (65.4%) and the Netherlands (64.9%). Only one country, Colombia, applies a reduced VAT rate to road fuels.

Excise levels for diesel fuel (Annex Table 4.A.3) are still lower than those for gasoline in all OECD countries, except Australia, Belgium, and the United Kingdom where the rates are the same and Switzerland where the excise duty on diesel is higher than the one applied to gasoline. From an environmental point of view, this is peculiar, as diesel consumption in vehicles has a much greater environmental impact than unleaded gasoline, largely due to the significant differences in nitrogen oxides (NOx) and particulate emissions. With more stringent motor vehicle regulations, the difference is becoming less pronounced for new vehicles, although there are concerns about differences between test cycle and on-road performance and the stock of vehicles is still weighted toward older, more polluting diesel vehicles.

In the European Union (EU), the Energy Taxation Directive (2003/96/EC) sets out common rules for the taxation of energy products in EU Member States. This Directive aims to reduce distortions of competition between mineral oils and other energy products, as well as tax competition between member states from rate differentiation in energy taxation. It also aims to incentivise more efficient energy use. The Directive sets common taxation rules for a range of fuels, including many oil products, coal and natural gas, and for electricity consumption. For each, it sets a minimum level of tax expressed in terms of the volume, weight, or energy content of the fuel. For example, minimum rates on road fuels are as follows: EUR 0.359/l for unleaded gasoline; EUR 0.330/l for gas oil and EUR 0.125/kg for LPG. The Directive does not specify which taxes should be used to reach the minimum level of taxation. These may include a diversity of specific taxes such as excise, carbon tax, energy tax, etc. This directive is currently being revised as part of the general review of climate-related legislation of the Green Deal.

Excise taxes on transport fuels are usually much higher than on mineral oils and, more generally, than on fossil fuels used in other sectors (OECD, 2013[2]). This can be for various reasons, including a lower elasticity of the tax base in transport; the use of excises to cover (more or less directly) external costs that are relevant only in the transportation context (most notably congestion); and equity concerns. Equity considerations have notably motivated the differences in taxation of diesel used for household heating compared to diesel used for transportation (Flues and Thomas, 2015[3]). The vast majority of OECD countries (except Greece, Hungary, Israel and the Netherlands) tax heating oil for households at a lower rate than diesel for transport use even though both products are more or less identical (see Annex Table 3.A.8).

Excise rates on automotive fuels should not be considered in isolation when assessing the overall tax burden on automotive transport (van Dender, 2019[4]). Vehicles may also be subject to distance-based taxes, parking taxes, road tolls, registration taxes and recurrent circulation taxes and many countries differentiate those taxes according to the type of fuel used or according to CO_2 emissions per unit distance (see Section 4.4 below). Furthermore, the tax treatment of company car use is often more favourable – sometimes considerably so – than that of other car use (Harding, 2014[1]).

4.3.2. Taxation of aviation fuels

This section describes the VAT and excise taxes applied to the two main categories of fuels destined to aircrafts, i.e. JET A-1 fuel used in turbine engines and AVGAS used in piston-engine aircrafts. Annex Table 4.A.5 shows the excise and VAT rates applied to these types of fuels (hereafter "aviation fuels") in OECD member countries and, where applicable, other specific taxes on the provision of those fuels to aircrafts (e.g. carbon tax).Other taxes applied to air transport (ticket taxes, airport taxes, etc.) are not covered in this publication.

The provision of aviation fuels to enterprises operating aircrafts for international commercial flights (i.e. passenger transport or cargo) is subject to a zero rate of VAT in all OECD countries or subject to a full refund of input VAT (Chile), except Colombia, where it is subject to the reduced VAT rate of 5% and the United States where there is no federal VAT. By contrast, the provision of aviation fuels for domestic commercial flights is subject to VAT in all OECD countries (except in the United States) at the standard VAT rate, except for Colombia where it is subject to the reduced VAT rate of 5%. Since aviation fuel will typically be a business input of an enterprise large enough to be registered for VAT, this component of tax will generally be fully deductible and thus ultimately have no economic impact. The provision of aviation fuels for domestic non-commercial or pleasure flights is taxed at the standard VAT rate in all OECD countries, except Colombia where it is subject to the reduced VAT rate of 5% and the United States, where it is taxed at the state level, with rates varying across them. In theory, the VAT zero-rating of aviation fuel for international flights reflects the objective of relieving exports from VAT in the jurisdiction of origin so as to avoid double taxation in the jurisdiction of destination, which normally has the right to levy VAT on internationally traded goods in accordance with the destination principle. However, unlike most exported items that are normally subject to VAT in the destination country, aviation fuel used in international flights will generally remain untaxed as most of it is consumed during the international flight and the remainder remains generally untaxed in accordance with the International Civil Aviation Organisation (ICAO) Convention (also known as the Chicago Convention; see below) requiring contracting states not to charge duty on aviation fuel already on board any aircraft arriving on their soil from another contracting state (all OECD countries are parties to the Convention).

Excise Annex Table 4.A.5 shows that all OECD countries exempt aviation fuels from excise duties for commercial international flights, in contrast to fuels used on road and rail transport. They also all exempt aviation fuel for domestic commercial flights, except Australia, Canada, Japan, Switzerland and the United States. The landscape is more diverse for aviation fuel used for non-commercial and pleasure flights, which is taxed in 14 countries for international flights (Belgium, Finland, Germany, Greece, Hungary, Ireland, Latvia, Lithuania, Luxembourg, Poland, Portugal, Slovenia, Spain and Sweden) and in a majority of OECD countries for domestic flights (in 22 countries out of 37).

Two OECD countries apply other (environmental) taxes to aviation fuels. Norway exempts aviation fuel from excise tax but submits it to a carbon tax and Slovenia applies a surcharge to all aviation fuels (including for international flights) in addition to excise duties (for non-commercial and pleasure flights).

As explained above, the exemption of aviation fuels for international flights in countries of arrival results from the Chicago Convention, which lays down the basic standards and principles governing international aviation. Article 24 of the Convention forbids the taxation of fuel on board aircrafts arriving in the territory of a contracting party. The Convention does however not forbid imposing any taxes on fuel supplied to an aircraft at the point of departure (Faber and O'Leary, 2018[5]) This tax exemption for fuels supplied to aircrafts rather result from the network of bilateral "Air Service Agreements" (ASAs) between individual countries, which generally provide for such an exemption on the basis of reciprocity (Antony Seely, 2019[6]).

The Chicago Convention is not applicable to domestic air transport and therefore nothing prevents countries from taxing aviation fuels on domestic flights.

4.4. Taxes on vehicles are increasingly used to curb transport externalities

Although excise on transport fuels has been around for many years, it was originally motivated primarily if not exclusively by non-environmental objectives, such as general revenue generation or to finance infrastructure spending in some cases. When the more environmentally-friendly unleaded gasoline appeared on the market, it was not commercially competitive with leaded gasoline as a retail product because it was more expensive to produce. Energy taxation was used to overcome this handicap by making unleaded gasoline cheaper at the pump. Today, leaded gasoline has disappeared and is even no longer allowed on the market. Lower taxes on Liquefied Petroleum Gas (LPG) used as propellant had a much less significant effect on consumer behaviour. The characteristics of this fuel (not liquid at standard temperature and atmospheric pressure; more difficult to stock; need for specifically equipped stations) have hindered its development. The use of LPG is globally very low compared to diesel and gasoline.

Taxation has increasingly been used over the last decades to influence customer behaviour and encourage the purchase of low polluting or more fuel-efficient vehicles. In 2020, all OECD member countries except Chile and Colombia take environmental or fuel efficiency criteria into account when determining the level of taxation for the purchase or use of vehicles (see Annex Table 4.A.1 and 4.A.2). In 21 of these countries, the polluting emissions (CO, NOx, particulate matter per kilometre) or CO_2 emissions are taken into account to determine the level of taxation and 24 apply tax rebates or exemptions for electric or hybrid vehicles. A number of EU Member States use the polluting emission norms set by European legislation (Directive 2007/46/EC and subsequent regulations) as a benchmark for their vehicle taxes although there is currently no European rule regarding car taxation. Three OECD countries (Belgium, Japan and Poland) apply rebates or exemptions on taxes on purchase or use of hydrogen fuel cell electric vehicles (FCEVs).

Differentiating motor vehicle purchase/registration taxes according to the fuel-efficiency or polluting emissions (as in 26 out of 37 OECD countries) can give potential vehicle purchasers an immediate incentive to buy a vehicle that pollutes less, is more fuel-efficient, or both. Differentiating annual charges on similar principles (as in 26 out of 37 countries) can also provide such an incentive, but somewhat less directly. Sixteen OECD countries (Austria, Belgium, France, Greece, Iceland, Ireland, Italy, Japan Luxembourg, Mexico, Netherlands, Norway, Portugal, Slovenia, Switzerland and Turkey) apply such differentiation on both purchase/registration and annual taxes. One approach is to estimate vehicles' usage over their lifetime, and to calculate tax rates based on the estimated tonnes of CO_2 a vehicle is estimated to emit over its lifetime. Research in this context show that tax rates applied per tonne CO_2 emitted over a vehicle's estimated lifetime vary significantly between countries (for an in-depth study on this topic, see (Nils Axel Braathen, 2009[7])

High registration taxes are likely to reduce the number of new motor vehicle purchases. However, while this would, at first sight, appear to favour environmental objectives, higher purchase taxes on vehicles can not only reduce the size of the vehicle fleet but also cause some purchasers to defer their purchase or to purchase a used vehicle, increasing the population of older, more polluting, cars.

At the local level, other taxes and charges have been implemented or are considered to reduce local air pollution and other social costs of vehicle usage more generally, particularly in urban areas (Kurt van Dender, 2019[8]) Local traffic emits air pollutants in addition to CO_2 emissions, especially fine particulates, which create health damages whose economic costs can be estimated. Expressed per vehicle-kilometre, these external environmental costs of car traffic have been estimated at up to EUR 0.01 (gasoline cars) to EUR 0.037 (diesel cars). Traffic congestion also creates marginal external costs that are estimated to range from EUR 0.30 to EUR 2.42 per vehicle/kilometre when traffic volumes exceed road capacity. Other vehicle transport externalities include traffic accidents (costs estimated at up to EUR 0.03 per vehicle kilometre), noise (up to EUR 0.36/km for heavy goods vehicles in urban areas) and road damage (from EUR 0.05 per vehicle kilometre for cars to 0.52 for heavy trucks). Taxes can efficiently internalise these external costs and ensure their cost-effective reduction (Braathen et al., 2017[9]), provided that they are carefully targeted. While fuel taxes are well suited to reflect external costs from CO_2 emissions, distance-based taxes and, to some extent, parking charges have the potential to effectively reflect specific costs such as congestion, road damage and other infrastructure-related costs. Distance-based taxes that take into account vehicle characteristics can also help address air pollution (OECD/ITF, 2019[10]).

The OECD's Taxing Energy Use publication (OECD, 2019[11]) provides a comprehensive overview of specific taxes on energy for 43 OECD and G20 countries. It shows that these taxes are strongly heterogeneous and are in general too low from an environmental point of view. In all countries covered, fuel excise taxes are the largest component in the average effective energy tax rate. Taxes on road transport are much higher than taxes in other sectors, but they are still too low to cover the external costs of road transportation in many cases. Although it is recognised that well-designed systems of energy taxation encourage citizens and investors to favour clean over polluting energy sources, the politics of carbon pricing often prove to be challenging and too many energy users do not pay the energy and carbon prices needed to curb dangerous climate change, even when comparing carbon price signals against a low-end carbon benchmark of EUR 30 per tonne of CO_2.

In addition to tax policies, governments generally operate rules for reducing motor vehicle pollution by imposing technical norms to the car industry and many of the tax systems discussed above define tax bases and rates assuming compliance with the CO_2 or polluting emissions standards. For example, in the European Union polluting emissions have been regulated since 1970 and a series of amendments have been issued since then to gradually tighten the limit values. The current norms set maximum emissions of carbon monoxide (CO), Volatile Organic Compounds (VOC), nitrogen oxides (NOx) and particles. These are reflected in the Euro 6 (setting lower emission limits for the registration and sale of new types of cars and vans as of 1 September 2015) and in the Euro VI standards for heavy duty vehicles. Emissions of carbon dioxide (CO_2) have also been targeted by the European Commission since 2007 and the EU has put in place a comprehensive legal framework to reduce CO_2 emissions from new light duty vehicles as part of its efforts to ensure it meets its greenhouse gas emission reduction targets.

For the tables in annex, references to the 'European Union and its Member States' includes the UK as a Member State for January 2020 and as an addition to the Member States ('Member States and the UK') for the period 1 February 2020 until the end of December 2020.

References

Antony Seely (2019), "Taxing aviation fuel", *Briefing Paper*, No. 523, House of Commons, London. [6]

Braathen, A. et al. (2017), *Environmental Fiscal Reform PROGRESS, PROSPECTS AND PITFALLS*, http://www.oecd.org/tax/tax-policy/tax-and-environment.htm. [9]

Faber, J. and A. O'Leary (2018), *Taxing aviation fuels in the EU*, CE Delft, Delft. [5]

Flues, F. and A. Thomas (2015), "The distributional effects of energy taxes", *OECD Taxation Working Papers*, No. 23, OECD Publishing, Paris, https://dx.doi.org/10.1787/5js1qwkqqrbv-en. [3]

Harding, M. (2014), "Personal Tax Treatment of Company Cars and Commuting Expenses: Estimating the Fiscal and Environmental Costs", *OECD Taxation Working Papers*, No. 20, OECD Publishing, Paris, https://dx.doi.org/10.1787/5jz14cg1s7vl-en. [1]

Kurt van Dender (2019), *Taxing vehicles, fuels, and road use Opportunities for improving transport tax practice*, OECD, Paris. [8]

Nils Axel Braathen (2009), *Incentives for CO2 Emission Reductions in Current Motor Vehicle Taxes*, http://www.oecd.org/env/transport. [7]

OECD (2019), *Taxing Energy Use 2019: Using Taxes for Climate Action*, OECD Publishing, Paris, https://dx.doi.org/10.1787/058ca239-en. [11]

OECD (2013), *Taxing Energy Use: A Graphical Analysis*, OECD Publishing, Paris, https://dx.doi.org/10.1787/9789264183933-en. [2]

OECD/ITF (2019), *Tax Revenue Implications of Decarbonising Road Transport: Scenarios for Slovenia*, OECD Publishing, Paris, https://dx.doi.org/10.1787/87b39a2f-en. [10]

van Dender, K. (2019), "Taxing vehicles, fuels, and road use: Opportunities for improving transport tax practice", *OECD Taxation Working Papers*, No. 44, OECD Publishing, Paris, https://dx.doi.org/10.1787/e7f1d771-en. [4]

Annex 4.A. Taxes on vehicles

Annex Table 4.A.1. Taxes on sale and registration of motor vehicles

Country	Taxes	Criteria	Rebates/Exemptions[1]
Australia	**GST:** 10% **Luxury Car Tax**: 33% calculated on the value of most cars that exceed the luxury car tax threshold. The luxury car tax threshold is generally AUD 67 525 (in 2019-20), tax inclusive (including GST) or AUD 75 526, tax inclusive (including GST) if the car's fuel consumption is less than 7 litres per 100 kilometres. **Registration fee** – varies between states/territories – may be calculated on the tare weight, value or type of vehicle **Stamp duty** - varies between states/territories - calculated on the tare weight (heavy vehicles) or value (light vehicles)	Value Fuel efficiency Weight (registration or stamp duty only)	Some exemptions apply from luxury car tax including: - emergency vehicles such as ambulances etc. - sale of vehicle is more than two years after manufacture or importation - vehicles modified to transport a person in a wheelchair (provided it is not GST-free) - commercial vehicles primarily used for carrying goods in business or trade - imported by museum for public display Eligible tourism operators and primary producers are eligible to claim a refund of Luxury Car Tax paid up to AUD 10 000 for certain cars. GST: exemption is provided to veterans and persons with a disability that fulfil legal requirements.
Austria	**VAT:** 20%. **New Car Registration Tax:** while the tax base is the selling price, the tax rate depends on the CO_2-emissions of the car* i.e. CO_2 emissions in gram/km, reduced by 115 grams WLTP (90 NDEC), divided by 5. The rate cannot exceed 32%. For CO_2 emissions above 275g/km WLTP (250 g/km NDEC), the tax increases by EUR 40 for each g/km exceeding the limit of 275g/km WLTP (EUR 20 for each g/km exceeding the limit of 250g/km NDEC. An amount of up to EUR 350 has to be deducted from the amount of tax calculated following the above rules. *Starting from 1.1.2020 the relevant CO_2-emissions are determined by WLTP (NEDC before that). **Registration fee** (tax): fixed rate of Registration fee: motor vehicles registered for the state or local authorities EUR 119.80 per motor vehicle (+ up to EUR 49,70 processing fee for the registration office + approx. EUR 20 for other expenditures)	Value CO_2 emissions	New Car Registration Tax: exemptions for demonstration vehicles, motor vehicles for driving schools, vehicles that are hired, used for guests or as taxis, motor vehicles used for short time hiring out, motor vehicles used for the transport of sick persons and for rescue services, vehicles used for the transport of corpses, vehicles used by fire brigades and accompanying vehicles for special transports, vehicles used for disabled persons. Registration fee: exemption for motor vehicles registered for the state or local authorities

Belgium	**VAT**: 21% **Entry into Service Tax** *Flemish Region*: for non-leasing passenger cars, the tax rate depends on vehicle age, environmental characteristics (including CO_2 emissions), the type of fuel and the euro standard. The tax for leased vehicles is still calculated based on the engine power of the vehicle. *Wallcon Region*: the tax rate depends on engine power or the fiscal power (which is derived from the combustion engine capacity). When the tax, determined on the bases of one parameter exceeds the tax determined on the bases of the other, the highest tax is retained. For motorcycles the amount is calculated with respect to the kilowatt. For electric cars and electric motorcycles, the tax is set at EUR 61.50 as of fiscal year 2019. For all hybrid vehicles (cars and motorcycles), the power taken in consideration is the one supplied by the combustion engine. Cars and mixed cars are also subject to a second constitutive element of the tax on registration of vehicles, the so-called "ecomalus", which is based on the CO_2- emission of the vehicle. *Brussels Capital Region*: for passenger cars the tax rate depends on engine power expressed in fiscal horsepower and is set according to a degressive scale based on the age of the vehicle (fuel and gasoil from EUR 61.50 to EUR 4.957 and Liquefied Gas Petroleum from EUR 61.50 to EUR 4.659). If the engine power corresponds to different amounts expressed in hp than in kilowatt, the highest amount has to be taken into consideration. For electric cars, the tax is set at EUR 61.50.	Age Engine power Cylinder capacity Environmental characteristics (incl. CO_2 emissions) Type of fuel/gas	*Flemish Region*: exemption for certain fuel types (pure electric, hydrogen-powered, plug-in hybrid (until 2021), powered by CNG/LNG (until 2021). Vehicles of more than 28 years old are subject to a uniform rate of EUR 45.56. As from fiscal year 2022 this uniform rate is only applicable to cars of 30 years of age or older. An age correction will be accorded within the tariff formula for used cars (in a progressive scale from 90% to 10% of the registration tax or a lump sum depending on the age of the vehicle). There is also a rebate for cars entirely or partially powered by Liquefied Gas Petroleum. All regions provide exemptions for some vehicles used by public authorities and vehicles for disabled people and war invalids.
Canada	**GST**: 5% **HST**: 13% or 15% for sales in the participating provinces. The following provinces have harmonised their provincial sales taxes with the federal Goods and Services Tax and therefore levy a rate of **GST/HST** of: New Brunswick, Newfoundland and Labrador, Prince Edward Island, Nova Scotia 15%; Ontario: 13%; Québec applies GST at a rate of 5% and Québec Sales Tax at a rate of 9.975%. **Provincial tax** rates are applicable for sales made in provinces not applying HST **Automotive Air Conditioning Tax:** CAD 100 per unit. **Excise tax on Fuel Inefficient Vehicles:** vehicles with a weighted fuel consumption rating of 13 or more litres per 100 kilometres (55 % city and 45% highway) are subject to an excise tax at the following rates: at least 13 but less than 14 litres per 100 kilometres, CAD 1 000; at least 14 but less than 15 litres per 100 kilometres, CAD 2 000; at least 15 but less than 16 litres per 100 kilometres, CAD 3 000; and 16 or more litres per 100 kilometres, CAD 4 000.	Value Fuel efficiency Air conditioning	Rebate of GST/HST to purchasers of specially equipped motor vehicles for persons with disabilities. The rebate is only available on the GST/HST paid on the portion of the purchase price that is attributable to the special features. Rebate of Excise Tax on Fuel Inefficient Vehicles – Specially Equipped Van: to end-users of vans equipped with a device designed exclusively to assist in placing a wheelchair in the van without having to collapse the wheelchair

Chile	**VAT:** 19% (used cars are exempt with some exceptions) **Registration fees** payable to Civil Registry: first registration fee, new plate fee, fee for transfer and registration of vehicles. **Tax on transfer of used motor vehicles** (levied by municipalities): 1.5% of the value of the vehicle.	Value Fixed fee	
Colombia	**VAT:** 19%. **Vehicle registration fee:** COP 152 000 for cars and COP 74 000 for motorcycles. **National Consumption Tax:** the 16% tax rate applies to family-type motor vehicles, camper vehicles and pick-ups whose FOB value (or the equivalent) is greater than or equal to USD 30 000 and Pick-ups whose FOB value (or the equivalent) is greater than or equal to USD 30.000. The 8% tax rate applies to family-type motor vehicles, camper vehicles and pick-ups and whose FOB value (or the equivalent) is less than USD 30.000 and to motorcycles with cylinder capacity greater than 200cc.	Type of vehicle Value	
Czech Republic	**VAT**: 21% **Registration fee**: motorcycles CZK 300 or 500 (depending on cylinder capacity); other motor vehicles CZK 800. The fee includes the registration plate. **Permit fee** on non-standard motor vehicles	Value Cylinder capacity	
Denmark	**VAT**: 25% **Vehicle registration tax:** payable on first registration of the vehicle. Graduated tax rates according to the value of the vehicle (with lower rates for commercial vehicles) from 105% to 150% (on the remainder above DKK 82 800) for private vehicles and from 0% to 50% (on the remainder above DKK 17 500) for commercial vehicles.	Value Utilisation Fuel efficiency Safety equipment Anti-pollution equipment	Rebate for low fuel consumption vehicles: registration tax is reduced by DKK 4000 for every kilometre the vehicle can run in excess of 16 km with 1 litre of petrol or in excess of 18 km with 1 litre of diesel. A supplement of DKK 1000 is payable for cars for every kilometre less than 16 km (petrol) or 18 km (diesel) they can run on one litre of fuel. Traffic Safety Equipment: for motor vehicles with major traffic safety equipment the value liable to registration duty is reduced up to DKK 13 370. For motor vehicles with minor traffic safety equipment reduction is between DKK 200 and DKK 600.
Estonia	**VAT:** 20% **Vehicle registration fee (State fee):** vehicle: EUR 130; temporarily imported vehicle: EUR 335	Value Type of vehicle	
Finland	**VAT**: 24% **Vehicle Registration Tax** is based on CO_2 emissions. Rates vary from 2.7% of the general consumer price of the vehicle for cars emitting 0g/km or less to 48.9% for cars emitting 360g/km or more. **For delivery vans** there is a deduction based on maximum laden weight of the vehicle for vans over 2 500 kg. **For motor cycles** rates vary according to the cylinder capacity, between 9.8% and 24.4%, and the base is general retail value.	Value CO_2 emissions Utilisation Cylinder capacity Type	Exemption for disabled people, taxis, motor homes, cars used for veterinary purposes, rescue vehicles and funeral cars.

France	**VAT**: 20% **Tax on Registration Certificates** or regional tax on certificates is based on horsepower. Rates vary between EUR 33 and EUR 51.20 per horsepower according to the region. The rate is reduced by half for some vehicles depending on their nature (trucks weighing more than 3.5 tons, motorcycles) or age (more than 10 years old). **Additional tax on Registration certificates for first registration in France:** CO_2 emission component of the tax varies from EUR 0 for vehicles emitting less than 138g CO_2/km to EUR 20 000 for vehicles emitting more than 212g CO_2/ km. (CO_2 emissions are determined according to the Worldwide harmonised light-duty vehicles test procedure 6 WLTP) The horsepower component of the tax (vehicles that have not been subject to an EU-type approval) varies from EUR 3125 (6HP) to EUR 20 000 (18HP). The tax is not applicable to vehicles belonging to disabled people. **Additional tax on Registration certificates for registration after first registration in France:** the tax is based on horsepower Horsepower component of the tax varies from EUR 100 (10HP) up to EUR 1000 (15HP) The tax is not applicable to vehicles belonging to disabled people. **Additional tax on Registration certificates for cars with horsepower of 36HP or more**: the tax is EUR 500 per horsepower from 36HP with a maximum of EUR 8 000. Collection vehicles are exempt from this tax. **Additional Lorry Tax** is levied on the regional certificate tax for lorries according to their weight (from EUR 38 for less than 3.5 tons to EUR 305 for more than 11 tons or trailers and buses for public transport of passengers);	Value Engine power Weight Utilisation Age CO_2 emissions Type of fuel Electric propulsion	Exemption for new demonstration models weighing less than 3.5 tons, state vehicles, certain motorcycles Rebate for electricity or gas propelled cars: from 50% or 100% of the Tax on Registration Certificates. Rebate for Ethanol propelled cars: the Tax on Registration Certificates is reduced by 50% or 100% for cars that run with E85 fuel (super ethanol). Bonus system: a premium is granted for the purchase of a new car when its CO_2 emissions are 125 g/km or less. The maximum premium is EUR 5000 (below 60 g/km).
Germany	**VAT**: 19% *From 1 July to 31 December 2020 the VAT rate is reduced from 19% to 16% to offset the economic impact of the Covid-19 pandemic.*	Value	
Greece[2]	**VAT**: 24% **Registration tax:** rate varies - from 3.8% up to 64,00% of the taxable value, according to the retail price before taxes and to the CO_2 emissions for passenger cars that belong to the current emissions standard. - from 5.7% to 96.00% of the taxable value, according to the retail price before taxes and to the CO_2 emissions for passenger cars that belong to the previous emissions standard. - from 11.40% to 192.00% of the taxable value, according to the retail price before taxes and to the CO_2emissions for passenger cars that belong to other emissions standard. - from 48.00% to 384.00% of the taxable value, according to the retail price	**Cars:** value (retail price before taxes), CO_2 emissions, "Euro" emissions standards, electric propulsion **Lorries**: weight, emissions standards, body type. **Motorcycles:** cylinder capacity	Exemptions from registration tax: Hybrid cars are relieved from the registration tax by 50%. Electric cars are not subjected to registration tax Cars used by public authorities Cars used by disabled persons. Cars used by parents having at least three (3) children. Ambulances used by public hospitals Cars used by people who have moved their normal residence to Greece Cars donated to the Greek Police, Fire Brigade or Greek Coast Guards.

	before taxes and to the CO_2 emissions for conventional technology cars. - from 5% to 13% of the taxable value, for lorries-trucks etc. (less or more than 3.5 tonnes), according to emissions standard. - from 0% to 25% of the taxable value for motorcycles according to cylinder capacity. **Registration tax for buses** depends on the number of seats etc.		
Hungary	**VAT**: 27% **Registration Tax**: from HUF 45 000 to HUF 400 000 on new passenger cars according to engine type (diesel or petrol) and engine cylinder capacity, and from HUF 15 000 to HUF 230 000 on motorcycles according to engine cylinder capacity. For cars with lower environmental category of engine higher rates are levied (400, 600, 800 or 1200% higher), but rate is reduced according to a scale based on age (until 90%). Reduced rate is levied to hybrid cars and HUF 0 is levied to electric cars. **Transfer of motor vehicles**: the rate of duty shall be determined based on the capacity of motor vehicle's engine (in kW). The tax rate is from HUF 300/kW to HUF 850/kW depending on the age of the vehicle (the older the vehicle, the less is due).	Engine type Cylinder capacity Engine power Polluting emissions Type of fuel Age Electric propulsion	Reduced registration tax for cars with hybrid engines or with gas-powered engines (HUF 76 000) and for cars with electric engines as well as for hybrid and electric motorcycles (HUF 0).
Iceland	**VAT**: 24% **Vehicle Registration Fee** of ISK 5 000 on initial registration and ISK 2 130 for subsequent changes. **Motor vehicle excise duty:** based on CO_2 emissions ranging from 0-65% **Excise duties on motor vehicles other than private automobiles:** a percentage of value **Small goods vehicles**, small special purpose vehicles, vehicles over 40 years old, motor vehicle bodies13% **Small coaches**, motorbikes, other vehicles30%.	Value CO_2 emissions Electric propulsion	Temporary VAT exemption with a cap at import and domestic sales of electric-, hydrogen or plug-in hybrid vehicles, including busses. Large goods vehicles, large special purpose vehicles, tractors, agriculture trailers, large snow-mobiles, amphibious vehicles, competition cars and motorbikes, vehicles for transport of disabled persons, rescue vehicles and large coaches is exempt.
Ireland	**VAT**: 23% **Registration Tax**: based on CO_2 emissions and NOx emissions for passenger vehicles with not more than 9 seating positions and certain commercial vehicles with greater than 4 seats. For the CO_2 element of the charge, rates vary from 14% of the value of such a vehicle with CO_2 emissions of up to 80 g/km to 36% for such a vehicle with CO_2 emissions above 225 g/km. The NOx element of the charge is EUR 5 per mg/km for the first 60 mg/km, EUR 15 per mg/km for the next 20 mg/km, and EUR 25 per mg/km thereafter. The NOx element of the charge is capped at EUR 4 850 for diesel vehicles and EUR 600 for other vehicles. Flat rate applies to vehicles designed and constructed for the carriage of goods and having a maximum laden mass not exceeding 3.5 tonnes not	Value CO_2 emissions NOx emissions Electric propulsion Type Age Max laden mass Body type	Relief for hybrid electric vehicles: age dependent with a maximum tax relief of EUR 1500 for a new vehicle. Relief for plug-in hybrid electric vehicles: age dependent with a maximum tax relief of EUR 2500 for a new vehicle. Relief for new series production electric vehicles: subject to a maximum of EUR 5000 Remission/repayment for vehicles specially adapted for persons with certain severe and permanent physical disabilities: subject to a maximum of EUR 10 000, EUR 16 000 and EUR 22 000 for a disabled driver and EUR 16 000 and EUR 22 000 for a disabled passenger. The amount is depended on the adaptations carried out on the vehicle. Relief for certain charitable organisations is subject to a maximum of EUR 16 000 when the vehicle is adapted to carry less than five such

	included above and motor caravans (13.30% of the value). Motor cycles are charged EUR 2 per cc up to and including 350cc and EUR 1 per cc above. Large vehicles designed and constructed for the carriage of goods (maximum laden mass over 3.5 tons), buses, tractors and "vintage' (over 30 years old) vehicles are charged EUR 200. Special purpose vehicles such as ambulances and fire engines are subject to a nil rate.		persons. Exemptions: Transfers of permanent residence, transfers of permanent business undertakings, inheritances, donations by certain organisations, international air services, diplomatic agents and EU officials, vehicles for use by EU or UN organisations
Israel	**VAT**:17% **Purchase Tax**: private and commercial vehicle weight not exceeding 3500 kg are taxed at 83% of the value; Additional luxury tax is levied on the value of the vehicle that exceeds 300 000 NIS, according to the following formula: 20%*(vehicle price - 300 000)/vehicle price; Taxi < 3 500 kg – 8%; Taxi >3 500 kg – 0%; Commercial vehicles over 3500 kg are taxed at 72% of their value but not eligible for a rebate.	Weight Polluting emissions Electric propulsion Safety system Engine power	Rebates according to the polluting emissions: vehicles weighing up to 3500 kg benefit of a rebate on the Purchase Tax according to their degree of pollution. There are 15 levels of polluting emissions according to a "Green Score" (weighting the emission of five major pollutants). Rebate is up to the amount of NIS 16 629 Hybrid vehicles - Pollution level 1 or 2 –; battery capacity > 3 KWH and green score < 100 – 20% are taxed at a rate of 45% but the tax benefit is capped at ILS 20 000. Plug-in Hybrid vehicles are taxed at a rate of 25% but the tax benefit is capped at ILS 60 000. Electricity powered vehicles are taxed a rate of 10% of their value depending on the customs and purchase tax rate. Since June 2018 luxury tax is also levied on hybrid vehicles and electric vehicles. Vehicles weighing up to 3500 kg benefit of a rebate on the Purchase Tax (up to 2400 NIS) according to their safety level. There are 9 safety levels (0-8) depending on the number of safety systems.
Italy	**VAT**: 22% Anyone who buys, incl. through financial leasing, and registers a new M1 vehicle (i.e. vehicles designed and constructed for the carriage of passengers and comprising no more than eight seats in addition to the driver's seat) in Italy, as well as registers in Italy an M1 vehicle already registered in another State, is required to pay a **tax based on the number of grams of CO_2 emitted** per km exceeding the threshold of 160 CO_2 g/km as follows: 161-175 CO_2 g/km: EUR 1100; 176-200 CO_2 g/km: EUR 1600; 201-250 CO_2 g/km: EUR 2000; above 250 CO_2 g/km: EUR 2500.	CO_2 emissions	Exemption from the tax: special purpose vehicles such as vehicles for disabled people.
Japan	**VAT:** 10% **Environmental performance excise (automobile tax - light motor vehicle tax):** 0-3% of acquisition price (0-2% for commercial and light vehicles) according to environmental criteria (e.g. vehicle type, fuel efficiency, etc.)	Value Environmental criteria Fuel efficiency	Extension of temporary reduction of environmental performance excise (automobile tax - light motor vehicle tax): reduced tax rate (environmental performance excise) for private passenger cars acquired between October 2019 and March 2021 by 1% Special measures of reduced environmental performance excise (automobile tax): vehicles with small burden of environment, barrier-free buses and taxis, trucks with collision damage alleviation brake control device, etc., buses for ordinary passengers used on the bus routes provided for in prefectural ordinance.

Korea	**VAT**: 10% **Special Excise Tax:** from zero to 5% of the manufacturer's price according to cylinder capacity **Education Tax**: 30% on the amount of Excise Tax **Acquisition Tax**: 2-7% of the retail price excluding VAT	Value Cylinder capacity Electric propulsion	Exemptions from special excise tax and education tax Cars used by disabled persons; ambulances used by hospitals; cars used for transportation business(public passenger transportation only); cars used for car-rental business. Exemptions from acquisition tax Cars used by disabled persons, cars used by parents having at least 3 children, small cars for non-commercial activities Rebate for hybrid and electricity powered vehicles: relief of the Special Excise tax not exceeding KRW 1 000 000 (hybrid) and KRW 2 000 000 (electricity powered vehicles).
Latvia	**VAT:** 21% **Vehicle registration (state fee):** for registration, registration certificate and registration number plates - EUR 43.93 **Natural resource tax:** EUR 55 per vehicle	Value	-
Lithuania	VAT**: 21 %** **Registration fee:** a flat rate fee of EUR 14.48 is payable on the first registration of a new vehicle (passenger cars, heavy vehicles) and a flat rate fee of EUR 12.45 is payable on the first registration of other vehicle – e.g. used cars (passenger cars, heavy vehicles). From 1 July 2020, a car registration tax applies payable by all car owners (individuals and legal entities) when registering the car. The fee will vary depending on CO_2 emissions and fuel type and will range from 15 Euro to 540 Euro.	Value Age of vehicle CO_2 Emissions	Rebate for disabled people (only owners of passenger cars (once every 3 years): 90% rebate on registration fee for owner who has a disability percentage of 75-100% 75% rebate on registration fee for owner who has a disability percentage of 60-70% 50% rebate on registration fee for owner who has a disability percentage of 45-55%
Luxembourg	**VAT**: 17% **Registration Tax**: the tax is calculated per 100 cm3 according to the following formula: Tax = a * b * c, where a = CO_2 emissions component; b = multiplier (= 0.9 for cars using gasoil & 0.6 for cars not using gasoil). c= additional multiplier when CO_2 emissions >90 g/km (= 0.5 plus 0.1 per additional 10 g/km).	Value CO_2 Emissions Type of fuel Electric propulsion	Bonus system : purchasers of new hybrid cars emitting less than 60g CO_2/km and electricity powered vehicles are entitled to a bonus of EUR 5 000.
Mexico	**VAT**: 16% **New vehicles tax**: from 2% to 17% plus a fixed fee according to vehicle value. For vehicles with a price higher than MXN 782 125.30 (for 2020), an additional discount applies consisting of the reduction of the tax at 7% of the difference between the sales price and the price threshold mentioned above. The tax tariff limitations are updated every year.	Value Electric propulsion	Exemption of 100% of the New Vehicles Tax for vehicles with value of up to MXN 263 690.54 Exemption of 50% of the New Vehicles Tax for vehicles with value from MXN 263 690.55 to MXN 334 008.02 Exemption of 100% of the New Vehicles Tax for hybrid electricity powered vehicles.

Netherlands	**VAT**: 21% **Registration Tax:** for passenger cars, it is fully based on CO_2 emissions and the type of motor fuel used. For passenger cars, the registration tax is progressive and varies between EUR 356 and EUR 458 per g/km exceeding the level of 1g/km. Passenger cars using diesel are charged with an additional EUR 86.43 per g/km exceeding the level of 67 g/km. Registration tax for motorcycles and delivery vans is based on the value of the vehicle	CO_2 Emissions Motor fuel Value Electric propulsion	Zero-emission vehicles (e.g. electricity powered vehicles) are exempt from Registration Tax Other examples of exemption are: delivery vans owned by entrepreneurs and used for business purposes for at least 10%; Tax refunds are provided for vehicles such as: vehicles used by fire brigades, vehicles used by the police, funerary vehicles, vehicles used for the transport of prisoners, vans used by disabled persons, (animal) ambulances, taxis and vehicles that are used for secure transport
New Zealand	**GST:** 15% **Registration Fee on initial registration**: the registration fee varies depending on the type of vehicle being registered. The base registration fee for a private passenger vehicle varies from NZD 74.00 to NZD 232.00 depending on the size of the engine. **Road user charges**: all diesel vehicles and any vehicle with a GVM of 3.5 tonnes or more are required to pay road user charges. Road user charges are distance based (purchased in 1000 kilometre increments) and charges vary based on the weight and configuration of the vehicle.	Vehicle type Cylinder capacity Electric propulsion	Electric vehicles are currently exempt from road user charges.
Norway	**VAT**: 25% **Registration Tax**: rates vary according to weight, CO_2-emissions and NOx-emissions. When CO_2-emissions information is not stated, the tax is calculated based on cylinder capacity instead of CO_2-emissions.	Weight CO_2 emissions NOx emissions Type of fuel Electric range	Electricity powered vehicles are exempt from the Registration Tax Plug-in hybric vehicles (both electric and combustion engine, with external charging) benefit from a rebate from Registration Tax: 23% of the total weight is not included in the tax base. From 1 July 2018 the weight deduction is differentiated by electric range. Flexifuel vehicles (can use fuel with at least 85 pct. Ethanol) benefit from a rebate of NOK 10 000 per vehicle.
Poland	**VAT**: 23% **Excise Duty** is levied on passenger cars prior to their first registration at the time of their sale, intra-community acquisition and import. The tax base is the sales price or the customs value (for imports). Rates for passenger cars depend on engine capacity i.e. 18.6% for cars with engine cubic capacity over 2000 cm^3 and 3.1% for the others. For hybrid fuelled passenger cars combining conventional combustion engine with an electric propulsion (hybrid electric vehicle - HEV) the tax rate is reduced by half compared to standard rate. For passenger cars with combustion engine capacity of 2 000 cubic centimetres or less, the tax is paid at a rate of 1.55% of the tax base and for passenger cars with engine capacity exceeding 2 000 cubic centimetres but not exceeding 3 500 cubic centimetres excise tax is paid at a rate of 9,3% of the tax base. A reduced tax rate of 9.3% of the tax base for hybrid fuelled vehicles (plug-in) with combustion engine capacity higher than 2 000 cubic centimetres but not exceeding 3 500 cubic centimetres also applies.	Value Cylinder capacity Electric/hydrogen propulsion	Are exempt from the Excise Duty: certain types of ambulance vehicles; electric, hybrid (plug-in) with engine capacity of 2 000 cubic centimeters or less and hydrogen fueled vehicles (the exemption for hybrid vehicles is temporary and shall apply until 1 January 2021; passenger cars introduced in Poland for permanent stay or returning from a temporary stay in the EU or EFTA (under certain conditions).

Portugal	**VAT**: 23% **Motor vehicle tax release for consumption (ISV)** is based on cylinder capacity and CO_2 emissions (light passengers vehicles) or only on cylinder capacity (other light vehicles, and cycles with two, three or four wheels). Other rate brackets are applicable for light commercial vehicles and some segments of combined (passenger and freight) vehicles.	Value Engine capacity CO_2 Emissions Particles emissions Electric propulsion	Are exempt: vehicles owned by the State (central, regional or local administration), fire brigades, foreign States, diplomatic and consular missions, international organisations and European agencies. Are also exempt: vehicles for disable persons, passenger vehicles for rental or taxi services. Non-motorized vehicles that are purely electric vehicles or moved by renewable energies, and ambulances and heavy vehicles (above 3.500 kg) are out of motor vehicle tax incidence.
Slovak Republic	**VAT**: 20% **Administrative fees**: registration in the vehicle register is subject to a registration fee payable by the holder of a motor vehicle (applies to new, imported and used cars). The fee is calculated by formula with given parameters: RP = Pkw x RV1-n where RP is fee rate, Pkw is power of engine, RV1-n is coefficient of vehicle residual value, but the rate shall not be lower than EUR 33. Pkw values vary in 16 brackets from EUR 33 (engine capacity up to 80kw) to EUR 3900 (engine capacity above 254kw). RV1-n coefficient varies in 17 brackets from 1 (first registration) to 0.06 (vehicles over 16 years old). First record of electric car in the cars register is subject to a fee of EUR 33 payable by the holder of the vehicle. **Plate fee:** for the release of a license plate number: EUR 16.50 per plate i.e. EUR 33 for 1 vehicle.	Value Engine power Residual value Type of fuel Electric propulsion	Disabled persons: 50% rebate (max. 100 EUR) in administrative fee are applied for disabled persons. Hybrids, CNG, LNG vehicles: 50% rebate in administrative fee for vehicle holder. Family vans: 50% rebate in administrative fee for vehicle holder with maximum power of engine of 110 kW; holder has at least 4 children in parenting. Other exemptions: 100% rebate for state authorities, higher territorial units, budget organisation, diplomats, court of justice, prosecution, police, Slovak red cross and legal person owned by state authority (100% of shares).
Slovenia	**VAT**: 22% **Motor vehicle tax** is levied for passenger motor vehicles, motorcycles and camper vans put into circulation for the first time; imports and acquisitions from other EU Member States are also subject to the tax. The tax base is the selling price of an individual motor vehicle, excluding VAT and the motor vehicle tax itself. The tax rate is determined according to environmental criteria (CO_2, Euro emission standards) and the rates are determined from 0.5% to 28% for petrol cars and from 1% to 31% for diesel cars. Passenger cars with cylinder capacity over 2500 cm³ are subject to an additional tax. Rates vary from 8% (2500 cm³ and more) to 16% (4000 cm³ and more). For diesel cars particulate matter (PM) emissions are also considered. Tax rates for motorcycles and camper vans are set upon engine power in the range from 1.5% to 5% for motorcycles and 6% to 18% for camper vans. Motorcycles with cylinder capacity over 1000 cm³ are subject to the additional tax of 5%. Motor vehicle tax is levied only at the time of first registration of a vehicle and not on an annual basis.	Value Selling price CO_2 emissions Particulate matter emissions EURO emissions standards Engine power Cylinder capacity Weight	Motor vehicle tax exemptions: vehicles acquired for transport of families with three or more children; vehicles purchased for carrying disabled people; vehicles intended for (1) official use by diplomatic and consular representations accredited to Slovenia; (2) official use by international organisations, if so stipulated by international treaties binding on Slovenia; (3) personal use by foreign staff of diplomatic and consular missions, accredited to Slovenia, including their family members; (4) personal use by foreign staff of international organisations, including their family members, if so stipulated by international treaties binding on Slovenia. Are also exempt: used vehicles (old-timers); vehicles imported on a temporary basis (the temporary change of residence of the vehicle's proprietor who does not maintain his permanent residence in Slovenia); sports vehicles that have not been adapted for road use and are intended only for driving on circuits; transfer of vehicles in the case of reorganisations of vehicle's proprietor; emergency rescue motor vehicles used for transport of victims and patients; financial leasing of the vehicles. Tax exemptions listed in this box also apply to financial leasing of these vehicles. There is no exemption for the environmental tax
Spain	**VAT**: 21% **Vehicle Registration Tax (VRT)** is based on CO_2 emissions. Rates vary from 0% (up to 120 g CO_2/km) to 14.75% (200 g CO_2/km and more).	Value CO_2 emissions	VRT exemptions: taxis, driving school vehicles, rental service vehicles; vehicles acquired and used by disabled people; vehicles with special diplomatic registration; transfer of vehicles in the case of change of residence of vehicle's owner.

Sweden	**VAT**: 25%	Value	
Switzerland	**VAT**: 7.7% **Automobile duty:** 4% of the vehicle's value is levied on light commercial vehicles with a unit weight of no more than 1600 kg, as well as on passenger vehicles. The duty is payable on the importation of automobiles into the domestic territory and the delivery and own use of automobiles produced domestically. No registration tax (but small fees for number plates and registration papers)	Value Electric propulsion	Electrically powered vehicles are exempt from acquisition tax
Turkey	**VAT**: 18%. **Special Consumption Tax (SCT)** is collected once on first acquisition of vehicles. Criteria: engine capacity, SCT tax base, motor power for electric and hybrid vehicles in kw.	Value Cylinder capacity Electric propulsion	Exemption: vehicles for diplomatic use, vehicles for people with disabilities, acquisition of aircraft and helicopters by T.A.A., the first acquisition of vehicles by the headquarters of the Presidency, the vehicles acquired exclusively for use in petroleum exploration activities, the exemption for vehicle purchases of relatives of martyrs, exemption for renewed of commercial vehicles. Rebate: discounted SCT rate applied for only electric vehicles in the 87.03 and 87.11 tariff positions and motor vehicles that have electric motors along with fuel engines (hybrids) in the 87.03 tariff position.
United Kingdom	**VAT**: 20% **Vehicle First Registration Fee**: a flat rate fee of GBP 55.0 is payable on the first registration or licensing of a motor vehicle in the United Kingdom	Value	Rebate for disabled people: disabled people are exempt from the Vehicle First Registration Fee. Other exemptions: vehicles previously registered in Northern Ireland; vehicles registered for off road use; Crown Exempt Vehicles; historic vehicles previously registered with the old Local Authorities (late conversions); imported vehicles previously registered under the Personal Export Scheme and New Means of Transport Scheme; Visiting Forces Vehicles.
United States	**A gas guzzler tax** is imposed on the sale, use, or lease by the manufacturer or importer of an automobile of a model type that does not meet certain standards for fuel economy. Automobiles imported for business or personal use are also subject to the tax. "Automobile" means any four-wheeled vehicle (including limousines) rated at 6 000 pounds or less unloaded gross weight that is propelled by an engine powered by gasoline or diesel fuel and is intended for use mainly on public streets, roads, and highways. In 2017, the tax applied to motor vehicles that achieved less than 22.5 miles per gallon. The tax was USD 1 000 for automobiles that got between 21.5 and 22.5 miles per gallon and increased in stages, reaching USD 7 700 for vehicles that got less than 12.5 miles per gallon. **A retail tax on heavy trucks, trailers, and tractors**.12 percent of the sales price applies to the first retail sale of a truck chassis or body, a truck trailer and semitrailer chassis or body, and tractors that are primarily used for highway transportation in combination with a trailer or semitrailer. **A taxable tire tax** is imposed on tires sold by the manufacturer, producer, or	Fuel efficiency Value Weight Tires	The gas guzzler tax is widely applied and must be paid by vehicles sold to the federal government, state and local governments, and non-profit educational organizations. Vehicles used for police, other law enforcement purposes, or firefighting purposes or as ambulances are exempt. Limousines weighing more than 6 000 pounds or designed to carry more than 10 people are exempt. Tires for use on local and school buses or for the exclusive use of the Department of Defense or the Coast Guard are exempt.

	importer at the rate of USD 9.45 cents (USD 4.725 cents in the case of a biasply tire or super single tire not designed for steering) for each 10 pounds of the maximum rated load capacity over 3 500 pounds.		

Notes:

This table does not include customs duties; specific regimes for second-hand cars (e.g. margin scheme, old timers); diplomatic sales; export/import and transit schemes and insurance premium tax.

1. Rebates and exemptions mentioned in this table do not include those that are granted to vehicles used by embassies and other diplomatic missions, international organisations and under a specific customs regime.

2. **Greece.** Since 31.7.2020 new registration tax rates with a progressive tax scale on the taxable value (retail price before taxes) have been defined, which are further differentiated on the basis of CO_2 emissions for passenger cars and the emissions standard. Exemptions from registration tax since 31.7.2020 is granted to hybrid cars with CO_2 emissions less than or equal to 50 g/km are released from the registration tax by 75%; hybrid cars with CO_2 emissions more than or equal to 51g/km are released from the registration tax by 50%; automotive wheelhouses are released from the registration tax by 75%.

Source: national delegates. Position as at 1 January 2020

Annex Table 4.A.2. Taxes on ownership or use of motor vehicles

Country	Taxes	Criteria	Rebates/Exemptions[1]
Australia	**Annual registration fees**. States and Territories levy fees for annual registration, third party compulsory insurance and drivers' licenses. Fees for commercial vehicles are generally higher than the fees for private vehicles. In most States, fees for trucks vary depending on the type of vehicle and the gross vehicle mass. Licence renewal fees vary to reflect validity periods from one to five years.	Commercial/private use Gross vehicle mass	
Austria	**Motor Vehicles Tax**: motor vehicles above a permissible gross weight of 3.5 tonnes are subject to a Motor Vehicle Tax based on the weight of the vehicle (from EUR 1.55 to EUR 1.90 per month and ton depending on the weight). **Motor Vehicle Insurance Tax**: applicable to motor vehicles up to and including a maximum permissible gross weight of 3.5 tons. For first registrations before 1.10.2020: the tax is based on engine power in kilowatt (cars) or cubic capacity (motorbikes). For first registrations after 1.10.2020: CO_2-emssions are taken into account in addition to engine power/cubic capacity. For cars: (engine power in kilowatt – 65) * 0.72 EUR + (CO_2 emissions – 115) * EUR 0.72 per month. For motorbikes: (cubic capacity – 52) *0,014 + (CO_2-emissions – 52) * EUR 0.20 per month.	Weight Engine power Cubic capacity CO_2 emissions Electric propulsion	Vehicles used by diplomatic missions and consular offices; armed forces; police; fire brigade; ambulances; mountain rescue; electrically propelled vehicles; self-propelled working machines; trial moving vehicles; taxi services; mopeds and motorcycles with a cubic capacity of maximum 100 CC; vehicle used solely in agricultural production and forestry; vehicles used for disabled persons.
Belgium	**Federal tax:** the calculation of the taxable benefit from the private use of a company car is based on $C0_2$ emissions. The deductibility of professional expenses related to the use of the car, including fuel expenses, (50 to 120%) is linked to CO_2 emissions. **Annual Road Tax:** *Walloon Region*: the tax rate depends on fiscal hp. and cylinder capacity and is set according to a progressive scale from EUR 80.52 to EUR 2060.92. For vehicles above 20 hp (more than 41 cylinder capacity) an additional amount of EUR 112.33 by hp is levied. Vehicles of more than 30 years old (25 years old in the Brussels Capital Region) are subject to an annual tax of EUR 36.53. *Flemish Region:* for passenger cars, dual-use cars and minibuses that were registered as from 1 January 2016 as well as for vehicles, intended for the transport of goods, hearses, tractors or trailers of an MMA of less than or equal to 2500 kg that were registered 30 June 2017, the tax rate depends on fiscal h.p. and cylinder capacity, but includes "ecoboni" and "ecomali". This implies that the tax is modulated depending on the $C0_2$ emission, the euro standard and the type of fuel (except for leasing cars). For leasing vehicles and other non-leasing vehicles, the tax rate depends only on fiscal h.p. and cylinder capacity and is set according to a progressive scale from EUR 80.52 up to EUR 2060.92. For vehicles above 20 hp (more than 41 cylinder capacity) an additional amount of EUR 112.33 h.p. is levied. Vehicles of more than	Engine power Cylinder capacity Fuel used Environmental characteristics CO_2 emissions	All regions provide exemptions for cars used by public authorities, vehicles for disabled people and war invalids, agricultural vehicles, rescue vehicles, trial moving vehicles, ships and little boats, taxi services, mopeds and motorcycles with a cylinder capacity of maximum 250 CC. Flemish Region: as of fiscal year 2016 a tax reduction of EUR 100 is applicable to cars running on Liquefied Gas Petroleum. Exemption is provided to cars using certain fuels: pure electric, hydrogen-powered, plug-in hybrid (until 2021), CNG/LNG (until 2021). Brussels region: an exemption of the tax is granted to victims of a terrorist attack that have an invalidity pension of minimum 60%.

	28 years old are subject to an annual tax of EUR 38.08. As from the fiscal year 2022 this annual tax is only applicable for cars of 30 years of age or older. *Brussels Capital Region*: for passenger cars the tax rate depends on engine power expressed in fiscal hp and is set according to a progressive scale from EUR 83.83 to EUR 2148.30. For vehicles with an engine power exceeding 20 hp (more than 41 cylinder capacity) an additional amount of EUR 117.21 per hp is levied. For electric cars the minimum rate applies. Vehicles of more than 25 years old are subject to an annual tax of EUR 38.08. (The age at which a vehicle is considered to be an "old-timer" is to be increased gradually from 25 to 30 years by 2025.). For motorcycles an annual flat-rate tax of EUR 59.27 applies. For light goods vehicles up to and including a maximum permissible laden weight of 3.5 tons, as well as for camping cars the tax rate depends on the maximum permissible laden weight. For heavy goods vehicles with a maximum permissible laden weight of over 12 tons the tax rate depends on the maximum permissible laden weight, the number of axles and the suspension type. **Additional annual road tax** is levied in all the regions on cars entirely or partially powered by Liquefied Gas Petroleum. This tax is based on a progressive scale depending on the engine power from EUR 89.16 to EUR 208. 20 **Kilometre charge**: a kilometre charge is levied in all the Regions on motor vehicles or articulated vehicle combinations intended or used for the carriage by road of goods having a maximum permissible laden weight of over 3,5 tonnes.		
Canada	**Annual fees**. All provinces impose annual fees for the use of motor vehicles. In general, the fees depend on the type of vehicles and in most cases on the weight of the vehicle	Type Weight	
Chile	**Annual Motor Vehicle Tax** (levied by municipalities) for the use of motor vehicles on public roads depending on the commercial value of the vehicle. Lightweight vehicles: depending on the commercial value of the vehicle Passenger vehicles: fixed fee Cargo vehicles: according to loading capacity	Commercial value Fixed fee Loading capacity (trucks)	
Colombia	**Annual Motor Vehicle Tax**. This tax is levied by municipalities for the use of motor vehicles on public roads and the rates depend on the commercial value of the vehicle, as follows: (a) 1,5% of the commercial value of the vehicle when the value of the vehicle is less than COP 48 029 000; (b) 2,5% of the commercial value of the vehicle when the value of the vehicle is greater than COP 48 029 000 and less than COP 108 063 000; (c) 3.5% of the commercial value of the vehicle when the value of the vehicle is greater than COP 108 063 000.	Commercial value	

Czech Republic	**Road tax** is imposed on all road motor vehicles and their trailers registered and operated in the Czech Republic if they are used by: - corporate income tax payers (except for vehicles used by public benefit taxpayer for activities which are not subject to corporate income tax); - personal income tax payers, for an independent from which they derive income as defined under the Act on Income Tax or in direct connection with such activities. Vehicles with a total permitted weight above 3.5t registered in the Czech Republic and destined solely for freight transport are always liable to road tax. For passenger cars the tax base is the engine's cylinder capacity in cubic centimetres, with the exception of electric-driven passenger cars; For semi-trailers and other motor vehicles the tax base is: the total of the maximum permitted weight on axles in tonnes and the number of axles of semi-trailers; in the case of other vehicles the maximum permitted weight in tonnes and the number of axles. The annual tax rate of passenger cars varies from CZK 1 200 to CZK 4 200 and in the case of other vehicles vary from CZK 1 800 to CZK 33 100.	Cylinder capacity (passenger cars) Type of propulsion Electric propulsion Type of fuel Total max. permitted weight on axles and number of axles (semi-trailers) Max. permitted weight and number of axles (other vehicles)	Tax exemption: vehicles usually with less than four wheels (motorcycles); vehicles used by diplomatic missions and consular offices (where there is a reciprocal arrangement); vehicles ensuring domestic line passenger transport, vehicles operated by the armed forces and civil defence; vehicles which are state mobilisation reserve or emergency reserve; vehicles of the Police of the Czech Republic; fire protection vehicles; ambulances; mining and mountain rescue vehicles; gas emergency service and power engineering emergency service vehicles. Special road sweeping vehicles; special single-purpose vehicles (e.g. vehicles used in road marking) and vehicles belonging to road authorities or to persons authorized by road authorities exclusively used to maintain land communications, except for passenger cars, electrically propelled vehicles, hybrid driven vehicles, vehicles using as fuel either LPG or CNG or vehicles equipped with an engine determined by his producer for combustion of E85. Tax reduction (25% to 100%) for vehicle exclusively used for carriage in the combined transport for which railway transport or inland waterway transport is made use of. The tax rate is reduced for the period of 108 months from the date of the first registration of vehicle (for the first 36 months by 48%, for the next 36 months by 40% and for the next 36 months by 25%.
Denmark	**Passenger cars semi-annual tax**: the tax is based on fuel consumption, with different rates for petrol/diesel. Rates range from DKK 310 (>20km/l) up to DKK 10830 (<4.5km/l) for petrol cars, and from DKK 130 (>32.1km/l) up to 16 100 (<5.1km/l) for diesel cars. **Lorries' annual tax**: Vehicles registered for the first time until 24 April 2007: the charge for private use is DKK 1 060 annually for cars with total permissible weight (tpw) up to 2000 kg and DKK 5 920 annually for cars with tpw between 2000 and 4000 kg. **Charge for private use**. Vehicles registered on 25 April 2007 or after: the charge for private use is DKK 5920 annually for cars with total permissible weight (tpw) up to 3000 kg and DKK 17 590 annually for cars with tpw between 3000 and 4000 kg. For cars used for both private and commercial purposes the rates are 50%. Cars used exclusively for commercial purposes are free of charge.	Fuel efficiency Weight (for lorries)	
Estonia	**Heavy goods vehicle tax**. Varies from 0 to 232,60 (per quarter) EUR depending on the combination of following factors: weight range (12 tonnes to 40 and more tonnes), axel combination (2, 3, 4, 2+1, 2+2, 2+3, 3+2, 3+3), type of suspension (air, other)..	Weight range, Axle combination, Type of suspension	Exemptions apply for Defence Force, Defence League, Enforcement Force and Rescue Service, local authorities, NGOs, Foundation and business vehicles intended for rescue operations, heavy goods vehicles.
Finland	**Annual tax for passenger cars and delivery vans** based on CO_2 emissions. If the car does not have emission data in the Vehicular and Driver Data Register, the tax is based on the total mass of the vehicle. Tax rates vary from EUR 53.29 for	CO_2 emissions Weight	

	vehicles emitting from 0g CO_2/km up to EUR 654.44 for vehicles emitting 400g CO_2/km or more. **A tax on driving power** is applicable for diesel passenger cars and vans, based on the total mass of the vehicle. The tax on driving power also applies to other cars and vans using less taxed fuels than petrol. For lorries there is an annual tax based on maximum gross weight, number of axles and use of trailer	Number of axles (lorries)	
France	**Company car tax** based on two components: CO_2 emissions and other air pollutants. For CO_2 emissions, rates vary from EUR 1 for each gramme emitted for cars emitting from 20g CO_2/km up to 60g CO_2/km, to EUR 29 for each gramme emitted for cars emitting more than 250g CO_2/km. For other air pollutant, the rate is EUR 20 for unleaded gasoline and EUR 40 for diesel fuel. **Annual tax on polluting vehicles**. An annual tax is payable by owners of vehicles emitting from 250g CO_2/km for car registered in 2009 to 190g CO_2/km for cars registered as of 2012. The rate is EUR 160 a year.	Engine power Electric propulsion Type of fuel CO_2 emissions	**Exemptions**: cars more than 10 years old; cars used for public passenger transport and cars used for leasing or sale; electrically or gas propelled cars (for mixed oil and gas propelled vehicles exemption is reduced by half). Vehicles using both petrol and GPL are exempt at rate of 50%.
Germany	**Motor Vehicle Tax**. For passenger cars with a first registration from 1 July 2009, the Motor Vehicle Tax is based mainly on CO_2 emissions. It consists of a base tax (according to cylinder capacity) and a CO_2 tax. The rates of the base tax are EUR 2 per 100 cc (petrol) and EUR 9.50 per 100 cc (diesel) respectively. The CO_2 tax is linear at EUR 2 per g CO_2/km. Cars that were first registered before 1 July 2009 are taxed according to their polluting emissions (EURO-Norm) and cylinder capacity.	Polluting emissions Cylinder capacity CO_2 emissions Electric propulsion	Cars with CO_2 emissions below 95 g/km are exempt from the CO_2-element. Only the base tax is due. Exemption for pure electric cars for ten years after the first registration, if the car is registered between 18 May 2011 and 31 December 2025. The time-limited tax exemption is only available until 31 December 2030 at the latest.
Greece	**Annual road tax on private passenger cars** registered for the first time in Greece/European Union/ European Economic Space before 31.10.2010 (as well as those with international initial registration before 2002), and also motorcycles regardless of their date of registration: based on cylinder capacity from EUR 22 to EUR 1 380. For the above category, there is an extra criterion of years of circulation of cars. Private passenger cars and taxis registered for the first time in Greece/European Union/ European Economic Space after 1.11.2010: based on CO_2 emissions from EUR 0 to EUR 3.72 per gram of CO_2. Annual road tax on trucks based on gross weight and on buses on the number of seats. Since 31.7.2020 new registration tax rates with a progressive tax scale on the taxable value (retail price before taxes) have been defined, which are further differentiated on the basis of CO_2 emissions for passenger cars and the emissions standard.	Cylinder capacity CO_2 emissions Electric propulsion Gross weight (trucks) Number of seats (buses)	The main exemptions are: cars used by public authorities, municipalities, ambulances etc., cars used by disabled persons and members of foreign diplomatic services; electric cars, hybrid cars registered until 31.10.2010, with engine displacement under 1.549 cc; private passenger cars, registered after 1.11.2010 with CO_2 emissions under 90g/km Motorcycles up to 300 cc cylinder capacity used in order to replace old technology ones (replacement should take place up to 31.12.2009). For motorcycles with cylinder capacity over 300 cc used in order to replace old technology motorcycles exemption applies for 5 years only following the date of first registration of the new motorcycle. Cars and motorcycles, registered with a valid permission of circulation, may be imported for a limited period up to six months per year, by the customs procedure of temporary importation. Exemptions from registration tax since 31.7.2020 is granted to hybrid cars with CO_2 emissions less than or equal to 50 g/km are released. These are exempt from the registration tax by 75%; hybrid cars with CO2 emissions more than or equal to 51g/km are exempt released from the registration tax by 50%; Moreover, caravans are also exempt automotive wheelhouses are released from the registration tax by 75%.

Hungary	**Motor vehicle tax** levied according to capacity of engine (in Kw) of passenger cars and motorcycles. The tax base for busses, semi-trailers and caravans is the unladen weight of the vehicle. For lorries the tax is based on net weight plus 50 % of cargo weight. The tax rate for passenger cars and motorcycles is from HUF 140/kW to HUF 345/kW depending on the age of the vehicle (the older the vehicle, the less is due). For lorries, busses, semi-trailers the tax rate is HUF 850/100 kg of the tax base, if the vehicle is equipped with road-saving axles. The tax rate for other lorries trailers is HUF 1380/100 kg.	Engine capacity Weight (for lorries) Type of axles (for high-duty vehicles) Electric propulsion	Exemption for vehicles: owned by budgetary agencies and religious organisations; owned by social organisations, foundations not subject to profit tax, used for public transport or fire service; owned by persons seriously disabled or by persons who regularly transport seriously disabled persons up to 13 000 HUF. The tax exemption is available for one vehicle, if its engine capacity does not exceed 100 kW; passenger cars equipped with environment- saving engine.
Iceland	**A disposal charge** of ISK 900 is levied on each vehicle for each six-month period. This charge is payable for fifteen years from the date of the first registration of the vehicle in Iceland, except when the vehicle is already 25 years old at the beginning of the payment year. The charge is an environmental tax that is intended to finance the disposal of the vehicle at the end of its useful life. Once the vehicle is delivered for scrap, an ISK 20 000 refund will be paid to the owner. Motor vehicles fuelled with diesel in excess of 10 tonnes are subject to a special weight/distance tax, calculated on the basis of the weight of the vehicle and the number of kilometres driven. Owners of diesel vehicles that weigh less than 10 tonnes do not pay a weight/distance tax. **A semi-annual road tax on passenger cars** is levied based on the vehicle's carbon dioxide emissions declared by the car manufacturer for combination of city and road driving. Where emission data are not available the tax rate is based on the weight of the vehicle. The semi-annual road tax is ISK 150 for each gram of carbon dioxide emission for emission above 121 grams, in addition to the minimum fee which is ISK 6 225.	Weight Distance CO_2 emissions	
Ireland	**Road tax on private cars** based on CO_2 emissions. Rates vary from EUR 120 (for 0g CO_2/km) to EUR 2350 (above 225g CO_2/km). Tax on commercial vehicles based on net weight: from EUR 333 (<3000 kg) up to EUR 5195 (>20 000 kg)	CO_2 emissions Weight (commercial vehicles) Electric propulsion	Electrically propelled vehicles: EUR 120 flat rate – private and EUR 92 flat rate – commercial not over 1 500kg
Israel	**Annual licensing fees**: private and commercial vehicles weighing up to 3500 kg in total: the vehicles are divided into seven groups (generally the price). The annual licensing fees differentiate according to the year of vehicle production and the group the vehicle belongs to The annual licensing fees range between NIS 720 to NIS 4 548. Commercial vehicles above 3 500 kg, with diesel engine are subject to a different tariff.	Price Age Category	Vehicles for disabled person, diplomats, United Nations Organisations, specific charity institutions.
Italy	**Annual Ownership Tax**: From EUR 2.58 per KW to EUR 4.95 per KW according to engine cylinder capacity and polluting emissions. Regions are entitled to vary the national rate. A surtax on use of cars and vehicles intended for the transport of persons or goods applies at a rate of EUR 20.00 for each KW exceeding 185 KW in engine power.	Engine power Polluting emissions Electric propulsion	Exemption for historical vehicles over 30 years old recognised as having special historical or collectors' interest; flat rate road tax on other vehicles over 30. An exemption of 100% from ownership tax is allowed for electric, LPG and CNG vehicles in the first 5 years (from the first registration) and an exemption

	Such surtax is reduced after five, ten or fifteen years from the construction of the vehicle by 40%, 70% and 85%, respectively		of 75% afterwards in many regions. 100% exemption also applies to vehicles for disabled persons.
Japan	**Motor Vehicle Tonnage Tax** (National) levied on commercial vehicles according to weight. The tax rate for passenger vehicles varies from JPY 4 100 per 0,5 ton up to JPY 6 300 per 0,5 ton (from JPY 2 600 up to JPY 2 800); for lorries from JPY 3 300 per ton up to JPY 6 300 per ton(from JPY 2 600 up to JPY 2 800) **Automobile Tax** (Prefecture) levied on commercial vehicles according to cylinder capacity. For passenger vehicle from JPY 25 000 up to JPY 110 000 (from JPY 7 500 up to JPY 40 700); for lorries: (4-5 tons maximum load) JPY 25 500 (JPY 18 500); for buses: (41-50 passengers capacity) JPY 49 000 (JPY 17 500). **Light Vehicle Tax** (Local): levied on light vehicles and motorcycles according to cylinder capacity and standards.	Weight Cylinder capacity Impact on the environment (incl. Electric/fuel cell propulsion)	Special measures of reduced Motor Vehicle Tonnage Tax Vehicles with low impact on the environment, barrier-free buses and taxis, trucks with collision damage alleviation brake control device, etc. Special measures of refunded Motor Vehicle Tonnage Tax Used vehicles properly scrapped or destroyed by certain disasters before the expiry date of valid period of inspection certificate. Special measures of reduced Automobile Tax and Light Vehicle Tax Vehicles with low impact on the environment.
Korea	**Automobile Tax**: rates are applicable according to cylinder capacity from KRW 80 per cc up to KRW 200 per cc for non-commercial vehicles; and from KRW 18 per cc to KRW 24 per cc for commercial vehicles.	Cylinder capacity	Full exemption for disabled persons
Latvia	**Annual tax for passenger cars:** based on CO_2 emissions for cars with first registration after 31 December 2008. For cars with first registration from 2005 to 2008, the tax is based on gross weight, motor capacity and maximum motor power. The annual tax for passenger cars registered before 2005 is based only on gross weight. **Annual tax for motorcycles**: based on motor capacity **Annual tax for heavy goods vehicles:** based on gross weight and number of axes and type of suspension if gross weight exceeds 12 000 kg.	CO_2 emissions Weight (passenger cars and heavy goods vehicles) Motor capacity (passenger cars and motorcycles) Maximum motor power (passenger cars) Number of axes and type of suspension (heavy good vehicles) Electric propulsion	The main exemptions are for: -a car, motorcycle, tricycle or quadricycle, the owner, holder or driver of which is a disabled person -a vehicle, the owner, holder or driver of which is a representative of a diplomatic, consular or international organisation or a person who has diplomatic or consular privileges and immunities -an emergency vehicle - vehicles having been registered or being registered with the status of historic motor vehicle - electric vehicles
Lithuania	**Charge for busses and heavy vehicles** (vignettes). Applicable annual tax rate threshold - from EUR 304 (for busses) up to EUR 1071 (for heavy vehicles of more than 12 tonnes of gross laden weight).	Vehicle type, category, class and group, emission class, gross laden weight.	Exemptions: vehicles used by public authorities; vehicles specially designed for the use and (or) transport of disabled persons; vehicles of health care institutions (ambulance and resuscitation cars); buses on local (city and suburban) regular routes.
Luxembourg	**Automobile Tax**: the annual circulation tax is based on CO_2 emissions. Tax rates are calculated by multiplying the CO_2 emissions in g/km with 0.9 for diesel cars and 0.6 for cars using other fuels respectively and with an exponential factor (0.5 below 90 g/km and increased by 0.1 for each additional 10 g of CO_2 /km). Tax on heavy vehicles (also known as "Eurovignette") is levied on vehicles (lorries) with a gross weight of 12 tons or more for the use of motor ways. Tax also varies according to Euro norms.	CO_2 emissions Electric propulsion	Exemptions: vehicles for disabled people; historical vehicles; cars used by public authorities; electrically propelled cars

Mexico	Starting 2012, the tax on ownership was eliminated as a Federal Tax. State governments may impose a tax on ownership and/or periodic registration. **Registration fee** is MXN 990 on average and **Tax on ownership** usually varies from 3.0% to 19.1% based on value, type of vehicle and number of passengers.	Value Type of vehicle Number of passengers Electric propulsion	States exempt hybrid and electric vehicles used for public passenger transport; Some states provide exemptions for particular uses. Some states provide a subsidy of 100% for vehicles of any value.
Netherlands	**Motor vehicle tax** is based on the dead-weight and the fuel type used. A Provincial surtax is applicable. Tax on heavy vehicles (also known as "Eurovignette") is levied on vehicles (lorries) with a gross weight of 12 tons or more for the use of motor ways in the Netherlands. Tax also varies according to Euro norms (diesel category)	For motor vehicle tax: Fuel used Weight Region (province) CO_2 emissions For tax on heavy vehicles: Number of axles Polluting emissions	Vehicles with a CO_2 emission of 0 are exempt. Low-emissions vehicles (CO_2 is not exceeding a level of 50 g/km) pay 50% of the taxes. Other examples of exemptions are: (Animal) ambulances; vehicles used by fire brigades and by the police/defence; funerary vehicles; vehicles used to clean, maintain or construct roads; taxis and vehicles older than 40 years. Other special regimes apply such as reduced tax rate for delivery vans owned by entrepreneurs and used for business purposes for at least 10% and for vans equipped for and used by disabled persons.
New Zealand	**Vehicle license fees**. Most vehicles are required to be continuously licensed in order to operate on public roads. Vehicle licenses are valid for up to 12 months. Fees vary depending on the type of vehicle being licensed. For a private passenger vehicle, the base fee for a 12 month license is NZD 52.11.	Vehicle type	
Norway	**The traffic insurance tax** replaced the annual motor vehicle tax from 2018. Daily tax: NOK 9.47 for diesel cars without factory-fitted particle filter and NOK 8.12 for other cars, NOK 5.65 for motorbikes. NOK 1.31 for moped, tractors etc.	Vehicle type Electric propulsion Particle filter	Electricity powered vehicles are exempt from the Traffic insurance tax.
Poland	**Annual Motor Vehicles Tax** levied at municipal level on heavy goods vehicles of maximum permissible gross laden weight over 3.5 tons, road and ballast tractors, trailers and semi-trailers and buses.	Weight Type of vehicle Number of passengers for busses	Vehicles belonging to diplomatic representations, consular offices and other foreign missions. Transport vehicles constituting mobilisation supply. Special vehicles and vehicles used for special purposes. Historic vehicles.
Portugal	**Annual state and municipal tax** on the ownership of a vehicle (reformed on 1st July 2007). For passenger vehicles and mixed use cars with gross weight not exceeding 2500 Kg registered after the reform, tax rate is based on motor capacity and CO_2 emissions. For vehicles registered since 1981 up to the reform rates vary depending on motor capacity or voltage, date of registration and fuel type. **Vehicle excise duty on lorries** above 2.5 tonnes used in public and private transport of merchandise.	Motor capacity CO_2 emissions Electric propulsion Weight Number of axels Vehicle type and fuel Type of suspension	Vehicles owned by the State (central, regional or local administration), fire brigades, foreign States, diplomatic and consular missions, international organizations, specialized European agencies and disabled persons; vehicles seized by the State for as part of a criminal procedure. Are also exempt ambulances, passengers vehicles destined to rental or taxi services, tractors, funerary vehicles, non-motorized vehicles that are purely electric or moved by renewable energies. From 1st April 2020, a tax exemption is also applied to certain types of vehicles with less than 30 years old, considered of historic interest and whose annual circulation does not surpass 500 kilometres.
Slovak Republic	**Motor Vehicle Tax** is imposed only on vehicles that are registered in the Slovak Republic and are used to conduct business activities during the tax period. Rates vary depending on type, weight, cylinder capacity, number of axles (for utility vehicles and buses) of the vehicle and type of engine.	Usage Vehicle type (passenger cars)	**Exemption:** vehicles for diplomats - vehicles used by diplomatic missions and consular offices, vehicles used for emergency services (first aid), vehicles for public services - public buses, vehicles used solely in agriculture or forestry. **Tax reduction (50%)** for hybrid motor vehicles or hybrid electric vehicles,

		Weight Cylinder capacity (utility vehicles and buses) Number of axles Type of engine	vehicles using compressed natural gas (CNG) or liquefied natural gas (LNG), hydrogen-powered vehicles, vehicles which were used for combined transport at least 60 times. The tax rate is reduced for the period of 108 months from the date of the first registration of vehicle (for the first 36 months by 25%, for the next 36 months by 20% and for the next 36 months by 15%).
Slovenia	**Circulation tax** (levied on an annual basis) – an annual fee for the use of road transport vehicles is paid once a year for the use of motor vehicles and trailers in Slovenia by vehicle owners. The fee is paid at the time of renewal of registration certificate. By paying an annual duty a person acquires the right to use a registered vehicle in road traffic for the next 12 months. The amount of tax depends on the category of the vehicle and is proportionate to the duration of the registration period in a certain year. Vehicle deregistration duty is paid for motor vehicle category M1, N1 and L2e for the first time after 1 year of vehicle deregistration and then every year at vehicle deregistration date. Duty is paying for 10 years from the last deregistration. The duty is 25% of circulation tax, but not less than EUR 25. The duty for three-wheeled cycles with electric engine, is EUR 20.	Cylinder capacity, Engine power, Weight Polluting emissions Electric propulsion Type of suspension Number of seats	Tax exemptions: Vehicles exclusively using electricity for power, tractors and tractor trailers, motorcycles, three-wheeled cycles with engine capacity up to 50 cc and light four-wheeled cycles, light trailers with maximum permissible weight up to 750 kg, motor vehicles registered to the Slovenian Army, Civil Protection, Mountain Rescue Service, Cave Rescue Service, Underwater Rescue Service, Disaster Response Service for Ecological and other Disasters and for Search Operations at Sea, Ecological Laboratory with mobile unit, police and fire-fighting vehicles, ambulances, motor vehicles and trailers registered for diplomatic and consular missions, vehicles owned by certain international organizations, and vehicles used for the transport of disabled persons and old timers. Tax reduction for low polluting trucks Trucks of category N1: tax reduction for EURO 5 (-25%) and EURO 6 and higher (-35%) and tax increase for EURO 3 (+10%), EURO 2 (+20%), EURO 1 (+30%) and EURO 0 or lower (+40%); Trucks of category N2, N3 and buses (M2, M3): tax reduction for EURO 5 (-25%) and EURO 6 and higher (-35%) and tax increase for EURO 3 (+10%) EURO 2 (+20%), EURO 1 (+30%) and EURO 0 or lower (+40%) Tax reduction for buses and trucks with air suspension (-15%) Tax reduction for old-timers (-80%) and vehicles acquired for transport of families with four or more children (-50%).
Spain	**Motor Vehicle Tax** (levied by municipalities) based on engine power for passenger cars, passenger capacity for buses, loading capacity for trucks and cylinder volume for motorcycles.	Vehicle type Engine power Cylinder capacity	**Tax exemptions:** Official vehicles belonging to public bodies of diplomatic offices, ambulances, vehicles adapted to disabled people, public transport vehicles over nine seats, tractors and other vehicles of agricultural use; historic vehicles.
Sweden	**The annual circulation tax** for cars from 2006 and later or, older cars that meet at least Euro 4 exhaust emission standards, is based on CO_2 emissions. Also campers, light goods vehicles and light buses that are taken in to use in 2011 or later are taxed based on the CO_2 emissions. The tax consists of a basic rate of SEK 360 plus SEK 22 for each gram CO_2 the vehicle emits above 111 g/km. If the vehicle can be driven with diesel fuel this sum is multiplied by 2.37 plus SEK 250 or 500 depending on vehicle year. For vehicles that can be driven with alternative	Weight CO_2 emissions Type of fuel. Electric propulsion Electric consumption	An exemption from annual circulation tax applies to green cars during the first five years. That set of rules has expired but still applies regarding vehicles that are taxable for the first time before the 1 of July 2018. New rules entered into force the 1 July 2018 for new vehicles taxable for the first time after the 1 of July 2018 and classified as green vehicles with low emissions of CO_2 qualifying for a bonus at purchase. The exemption applies to cars, campers, light goods vehicles and light buses with low emissions of CO_2 in proportion to

	fuels, the tax is SEK 360 plus SEK 11 for each gram CO_2 the vehicle emits above 111 g/km. New vehicles taxable for the first time after the 1 July 2018, vehicle model year 2018 or later, with high emissions of CO_2 will be taxed at a higher rate for the first three years. Vehicles running on gasoline fuel, the tax consists of a basic rate of SEK 360, plus a CO_2 amount consisting of SEK 82 for each gram of CO_2 the vehicle emits above 95 g/km up to 140 g/km and SEK 107 for each gram of CO_2 the vehicle emits above 140 g/km. If the vehicle can be driven with diesel fuel the same principles apply plus that the amount of CO_2 g/km the vehicle emits is multiplied with 13.52 plus SEK 250. After the first three years the CO_2 related amount is SEK 22/gram over 111 gram per kilometre		the vehicle's weight. The vehicle's emissions of CO_2 shall not exceed a calculated value of (95 + 0,0457 x (the vehicle's weight in kg – 1 372)). For alternative fuel vehicles the value is calculated; (150 + 0.0457 x (the vehicle's weight in kg – 1 372)). Electric cars should not consume more electricity than 37 kWh/100 km.
Switzerland	**Annual motor vehicle tax - Cantonal (provincial) tax,** levied according to the weight or engine volume of the vehicle. **Use of Swiss motorways** (first and second-class motorways) is generally subject to a federal charge levied in the form of a motorway charge sticker, which costs CHF 40. The obligation to display a motorway charge sticker generally applies to motor vehicles and trailers with a total weight of up to 3.5 tons each. This group comprises primarily passenger vehicles, motorbikes, vans, trailers, etc. Motor vehicles and trailers with a total weight exceeding 3.5 tons (so-called heavy vehicles) require a motorway charge sticker if they are not subject to the heavy vehicle charge. These include, for example, heavy utility vehicles (e.g. crane lorries). The performance-related heavy vehicle charge (LSVA) depends on the total weight, polluting emissions and kilometres driven in Switzerland. It is levied on all motor vehicles and trailers that have a total permissible laden weight of more than 3.5 tons, are used to transport goods, are registered in Switzerland or abroad and are driven on the Swiss public road network. The lump-sum heavy vehicle charge (PSVA) is levied in the form of a lump sum on heavy motor vehicles for the following vehicle types that are driven on the Swiss public road network: heavy passenger vehicles, heavy campervans, motor-homes and caravans, vehicles used for transporting passengers (coaches, buses), tractors and motor carriages, motor vehicles for fun fairs and circuses. Other motor vehicles for the carriage of goods and with a maximum speed of 45 km/h.	Weight Engine volume Kilometres driven Polluting emissions Electric propulsion	A reduced rate of the motor vehicle tax usually applies to electric and agricultural vehicles.
Turkey	**Motor Vehicle Tax**. Motor vehicles that are in scales specified in the Law and registered at the related government institution are subject to motor vehicle tax. The tax is paid in two instalments. Scales: automobiles, off road vehicles and similar vehicles and motorcycles which are registered after 31/12/2017 are taxed under the scale No 1, Automobiles, off road vehicles and similar vehicles which are registered before 31/12/2017 (this day included) are taxed under the scale No 1/A, Minibuses, vans, motor caravans, buses and similar vehicles, small trucks, trucks, tow trucks and similar vehicles are taxed under the scale No II,-Planes and helicopters are	Weight Number of seats Age Value Vehicle type Cylinder capacity Engine power	Vehicles in scales No I, I/A and II that have only electric motors are taxed over 25% of the tax amounts applied to the same type of vehicles. Vehicles that are registered in the name of government institutions under general budget, government institutions under special budget, social security institutions, special provincial administrations, municipalities, village legal personalities, Turkish Red Crescent Society and Disabled people are exempt from motor vehicle tax.

	taxed under the scale No IV.	Electric propulsion	
United Kingdom	**Vehicle Excise Duty (VED)** on lorries is set according to the number of axles, weight and type of vehicle. Cars that are presented for registration in the UK on or after 1 March 2001 – and before 01/04/17, on the basis of a type approval certificate specifying a carbon dioxide (CO_2) emission figure, attract a rate of VED according to the amount of CO_2 emitted and the type of fuel used. These cars fall within a 13-banded graduated VED system. The bands are labelled A-M, with band A containing the least polluting vehicles and band M comprising of vehicles that have high CO_2 emissions. Full details can be found at www.direct.gov.uk/Motoring Cars registered on or after 01/04/18 on the basis of a type approval certificate specifying a carbon dioxide (CO2) emission figure, attract a rate of VED for its first vehicle licence according to the amount of CO_2 emitted and fuel used. For the second vehicle licence, vehicles with a list price exceeding GBP 40 000 attract a standard rate of VED plus an additional rate of VED. Vehicles with a list price of GBP 40 000 or less attract a standard rate of VED. For private cars which do not fall into the above graduated VED system there is a two-tier threshold: vehicles not over 1549cc pay an annual rate of duty of GBP 145, and those over 1549cc pay a rate of duty of GBP 230.	Vehicle type CO_2 emissions Type of fuel Electric propulsion	Tax exemption applies to vehicles for disabled people, historic vehicles, which are 40 years old, limited use vehicles, agricultural machines, mowing machines, steam powered vehicles, electrically propelled vehicles, and electrically assisted pedal cycles. Vehicles belonging to public bodies such as ambulances, fire engine, police cars, etc.
United States	**Heavy Highway Vehicle Use Tax** is imposed on the use of trucks weighing 55 000 pounds or above. For those trucks (except logging trucks) weighing no more than 75 000 pounds, the tax is USD 100 per year plus USD 22 for each 1 000 pounds in excess of 55 000 pounds. For those trucks weighing more than 75 000 pounds, the tax is USD 550. For logging trucks, the tax is USD 75 per year for trucks weighing at least 55 000 pounds plus USD 16.50 per 1 000 pounds in excess of 55 000 pounds. For logging trucks weighing more than 75 000 pounds the tax is USD 412.50. A credit may be claimed for the tax in the following year if the vehicle was driven 5 000 miles or less (7 500 miles or less for agricultural vehicles.). State and local governments may impose a **periodic registration, operators' license, parking and inspection fees as well as property taxes.**	Weight (for trucks)	

Note:
Excluding insurance premium tax.
1. Rebates and exemptions mentioned in this table do not include those that are granted to vehicles used by embassies and other diplomatic missions, international organisations and under a specific customs regime.
Source: national delegates; position as at 1 January 2020

Annex Table 4.A.3. Taxation of premium unleaded (94-96 RON) gasoline (per litre, 2019)

Country		Ex-tax price[1]		Excise[2]	VAT rate[3]	VAT amount	Total tax	Total price		Total tax as % of total price
	Currency	National currency	USD	National currency	%	National currency	National currency	National currency	USD	
Australia	AUD	0.998	0.694	0.418	10.00	0.142	0.560	1.558	1.083	35.9
Austria*	EUR	0.538	0.602	0.482	20.00	0.204	0.686	1.224	1.371	56.0
Belgium	EUR	0.617	0.691	0.600	21.00	0.256	0.856	1.473	1.650	58.1
Canada*	CAD	0.814	0.613	0.254	12.14	0.132	0.386	1.200	0.904	32.2
Chile*	CLP	411.618	0.585	315.799	19.00	78.207	394.006	805.624	1.145	48.9
Colombia*	COP	1879.36	0.573	414.74	5.00	114.705	529.445	2408.805	0.734	22.0
Czech Republic	CZK	13.315	0.581	12.840	21.00	5.493	18.333	31.648	1.367	57.9
Denmark*	DKK	4.835	0.725	4.673	25.00	2.377	7.050	11.885	1.782	59.3
Estonia	EUR	0.455	0.510	0.563	20.00	0.244	0.807	1.262	1.413	63.9
Finland*	EUR	0.529	0.592	0.703	24.00	0.295	0.998	1.527	1.710	65.4
France*	EUR	0.565	0.633	0.691	20.00	0.251	0.942	1.507	1.688	62.5
Germany*	EUR	0.559	0.626	0.655	19.00	0.231	0.885	1.444	1.617	61.3
Greece	EUR	0.573	0.641	0.700	24.00	0.305	1.005	1.578	1.767	63.7
Hungary	HUF	201.622	0.694	122.674	27.00	81.288	203.962	382.356	1.316	53.3
Iceland*	ISK	82.330	0.671	82 350	24.00	39.523	121 870	204.200	1.665	59.7
Ireland	EUR	0.551	0.621	0.588	23.00	0.262	0.850	1.405	1.584	62.3
Israel	ILS	2.209	0.620	3.074	17.00	0.897	3.971	6.180	1.734	64.3
Italy	EUR	0.562	0.629	0.728	22.00	0.284	1.012	1.574	1.763	64.3
Japan*	JPY	79.155	0.726	56.600	10.00	13.576	70.176	149.331	1.369	47.0
Korea	KRW	878.146	0.754	745.890	10.00	162.404	908.294	1786.440	1.533	50.8
Latvia	EUR	0.553	0.619	0.509	21.00	0.219	0.732	1.285	1.439	57.0
Lithuania	EUR	0.516	0.578	0.434	21.00	0.223	0.634	1.150	1.288	55.1
Luxembourg*	EUR	0.621	0.695	0.472	17.00	0.186	0.658	1.279	1.432	51.4
Mexico*	MXN	16.681	0.868	0.000	16.00	2.669	2.669	19.350	1.007	13.8
Netherlands	EUR	0.581	0.651	0.788	21.00	0.287	1.066	1.656	1.844	64.9
New Zealand*	NZD	1.212	0.798	0.754	15.00	0.295	1.075	2.260	1.489	46.4
Norway*	NOK	6.222	0.707	6.430	25.00	3.163	9.593	15.815	1.797	60.7
Poland*	PLN	2.394	0.624	1.673	23.00	0.935	2.608	5.002	1.303	52.1
Portugal	EUR	0.570	0.638	0.643	23.00	0.279	0.921	1.491	1.670	61.8
Slovak Republic*	EUR	0.579	0.648	0.514	20.00	0.219	0.733	1.312	1.469	55.9
Slovenia*	EUR	0.506	0.567	0.535	22.00	0.229	0.764	1.270	1.422	60.1
Spain*	EUR	0.600	0.671	0.473	21.00	0.225	0.698	1.298	1.453	53.8
Sweden*	SEK	6.016	0.636	6.570	25.00	3.147	9.717	15.733	1.664	61.8
Switzerland	CHF	0.728	0.732	0.754	8.00	0.119	0.873	1.596	1.605	54.5
Turkey	TRY	3.418	0.602	2.377	18.00	1.043	3.420	6.837	1.205	50.0
United Kingdom	GBP	0.461	0.588	0.580	20.00	0.208	0.788	1.249	1.593	63.1
United States*	USD	0.636	0.636	0.121	-	-	0.145	0.781	0.757	18.6

Notes

Conversion of national currency in USD: conversion rates are average market rates (2019) published in OECD Monthly Monetary Statistics (stats.occd.org). See also Annex B.

Prices are average prices for the year 2019. Tax rates are those applicable as at 1 October 2019.

1. Ex-tax price is the price excluding VAT and excise.

2. Excise taxes include all non-VAT taxes levied on the product. For the purposes of this table, payments made to specific bodies that use all the amounts collected to accomplish specific missions (e.g. some emergency stock fees) are not considered as "taxes" and are included in the ex-tax price. When different rates apply to the same product depending e.g. on its biofuel or sulphur content, the rate shown is the one applicable to the most commonly used fuel in the country.

3. GST for Australia, and New Zealand; volume-weighted GST-HST/retail sales taxes for Canada; sales taxes for the United States and Consumption Tax for Japan. VAT for all other countries.
Source: International Energy Agency, IEA Energy Prices, 2020 edition https://www.iea.org/reports/world-energy-prices-2020 and country delegates

StatLink https://doi.org/10.1787/888934220287

Annex Box 4.A.1. Country notes to Table 4.A.3

Austria. The excise amount of EUR 0.482/l applies to unleaded gasoline with minimum 4.6% biofuel content and sulphur content ≤ 10mg/kg. Otherwise the excise duty is EUR 0.515/l.

Canada. The excise rate includes federal and provincial taxes (the federal excise rate is CAD 0.1 per litre). The federal GST rate is 5%. The volume weighted GST/HST rate including the provincial component was 10.69% and the volume weighted GST/HST retail sales tax rate was 12.14%. Municipal taxes and carbon pollution pricing are not included in the excise taxes.

Chile. The Fuel Price Stabilisation Mechanism (*Mecanismo de Estabililización de Precios de los Combustibles* - MEPCO), introduced in 2014 by Law 20.765 has incorporated a variable component to the excise. In order to stabilise consumer price where there are international market price variations, this mechanism operates weekly either as a tax or as a tax credit. The excise is not included in the VAT base.

Colombia. From 1 May 2019 onwards, the VAT rate of 5% applies instead of 19%

Denmark. The excise amount is for fuel with a minimum amount of 4.8% of biofuels. It includes the Excise Tax, the Environment Tax and the NOx Tax.

Finland. The excise amount for premium unleaded gasoline includes taxes of energy and CO_2 components and strategic stockpile fee of EUR 0.0068/l.

France. Tax rate is reduced by EUR 0.01/l in Corsica. An additional tax of max. EUR 0.0073/l is applied by region councils (except in Corsica) to finance sustainable, railway or river navigation substructure. In addition, in the Ile-de-France region, tax rate is inflated up to EUR 0.0102/l.

Germany. The excise amount is for unleaded gasoline with sulphur content ≤ 10mg/kg. Otherwise the excise amount is EUR 0.6698/l. *From 1 July to 31 December 2020 the VAT rate is reduced from 19% to 16% to offset the economic impact of the Covid-19 pandemic.*

Hungary. Excise amount depends on the world market price of crude oil. If the world market price of crude oil is higher than 50 USD/barrel the excise amount is HUF 122.674/l (including the excise duty of HUF 120/l and the strategic stock fee of HUF 2.674/l). If the world market price of crude oil is 50 USD/barrel or less the excise amount is HUF 127.674/l (including the excise duty of HUF 125/l and the strategic stock fee of HUF 2.674/l).

Iceland. Since this country is not member of the IEA or the EU, price data is taken from European Automobile Manufacturers Association. The excise rate of ISK 82.35/l includes the general excise on petrol (ISK 28.05/l), the special excise (ISK 45.02) and the carbon tax (ISK 9.2/l).

Ireland. The 'Ex-tax price' includes a National Oil Reserves Agency (NORA) levy which is charged at a rate of EUR 0.02 per litre. From 9 October 2019 the 'Excise' rate on unleaded gasoline increased to EUR 0.602 per litre.

Japan. This amount includes the Gasoline Tax (JPY 48.6/l), the Local Gasoline Tax (JPY 5.2/l) and the Petroleum and Coal Tax (JPY 2.8/l). The prices and taxes are given for the Tokyo prefecture.

Mexico. There are no excise duties on volume. A tax (Impuesto Especial sobre Producción y Servicios) is charged as a percentage of the value of the product at wholesale level. It is included in the ex-tax price.

Netherlands. For gasoline a stockpiling tax of 0.008/l applies, this is not included in the mentioned excise rate.

New Zealand. The excise amount includes the National Land Transport Management Fund excise tax, the Accident Compensation Commission Levy, the Petroleum or Engine Fuels Monitoring Levy and the Local Authority Fuel Tax.

Norway. The excise amount includes the Excise tax and the CO_2 tax.

Poland. The excise amount includes excise tax and fuel charge.

Slovak Republic. The excise amount is EUR 0.514/l for gasoline with biofuel content lower than the minimum of 6.2%.

Slovenia. The excise duty amount of EUR 534.55 per 1000 litres includes: the excise duty of EUR 478.29; EUR 7.36 surcharge on energy end-use efficiency on petrol; EUR 9.11 surcharge for the promotion of electricity generation from renewable energy sources and high-efficiency cogeneration on petrol and EUR 39.79 CO_2-tax.

Spain. The excise amount of EUR 0.462/l includes the Excise tax (EUR O.424/l) and the average Regional authorities tax (EUR 0.038/l).

Sweden. The excise tax amount includes the Energy Tax (SEK 3.950/l) and CO_2 Tax (SEK 2.620/l).

United States. Average federal and state taxes - there is no VAT

European Union. Directive 2003/96/EC sets minimal excise rates for energy products and electricity

Annex Table 4.A.4. Taxation of automotive diesel (per litre, 2019)

Country		Ex-tax price[1]		Excise[2]	VAT rate[3]	VAT amount	Total tax	Total price		Total tax as % of total price
	Currency	National currency	USD	National currency	%	National currency	National currency	National currency	USD	
Australia	AUD	0.915	0.636	0.418	10.00	0.133	0.551	1.466	1.019	37.5
Austria*	EUR	0.595	0.667	0.410	20.00	0.201	0.611	1.206	1.351	50.6
Belgium	EUR	0.657	0.736	0.600	21.00	0.265	0.864	1.522	1.704	56.8
Canada*	CAD	0.869	0.655	0.192	12.14	0.129	0.321	1.190	0.897	27.0
Chile*	CLP	425.903	0.606	77.410	19.00	84.953	166.656	592.559	0.843	28.1
Colombia*	COP	1951.620	0.595	216.880	5.00	108.425	325.305	2266.930	0.691	14.4
Czech Republic	CZK	15.232	0.664	10.950	21.00	5.498	16.448	31.681	1.382	51.9
Denmark*	DKK	4.996	0.749	3.184	25.00	2.045	5.229	10.225	1.533	51.1
Estonia	EUR	0.470	0.526	0.493	20.00	0.193	0.686	1.120	1.257	61.3
Finland*	EUR	0.604	0.677	0.530	24.00	0.272	0.802	1.407	1.575	57.0
France*	EUR	0.591	0.662	0.609	20.00	0.240	0.849	1.441	1.614	58.9
Germany*	EUR	0.617	0.691	0.470	19.00	0.207	0.677	1.294	1.449	52.3
Greece	EUR	0.698	0.781	0.410	24.00	0.266	0.676	1.373	1.538	49.2
Hungary	HUF	201.622	0.694	112.855	27.00	84.909	197.770	399.392	1.374	49.5
Iceland*	ISK	88.770	0.724	73.250	24.00	38.880	112.130	200.900	1.638	55.8
Ireland	EUR	0.593	0.669	0.479	23.00	0.247	0.726	1.324	1.492	54.9
Israel	ILS	2.775	0.779	2.945	17.00	0.972	3.915	6.690	1.877	58.5
Italy	EUR	0.595	0.667	0.617	22.00	0.266	0.884	1.480	1.657	59.8
Japan*	JPY	84.552	0.775	34.900	10.00	8.735	43.635	128.187	1.176	34.0
Korea	KRW	689.905	0.592	528.750	10.00	121.870	650.616	1340.520	1.150	48.5
Latvia	EUR	0.607	0.680	0.414	21.00	0.214	0.628	1.235	1.383	50.9
Lithuania	EUR	0.612	0.685	0.347	21.00	0.201	0.548	1.160	1.299	47.2
Luxembourg*	EUR	0.594	0.665	0.355	17.00	0.162	0.509	1.102	1.234	46.1
Mexico*	MXN	32.780	1.706	0.000	16.00	5.250	5.250	38.030	1.979	13.8
Netherlands	EUR	0.627	0.702	0.496	21.00	0.239	0.729	1.356	1.519	53.8
New Zealand*	NZD	1.219	0.803	0.044	15.00	0.185	0.232	1.451	0.956	16.0
Norway*	NOK	6.832	0.776	5.160	25.00	2.998	8.138	14.990	1.704	54.3
Poland*	PLN	2.637	0.687	1.469	23.00	0.935	2.413	5.050	1.316	47.8
Portugal	EUR	0.622	0.697	0.486	23.00	0.256	0.741	1.363	1.526	54.3
Slovak Republic*	EUR	0.649	0.727	0.368	20.00	0.203	0.571	1.220	1.366	46.8
Slovenia*	EUR	0.556	0.623	0.457	22.00	0.223	0.680	1.236	1.384	55.0
Spain*	EUR	0.625	0.700	0.379	21.00	0.211	0.590	1.215	1.361	48.5
Sweden*	SEK	7.832	0.828	4.625	25.00	3.114	7.739	15.571	1.647	49.7
Switzerland	CHF	0.837	0.842	0.782	8.00	0.124	0.907	1.743	1.754	52.0
Turkey	TRY	3.624	0.638	1.795	18.00	1.001	2.770	6.394	1.126	43.3
United Kingdom	GBP	0.516	0.658	0.580	20.00	0.218	0.799	1.315	1.677	60.7
United States*	USD	0.648	0.648	0.141	-	..	0.163	0.811	0.811	20.1

Notes

* See Country notes

Conversion of national currency in USD: conversion rates are average market rates (2019) published in OECD Monthly Monetary Statistics (stats.oecd.org). See also Annex B.

Prices are average prices for the year 2019. Tax rates are those applicable as at 1 October 2019.

1. Ex-tax price is the price excluding VAT and excise.

2. Excise taxes are expressed in local currency per litre. They include all non-VAT taxes levied on the product. For the purposes of this table, payments made to specific bodies that use all the amounts collected to accomplish specific missions (e.g. some emergency stock fees) are not considered as "taxes" and are included in the ex-tax price. When different rates apply to the same product depending e.g. on its biofuel or sulphur content, the rate shown is the one applicable to the most commonly used fuel in the country.
3. GST for Australia, and New Zealand; volume-weighted GST-HST/retail sales taxes for Canada; sales taxes for the United States and Consumption Tax for Japan. VAT for all other countries.
Source: International Energy Agency, IEA Energy Prices, 2020 edition https://www.iea.org/reports/world-energy-prices-2020 and country delegates.

StatLink https://doi.org/10.1787/888934220306

Annex Box 4.A.2. Country notes to Table 4.A.4.

Austria. The excise amount of EUR 0.397/l applies to automotive diesel with minimum 6.6% of biofuel and sulphur content ≤ 10mg/kg. Otherwise the excise amount is EUR 0.425/l.

Canada. The excise rate includes federal and provincial taxes (the federal rate is CAD 0.04 per litre). The federal GST rate is 5%. The volume weighted GST rate, including provincial GST rates, was 10.69% and the volume weighted GST/sales tax rate was 12.14%. Municipal taxes and carbon pollution pricing are not included in the excise taxes.

Chile. The Fuel Price Stabilisation Mechanism (*Mecanismo de Estabililización de Precios de los Combustibles* or MEPCO, introduced in 2014 by Law 20.765) has incorporated a variable component to the excise. In order to stabilise consumer price where there are international market price variations, this mechanism operates weekly either as a tax or as a tax credit. The excise is not included in the VAT base.

Colombia. From 1 May 2019 onwards, the VAT rate of 5% applies instead of 19%

Finland. The excise includes energy content tax, CO_2 tax and strategic stockpile fee EUR 0.0035/l.

France. An additional tax of max. EUR 0.0135/l is applied by region councils (except in Corsica) to finance sustainable, railway or river navigation substructure. In addition, in the Ile-de-France region, tax rate is inflated up to EUR 0.0189/l.

Germany. The excise amount is for unleaded gasoline with sulphur content ≤ 10mg/kg. Otherwise the excise amount is EUR 0.48517/l. From 1 July to 31 December 2020 the VAT rate is reduced from 19% to 16% to offset the economic impact of the Covid-19 pandemic.

Hungary. Excise amount depends on the world market price of crude oil. If the world market price of crude oil is higher than 50 USD/barrel the excise amount is HUF 112.588/l (including the excise duty of HUF 110.35/l and the strategic stock fee of HUF 2.505/l). If the world market price of crude oil is 50 USD/barrel or less the excise amount is HUF 122.588/l (including the excise duty of HUF 120.35/l and the strategic stock fee of HUF 2.505/l).

Iceland. Since this country is not member of the IEA or the EU, price data is taken from European Automobile Manufacturers. The excise rate of ISK -73.25/l includes the excise on diesel (ISK 62.85/l) and the carbon tax (ISK 10.04/l).

Ireland. The 'Ex-tax price' includes a National Oil Reserves Agency (NORA) levy which is charged at a rate of EUR 0.02 per litre. From 9 October 2019 the “Excise” rate for automotive diesel increased to EUR 0.495 per litre.

Lithuania. As of 1st January 2020 there was an increase in excise rate: rate for automotive diesel used for agriculture was set at EUR 0.06/l, normal rate for automotive diesel was set at EUR 0.372/l.

Mexico. Excise taxes on gasoline and diesel in 2015 had three components: (1) the excise-carbon tax, set proportionally to the carbon content of the fuel and implemented through a fixed amount per litre, whose main purpose is to send a carbon price signal to contribute to Climate Change commitments; (2) the excise tax specifically earmarked as transfers to the State's governments, proportional to their consumption, also implemented as a fixed amount per litre; and (3) the main excise tax, which, changed each month in value according to a set of criteria which essentially subtracted from the fuel's controlled price the cost of importing or producing fuel, plus the costs of distribution, logistics, related items, and the retail profit for gas station owners. This general excise tax could even become a negative tax (a subsidy) if domestic prices for fuel were low and international reference prices were high, and this was the case for the first 3 years of the decade. The 2016 excise tax reforms changed completely this latter component. Now, the general excise tax on gasoline and diesel is also a fixed quota tax per litre. During the transition period before full price liberalisation of fuels in 2018, the fixed quota of the excise tax will have a complementary quota component (positive or negative) to ensure that the final fuel prices do not vary outside a price band of +/- 3% of the price they had in 2015. This complementary quota can never become equal in size to the excise tax, so general fossil fuel subsidies would be precluded from happening again.

Netherlands. For diesel a stockpiling tax of 0.008/l applies, this is not included in the mentioned excise rate.

New Zealand. The excise tax on diesel is a local authorities' fuel tax and diesel vehicle owners are also required to pay road user charges.

Norway. The excise amount includes the Excise tax and the CO2 tax.

Poland. The excise amount includes excise tax and fuel charge.

Portugal. Automotive diesel used for agriculture is taxed at a lower VAT rate of 13%.

Slovak Republic. The excise amount is EUR 0.393/l for diesel with biofuel content lower than minimum of 6.9%.

Slovenia. The excise duty of EUR 457.33 per 1000 litres includes the excise duty of EUR 392.72; EUR 8.00 surcharge on energy end-use efficiency on gasoil used as propellant, EUR 9.90 surcharge for the promotion of electricity generation from renewable energy sources and high-efficiency cogeneration on gasoil used as propellant, EUR 46.71 CO_2 tax.

Spain. The excise amount of EUR 0.368/l includes the Excise tax (EUR O.331/l) and the average Regional authorities tax (EUR 0.037/l).

Sweden. The tax amount of SEK 4.625/l relates to Class 1 automotive diesel (aromatic content < 5%vol.; max sulphur content of 10 wppm. Higher taxes apply to Class 2 (SEK 4.930/l) and Class 3 (SEK 5.088/l) diesel.

United States. Average federal and state taxes - there is no VAT

European Union. Directive 2003/96/EC sets minimal excise rates for energy products and electricity.

Annex Table 4.A.5. Taxation of aviation fuel

Country	Tax	Commercial aviation[1] (JET A-1)[2]		Private/pleasure flights[3] (JET A-1/AVGAS)[4]	
		Domestic flights	International flights	Domestic flights	International flights
Australia*	Excise (AUD) per litre	0.03556	0	0.03556/0.03556	0
	GST (%)	10	0	10	0
	Other	-	-	-	-
Austria	Excise (EUR) per litre	0	0	0	0
	VAT (%)	20	0	20	0
	Other	-	-	-	-
Belgium	Excise (EUR) per litre	0	0	0.6325307 / 0.6678350	0.6325307 / 0.6678350
	VAT (%)	21	0	21	0
	Other	-	-	-	-
Canada	Excise (CAD) per litre	0.04	0	0.04/0.1	0
	GST (%)	5	0	5	0
	Other	-	-	-	-
Chile*	Excise (CLP) per litre	0	0	0	0
	VAT (%)	19	19	19	19
	Other	-	-	-	-
Colombia	Excise (COP) per litre	0	0	0	0
	VAT (%)	5	5	5	5
	Other	-	-	-	-
Czech Republic	Excise (CZK) per litre	0	0	0	0
	VAT (%)	21	0	21	0
	Other	-	-	-	-
Denmark	Excise (DKK) per litre	0	0	0	0
	VAT (%)	25	0	25	0
	Other	-	-	-	-
Estonia	Excise (EUR) per litre	0	0	0	0
	VAT (%)	20	0	20	0
	Other	-	-	-	-
Finland	Excise (EUR) per litre	0	0	0.7635/0.6959	0.7635/0.6959
	VAT (%)	24	0	24	0
	Other	0	0	0	0
France	Excise (EUR) per litre	0	0	0.397/0.4549	0
	VAT (%)	20	0	20	0
	Other	-	-	-	-
Germany	Excise (EUR) per litre	0	0	0.6545/0.721	0.6545/0.721
	VAT (%)	19	0	19	0
	Other	-	-	-	-
Greece	Excise (EUR) per litre	0	0	0.410/0.697	0.410/0.697
	VAT (%)	24	0	24	0

	Other	-	-	-	-
Hungary	Excise (HUF) per litre	0	0	126.432	126.432
	VAT (%)	27	0	27	0
	Other	-	-	-	-
Iceland	Excise (ISK) per litre	0	0	0	0
	VAT (%)	24	0	24	0
	Other	-	-	-	-
Ireland	Excise (EUR) per litre	0	0	0.495/0.602	0.495/0.602
	VAT (%)	23	0	23	0
	Other	-	-	-	--
Israel	Excise (ILS) per litre	0	0	0	0
	VAT (%)	17	0	17	0
	Other	-	-	-	-
Italy	Excise (EUR) per litre	0	0	0.3375 / 0.7284	0
	VAT (%)	22	0	22	0
	Other	-	-	-	-
Japan	Excise (JPY) per litre	18	0	18/18	0
	VAT (%)	10	0	10	0
	Other	-	-	-	-
Korea	Excise (KRW) per litre	0	0	0	0
	VAT (%)	10	0	10	0
	Other	-	-	-	-
Latvia	Excise (EUR) per litre	0	0	0,33017 / 0,57924	0,33017 / 0,57924
	VAT (%)	21	0	21	0
	Other	-	-	-	-
Lithuania	Excise (EUR) per litre	0	0	0,33017 / 0,57924	0,33017 / 0,57924
	VAT (%)	21	0	21	0
	Other	-	-	-	-
Luxembourg	Excise (EUR) per litre	0	0	0.33	0.33
	VAT (%)	17	0	17	17
	Other	-	-	-	-
Mexico	Excise (MXN) per litre	0	0	0	0
	VAT (%)	16	0	16	0
	Other	-	-	-	-
Netherlands*	Excise (EUR) per litre	0	0	0.50	0.50
	VAT (%)	21	0	21	0
	Other	-	-	-	-
New Zealand	Excise (NZD) per litre	0	0	0	0
	VAT (%)	15	0	15	0
	Other	-	-	-	-
Norway	Excise (NOK) per litre	0	0	0	0
	VAT (%)	25	0	25	0

	Other (CO_2 Tax)	1.39	0	1.39/1.39	0
Poland*	Excise (PLN) per litre	0	0	1.581/1.945	1.581/1.945
	VAT (%)	23	0	23	0
	Other	-	-	-	-
Portugal*	Excise (EUR) per litre	0	0	0.396/0.667	0.396/0.667
	VAT (%)	23	0	23	0
	Other	-	-	-	-
Slovak Republic	Excise (EUR) per litre	0	0	0	0
	VAT (%)	20	0	20	0
	Other	-	-	-	-
Slovenia	Excise (EUR) per litre	0	0	0.330/0.42161	0.330/0.42161
	VAT (%)	22	0	22	0
	Other	0,00911	0,00911	0.0489/0.05238	0.0489/0.05238
Spain	Excise (EUR) per litre	0	0	0	0
	VAT (%)	21	0	21	0
	Other	-	-	-	-
Sweden	Excise (SEK) per litre	0	0	5.187/6.720	5.187/6.720
	VAT (%)	25	0	25	0
	Other	-	-	-	-
Switzerland	Excise (CHF) per litre	0.7395	0	0.7395/0.7312	0
	VAT (%)	7.7	0	7.7	0
	Other	-	-	-	-
Turkey	Excise (TRY) per litre	0	0	0	0
	VAT (%)	18	0	18	0
	Other	-	-	-	-
United Kingdom	Excise (GBP) per litre	0	0	0.5795/0.3770	0
	VAT (%)	20	0	20	0
	Other	-	-	-	-
United States*	Excise (USD) per litre	0.0116	0	0.0579/0.0512	0
	Sales taxes (%)				
	Other	-	-	-	-

Notes

Fuels considered in this table are JET A-1 used in turbine engines and AVGAS used in piston-engine aircrafts. This table does not include fuels on board of aircrafts when they land in a jurisdiction covered by the ICAO Chicago Convention and specific fuels for military use or for use in Nordic areas.

1. For the purpose of this table, "commercial aviation" means aviation for the transport of goods or passengers for consideration, whatever the type of plane.
2. For the purpose of this table, it is assumed that commercial flights (passenger and cargo) only use JET A-1 fuels.
3. For the purpose of this table, "private/pleasure flights" means flights that are not considered as commercial flights.
4. For private/pleasure flights, both rates for JET A-1 and AVGAS fuels are shown.

Source: national delegates. Situation as at 1 January 2020

StatLink https://doi.org/10.1787/888934220325

Annex Box 4.A.3. Country notes to Table 4.A.5

Australia. *As part of measures to combat the Covid-19 crisis, the excise tax on jet fuel used in commercial aviation is suspended from 1 February 2020.*

Canada. The federal Goods and Services Tax is levied at a rate of 5% on aviation fuel and gasoline used in domestic flights. The federal excise rate, when applicable, is CAD 0.04 per litre of aviation fuel and CAD 0.10 per litre of aviation gasoline. Provinces and territories may also impose additional sales taxes and excise rates over and above the applicable federal rate.

Chile. Commercial services provided by aviation companies (notably, international cargo and/or passenger flights) and services provided to non-residents are considered exports. The aviation companies are therefore entitled to claim the refund of the input VAT, including on the fuel. In those cases, the practical effect can be similar to the application of a zero-rate (for ease of reading of the table, the VAT rate indicated in the table is 0 although in practice it is taxed and refunded to the aviation companies and to non-residents).

Germany. Fuels used for private pleasure flights are taxed at an excise rate of EUR 654,50 /1000 l (JET A-1) and 721 /1000l (AVGAS). *From 1 July to 31 December 2020 the VAT rate is reduced from 19% to 16% to offset the economic impact of the Covid-19 pandemic.*

Greece. The VAT rate for aviation fuel is 24%. However, in each case the Directive 2006/112/EC is applied and a conditional exemption is provided, which is reflected as 0%. For Private/pleasure flights Excise Duties rates for AVGAS (CN code 27101231, 27101270) is EUR 697/1000 litres and for JET A-1 (CN codes 2710 1921, 2710 1925) is EUR 410/1000 litres.

Hungary. Excise amount depends on the world market price of crude oil. If the world market price of crude oil is higher than 50 USD/barrel the excise amount is HUF 126.432/l (including the excise duty of HUF 124.2/l and the strategic stock fee of HUF 2.232/l). If the world market price of crude oil is 50 USD/barrel or less the excise amount is HUF 131.432 (including the excise duty of HUF 129.2/l and the strategic stock fee of HUF 2.232/l).

Ireland. AVGAS used for commercial aviation is partially relieved from excise. The rate of relief is EUR 0.232 per litre giving an effective 'Excise' rate of EUR 0.369 per litre.

Netherlands. A zero VAT rate applies to fuels for aircrafts that are used by airlines that are mainly occupied by international transport of persons or goods against remuneration.

Poland. Both fuel charge and excise tax are imposed on aviation fuels. The rate shown in the table includes the excise duty of PLN 1.446/l (JETA-1) and PLN 1.822 (AVGAS) and the fuel charge of PLN 0.17055 per kg). As the national excise rates are expressed in PLN per litre whereas fuel charge rate is expressed per kg, the rate for the fuel charge has been converted into a rate per litre by applying the appropriate density of the fuel.

Portugal. Aviation fuels used for commercial flights (i.e. flights for the transport of goods or passengers for consideration, whatever the type of plane) are exempt from excise duties. Fuels used for pleasure private flights are taxed at an excise rate of EUR 667.29 per 1000 litres for aviation gasoline (AVGAS) and EUR 395.54 per 1 000 litres for jet fuel (JET A-1).

Slovenia. Aviation fuels used for private/pleasure flights are taxed at an excise rate of EUR 330.00 per 1000 litres JET A-1 and EUR 421.61 per 1000 litres AVGAS and CO_2 tax EUR 39.79 per 1000 litres JET A-1 and EUR 43.25 per 1000 litres AVGAS. Aviation fuels are also subject to surcharge for the promotion of electricity generation from renewable energy sources and high-efficiency cogeneration in amount EUR 9.11 per 1000 litres JET A-1 and 9.13 per 1000 litres AVGAS.

United States. For commercial aviation, the federal tax rate in the US is USD 0.044 per gallon (€ 0.010 per litre). For non-commercial aviation, kerosene is generally taxed at USD 0.244 per gallon. In addition, states or local authorities can levy additional taxes on aviation fuel varying from USD 0 (Texas, Ohio and Delaware) and USD 0.328 (Illinois) per gallon. There is no federal sales tax; States and local sales rates vary from 0% (Delaware, Montana, New Hampshire and Oregon) to more than 9.5% (Tennessee and Louisiana). *As part of measures to combat the Covid-19 crisis, the federal fuel excise tax on jet fuel used in commercial aviation is suspended from 28 March to 31 December 2020.*

Annex A. Countries with VAT

Almost all countries levy general consumption taxes i.e. taxes on the sale of most goods and services. The general consumption tax applied by the majority of those countries is value added tax (VAT[1]) i.e. a tax collected at all stages of the processes of production and distribution of goods and services, accumulation of the tax being prevented by allowing businesses to deduct the tax they incur on their inputs from the tax they collect on their outputs. Exports of goods and services are generally within the scope of VAT, although they are commonly zero rated. On the other hand, the importation of goods and services is subject to tax to ensure the neutrality of the tax system (see Chapter 1). A minority of countries (and some sub-national entities) apply retail sales taxes, i.e. single-stage taxes on goods and services supplied to final consumers (these are not listed in the table below). All OECD countries levy VAT, except the United States, where sales taxes are levied at sub-national level (see Chapter 1).

As of 1 November 2020, 170 countries and territories in the world have implemented a VAT.

Table A A.1. Countries and territories operating a VAT

No.	Country	Implementation	Rates 2020 (%)		
			Standard[1]	Reduced[2]	Increased
1	Albania	1995	20	0, 6	
2	Algeria	1992	19	0, 9	
3	Andorra	2013	4.5	0, 1, 2.5	9.5
4	Angola	2019	14		
5	Antigua and Barbuda[3]	2007	15	0, 13, 14	
6	Argentina	1974	21	2.5, 5, 10.5	27
7	Armenia	1993	20	0	
8	Australia	2000	10	0	
9	Austria[4]	1973	20	10, 13	
10	Azerbaijan	1992	18	0	
11	Bahamas	2015	12		
12	Bangladesh	1991	15	5, 7	
13	Barbados	1997	17.5	0, 7.5	
14	Bahrain	2018	5	0	
15	Belarus	1991	20	0, 10	25
16	Belgium	1971	21	0, 6, 12	
17	Belize	2006	12.5	0	
18	Benin	1991	18	0	
19	Bolivia	1986	13	0	
20	Bosnia Herzegovina	2006	17		
21	Botswana	2002	12	0	
22	Brazil	1964	17, 18	4, 7, 12	25, 30
23	Bulgaria	1994	20	9	
24	Burkina Faso	1993	18	0	
25	Burundi	2009	18	0, 10	
26	Cambodia	1999	10		
27	Cameroon	1999	19.25	0	
28	Canada[5]	1991	GST/HST: 5, 13, 15		
29	Cape Verde	2004	15	0	
30	Central African Republic	2001	19	0, 5	
31	Chad	2000	18	0, 9	
32	Chile	1975	19		
33	China (People's Republic)	1994	13	1, 3, 6, 9	
34	Colombia	1983	19	0, 5	
35	Commonwealth of Dominica	2006	15	10	
36	Congo (Dem. Republic)	2012	16	0	
37	Congo (Republic)	1997	18	0, 5	
38	Cook Islands	1997	15	0	
39	Costa Rica	2019	13	4, 2, 1	
40	Côte d'Ivoire	1960	18	0, 9	
41	Croatia	1998	25	5, 13	
42	Cyprus[6]	1992	19	0, 5, 9	
43	Czech Republic	1993	21	10, 15	
44	Denmark	1967	25	0	
45	Djibouti	2009	10	0, 7	
46	Dominican Republic	1983	18	0, 16	-
47	Ecuador	1970	12	0	
48	Egypt	2017	14	0, 5	
49	El Salvador	1992	13	0	
50	Equatorial Guinea	2005	15	0, 6	

51	Estonia	1991	20	0, 9	
52	Eswatini	2012	15	0	
53	Ethiopia	2003	15	0	
54	Faroe Islands	1993	25	0	
55	Fiji	1992	9	0	
56	Finland	1994	24	0, 10, 14	
57	France[7]	1968	20	2.1, 5.5, 10	
58	Gabon	1995	18	0, 5, 10	
59	Gambia	2013	15	0	
60	Georgia	1993	18	0	
61	Germany	1968	19	7	
62	Ghana	1998	12.5	0, 3	
63	Greece[8]	1987	24	6, 13	
64	Grenada	2010	15	0, 10	20
65	Guatemala	1992	12	0	
66	Guinea	1996	18	0	
67	Guinea-Bissau	2001	17	0, 10	20
68	Guyana	2007	14	0	
69	Haiti	1982	10		
70	Honduras	1964	15	0	18
71	Hungary	1988	27	5, 18	
72	Iceland	1990	24	0, 11	
73	India	2017	12, 18	0, 5	28
74	Indonesia	1985	10	0	10 – 125
75	Iran[9]	2008	9	0	12+3, 20 (5 or 10) 25-30
76	Ireland	1972	23	0, 4.8, 9, 13.5	
77	Isle of Man	1973	20	0, 5	
78	Israel[10]	1976	17	0	
79	Italy	1973	22	0, 4, 5, 10	
80	Jamaica	1991	16.5	2, 10	21.5, 25
81	Japan	1989	10	8	
82	Jersey	2008	5	0	
83	Jordan	2001	16	0, 4, 5, 10	26
84	Kazakhstan	1992	12	0	
85	Kenya	1990	14	0	
86	Kiribati	2014	12.5	0	
87	Korea (South)	1977	10		
88	Kosovo[11]	2001	18	8	
89	Kyrgyzstan	1999	12	0	
90	Lao (People's Democratic Republic)	2010	10	0	
91	Latvia	1995	21	5, 12	
92	Lebanon	2002	11	0	
93	Lesotho	2003	15	0, 9	
94	Liechtenstein	1995	7.7	2.5, 3.7	
95	Lithuania	1994	21	5, 9	
96	Luxembourg	1970	17	3, 8, 14	
97	Madagascar	1994	20	0	
98	Malawi	2002	16.5	0	
99	Maldives	2011	6	0	12
100	Mali	1991	18	5	
101	Malta	1999	18	0, 5, 7	
102	Mauritania	1995	16		18
103	Mauritius	1998	15		

104	Mexico	1980	16	0	
105	Moldova	1998	20	0, 8	
106	Monaco	1968	20	2.1, 5.5, 10	
107	Mongolia	1998	10	0	
108	Montenegro	2003	21	0, 7	
109	Morocco	1986	20	0, 7, 10, 14	
110	Mozambique	1999	17	0, 5	
111	Namibia	2000	15	0	
112	Nepal	1997	13	0	
113	Netherlands	1969	21	9	
114	New Zealand	1986	15	0	
115	Nicaragua	1975	15	0, 7	
116	Niger	1986	19	0, 5, 10	
117	Nigeria	1994	7.5	0	
118	Niue	2009	12.5	0	
119	North Macedonia	2000	18	5	
120	Norway	1970	25	0, 12, 15	
121	Pakistan	1990	17	0	18.5, 21, 22 and 25
122	Panama	1977	7		10, 15
123	Papua New Guinea	1999	10	0	
124	Paraguay	1993	10	0, 5	
125	Peru[12]	1991	16, 2	0	
126	Philippines	1988	12	0, 5	
127	Poland	1993	23	0, 5, 8	
128	Portugal[13]	1986	23	6, 13	
129	Romania	1993	19	5, 9	
130	Russia	1991	20	0, 10	
131	Rwanda	2001	18	0	
132	Saint Kitts and Nevis	2010	17	10	
133	Saint Lucia	2012	16	0, 10	
134	Saint Vincent and the Grenadines	2007	15	0, 10	
135	Samoa	1994	15	0	
136	Saudi Arabia	2018	5	0	
137	Senegal	1980	18	0, 10	
138	Serbia	2005	20	10	
139	Seychelles	2012	15	0	
140	Sierra Leone	2009	15	0	
141	Singapore	1994	7	0	
142	Slovak Republic	1993	20	10	
143	Slovenia	1999	22	5, 9.5	
144	South Africa	1991	15	0	
145	Spain[14]	1986	21	4, 10	
146	Sri Lanka	1998	8	0	15
147	Sudan	2000	18	0	
148	Sweden	1969	25	0, 6, 12	
149	Switzerland	1995	7.7	2.5, 3.7	
150	Chinese Taipei	1986	5	0	
151	Tajikistan	1992	18	5	
152	Tanzania	1998	18	0	
153	Thailand[15]	1992	10	0, 7	
154	Togo	1995	18	10	
155	Tonga	2005	15		
156	Trinidad and Tobago	1990	12.5	0	
157	Tunisia	1988	19	0, 7, 13	

158	Turkey	1984	18	1, 8	
159	Turkmenistan	1992	15	0	
160	Uganda	1996	18	0	
161	Ukraine	1992	20	0, 7	
162	United Arab Emirates	2018	5	0	
163	United Kingdom	1973	20	0, 5	
164	Uruguay	1972	22	0, 10	
165	Uzbekistan	1992	20	0	
166	Vanuatu	1998	12.5	0	
167	Venezuela	1993	16	8	31
168	Vietnam	1999	10	0, 5	
169	Zambia	1995	16	0	
170	Zimbabwe	2004	14.5	0	
	Bhutan[16]				
	Oman[17]				
	Malaysia[18]				

Notes:

The acronym "VAT" refers to any national tax that embodies the basic features of a value added tax as described in Chapter 1, by whatever name or acronym it is known e.g. "Goods and Services Tax" ("GST")

1. The standard rate is the rate that generally applies, unless the legislation explicitly provides that specific goods and services are subject to different (reduced or increased) rates.

2. Reduced rates include zero-rates applicable to domestic supplies (i.e. an exemption with right to deduct input tax). This does not include zero-rated exports or other supplies subject to similar treatment such as international transport or supplies to embassies, international organisations and diplomatic missions. VAT rate measures taken by countries as part of the Covid-19 crisis are not reflected in this table given their temporary nature.

3. **Antigua and Barbuda**: the reduced rate of 12% was replaced with reduced rates of 13% and 14% on 13 March 2020.

4. **Austria**: The standard VAT rate is 19% in Jungholtz and Mittleberg.

5. **Canada:** additional HST rates apply on the top of the federal 5% GST rate in several provinces (see Annex Table 2.A2.1)

6. **Cyprus:** Footnote by Turkey: the information in this document with reference to « Cyprus » relates to the southern part of the Island. There is no single authority representing both Turkish and Greek Cypriot people on the Island. Turkey recognizes the Turkish Republic of Northern Cyprus (TRNC). Until a lasting and equitable solution is found within the context of United Nations, Turkey shall preserve its position concerning the "Cyprus issue".

Footnote by all the European Union Member States of the OECD and the European Union: the Republic of Cyprus is recognised by all members of the United Nations with the exception of Turkey. The information in this document relates to the area under the effective control of the Government of the Republic of Cyprus.

7. **France:** Specific rates also apply in some regions/territories: reduced rates 0.9/2.1/10.0/13.0 (Corsica); standard/reduced rates 8.5/2.1 (Martinique, Guadeloupe, Réunion); standard/reduced rates 16-13/5 (French Polynesia) (see also Annex Table 2.A.1)

8. **Greece:** Specific regional rates of 4.0%; 9.0% and 17.0% apply in the islands of Leros, Lesbos, Kos, Samos and Chios until 31 December 2020 (see also Annex Table 2.A.1).

9. **Iran:** In addition to VAT (at the rate of 6%) an additional levy of 3% is collected and treated in the same way as VAT.

10. **Israel:** The statistical data for Israel are supplied by and under the responsibility of the relevant Israeli authorities. The use of such data by the OECD is without prejudice to the status of the Golan Heights, East Jerusalem and Israeli settlements in the West Bank under the terms of international law.

11. **Kosovo** This designation is without prejudice to positions on status, and is in line with United Nations Security Council Resolution 1244/99 and the Advisory Opinion of the International Court of Justice on Kosovo's declaration of independence.

12. **Peru:** in addition to the standard IGV rate of 16%, a 2% sales tax (IPM) is levied at municipal level

13. **Portugal:** In the Islands of Azores, the standard VAT rate is 18% and the reduced rates are 4% and 9%. In the Islands of Madeira the standard rate is 22% and reduced rates are 5% and 12%.

14. **Spain:** Rates of 0.0%, 3.0%; 7.0%, 9.50%; 13.50%, 20% apply in the Canary Islands.

15. **Thailand**: the standard VAT rate was increased from 7% to 10% on 1 October 2020.

16. **Bhutan**: a GST Act was approved by Parliament in 2020 for a possible implementation in 2022

17. **Oman:** The government has announced the introduction of VAT in early 2021

18. **Malaysia :** GST was abolished and a single-stage sales tax system was reintroduced on 1 September 2018, three years after GST was first introduced

Source: F. Annacondia, International - Overview of General Turnover Taxes and Tax Rates, International VAT Monitor, Journals IBFD, cited with permission of IBFD, see http://online.ibfd.org/kbase/, All rights reserved.

Annex B. Exchange rates

Country	Currency	PPP exchange rate for GDP 2019[1]	Market exchange rate for 2019[2]
Australia	AUD	1.44	1.44
Austria	EUR	0.76	0.89
Belgium	EUR	0.76	0.89
Canada	CAD	1.19	1.33
Chile	CLP	416.25	702.90
Colombia	COP	1 349.01	3 280.83
Czech Republic	CZK	12.44	22.93
Denmark	DKK	6.67	6.67
Estonia	EUR	0.54	0.89
Finland	EUR	0.85	0.89
France	EUR	0.73	0.89
Germany	EUR	0.74	0.89
Greece	EUR	0.56	0.89
Hungary	HUF	140.94	290.66
Iceland	ISK	136.66	122.61
Ireland	EUR	0.80	0.89
Israel	ILS	3.69	3.56
Italy	EUR	0.67	0.89
Japan	JPY	101.47	109.01
Korea	KRW	860.21	1 165.50
Latvia	EUR	0.49	0.89
Lithuania	EUR	0.45	0.89
Luxembourg	EUR	0.84	0.89
Mexico	MXN	9.31	19.26
Netherlands	EUR	0.78	0.89
New Zealand	NZD	1.45	1.52
Norway	NOK	9.93	8.80
Poland	PLN	1.75	3.84
Portugal	EUR	0.57	0.89
Slovak Republic	EUR	0.51	0.89
Slovenia	EUR	0.57	0.89
Spain	EUR	0.63	0.89
Sweden	SEK	8.75	9.46
Switzerland	CHF	1.15	0.99
Turkey	TRY	1.84	5.67
United Kingdom	GBP	0.68	0.78
United States	USD	1.00	1.00

Notes:

1. Purchase Parity Rates (PPP) for GDP 2019. Accessed on 28 August 2020. For further detail, see *www.oecd.org/std/ppp.*
2. Average market rates 2019. OECD Monthly Monetary Statistics. For further details see *stats.oecd.org*.

Note on exchange rates: Cross-country comparisons of thresholds or tax amounts expressed in national currency require their conversion into one single currency. By convention, the currency used in this publication is the United States Dollar (USD). Two exchange rates can generally be used for converting national currencies into USD: (1) market exchange rates, which are currency exchange rates observed on the markets. The rate used in this publication is the average rate for 2019 as published in the OECD Monetary and Financial Statistics. However, the rate used for Table 3.5 is the average market exchange rate for 2018 as prices and taxes refer to the year 2018. (2) The purchasing power parity rates (PPP) for GDP, which equalise the purchasing power of different countries by eliminating differences in price levels between them; they show the specified number of monetary units needed in each country to buy the same representative basket of consumer goods and services that costs USD 1 in the United States. PPP exchange rates (for 2019) are used for Tables 2.5, 2.8 and 2.9 as they provide for a better comparison of the value of VAT relief thresholds. Market exchange rates are used for the other tables as they allow easier comparison of prices and the level of taxes in countries.
Source: OECD.

Annex C. Most sold brands of cigarettes in OECD countries

Country	Most sold brand 2018
Australia	Winfield
Austria	**Marlboro**
Belgium	Marlboro
Canada[2]	—
Chile	Pall Mall
Czech Republic	L&M
Denmark	Prince
Estonia	Marlboro
Finland	L&M
France	Marlboro
Germany	Marlboro
Greece	Marlboro
Hungary	Marlboro
Iceland	Winston
Ireland	Silk Cut
Israel	Marlboro
Italy	Marlboro
Japan	Mevius
Korea	Esse
Latvia	Winston
Lithuania	Marlboro
Luxembourg	Marlboro
Mexico	Marlboro
Netherlands	Marlboro
New Zealand	Pall Mall
Norway	Prince
Poland	L&M
Portugal	Marlboro
Slovak Republic	L&M
Slovenia	Marlboro
Spain	Marlboro
Sweden	Marlboro
Switzerland	Marlboro
Turkey	Parliament
United Kingdom	Mayfair
United States[1]	—

Notes:
Data as at 1 July 2018.
1. No most sold brand is available for the United States and Canada as an average price weighted by consumption in each State/Province was used.
Source: World Health Organisation.

www.ingramcontent.com/pod-product-compliance
Ingram Content Group UK Ltd.
Pitfield, Milton Keynes, MK11 3LW, UK
UKHW051500290926
15471UKWH00008B/1326

9 789264 763869